AMERICAN BOMBER AIRCRAFT DEVELOPMENT

IN WORLD WAR 2

AMERICAN BOMBER AIRCRAFT DEVELOPMENT
IN WORLD WAR 2

Bill Norton

MIDLAND

American Bomber Aircraft Development in World War 2
Bill Norton

First published 2012

ISBN 978 1 85780 330 3

Published by Midland Publishing

an imprint of Ian Allan Publishing Ltd, Hersham, Surrey KT12 4RG.
Printed in England by Ian Allan Printing Ltd, Hersham, Surrey KT12 4RG.

Visit the Ian Allan Publishing website at www.ianallanpublishing.com
Distributed in the United States of America and Canada by BookMasters Distribution Services.

Contents

Introduction

This is the third of my planned four-volume set presenting America's development of military aircraft during World War 2, with emphasis on experimental and lesser-known models. As the title indicates, this book addresses bombers. The first explored fighters and was published in 2008 by Specialty Press as *U.S. Experimental & Prototype Aircraft Projects, Fighters 1939-1945*, and the second *American Military Gliders of WWII*, published in 2012 by Schiffer.

I was motivated to undertake these projects by a desire to collect a clear and detailed examination of American accomplishments in aviation development during the war years. This would stand beside comparable texts on the work of other combatants of the period. Especially the German subjects are covered in a generous number of books, some going far afield in examining projects that never progressed beyond conceptual design. By comparison, the scope of what the United States accomplished during the war was of considerably more breadth, technical success and greater import for the future.

Some aircraft are widely recognised as bombers while others, like those of the Attack (A) designation, are less clearly denoted as bombers in popular literature. Likewise, American bombers employed in anti-submarine warfare and those employed solely by foreign operators are seldom included in general accounts of wartime US bombers. Consequently, I have included all aircraft with a bombing

mission as a primary role. I have used my own judgement in selecting the aircraft to include (multi-engine, bomb bay, bombsight, bombardier) while also 'filling in the gaps' of the narrative begun in my fighters volume. For example, the text excludes all carrier-based Navy aircraft but includes flying-boat bombers and land-based naval bombers. This distribution helps ensure a focused yet even examination of the subject to a suitable depth. In seeking this goal, other material had to be set aside. Modifications of bombers by foreign operators or for non-bombing missions are left to other texts, as is the subject of bomb evolution and development of guided munitions. Likewise, this volume avoids design concepts or proposals that were never endorsed officially nor progressed far. Focusing exclusively on official programmes that entered development provides more than sufficient interesting material of adequate depth to fill these limited pages.

Although the United States of America entered World War 2 only in the last month of 1941, with the conflict already more than two years old, this book will encompass the period from September 1939 and the declaration of war in Europe to August 1945 and the cessation of hostilities with Japan. Foreign combatants operated American-built bombers from the first days of the conflict. There were official US military aviation operations in the early war years, albeit as a neutral force. Even before the outbreak of open warfare, American military expansion had begun

and the aviation industry was growing to support rearmament. These producers were soon the principal external supplier of combat aircraft to friendly countries at war or preparing to meet any eventuality. Aviation programs slowed little after the defeat of Germany, as Japan remained a determined foe of uncertain capabilities that was expected to require prodigious quantities of equipment to defeat completely. Hence, the time period examined is entirely appropriate.

The reader is expected to come to this book with knowledge of the general course of the air war in World War 2. The reader will find few references to actual combat experiences and associated personalities; instead, the 'war stories' are those of military personnel, engineering teams and test pilots struggling against short schedules and tight resource constraints to develop new aircraft pushing the bounds of technology. These epic and sometimes life-threatening endeavours were as vital to the war effort as actual combat. If I have done my job well, the reader will be intrigued and fascinated by the account. I can only regret that space limitations compelled exclusion of so much interesting detail and supportive material.

I welcome feedback and additional research material. Readers may contact me at williamnorton@earthlink.net.

Bill Norton
California City, USA
February 2012

Acknowledgements

For their kind assistance, the author would like to thank the following individuals and organisations: Gerald Balzer, Kase Decker, Hayden Hamilton and Paul Minert of the American Aviation Historical Society, Dan Hagedorn, Dennis Jenkins, Lloyd Jones, Tony Landis, Jay Miller and the people of the Jay Miller Collection, Alan Renga and the folks at the San Diego Air & Space Museum, Brett Stolle and the National Museum of the United States Air Force, Curtiss Utz and the staff of the Naval Aviation Archives, Stan Piet at the Glenn L. Martin Maryland Aviation Museum, personnel at the National Museum of Naval Aviation archives, Paul Oelkrug and the other finc folks at the University of Texas at Dallas History of Aviation Collection, Amy Heidrick and John Little at the Museum of Flight, George Larson, Dr. Jim Young and the people of the Air Force Flight Test Center History Office, the United States National Archives, Ray Wagner, Steve Roberts, and Dr. Bill Wolf.

Glossary

Adverse Yaw – the tendency of the aircraft to yaw away from the direction of a roll, reducing turn rate and increasing drag. It is normally countered by applying rudder to bring the sideslip to zero (coordinate the turn).

Air-Cooled Engine – a reciprocating engine in which cooling is derived from passing air channelled via the cowling, baffles, and cylinder fins.

Airfoil – a wing cross-section shape determining lift characteristics.

Angle-of-Attack – angle between the wing mean chord line and the incident airflow.

Axial-flow Jet engine – a turbine engine through which air flows along the longitudinal axis without being radically redirected as through a centrifugal compressor.

Block – a group of aircraft in a production model series with like physical attributes.

Bombsight – an optical device for estimating the impact point of bombs dropped from an aircraft at considerable altitude.

Boundary Layer – the thin layer of air adjacent to a surface in an air stream in which the flow goes from zero velocity at the surface to freestream velocity. A thick or turbulent layer would possess greater skin friction drag than a thin or laminar boundary layer.

Centre of Gravity – (CG) is the point at which the aircraft would balance if suspended from that point, or the centre of gravitational attraction acting on the mass of the machine. A CG too far forward or too far aft could make the aircraft uncontrollable.

Centrifugal-flow Jet Engine – a turbine engine through which air flows through a centrifugal compressor, redirecting the air radially outward to pass through combustors on the outer perimeter of the powerplant.

Chord – the width of a wing or the line between the leading and trailing edges, usually referred to as chord length or a mean chord for a tapered wing.

Compressibility Effects – refers to the effects on aircraft performance and control resulting from air compressing into shock waves as the aircraft approaches the speed of sound at the operating altitude.

Contra-rotating Propeller – also known as a dual-rotation propeller or 'contraprop', this employs two propellers, front to back, turning in opposite directions on the same power shaft.

Counter-rotating Propeller – propellers on opposite sides of the aircraft (as in a twin-engine aircraft) that rotate in opposite directions to eliminate torque effects.

Drag – the resistance of the air to passage of an aircraft. It is made up of induced drag from the creation of lift and profile drag created by moving the aircraft through an air mass. Profile drag includes skin friction drag, the overall frontal area offered to the incident air, cooling drag from air passing through a cowling and engine baffling, and other elements.

Dual-rotation Propeller – (see Contra-rotating Propeller).

Flaps – an articulated portion of a wing trailing edge that enhances lift at the expense of drag, and is usually employed on approach to allow a reduced landing speed. The split flap is a lower portion of the trailing edge that rotates down. The Fowler flap slides aft and down, usually creating a slot between the wing mainplane and flap surfaces through which air accelerates.

Flutter – an unstable oscillation of a portion of the aircraft or control surface that can grow to catastrophic levels. The instability is induced by unsteady air loads interacting with elastic deformation of the structure or control surface rotation at like frequencies (resonance).

Gunsight – a mechanism for aligning aircraft projectile weapons with a target. This is usually in front of the pilot or gunner allowing a visual sighting through an optical device.

Hardpoint – a strengthened structural portion within the bottom surface of a wing or fuselage with fittings for carriage of weapon or fuel tank mounts.

Inline Engine – a reciprocating engine in which the cylinders are disposed longitudinally adjacent to the power shaft, typically in two opposing rows of flat or V arrangements.

Intercooler – one or more heat exchangers cooling air passing to a supercharger to increase density.

Laminar flow – boundary layer of air adjacent to a surface in an air stream with an even pressure distribution as opposed to turbulent and possessing less skin friction drag. A laminar-flow wing is one with an airfoil designed to maintain laminar flow for more of the chord length than typical airfoils.

Lend-Lease – US government policy by which weapons and other materiel assistance was purchased by the United States and provided as a form of loan to nations fighting or arming to fight the Axis powers.

Pressurisation – a system that pumps compressed air into the sealed cockpit to maintain pressure at a safe 'cabin altitude' as the aircraft climbs into the rarefied air at high altitude.

Propeller Cuff – fitting near the base of a propeller blade that expands the width (chord) to improve thrust or alter the flow off that portion of the blade for improved cooling air passage into an engine cowling immediately aft.

Propwash – the flow of air off a propeller passing back over the aircraft directly aft (assuming a tractor propeller). The propwash can create asymmetrical moments on the aircraft but also ensures control effectiveness at low aircraft velocities for those surfaces within the wash.

Radio or Radar Altimeter – a device measuring height above the ground or sea by reflected electromagnetic waves and permitting safer night flying at low altitude.

Radial Engine – a reciprocating engine in which the pistons are arranged radially about the centre power shaft. One or two rows of these radially grouped cylinders was typical.

Slot – a narrow spanwise opening between the lower and upper surface of a wing allowing the high-pressure air below to accelerate up and over the top of the wing to energise the flow and delay stall. Also a gap created when moving a control surface or flap (two slots if the flap has a leading-edge vane), the flow through the slot enhancing the effect of the surface deflection.

Specifications – ('Specs') is an agreement between a manufacturer and the customer as to the characteristics of an aircraft yet to be designed and built.

Stall – the turbulation and separation of air on a wing or other surface due to high angle of attack and adverse pressure gradients within the boundary layer that causes a large loss of lift.

Supercharger – a spinning compressor impeller, usually driven off the engine accessory gearcase, through which the fuel-air mixture from the carburetor is passed before entering the fuel-intake manifold to the carburetor. This 'boost' helps maintain intake pressure nearer sea level even with the lower air density at altitude for sustained high engine power output.

Torque – the moment (lateral displacement tendency) created by a propeller, especially at high power on takeoff and low speed on landing. This is a combination of mechanical effects from turning the heavy prop as well as the asymmetrical airflow effects on the aircraft elements aft of the propeller.

Turbojet – a turbine (jet) engine for which the motive output is an accelerated mass of air for thrust

Water-Cooled Engine – a reciprocating engine that is cooled via coolant circulated in jackets around the components and pumped to radiators in which heat is carried away by passing air.

Water Injection – the introduction of a metered flow of water (usually a water-alcohol mixture) into the cylinders of a piston engine or combustion chamber(s) of a jet engine to reduce temperatures, allowing more fuel to be burned in the combustor for greater power or thrust output. For the piston engine, the leaner fuel-air mixture (less fuel in the ratio) permits higher manifold pressure.

Wing Loading – aircraft gross weight divided by wing area. The advantage of a smaller wing for a given gross weight is reduced structural weight and aircraft drag, but this also yields lower manoeuvrability. Additionally, without high-lift devices like Fowler flaps, landing speed and distance can be uncomfortably great.

Acronym List

AAA	anti-aircraft artillery	inc.	including	pp.	pages
AAB	Army Air Base	int.	internal	psf	pounds per square foot
AAF	Army Air Force	JATO	Jet-Assisted Take-Off	psi	pounds per square inch
AC	alternating current	kg	kilogram	P&W	Pratt & Whitney
APU	auxiliary power unit	km	kilometres	RAAF	Royal Australian Air Force
ASV	air-to-surface vessel	km/h	kilometres per hour	RAF	Royal Air Force
ASW	anti-submarine warfare	kPa	kilopascals	RCAF	Royal Canadian Air Force
ATSC	Air Technical Service Command	kW	kilowatt	RCM	Radio Countermeasures
aux	auxiliary	LORAN	Long Range Aid to Navigation	RCT	remote controlled turret
BTO	Bombing Through Overcast	lbf	pounds force (thrust)	RNZAF	Royal New Zealand Air Force
BuAer	Bureau of Aeronautics	lb	pounds	rpg	rounds per gun
BVD	Boeing-Vega-Douglas	lit	litre, litres	R&D	research and development
cal	calibre	m	metre, metres	SAAF	South African Air Force
Caltech	California Institute of Technology	MAD	magnetic anomaly detector	sec	second, seconds
CBI	China-Burma-India theatre	max.	maximum	SWPA	Southwest Pacific Area
CFC	Central Fire Control	MG	machine gun	TBO	time between overhaul
CG	centre of gravity	mi	statute miles	TIPS	Thermal Ice Preventative System
cm	centimetre	min	minute(s)		
DC	direct current	min.	minimum	torp.	torpedo
dist.	distance	MIT	Massachusetts Institute of Technology	typ.	typical
ERCO	Engineering and Research Corporation			UK	United Kingdom
		Mk.	Mark	US	United States of America
ETO	European Theatre of Operations	mm	millimetre	USAAC	United States Army Air Corps
		mod	modification	USAAF	United States Army Air Forces
ext.	external	MPC	Motor Products Corporation	USCG	United States Coast Guard
fpm	feet per minute	mph	miles per hour	USMC	United States Marine Corps
ft	foot, feet	mps	metres per second	USN	United States Navy
gal	gallon, gallons (US units)	MTO	Mediterranean Theatre of Operations	USSR	Union of Soviet Socialist Republics
GE	General Electric				
GFE	government furnished equipment	N	Newtons	VE-Day	Victory in Europe Day
		NAA	North American Aviation	VHB	Very Heavy Bomber
GW	gross weight	NACA	National Advisory Committee or Aeronautics	VJ-Day	Victory over Japan Day
h	hour, hours			VLR	Very Long Range
hp	horsepower	NAF	Naval Aircraft Factory	V-S	Vought-Sikorsky
hr	hour, hours	NAS	Naval Air Station	WE	War Emergency
HVAR	High Velocity Aircraft Rockets	norm.	normal	WW1	World War 1
IFF	Identification Friend or Foe	obs.	obstacle	WW2	World War 2
in	inch, inches	p.	page		

Chapter One

Background on Expansion

Bombers in Ascendance

Since World War 1, bombers were seen as an essential element of airpower. However, the greater cost and complexity of bombers made for varying levels of commitment among the world's air arms. Prior to World War 2, the United States was among the more progressive in its earnestness to expand the bomber force. The US Army Air Corps (USAAC) sought capable and aggressive light bombers directly supporting troops in the field, medium bombers to interdict materiel en route to the front and heavy bombers for attacking enemy homeland infrastructure and morale. Such plans were consistently frustrated by meagre budgets, congressionally-mandated force limitations, isolationist sentiments and resistance by powerful and traditionalist Army leaders. The US Navy (USN) was continuing to build its carrier-based

aviation, but used flying boats for level bombing of maritime targets. Yet, naval aviation suffered under constraints similar to its Army brethren.

Few such restrictions were imposed abroad, especially by Germany, Japan, and Italy who engaged in small conflicts that confirmed the importance of bombers and how far behind America was falling. Things began to change given these emergent threats and the realisation America could be drawn into another global war. Visionary leadership, in and out of uniform, saw the essential contributions airpower could make and set out to correct the deficiencies.

In the latter half of the 1930s, the USAAC ranked about fifth in the world in number of front-line aircraft. Facing a rapidly worsening world milieu, President Roosevelt urged a dramatic jump in defence appropriations from Congress in January 1939 with the

purchase of 10,000 aircraft a noted goal. At the time, the entire War Department aircraft inventory was approximately 3,500 frontline machines. Developmental and experimental programs, in airframes, engines, bombsights, turrets and radar promised tremendous capability improvements, but taking these to production at quantities and rates to wage total war remained in doubt. Over the next two years, the proclaimed goals increased with each new appropriation bill, but actual procurement failed to match authorisation. However, the logjam over bombers was broken and

Below: In prewar years, War Department air elements conducted occasional design competitions to fill its equipment needs. These kept "creative juices flowing" and sought to ensure warplanes were abreast of recent aeronautical developments. The Air Corps' effort to develop a twin-engine attack bomber brought forth this 1938 Bell Model 17 concept. *Jay Miller Collection*

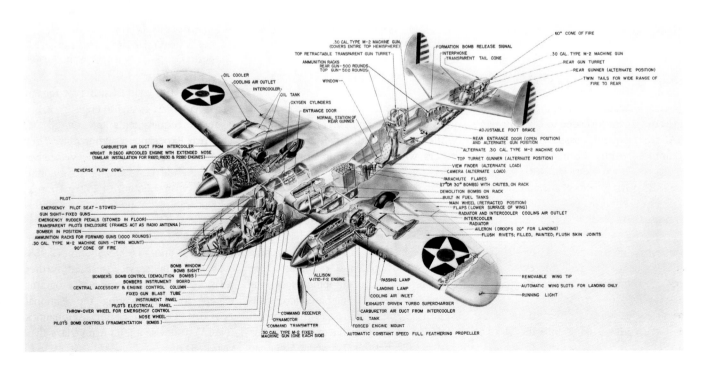

Left: American bombers fought from the earliest days of the war, long before the United States entered the conflict. Aircraft like this Douglas DB-7 were purchased prewar by rearming nations, but the buying grew considerably after war began. America's defence plants and the quality of the aircraft benefited from this interchange. *Ray Wagner Collection*

and German forces occurred there during September and October 1941. The Navy was then authorised to sink on sight any hostile submarine.

Services' Ambitions

the services were allowed to move forward. Orders were at first small and the products immature, bringing production capacity up to a total-war volume taking much time. As late as July 1941, the USAAF's chief assessed its actual combat bomber capability as essentially zero 'at zero strength as far as a major war is concerned'.[1]

While American aircraft manufacturing was under-utilised in the prewar years, it was also recognised as world-class. This attracted the interest of friendly nations seeking to expand rapidly their air arms. The resulting contracts produced an expansion of the US aircraft industry, garnering of current experience, and introduction of new bombers. With the advent of war in Europe on 3 September 1939, a 1935 Neutrality Act came into play, prohibiting shipment of war materiel to opponents. This embargo proved short-lived as enactment of Cash-and-Carry legislation on 4 November.[2] Direct delivery was finally permitted with signing of the Lend-Lease Act on 11 March 1941 whereby American arms were ostensibly passed to foreign nations under generous financial terms. Some of the equipment provided to Great Britain's RAF was frequently passed along to other Commonwealth nations including the Royal Canadian Air Force (RCAF), Royal Australian Air Force (RAAF), Royal New Zealand Air Force (RNZAF) and South African Air Force (SAAF). However, the US military worked with these countries to order new aircraft meeting their specific combat needs. The resulting evolution of designs and further expansion of national manufacturing capabilities, provided ready assets sustaining American airwar growth. With US entry into the war, the domestic users took priority.

The Americans keenly observed the air war between the European combatants, extracting lessons and requirements for aircraft improvements. Particularly observed were the tremendous logistical challenges for total war and how quickly men and equipment were expended. Unfortunately, they were less attentive to Japan's ongoing wars in Asia. British experience was highly valued, but not adopted entirely. The Americans had their own doctrine and tactics to which aircraft were developed and airmen trained.

Before the war, the prevailing concept was that bombers would fly so high and fast that interception by enemy fighters and targeting by anti-aircraft artillery (AAA or 'flak') would all be ineffective. War experience quickly showed the fallacy of such concepts. Between the wars, defensive measures had markedly grown in size and effectiveness. Bomber formations (during daylight) were developed to provide an optimal concentration and pattern of bomb dispersal, distributed mutual defensive fire to maximum effect, and allow 'follow-the-leader' procedures such that only one aircraft needed to perform full-time navigation and run-in to the target while reducing the workload of the others who would 'drop on the lead'. This still required formation flying skills and a suitably responsive aircraft.

Soon after 3 September 1939, the United States undertook the Neutrality Patrol with the mission of tracking and reporting belligerent forces approaching US waters. Lend-Lease extended these missions to Atlantic shipping escort, the Patrol Force establishing bases across this route. These units were on a virtual combat footing, building valuable experience. The first hostile actions between American

By summer 1937, Air Corps leadership had decided to focus on heavy bombers and attack-bombers, the B-18 having met twin-engine bomber needs. The heavies would support the strategic bombing they felt could be decisive in war and also clearly define a mission only the Air Corps could execute, thus supporting their cherished aim of a separate service. The USAAC had the greatest focus on aerial bombardment among the world air combat teams, and its chief, General Henry 'Hap' Arnold, was particularly disposed to expanding this capability. The strategic bombardment concept, long advocated but never demonstrated, was a tough sell. All wars had been won by occupation of territory and destruction of opposing armies and fleets, and the cost of vast heavy bomber groups was staggering. It was also a threat to the established Army and Navy tenets that saw aircraft as supporting elements.

The Kilner Board explored Air Corps acquisition priorities during 1939, drafting a research and development (R&D) outline to 1944. Given the evolving air war overseas in 1940, the Emmons Board reviewed requirements and revised this Five-Year Experimental Programme. They recommended developing a heavy bomber with 5,333mi (8,582km) range, medium bomber with 2,667mi (4,292km) range, a longer-range bomber and aero engines with power ranges of 1,700-2,400hp (1,268-2,535kW), 2,500-4,000hp (1,864-2,983kW) and 4,000-5,500hp (2,983-4,101kW). The service resisted further revision to its development programs except for empowering the National Advisory Committee for Aeronautics (NACA) to devise a joint Army/Navy five-year R&D plan.

The 20 June 1941 War Powers Act transformed the Air Corps into the semi-autonomous US Army Air Forces (USAAF). That summer, the President asked the War Department for an estimate of equipment required to defeat potential enemies. This suggested an offensive rather than the previous defensive posture – a notable change from the previous 'hemispheric defence' isolationist policy. An aspect to be considered was the secret agreement reached earlier in the year with the United Kingdom. Should the US enter the war, these allies would deal with Germany and Italy while holding actions contained Japan until resources were freed. For the first time, airmen prepared a separate document addressing airwar needs. Finalised on 12 August 1941, this AWPD-1 projected numbers and types of bombers to prosecute a strategic bombing campaign against Germany while also supporting a land invasion. It estimated nearly 10,000 four-and six-engine strategic bombers in addition to 1,000 medium bombers. Only later might these resources be employed against Japan. With the Navy's plan, it amounted to a 10-fold increase in the number of aircraft, almost all entirely new types or models. Only later might these resources be employed against Japan. The Air Forces' plan was updated in 1942 based on lessons and the changing situation, but even this was later greatly extended. Hence, over-arching plans formed the basis for the tremendous World War 2 aircraft acquisition programme. In the meantime,

America found itself at war with the resources at hand. The much-harried bombers contributed modestly in 1942, but made up for this as enormous fleets of superior aircraft began to fill the ranks.

The USAAF's principal aircraft acquisition team was at Wright Field in Dayton, Ohio, as elements of Materiel Division with procurement, engineering and flight test branches. It soon fell under the new Air Materiel Command. This and Air Service Command were merged to become Air Technical Service Command (ATSC) during 1945. Service trials were typically performed by the units at Wright Field, the Army Air Forces Proving Ground Command at Eglin Field, Florida and the Army Air Forces Tactical Center at Pinecastle Field, Florida.

In March 1941, the Royal Air Force (RAF) switched from daylight bombing to night area bombing because of heavy losses to flak and fighters. This caused concern with USAAF purchases of heavy bombers suited for exactly the tactics just abandoned by the very experienced British. However, Air Forces leadership held firm, as they believed the heavy armament in these aircraft, flying in mass formations, and precision daylight bombing owing to better navigation and superior bombsights, would bring the enemy to heel faster and so with fewer casualties. This element of the USAAF bomber programme remained the apple in the leadership's eye.

The first USAAF bombing mission into Europe came in June 1942, and by

autumn the first raids were flown from the UK. By then, Britain appeared secure and the United States free from direct enemy attack. Successes at Guadalcanal, the battles of Coral Sea and Midway, ended Japanese momentum. Bomber production was picking up steam. A corner had been turned.

While the US Navy's aviation focus was on carrier-based aircraft, it employed large patrol flying boats ('P-boats') for long-range surveillance, bombing and anti-submarine warfare work. The vast expansion programs also brought new models and types of P-boats, exploiting new technologies for greater capabilities. The bombing aspect took on more significance, as indicated by adoption of the Patrol Bomber (PB) designation. Such aircraft had many demanding and unique requirements and were more costly than land-based counterparts. They required additional development facilities such as hydrodynamic testing of models in water tanks and by towing large models on open waterways.

Despite much acclamation early in the war, high altitude and level bombing of manoeuvring vessels was largely fruitless. Ships were best attacked in a direct, albeit more hazardous fashion. The Army and Navy began using low-level attacks by twin-engine bombers. Torpedoes were supplanted by lighter, less complex bombs, rockets or heavy guns and cannon. Flying boats were slow and vulnerable, and such work was best left to bombers or carrier aircraft. Consequently, facing a vastly expanded sea control mission with the dawn of war, the Navy began moving toward more efficient and cost-effective land-based bombers.

The medium bombers in this mix were also operated by the Marine Corps whose aviation acquisition needs were addressed by the Department of the Navy. The Bureau of Aeronautics (BuAer) in Washington oversaw development and procurement of naval and Marine aviation assets. Testing was principally performed at Naval Air Station Anacostia,

Left: Examination and testing of allied and captured enemy aircraft gave insights into manufacturing techniques, equipment capabilities, and aircraft performance that supported tactics development. However, shared with local aircraft development teams, it potentially aided ongoing or future American programmes. This captured Junkers Ju 88 undergoes flight testing on 29 December 1943. *Jay Miller Collection*

Maryland, before the activity was moved to Patuxent River, Maryland, in late 1943.

Air Forces leadership was frustrated that, even as their heavy bomber strength increased in the European and Mediterranean theatres, their strategic bombing campaign continued to be diminished by diversion of resources against targets directly facilitating the coming invasion of the continent. Additionally, the Germans proved resilient and the USAAF suffered horrendous losses while grimly pressing on. With the introduction of long-range fighter escort in December 1943, the balance tilted again. By the end of 1944, the Americans alone were sending 2,000 heavy bombers per day against strategic and tactical targets on the continent.

The ultimate expression of the long-range, heavy bomber was the technologically superior B-29. It played a pivotal role in bringing Japan to capitulation. Yet, all theatres saw sustained use of heavy, medium, and light bombers by both services against a wide assortment of tactical and resupply targets. All these aircraft underwent an evolution in meeting combat needs throughout the war.

War Dictates Change

The extraordinary technological march of aviation was on the verge of yielding tremendous gains in the late 1930s. Although military aircraft orders were initially weak during this period, the US enjoyed a most vibrant commercial aviation sector. The NACA assisted these advances with research and test facilities. The services themselves conducted and funded research, to include experimental aircraft. Later, examination and test of allied and captured enemy equipment lent insights that were communicated to development teams.

Manufacturing

The surge in aircraft orders, with the urgency of war and restraints of materials shortages, required government committees to balance and prioritise requests. The war placed some raw materials out of reach and alternatives had to be found or developed. The industry also had to institute new and more efficient manufacturing techniques while rapidly training new workers. Construction techniques continued to be refined, reducing materials and weight, and optimising construction techniques for quicker builds. Everything was pushed as fast as possible. More use of subcontractors and joint production with previous competitors was necessary while plant capacity was expanded multifold, outstripping all of Axis production. This offered the opportunity to build plants in the centre of the country where more labor might be found and farther from potential enemy attack. The same approach was played out with engine production. Despite some cooperation, inter-service rivalries kept the Army and Navy as competitors for resources.

A new bomber or even a new model of an established design required hundreds of thousands of engineering manhours and typically hundreds or thousands of drawings. This was followed by tooling changes and tests of revised or new

Left: PBY production rocketed up in the early war years as Consolidated expanded its San Diego line (shown here with PBY-5As) and later in New Orleans, plus at two Canadian plants. As with all bombers, improvements and new models were introduced, keeping the manufacturing of the complex airplane a challenging task. *San Diego Air & Space Museum*

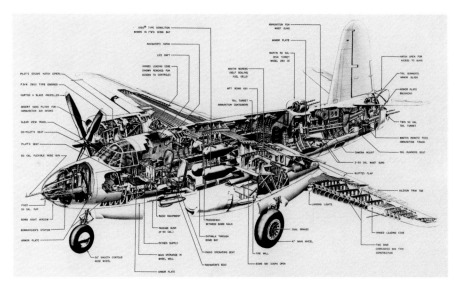

components, followed by flight testing of the aircraft itself. Production then had to ramp up as assembly of the new article became familiar. Training and deployment of operationally significant numbers followed. Consequently, it was typically a year before even an extensive aircraft change would appear in the field, and more for an entirely new design.

The demands from combat theatres for aircraft changes to meet emerging needs were best answered by incremental changes to existing models. However, there was persistent hesitancy to slow or stop a production line to introduce such changes. Consequently, modification centres were created to handle this work, with some undertaken by field shops. These incremental changes were reflected in Block numbers.

Chasing Rates

Speed is life in combat aircraft. High speed and the ability to climb at high rate assisted in evading enemy fighters and reducing exposure to AAA. Speed is facilitated with high engine power and conversion to thrust via the propeller, light weight of the airframe and low aerodynamic drag.

The prewar move to monoplanes, with elimination of struts and flying wires, greatly aided in drag reduction. Likewise, retractable landing gear cut drag, although the move to fully enclosed wheels while retracted was still underway. Advances in wing flaps, used to increase lift at low speed for landing, were also experienced. The simple split flaps were giving way to slotted flaps and sliding Fowler flaps that provided greater lift to keep approach airspeed low for landing distances of reasonable length despite the growing weight of

bombers. The NACA had devised a new wing airfoil that gave, laminar (smooth) airflow for more of the wing chord, delaying transition to the turbulent flow with attendant increase in drag. However, the laminar-flow wing required very tight tolerances on assembly for the benefit to be realised. For example, the upper surface skin of the XB-36 had to be within $\frac{1}{32}$in (1mm) tolerance.

A greater source of drag was landing gear, and bombers kept pace with evolving requirements that included being fully retractable and able to handle the growing weight of these machines. The latter concern also drove continuing wheel brake development to allow good landing distance without excessive heating. Typical wheel brakes were a caliper clamping to a steel disk attached to the rotating wheel, or pucks pressed to the disk with pneumatic or hydraulic pressure. The United States led in development of multi-disk brakes for greater energy capacity and multi-wheel bogies to reduce ground footprint load.

The United States also led in the adoption of tricycle landing gear, especially for bombers. This allowed easier control of the aircraft during ground manoeuvring, a safer takeoff attitude and a level deck angle on the ground for easier servicing and bomb loading. However, nose wheel steering remained rare during the war.* The tricycle landing gear for the Douglas XB-19 was a matter of concern, so the Air Corps bailed a OA-4B Dolphin amphibian to the company in May 1936 to be modified for testing. The Lockheed C-40B (38-582) was a Model 12 Electra Junior fitted with a nose gear delivered

*The reader is to assume no steering unless specifically stated.

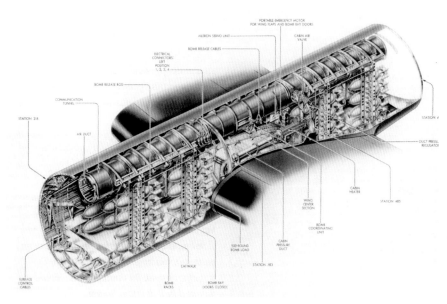

Left: This Boeing drawing of the B-29 centre-section, with bomb bays and communication tunnel, reveals a further level of complexity for what became the most advanced and capable bomber of the war. The addition of pressurization was a principal contributor to this growing intricacy and weight. *San Diego Air & Space Museum*

Above: The Air Corps had been interested in exploring tricycle landing gear as it offered advantages, especially for bombers. With Douglas developing the tricycle-gear XB-19, the USAAC bailed this OA-4B (photographed 21 December 1936) to the firm to be modified for undercarriage research. These results were subsequently applied to many military projects. *National Museum of the United States Air Force*

Above: Both the US Army and Navy converted Lockheed Electra Juniors with fixed tricycle landing gear during 1939, in essentially identical configuration, for flight testing. The Army example shown here was the C-40B while the USN's was the XJO-3. The engineering data and flight experience were most valuable. *Gerald Balzer Collection*

in June 1939 for testing. The USN also used an Electra Junior, the XJO-3 (1267), during summer 1939 as a tricycle gear testbed.† Consequently, experience and engineering data in tricycle gear aircraft was fresh when the military sought advanced bombers.

Aircraft weight continued to grow during the war as additional systems and defensive weapons were added. Also contributing weight was armour protection of critical systems and men against combat damage from anti-aircraft shell splinters, fighter gunfire and cannon, which took several forms. This included metal deflection and splash plates placed to protect vital

† US Army serial numbers and USN Bureau Numbers are provided in parenthesis for some of the more unique aircraft touched on in the text.

components, generally engine accessories and crew, from the most likely trajectories of incoming round and shell splinters. Crew members also had bullet-proof glass panels where needed and safety glass elsewhere, and flak curtains gave minimal protection from shell splinters.

Propulsion

Piston aero engine technology was reaching a performance pinnacle, and the excellent American models were a key to bomber performance. Several programs were underway to develop new aero engines with a leap in power. However, engine development time was even longer than that of airframes, and only new models of existing engines were fielded after America entered the

war. Still, a gain of even a few hundred horsepower required much effort to avoid excessive heat, wear and weight.

The 'competition' between air-cooled radial engines and liquid-cooled inlines that permeated fighter development was not evident in bombers. The most powerful, mass-produced aero engines were radials, and these were exploited to maximum effectiveness on bombers. The Army did undertake tests of inline engines on bomber testbeds and was not adverse to such combinations, but not at the expense of interrupting an ongoing production.‡

A short boost of additional power (called War Emergency, WE), usually at take off or to escape an enemy, was achieved by several means. Methods included operating an engine at excessive speeds, supercharging the air to the carburetor, or injecting water into the cylinders.§ The Americans led in the use of supercharging, or boost, to sustain intake manifold pressure of the fuel-air mixture and maintain power even in the thinner

‡ Lockheed-Vega installed the Allison V-1710, the most successful American inline aero engine, on a B-17E to become the Boeing XB-38, but it was not produced.
§ Water injection (usually a water-methanol mixture) produced a leaner fuel-air mixture but also kept heat down, slowing combustion to avoid detonation while allowing higher manifold pressure.

Left: This cutaway of a Pratt & Whitney twin-row R-2800-5 Double Wasps engine reveals the great complexity of high-performance aero engines as they reached the peak of their evolution during WWII. Development time for such powerplants were longer than for airframes. Wartime production presented just as many hurdles. *National Museum of the United States Air Force*

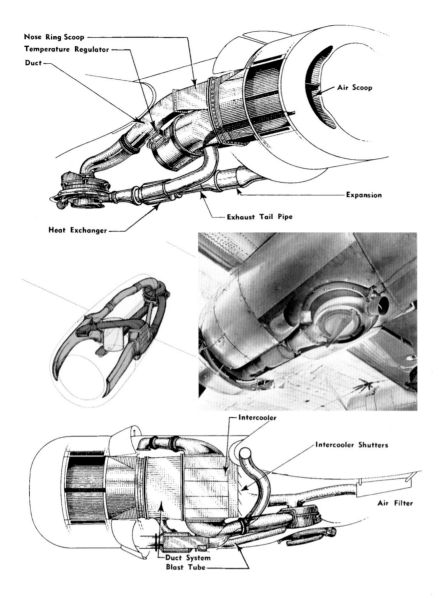

Nose Ring Scoop
Temperature Regulator
Duct
Air Scoop
Expansion
Exhaust Tail Pipe
Heat Exchanger

Intercooler
Intercooler Shutters
Air Filter
Duct System
Blast Tube

of high-performance propellers, Curtiss generally employed electric motors to achieve pitch change while Hamilton Standard preferred hydraulics. This also allowed the blades to be feathered, or turned edge-on to the airflow, for minimal drag when an engine had to be shutdown in flight. Cuffs at the base of blades could improved thrust and airflow into the cowling for enhanced cooling. Work was done to use various materials and make the blades hollow for reduced weight.

Ongoing cowling development sought to maintain suitable engine cooling while reducing drag. Instead of one or two exhaust pipes, ejector exhaust stacks expelled engine exhaust from several points around the periphery of the cowling exit, creating low pressure that drew additional air through the cowling for enhanced engine cooling. These might also extract some thrust with properly shaped stacks, and perhaps offer some exhaust flame damping effect. This latter was important for night combat, several supplemental flame dampers being employed but usually sacrificing some power output.

Fuel systems grew in complexity as multiple tanks became commonplace and the desire to crossfeed any tank ensured supply despite failures and battle damage. The growing complexity included submerged, electrical boost pumps and improved metering. Integral tanks or 'wet wing' eliminated rubber cells for more volume, but required sealed structure. However, the need for protection via self-sealing or leak-proof tanks to reduce the fire hazard if tanks were holed during combat essentially eliminated integral tankage as a design option. The self-sealing tanks were bladders made of layered fabric and rubber sheeting that also consumed volume and so reduced fuel capacity.

All-Weather Flying

The ability to operate without ground or celestial references at night and in inclement weather was a tremendous operational benefit for bombers. Passing through clouds

air at altitude. This was usually done with a compressor turned by engine gearing that could be operated at one or two speeds, with one or two stages of compression, and possibly one or two intercoolers to extract the heat added by the work. Where the aircraft dwelled mostly at low and medium altitudes, a single stage would suffice. This was taken a step further with a turbine turned by engine exhaust gases that, in turn, spun the compressor. The US had expended considerable resources since the early 1930s to develop this turbosupercharger and the results were superior to anything employed abroad. It was the only nation to subject such equipment to mass production, supplying 303,000 units during the war.[3] The introduction of automatic electronic turbo control greatly reduced the hazards and difficulty of manual control. Another advance just gaining traction was direct

fuel injection to eliminate the carburetor altogether.

Although the Americans had rigorous specifications for its military powerplants, war had a way of highlighting deficiencies. Sand and dust in North Africa and coral dust on Pacific islands quickly deteriorated engines. Some engine changes were required every 10 hours. In the desert, the addition of sand (tropical) filters on the carburetor intake was necessary. Fire detection and extinguishing systems (using carbon dioxide bottles) became common.

Propeller technology had advanced steadily to meet commercial demands. The fixed-pitch propeller could not be suitably optimised for all phases of flight. A two-position controllable pitch propeller was a good step forward, but the constant-speed propeller was the ultimate solution. This adjusted the blade pitch to match the power setting. Of the two principal manufacturers or rain showers risked accumulation of ice on the airframe that added weight and disturbed aerodynamics. The Americans were particularly focused on aircraft systems and training for these capabilities.

Prewar civil aviation industry was the incubator for many elements supporting all-weather flying. Heated pitot probes were long established, as was carburetor heat, but heated windscreen panels were new. De-icing boots were first employed on the Boeing Model 247 airliner in 1933, and so was established technology. These are rubber bladders fixed to the leading edge of flying surfaces and inflated with air to break away accreted ice. If employed incorrectly, they might not be effective. Also, the boots were easily cut by shell splinters and so required a close and lengthy inspection before missions or were simply removed. Boots damaged in combat could shred and interfere with flight controls. With Army sponsorship, NACA developed propeller de-icing using a fluid (isopropyl alcohol) ejected at the root of propeller blades to be carried to the tips via centrifugal acceleration. Addressing airframe icing, NACA began during 1941 with a specially modified Lockheed 12A Electra Junior, first redirecting engine exhaust into the leading edges then ducting ram air heated in an exhaust heat exchanger. General Arnold was so enthusiastic with their results that he directed in August 1942 that every B-17 and B-24 crossing the Atlantic be fitted with such systems by the next winter. Although this did not occur, the USAAF provided NACA with several bombers to support further icing research.[4] The work yielded information supporting the adoption of thermal de-icing in several models of bombers during the war.

'Blind flying' required precision flight instruments and intensive training. Radio navigation had advanced to permit bearings to radio stations and beacons at surveyed ground locations via direction-finding loop antenna. The Long Range Aid to Navigation (LORAN)

navigation system was developed during 1941 at the Radiation Laboratory, Massachusetts Institute of Technology (MIT). Bearings were taken from two stations transmitting on slightly different frequencies and pulse rates to calculate a position fix. Two successive readings over a set time determined course (drift) and ground speed. Three stations allowed a position fix within 4mi (6km) at a range of 1,200-1,500mi (1,931-2,414km). Instrument landings also employed radio beams and beacons for steering cues on cockpit instruments.

Radar was suitable for navigation by deriving position fixes by examining reflections off land masses or from radar beacons installed at surveyed locations. The latter was originally derived from the British 'Rebecca' system, but American equipment soon appeared. Radio altimetres (later radar altimetres) were used to determine height above the ground via microwave transmission reflections using a dedicated unit. Below 400ft (122m), it provided altitude readings to within 10ft (3m), permitting safe blind flight below 50ft (15m).

For bombers, radar had value for navigation, weather penetration or avoidance, and target location Another important use of radar was for Identification Friend or Foe (IFF) beacon with coded transmission and reception. The radar station could also acquire range and bearings to the emitting aircraft to direct interceptors or offer guidance instructions

if the aircraft was lost.

America had contributed to the development of radar, but was left to observe as the technology was militarised and airborne equipment emerged in the first years of the war. However, a 1940 joint development agreement with Britain permitted the US to benefit from the advanced work and manufacture early sets before expanding to further developments. The Radiation Laboratory became the centre of this effort. The first deployed gear, installed on hundreds of aircraft, was of British design and characterised by many external antennas for the long wavelength beams intended principally for air-to-surface vessel (ASV) detection supporting anti-ship and anti-submarine warfare (ASW) work. The objective of a centimetre wavelength, or microwave, radar would allow a single convene antenna under a 'radome' fairing and so reduce aerodynamic drag. The Americans flew their first such unit aboard a B-18 in spring 1941. The American ASD-1 (AN/APS-3) 3cm X-band radar was introduced in 1944. This unit could detect a large vessel at 58mi (93km), 35mi (56km) was more typical for a transport-sized ship, and 12mi (19km) for a submarine.

Systems Proliferate

The demands of an evolving battlefield plus enhanced safety and reliability drove a continuing growth in aircraft systems complexity. Flight engineers became

Right: The introduction of flight engineers on American bombers paralleled the unprecedented rise in complexity of these aircraft. The engineer assisted the pilots in handling the onboard systems, especially the engines and during emergencies. This B-29 flight engineer has a full set of engine controls in addition to other instruments. *National Archives*

Left: Even single-pilot bombers like this A-20G-15 twin (photographed 9 September 1943) had a cockpit considered to be overly complex by some, compared with foreign types of comparable mission. Nonetheless, all operators seemed to adapt to it and it worked well. Note the forward armoured glass, combiner glass for a reflector gunsight, and backup ring-and-bead sight. *National Archives*

Below, left: The flight deck of the four-engine B-24, with its long-range, heavy bomber mission, was necessarily "busier" than the A-20's. The Liberator had more extensive and complex systems, such as turbosuperchargers, and required two pilots for effective operation. Foreign operators continued to complain that the Americans insisted on controlling everything. *San Diego Air & Space Museum*

camera to record the immediate results of bomb impacts.

A particularly important addition to the electronic complement was the autopilot that reduced pilot workload and improved navigation for long cruise flight. More importantly, it could be coupled with the Norden bombsight to make the aircraft more stable for precision bombing. The Minneapolis Honeywell C-1 three-axis autopilot was the most common on American bombers. This had basic altitude hold and wing leveler for heading hold functions, plus 'fingertip control' to change heading with a knob to command a specific roll attitude.

The increase in crew complement paralleled the addition of advanced equipment and defensive weaponry. It reached its peak with 10-12 normally aboard a B-29. As mission length and altitude for bombers grew, the stress on the crew also grew and measures were taken in seeking some measure of comfort to ensure fighting effectiveness. However, insulation, sound proofing and air conditioning remained minimal to nonexistent to save weight and construction time. This ensured a stressful airborne environment even without enemies shooting at the aircraft.

Until the mid-1930s, most combat, including bombing, occurred below 10,000ft (3,048m). However, flight at high altitude got the aircraft above much of the weather, improved radio reception and could reduce the effectiveness of flak and interceptors. Supercharging allowed climbs to greater altitudes that presented significant physiological challenges owing to decreasing atmospheric pressure and temperature.

common on the larger bombers to assist pilots in attending to all these systems, especially in emergency situations. Design guidance for such systems were published by the services but were revised as technology advanced and combat survivability rose in importance. The latter required systems to be less centralised and with more redundancy.

Ever larger moving components saw greater application of hydraulic actuators. Electric motors gained in popularity, especially as they eliminated the potential hazard of hydraulic fluid leaks. This, in turn, required more power sources as engine accessories or separate Auxiliary Power Units (APU, usually a small gasoline motor). Electrical systems were important in supporting the growing number of electronic components added to support the bombing mission. Radios, for example, proliferated for communication, navigation and electronic warfare while growing in capabilities. Associated antenna collected on the aircraft exterior, including a trailing wire type that was reeled in when not required. Many bombers were also equipped with a strike

A supply of breathing oxygen to a mask is necessary to avoid hypoxia and systems of increasing this capability were introduced. Although bomber interiors could be heated, this became ineffective when gun ports were opened for attack or men moved into turrets that leaked conditioned air. The airman dressed in arctic gear and even electrically heated overalls, boots and gloves. Gun heaters were required to ensure operation. Survival in combat required parachutes, life rafts, emergency medical kits, rations, CO2 fire extinguishers, etc., plus training. The men might also wear flak vests, aprons and helmets.

Cabin pressurisation (or 'supercharged cabin') was judged essential for crew comfort and efficiency during high-altitude operations. Pressurised, it could maintain a pressure equivalent of 7,000ft (2,134m) altitude for a less-encumbered 'shirt-sleeve' environment. Such systems generally used a pump operating off engine power or a ram air turbine, also permitting air heating. Special construction and maintenance techniques were required to ensure an airtight cabin. In America, pressurised cabin efforts got a boost with a June 1936 USAAC contract to Lockheed for a 'sub-

stratospheric' research aircraft. This was based on a Model 10-A Electra but with turbosupercharged engines and new circular-cross-section cabin. The latter had pressure bulkheads and doors, internal bracing, small windows and windscreen, and ultimately used a construction technique involving Du Pont neoprene sealing strips between riveted interfaces. This XC-35 (36-353) first flew from Burbank in May 1937 and demonstrated a service ceiling of 31,000ft (9,449m).¶ The research lent confidence to the feasibility of turbosupercharging and pressurised

¶ Service ceiling is the altitude at which aircraft climb rate falls to 100fpm (0.5mps).

Above, left: These B-24J waist gunners model the wear and conditions for exposed high-altitude operations for typical WWII aircrew. They wear oxygen masks with microphones, earphones, and electrically-heated thermal suits. They might also don flak vests, be impeded by a parachute, armour and flak curtains, insulation, ammunition feeds, and be "fanny bumping" the other gunner. *Ray Wagner Collection*

Above: By contrast with the last photo, these gunners in an early-model B-17 are operating at low altitude in the tropics, and so are less encumbered swinging the heavy .50cal. One man wears a life vest for over-water flight. Note the gun-mounted ammunition canister feed via a belt or chute. *National Archives*

Right: The ubiquitous Martin electric turret, here in B-37 (interior) and B-24 (exterior), appeared on many aircraft because of its light weight and ready availability. The twin-.50cal guns were common with many turrets and the controls were also similar with other manned models. Evolution included addition of a computing gunsight and raised overhead canopy. *National Museum of the United States Air Force and National Archives*

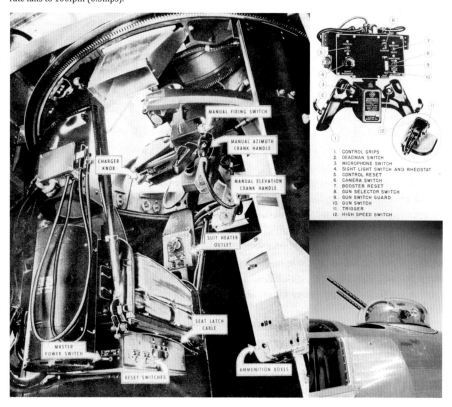

1. CONTROL GRIPS
2. DEADMAN SWITCH
3. MICROPHONE SWITCH
4. SIGHT LIGHT SWITCH AND RHEOSTAT
5. CONTROL RESET
6. CAMERA SWITCH
7. BOOSTER RESET
8. GUN SELECTOR SWITCH
9. GUN SWITCH GUARD
10. GUN SWITCH
11. TRIGGER
12. HIGH SPEED SWITCH

Left: The XC-35 was based on the Electra and was built by Lockheed under a Air Corps contract for a "sub-stratosphere" research aircraft. It had a new circular cross-section cabin and turbosupercharged Pratt & Whitney XR-1340-43s. Flying in May 1937, the machine soon achieved a service ceiling of 31,000ft (9,449m). *National Museum of the United States Air Force*

cabins, allowing direct application of these features to American bombers during the war.[5] Additionally, altitude chamber tests provided confidence in survivability from rapid decompression should the aircraft be holed. The USAAC unsuccessfully sought funds for an experimental pressurised 'substratosphere bomber' maintaining 8,000-8,900ft (2,438-2,713m) cabin altitude to 35,000-40,000ft (10,668-12,192m).[6]

Much had to be learned about building and operating pressurised aircraft in service. Instruments had to be sealed differently, and aircraft structural design and construction techniques were adjusted. Pressure leaks had to be found and repaired.

The advent of airborne electronic warfare during the war was particularly important and was most evident in the heavy bomber realm. The size, electrical systems and missions typically made them suitable candidates for carrying Radio Countermeasures (RCM) equipment. This included jamming of enemy radar and communications, plus 'spoofing' to misguide the enemy. This initially took the form of chaff ('window' or 'rope') to create false radar returns and later as specific signals from RCM gear. Allied systems were markedly superior to those of the Axis.

Window was first employed in the European Theatre of Operations (ETO) during December 1943 and continued to the end of the war over Japan. Crews would dispense the chaff either by hand out of gun ports or from specially installed chutes.

The size, electrical systems and missions of typical bombers made them suitable candidates for carrying RCM equipment. This included specialised receivers, signal analysers and transmitters operated by dedicated crewmen. Transmissions might seek to saturate a band with 'noise' or 'hash', jam specific frequencies or generate false indications. Jamming success was a function of output power and ability to match the enemy emitter characteristics. This included rotating directional finder antennas replacing fixed types. Formations would have one or more aircraft with such equipment.

Bombsights

A bombardier station normally had the man kneeling before the bombsight with observation out of a flat glass window to avoid optical distortion, so this had to be included in aircraft design. He had a few instruments giving the aircraft flight condition, a panel for commanding sequence of bomb release (intervalometer), bomb release, bomb bay doors controls and autopilot controls for fine adjustments.

The Norden bombsight had been standard equipment for both the US Navy and Army since the 1930s. It was subsequently manufactured by the C. L. Norden Company of New York City and was developed and procured by the Navy. The most produced wartime M-7 unit was considered so accurate that it was treated as sensitive equipment. The bombsight weighed 45lb (20kg) and included more than 2,000 parts. It was a synchronous stabilised instrument with gyroscopes, mirrors, gears and knobs. The gyros provided stabilisation to indicate drift from the straight and level. The bombardier sighted the target through a 2.5-power telescope while it lay ahead of the bomber. The bombardier had to make adjustments to account for the winds aloft (via a separate drift metre scope) and bombing ballistics given the bomber's altitude and airspeed (manually entered). All this required a steady lining up and run in to an aim point on the target from an initial point so that ground speed and drift could be accurately determined. The mechanical computer moved a mirror to keep the sight crosshairs on the target as the bomber advanced and provided an indication of when the bombs-away signal should be given for high certainty of bombs-on-target. It could also proceed automatically with the aircraft guided to keep the crosshairs on the target and the bombs released automatically.

The sighting portion of the Norden could be attached to a base component that contained the Automatic Flight Control Equipment, or Stabilised Bombing Approach Equipment to the Navy. The latter became standard Army-Navy equipment, but the Army eventually had Honeywell develop an electronics addition to the equipment that then morphed into the C-1 autopilot. With this interface, the bombardier could give lateral steering direction to the C-1 for final alignment on the target. If the gyros detected drift, the autopilot was sent correcting signals. The M-9 unit became available in late 1943 that required only 15-20 seconds of stable altitude and airspeed before release. Approximately 52,000 of the sights were manufactured during the war by a number of vendors at a unit cost of $6,000.

That the Army initially had to make all procurement and engineering change actions through the Navy was a source of frustration. Consequently, the USAAC had Sperry Gyroscope Company develop a similar bombsight. (The B-24 was delivered with Sperry gear for several years.) However, by fall 1943, the USAAF had decided to standardise on the Norden.

When war came, it appeared production would fall well short of demand, and this was the case into 1943. For this reason and security, the Sperry bombsight was fitted to bombers delivered to foreign operators. It was early 1942 before the US consented to releasing Norden to allied nations. However, the

British considered the bombsight inferior
for attacking heavily defended targets and
sought it only sparingly.

In 1943, the USAAF also had a low-
altitude bombing device developed
and added to the Norden to permit
descending bomb releases. In general,
the Norden was unsuitable for low-
altitude work and was replaced with
more simple devices, some employed
solely by the pilot. Likewise, a high-
altitude bombing addition was created.
The Automatic Gyro Leveling Device
attachment to the Norden was also
developed for the USAAF by Honeywell.

The advent of aircraft radar and the
prevalence of clouds over targets in Europe
compelled the development of bombing/
navigation radar. Targets were identified
by radar returns or this facilitated offset
bombing.** This 'blind bombing' was
introduced in the ETO during fall 1943.
The British H2S centimetric (10cm) came
first and saw some introductory use with
American units before the Americanised
H2X (AN/APS-15) Bombing Through
Overcast (BTO) units became dominant.
Development of a new X-band (3cm) AN/
APQ-13 Radar Bombing and Search Set,
or 'Mickey', began in August 1943 at Bell
Laboratories and the Radiation Laboratory.
The rotating antenna could image 360°
with a wide vertical beam matched to a
narrow horizontal. The installation of both
sets was characterised by the radome for
the 30in (76cm) antenna. This radome was
initially a retractable cylinder/hemisphere
but a teardrop shape was seen near the
end of the war.

** Offset bombing is flying a predetermined distance
and bearing from an easily identifiable landmark
distinguishable on radar to place the aircraft over the
target.

Range was a nominal 10-30mi (16-48km) with a maximum search range of 67mi (108km), but this was increased to 96mi (155km) with minor improvements. The final antenna was 16.0ft (4.9m) long and 3.3ft (1.0m) wide, weighed 1,100lb (499kg), and so envisioned as carried as a 'vane' under the bomber but that degraded bomber performance. Five pre-production sets were ordered in May 1943 and production orders reached 2,650 by February 1945. The Eagle was first tested aloft on 16 June 1943 on a B-24, and later tested on a B-25. The Eagle reached the ETO in October 1944, and just 24 B-24s and a handful of B-17s were modified. They did not see action. The B-29 used this radar to a limited degree in the closing months of the war with good results.

A programme to develop an improved radar bombing system combining optical and radar bombsight for improved accuracy, and suitable for high-speed aircraft like jet bombers, was initiated in spring 1944 under project Nosmo. The AN/APQ-23 was about ready for introduction at war's end as the first 'bomb/nav' system; however, range was on the order of 17mi (27km). This could be housed in a shallow blister radome in the belly of the aircraft.

Bombs and Other Weapons

By World War 2, bomb release was typically electrical, with control of which bombs were released in sequence for aircraft centre-of-gravity (CG) control. After configuring the bomb bay racks and shackles for the planned weapons load, each bomb was hoisted up individually, secured and armed. The process generally took a few hours.

Up to World War 2, American bomb sizes were 600lb (272kg), 1,100lb (499kg), and 2,000lb (907kg). In 1942, the Army and Navy adopted standard sizes of 500lb (227kg), 1,000lb (454kg), 2,000lb (907kg) and 4,000lb (1,814kg) Blockbuster. Larger weapons were introduced in an effort

Above: The APQ-7 was installed on a handful of B-17s and B-24s, some deployed to the ETO, but none were committed to combat before the war wound down. At top, a B-17G models the Eagle installation Stateside. At bottom, a B-24M-30-CO carries the antenna "vane" with little ground clearance. top *National Museum of the United States Air Force*, bottom *Author's Collection*

A more precise X-band radar (3cm) bombsight was initiated by the Radiation Laboratory in November 1941 under the title Every House in Berlin. This sought a high resolution by using the highest frequency then practical, and it became the AN/APQ-7 Eagle radar bombsight. It was particularly noteworthy for ten times the image resolution for more accurate bombing (equaling the Norden) with a shortened run-in (33mi/53km versus 70mi/113km, with the APQ-13) because of electrical scanning a narrow 60° arc forward from a fixed antenna.

to penetrate hardened targets via blast or kinetic energy, many being of British design. The M-17 incendiary was a cluster of 110 4lb (2kg) weapons. Fire bombs (napalm) were created from 108gal (409lit) compressed paper fighter drop tanks. Because of the close association with UK forces and potential difficulties with replenishment, provisions were made to employ British bombs from American racks.

The Pacific and sometimes China-Burma-India (CBI) theatres were seldom suited to high altitude bombing. Point targets in forest or jungles had to be hit

Right: This image is of 1,000lb bombs mounted in the bomb bay of a B-24C on 1 October 1941. It illustrates the stout frames with integral winches and release points for the bombs on either side of a central catwalk. Lighter bombers attached the bombs to mounts on the bay sidewalls. *San Diego Air & Space Museum*

Below: This shot of General Purpose Bombs reveals similarity in dimensions, save for scale. This allowed ballistic data to be readily computed and familiarity for armament personnel. Right to left are 100lb, 250lb, 500lb, 1,000lb, 2,000lb, 4,000lb, and 10,000lb weapons. The 2,000 or 4,000lb bombs were commonly the largest accommodated in bays. *National Museum of the United States Air Force*

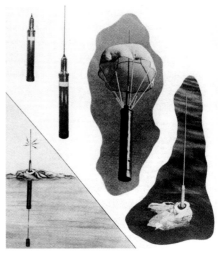

This 1945 diagram shows the sequence of sonobuoy operation, and the actual 3.75ft (1.14m) long AN/CRT-1 expendable device shown ready for drop from an aircraft bay. The sonobuoy revolutionized antisubmarine warfare from aircraft. This and other new technology blunted the submarine threat during the war. *National Archives*

from low altitude, sometimes in direct attack, and new techniques and weapons were employed. Among the preferred weapons was a parachute-retarded 23lb (10kg) fragmentation bomb (parafrag) with instantaneous fuze. The parafrags were employed for bombing of airfields and other 'soft' targets, the parachute allowing low-level release without risking the bomber being damaged by the blast. Skip bombing of vessels, by releasing the bomb at low altitude such that it skipped like a stone across the water, eliminated the long and vulnerable run-in with a torpedo which was often faulty. It was, however, tricky and required much practice to ensure the bomb did not exhaust its momentum short of the target or skip over.[7]

Rocket-propelled ordnance was introduced for greater direct-fire hitting power. Again following on the coattails of the British, the American aircraft rockets were developed at the California Institute of Technology (CalTech). These began with a 4.5in (11.4cm) diameter, 3.0ft (0.9m) long bazooka projectile with solid propellant fired from a 10.0ft (3.0m) tube. This heavy gear was soon replaced by a 3.5in (8.9cm) rocket with solid steel warhead weighing 34lb (15kg) and fired off 6.0ft (1.8m) rails. Initially air-launched in August 1943, it was in combat during January 1944. Adopting a 5.0in (12.7cm) artillery shell brought weight to 82lb (37kg) but velocity was cut significantly.

However, aircraft velocity was sufficient for firing stability, so the draggy rails soon gave way to zero-length launch stubs first introduced during spring 1944. A change to a 5in diameter motor yielded 1,375fps (419mps) as the 140lb (64kg) High Velocity Aircraft Rocket (HVAR) or 'Holy Moses'.

Submarines were primarily attacked with depth charges. However, waiting for a chance sighting or a radar contact with a surfaced sub was inadequate. Seeking to detect the boat beneath the waves brought forth the Magnetic Anomaly Detector (MAD) that employed a sensitive magnetometer. This device detected the alteration in the earth's magnetic field caused by the dense ferrous material of the submarine. Development began at the National Defence Research Committee during early 1941 and operational equipment was developed at Quonset Point, Rhode Island, with a Navy PBY serving as a testbed. The need to place the magnetometer as far from the influence of the aircraft's metallic structure meant MAD was evidenced by the tail boom 'stinger' projecting out of the aft fuselage. The first detection of a submarine from the aircraft was on 21 October 1941. The equipment could detect a submarine reliably at just 400ft (122m) range or at a depth of 300ft (91m) from 100ft (31m) altitude. Development of production models began in early 1942 and these

were flying in the spring.

Because of the small detection window of MAD, a depth charge released at the instant of detection would impact beyond lethal range of the submarine. Addressing this, the retro-bomb was developed. This weighed 65lb (30kg) with a 37lb (17kg) warhead and with a solid rocket motor. With the aircraft flying at the appropriate airspeed, rockets were fired backwards from launch rails to cancel the forward velocity such that the bombs would quickly assume a vertical descent such as to strike a target nearly below the aircraft. This was developed at CalTech and first tested from a PBY-5A in July 1942. Retro-bombs were deployed in mid-1943.

The difficulty in locating a submarine via MAD meant that its general location had first to be found via radar or sighting reports. However, research yielded sonobuoys equipped with passive hydrophone and radio transmitter. Descending by parachute, the buoy would float with the hydrophone hanging 24ft (7m) beneath the surface and the radio antenna projecting above. An operator aboard the aircraft would receive the transmissions and analyse the sounds. Until the advent of a directional capability, a line of sonobuoys would have to be laid to determine a bearing to the vessel. The sonobuoy's batteries soon expired and the unit was designed

to sink after a time to prevent capture. Detection range was a function of submarine speed (propellers cavitating), depth and sea state. It could vary from as little as 300ft (91m) to 3.5mi (6km). RCA built an experimental unit, the first flight trials performed with a blimp in March 1942 and a B-18 in July. The production device was the AN/CRT-1, 3.8ft (1.1m) long, 4in (10cm) diameter and 15lb (7kg) with 4hr life. The first units were deployed in August 1942. The US Navy bought 59,700 CRT-1s through 1944, and a directional model was under evaluation during 1945.[8]

Despite all the ASW hardware, the U-boats then took to remaining surfaced and engaging patrol aircraft with deck guns. The airmen then turned to rockets, cannon and heavy machine guns (MG).

Guns and Turrets

Defensive gun systems had always been an element of bombers. Prewar defences included exposed gun stations and manually operated enclosed turrets. The years leading to war and the initial

combat quickly rendered these anachronistic. Growing altitude and speed made exposed firing stations untenable. Manually moving a turret under airloads and with a heavy gun was an exceptionally strenuous activity made almost impossible by aircraft manoeuvring. Likewise, the American's favoured .30cal MG was shown to be too light to consistently knock down the latest fighters. Consequently, the .50 was phased in, although at 64lb (30kg) without ammunition box it further exacerbated manual gun laying. Powered

turrets remained in development. Cannon with explosive shells promised more damage to enemy aircraft and greater range, 20mm and 37mm weapons being explored. However, fewer shells could be carried and rate of fire was less, apart from added weight of the cannon (213lb/97kg for the M4 37mm weapon) and an automatic feed system. An answer to the cannon's slow rate of fire was the .60cal machine gun. This was under development during the war but never installed for combat. Bomber range briefly outpaced fighter escort until late in the war, so long-range bomber formations initially ventured out alone. This and the hardening of enemy opposition with more effective tactics meant bomber defences had to expand to cover all quarters with an intense volume of fire. This, in turn, drove up aircraft weight and larger crew size.[9]

At the start of the war the Americans were continuing to resist installation of tail guns. When combat demonstrated this a fatal lack, they scrambled to correct the deficiency. The initial cramped stations with one manually swung gun were belatedly replaced by proper

The Sperry ball turret was most noted for its installation under American heavy bombers. A smallish man entered from within the bomber, the hatch secured, and the ball extended. His legs lay between the computing gunsight and the .50cal guns. These armourers install the gun barrels before a mission.
National Museum of the United States Air Force

turrets, although this brought volume and CG issues. No sooner had this been resolved when the enemy changed tactics and engaged in head-on attacks. Forward firepower was inadequate and designers again hastened to adopt turrets to a nose mount for heavy bombers. Manual ventral gun stations were rapidly replaced by powered turrets as well, where practical.

Initially, ammunition was fed from boxes mounted on the guns. A 50-round box for a .50cal could be exhausted in less than 10sec of near-continuous fire, and likewise for a 100-round .30 box. Apart from the encumbering weight, reload meant vital seconds the aircraft was vulnerable. An alternative was a continuous feed of long belts from a nearby floor or wall-mounted box of larger capacity. However, the belts could become entangled with other items in the compartment. An innovation was flexible chutes – stiff enough to prevent belts from sagging yet flexible enough for unimpeded motion – channeling ammunition, with electric motor boosters, to turrets and other movable gun installations. This also allowed ammunition storage to be placed farther away to permit more area for the gunner to work and for a greater supply. Collecting spent shell casings in a bag or directed overboard was also important to keep them from gathering

on the deck and making for treacherous footing.

The programs to develop universal turrets initially lagged behind British work. The UK initially would not permit access to this sensitive technology, then production of an Anglo turret in the US was promoted.[10] However, US work continued apace and soon generated quality equipment. The service-developed turrets were not always available on time or in sufficient quantities. Consequently some airframe manufacturers developed their own. Ring-and-bead sights were eventually replaced with compensating optical sights.

The next step was remote controlled turrets (RCT), the gunner controlling the unit separately, allowing a lower profile and simplifying pressurisation design. Additionally, gunners could not practically perform manned turret operation at 30,000ft (9,144m) owing to the severe cold (assuming pressure breathing). Remote guns had to be charged other than manually, a CO2 gas cylinder being typical. Sighting was usually via a periscope, sometimes a bifurcated unit with head on top and below the aircraft. The system automatically switched between top and bottom periscopes based upon elevation of the gunner's sight as he tracked the target. The central fire control system permitted more than one gunner to

control an RCT.[††] Official development of a system began in 1940 and was intended for the newest-model heavy bombers, but development delays made necessary use of markedly improved manned turrets. A late-war innovation was radar-directed remote gun systems.

The demand for more ammunition, reload capability and higher calibre weapons had a weight penalty. For example, the 5,830 rounds of .50cal ammunition in the B-32 weighed 1,629lb (739kg). Mounts, some being articulated, had to allow the gun to be positioned as required, react or dampen recoil loads, and balance the weapon for ease of manual movement. Computing sights for defensive guns began appearing during 1942. Flash tubes fixed to the muzzles reduced pressures on the nearby aircraft skin.

Larger, fixed cannon were desired for ground attack. The M4 75mm cannon fitted to some aircraft weighed 1,800lb (817kg) and consumed 14.0ft (4.3m) of space with the recoil. Each round weighed 15lb (7kg) and only about two dozen could be accommodated in most aircraft installations. No automatic loader was devised, so it was serviced by a gunner.

†† A fire control system integrated the inputs from several gunners and directed a number of remote turrets as programmed for optimal defensive converage. An electronic system, it compensated for gun offset from the gunners' sights and adjusted fire for all the normal corrections.

Chapter Two

Twins Carry On

The Way It's Been Done

Twin-engine bombers were a natural extension of the USAAC's prewar fleet that was composed almost entirely of such types. Regardless of the focus on strategic bombing, doctrine and tactics still maintained a place for the twins, especially in the ground support mission, and fiscal limitations were ever-present. Consequently, as effort shifted to a rapid build-up of forces in the immediately prewar period, twins remained a major element. These would soon be labeled medium bombers as heavies came to the fore.

Initial tactics and training moved from level bombing to emphasised low-altitude attacks to meet combat requirements. While such was generally successful in the Asia and Pacific theatres, the more dense anti-aircraft defences in the Mediterranean and European regions forced the bombers back to medium altitude. Likewise, the typical lack of fighter escort and deficient self-defence weaponry in the early years contributed to serious losses to enemy interceptors.

As always, changing tactics demanded retraining and equipment adjustments that required time. For example, an increase of attack altitude could require a different bombsight and more emphasis on bottom defence. In later years, a return to low altitude with heavier firepower and new weapons again compelled changes. These pressures resulted in a steady evolution of the medium bomber types. The usual chase of escalating aircraft weight with added engine horsepower was in play, but the gradual losses in performance were acceptable as fighter escort became more plentiful and enemy counter-air resources strangled.

The pressures of a constantly changing airwar milieu saw the demise of older twin-engine American bombers, the maturation of a new generation and the looming retirement of these with the war's wrap-up. The future of such warplanes appeared in doubt even as they reached full potency late in the conflict with service leadership emphasising longer-range aircraft carrying heavier payloads mixed with multi-role fighters as the future of airpower. Such attitudes affected procurement decisions.

Put to Good Use (B-18)

The most numerous twin-engine American bomber in service at the dawn of World War 2 was the Douglas Aircraft Company B-18. This Model DB-1 adopted revised DC-2 airliner elements including the wings, empennage and two nine-cylinder Wright R-1820 Cyclone engines, but added 2,260lb (1,025kg) normal bomb load. Although the four-engine Boeing Model 299 was recommended by the Air Corps, and the future of the B-18 appeared limited, the Army General Staff decided on the latter. They noted the DB-1 met requirements and twice as many could be procured with available funds compared with the 299. In addition, the big Boeing bomber caused isolationists concern, so the twin was an easier political sell. The first of 129 B-18s was delivered from Santa Monica, California, in February 1937.

Below: The Douglas B-18 was conceived in 1935 as a spin-off of the DC-2 airliner. It was the most numerous bomber in the Air Corps at the dawn of war, yet was already antiquated: slow, under-armed, and without armour. A lineup of the bombers is shown on 25 April 1941. *National Archives*

The bombers were powered by the 930hp (694kW) R-1820-45 with two-speed, gear-driven supercharger. A single exhaust over the top of the nacelle shielded the flame from bottom observation. The typical crew of six included two pilots, a navigator/bombardier, and three gunners for the three .30cals. The guns were located in a manual nose turret (600 rounds), retractable and manually cranked dorsal turret (500 rounds), and a ventral station under a floor panel (500 rounds). The split flaps, landing gear, bomb bay doors and brakes were hydraulically actuated.* The main gear wheels remained partially exposed and the tail wheel non-retractable. Fuel capacity could be extended with two bomb bay tanks. De-icing boots were complemented by propeller anti-ice consisting of alcohol glycerin ejected at the root of the blades. Cabin heating was via circulated ram air heated by a steam radiator. Innovations included watertight outer wing panels that provided flotation in the event of ditching. Voids in the wing centre-section were likewise watertight and bilge pumps provided.

Responding to bitter complaints about the cramped bombardier station, Douglas proposed an alteration placing the bombsight above the gun in a projecting 'shark nose'. The revised B-18 was considered in early 1937 when seeking expansion of the bomber force. Requirement 36-528 included hauling up to 8,800lb (3,992kg) of bombs to 660mi

* Split flaps are hinged to simply rotate down from the parent surface, effectively adding camber to the wing and enhancing low-speed lift.

Douglas B-18A characteristics:

span	89.5ft	weight empty	16,321lb
length	57.8ft	gross	22,123lb
height	15.2ft	max.	27,673lb
wing area	959ft²	bomb load, maximum	4,400lb
fuel (int. + bay)	802+368gal	normal	2,260lb
service ceiling	23,900ft	speed, max. (10,000ft)	216mph
best climb rate	1,010fpm	cruise	167mph
takeoff distance, 21,123lb*	1,775ft	range, 4,000lb bombs	1,100mi
landing distance*	1,525ft	ferry	2,100mi
*over 50ft obstacle			

(1,062km), reach 225mph (362km/h) and ceiling of 25,000ft (7,620m). The crew of five was to range 2,000mi (3,219km) with a 2,200lb (998km) payload. Competing against the North American NA-21, the USAAC decided in favour of Douglas, although the bomber did not meet the requirements. The dorsal turret was bulging at the top to permit improved observation without extension. A Sperry A-2 autopilot was also fitted. The model featured the 1,000hp (746kW) R-1820-53 with 11.5ft (3.5m) diameter propellers that possessed a quick-feathering feature. The engine did not compensate entirely for the 1,000lb (454kg) additional aircraft weight, so there was a slight degradation of performance.

The first of 155 B-18A on order flew in April 1938, although 38 would be built as B-23s. The last was delivered to its operational unit in February 1940.

When the British delegation came to America in 1938 seeking military aircraft, they passed on the B-18 as a maritime reconnaissance bomber. They assessed it as underpowered, possessed of poor field performance, under-armed and pricey. Worse, Douglas said they would need more than two years to deliver the first RAF machine. This schedule must have been for significantly altered aircraft because Douglas did better against a Canadian order. They won a CAF contract for 20 machines for $117,300 each to serve the maritime role. Identified as the Digby Mk. I (Model DB-280), they were like the B-18A but with standard Commonwealth equipment and retaining the .30cal MGs.† Deliveries were from 29 December 1939 through 22 May 1940. They flew ASW patrols that lasted as long as 12hr, soon receiving ASV radar and operated through April 1943.

The Douglas aircraft were the US Army's standard medium bomber as war emerged in Europe. During 1940, 22 B-18s and 17 B-18As 'Bolos' had bomb shackles removed so that larger weapons to maximum capacity could be carried in the bomb bays. These became B-18Ms and B-18AMs, respectively. Despite these measures, the type was obsolete by the time of US entry into the war: slow, under-armed and vulnerable. Yet, it was the most widely deployed with 112 offshore on 7 December 1941.

The Bolos were to be replaced as

† Some sources state Vickers .303 inch guns were substituted.

Left: Although the B-18 was of little use as a frontline bomber, it found value in anti-submarine patrol. The USAAF quickly converted the B-18As to this role and Canada bought 20 new as the Digby. This RCAF example is fitted with ASV radar antennas on the spine. *Ray Wagner Collection*

Right: This B-18B (converted B-18A 37-530) models the nose radome and Magnetic Anomaly Detector (MAD) "stinger" on anti-submarine patrol over the Caribbean, a useful mission for the antiquated bomber. The insert shows the stinger as a test installation on B-18 36-262, in addition to radar receiver antennas along the aft fuselage. *National Museum of the United States Air Force*, insert *Ray Wagner Collection*

Below: The MAD was frequently used in conjunction with 65lb (30kg) retrobombs that fired rearward to descend vertically over the location fired. The B-18B could carry 16 of the projectiles fired from rails under the wings. A test firing from a B-18A is captured in this rare image. *Ray Wagner Collection*

frontline bombers during 1942, so efforts at upgrade were resisted. With most B-17s and B-24s husbanded for the strategic bombing campaign, the 'oldster' claimed the ASW role because it was suitable for bulky new equipment, could accommodate depth charges... and it was at hand. Although initially patrolling without radar, in early 1942, the B-18s began receiving 1.5m British ASV Mk. II units installed as the American SCR-521 (ASE). This was only marginally effective, especially after Germany deployed a radar detection system aboard its boats. A year later, centimetric ASV units, the 10cm SCR-517As developed as a joint US and British programme, were available. Also known as the ASV Mk. X or ASV-10, the radar could detect a surfaced submarine at 40mi (64km), but more practically, 25mi (40km), and a conning tower at

15-20mi (24-32km). The first tests were performed in March 1942 aboard a Bolo. The system proved immediately more successful, but only ten pre-production sets were available. Ten bombers were modified at Wright Field and deployed.

Owing to production delays, it was summer 1942 before significant numbers of SCR-517As were available. Some 122 B-18As were then modified in San Antonio, Texas, becoming B-18Bs. Adding 600lb (272kg) of equipment, the projecting nose of the B-18A was converted to a radome. The bombardier was again moved to the lower portion of the nose. Long-range navigational gear was also added. Some of the ASW-equipped aircraft also carried British Leigh searchlights to illuminate submarine targets at night. Deployment of B-18Bs began in October 1942.[1]

Later, 79 B-18Bs were given Mk. IV Magnetic Anomaly Detector gear, evidenced by the tail 'stinger' projecting out of the aft fuselage. This was soon complemented with retro-bombs in mid-1943, carrying eight under each wing and typically fired as salvoes of four from each wing and eight more half a second later. With sets of three rockets installed to fire at slightly different incidence, each group of eight projectiles struck the water in a 100ft (31m) line across the flight path, the second salvo impacting 90ft (27m) farther. The addition of sonobuoys completed this suite of high technology ASW weaponry on the least advanced bomber. Two B-18Bs in the Caribbean had a .50cal fixed in the nose by the combat unit to keep the submariners' heads down as the bomber made its bombing pass. These machines were dubbed B-18Cs.[2] The Bolo continued ASW patrols until replaced in August 1943 by B-24s. The type ultimately flew 46 per cent of the Army flight hours devoted to these missions and destroyed one U-boat.

Some Bolos were used for systems testing, to include evaluations of radar bombing, radio navigation gear and radio altimetres. The prototype B-18 (37-51) was modified at Wright Field in November 1938 with a M1898 75mm cannon in what had been the bomb bay. This was a purely experimental test installation that added considerable drag. It had the gun in a deep structure lacking forward fairing and with a periscopic

and stereo sight plus rangefinder projected far above the forward fuselage. The gun had a shortened barrel and was on a ball mounted for limited motion. Because the aircraft was involved in other tests, initial ground firing at Aberdeen Proving Ground, Maryland, was on a derelict B-18 similarly modified. The trials demonstrated adequacy of the installation's structural design. The flight testbed finally fired its cannon over Lake Erie in autumn 1939, but most work was performed at Philips Field, Aberdeen. This was the first testing of a large cannon for air and ground targets in an American aircraft. Vibration accompanying firing was prohibitive, but firing accuracy and general practicality of the concept was positively demonstrated.

Most Bolos ended their days in training, transport and target tow roles. Two were provided to Brazil in 1942. Three finding their way to Australia were employed as transports.[3] Consequently, the Bolo served to the end of the war, but with an R prefix (no longer combat-worthy) after October 1942, and 24 attrited.

Odds & Ends (XB-21)

Another older American bomber still lingering on at the dawn of World War 2 was the singular but uninspiring North American XB-21. Originally flying in December 1936 as the NA-21, it had competed in the 1937 competition won by the B-18A. A primary objective had been achieving an exceptionally high 40,000ft (12,192m) ceiling. Consequently, the two 1,200hp (895kW) Pratt & Whitney

(P&W) R-2180-1 Hornets were each fitted with a F-10 turbosupercharger. However, the combination had proven unreliable. Unusual features at the time were full-feathering propellers, a regulated oxygen system as opposed to local bottles and Sperry autopilot. Interestingly, the engine nacelles had a horizontal brace to the fuselage. Bomb capacity was an impressive 10,000lb (4,536kg), albeit with two 2,000lb (907kg) bombs carried

externally. The five .30cal MGs included one in each hydraulically powered nose ball and dorsal turrets, the first on an American bomber to have the gunner integral with the turret, plus one each in waist and ventral stations.

Competing without its turbos or turrets, the NA-21 was rejected, although primarily on price. The USAAC evaluated the aircraft again after it was rebuilt as the NA-39 and delivered in May 1938 as the XB-21 (38-485). It then sported de-icing boots and a .50 in the nose. An order for five YB-21 service test examples was considered but not

North American XB-21 characteristics:

span	95.0ft	weight empty	19,082lb
length	61.8ft	gross	27,253lb
height	14.8ft	max.	40,000lb
wing area	1,120ft²	maximum bomb load	10,000lb
fuel	2,400gal	speed, max. (10,000ft)	220mph
service ceiling	25,000ft	cruise	190mph
best climb rate	1,000fpm	range, 2,200lb bombs	1,960mi
takeoff distance*	2,000ft	8,800lb bombs	660mi
landing distance*	2,000ft	maximum	3,100mi
*over 50ft obstacle			

pursued. The aircraft simply did not have enough to recommend it and more promising bombers were under development. Nonetheless, the sole example was useful as a systems testbed and was purchased in January 1939. It continued to be employed in research projects at Wright Field for several years.

Sidelined (XB-22, B-23)

Seeking to improve on the B-18 as aeronautical science advanced during the 1930s, Douglas proposed a B-18A with the 14-cylinder, double-row, 1,600hp (1,193kW) Wright R-2600-1 Cyclone 14 engines with single-stage/single-speed supercharger. The USAAC designated this concept XB-22, but projected performance fell short of desires owing to high drag from the pot-belly fuselage.

Douglas initiated a major redesign, seeking a narrowed fuselage with lower frontal area. They employed strengthened and shortened DC-3 wings with watertight panels, landing gear and horizontal tails mated to a new fuselage and vertical tail. The undercarriage was fully retractable, albeit with the expedient of the nacelle base extended down and added doors that projected around the main wheels. The USAAC ordered 38 of these aircraft in November 1938 as B-23s. Although this was essentially a new design, the contract was awarded without competition, prototype or service test examples. The first B-23 was taken up for a maiden flight in July 1939, just nine months following concept proposal and less than eight months after contract award.

The B-23 was powered by two 1,600hp (1,193kW) Wright R-2600-3 turning three-blade, 13.5ft (4.1m) diameter props with a quick-feathering feature. It retained the 4,400lb (1,996kg) bomb bay capacity of the Bolo. A droppable 420gal (1,590lit) bay fuel tank augmented the four wing centre-section tanks.

The aircraft was potentially so fast that a nose turret was judged minimally necessary and a turret dismissed.

Douglas B-23 characteristics:			
span	92.0ft	weight empty	19,089lb
length	58.4ft	gross	26,500lb
height	18.5ft	max.	30,475lb
wing area	993ft²	bomb load, max.	4,400lb
fuel (int.+bay)	870+420gal	normal	2,500lb
service ceiling	31,600ft	speed, max. (12,000ft)	282mph
best climb rate	1,493fpm	cruise	225mph
takeoff distance*	1,475ft	range, 4,000lb bombs	1,400mi
landing distance*	1,875ft	ferry	2,750mi
*over 50ft obstacle			

Instead, a .30cal MG with 600 rounds was provided in a simple ball mount. Curiously, the nose lacked a bottom flat transparency for the bombsight. A .30cal was mounted to a bar off a bulkhead such that it could be swung to fire out either side hatch or a dorsal hatch. A ventral .30 fired out a drop-down panel. There were 600 rounds for each of these guns. A .50cal with 200 rounds was placed in the tail as the first American bomber to fly with such a heavy gun in this quarter. This had a fixed telescopic sight and transparent fairings that centred the barrel and ensured a streamlined aspect when not in use. The gunner was so confined that he could not crawl to the gun while wearing a parachute. The ship was manned by the single pilot, bombardier/nose gunner, navigator, radio operator, camera operator and rear gunner for all three aft guns. Sound-proofing and cabin heating helped crew efficiency.

Deliveries of the B-23 ran from October 1939 through September 1940. An order for 125 B-23As was contemplated but not consummated.‡ Although the bomber was superior to the B-18, the B-17 and newer twins showed that it was still 'old school'. The armament was too light, the beam/dorsal gun arrangement cumbersome, and the bomber lacked armour and self-sealing fuel tanks. Contemplated improvements were not consummated.

The B-23's service as a fleet bomber was brief and it flew equally briefly in patrol off the Pacific Coast after war was declared with Japan. Many were turned to test duties, including 39-28 serving with Emerson Electric as a platform for remote gun control and aiming systems, and 39-50 as a turbosupercharger testbed.

Multi-Tasking (B-25)

In light of worsening world events and the strides being made in foreign airpower, the Air Corps responded to national direction to acquire more advanced

‡ Differences of the B-23A from the baseline design are unclear.

combat aircraft. It issued specification AC 39-640 in March 1939 seeking a medium bomber. The salient requirements were a bomb load of 3,000lb (1,361kg), 300mph (483km/h) top speed with 350mph (563km/h) desired, 2,000mi (3,219km) range, 20,000ft (6,096m) service ceiling, armed with four .30cal. machine guns and a crew of five. It was to use either the R-2600, R-2800 or R-3350. To hasten the acquisition process, selection would be made from proposals alone, without a 'fly-off' of prototypes, with the intent that the winner would be bought 'off the shelf' with an order for 385 aircraft.

North American Aviation (NAA) prepared a proposal derived from an aircraft built earlier for the AC 98-103 competition won by the Douglas A-20. The NA-62's slotted flaps were hydraulically operated as was the fully retractable undercarriage.§ The fuselage accommodated the 3,000lb (1,361kg) bomb load, although a typical load was 2,000lb (907kg). The USAAC urged NAA to adopt the R-2600. Wright built some 50,000 of this twin-row engine during

the war at its Cincinnati, Ohio, and Paterson, New Jersey, plants. The 1,700hp (1,278kW) R-2600-9s had a two-speed mechanical supercharger and turned three-blade, 12.5ft (3.9m) propellers with anti-ice. The oil coolers were in the wing outboard of the nacelles, air taken in through leading edge openings and expelled out vents atop the wing.

The NA-62 crew was to consist of two pilots, the bombardier/gunner, the navigator/gunner and radio operator/rear gunner. The .30cal in the apex of the transparent nose was supplied with 600 rounds and was transferable between one of three ball mounts. Another gun

was mounted behind windows in the fuselage top, aft of the wing, requiring the navigator to crawl over the wing spar and bomb bay to gain the weapon. A .30 was mounted on an arm such that it could be fired by the radio operator out a ventral hatch or either waist window. A tail .50cal with telescopic sight was found in a mounting like that from the B-23, the gunner lying prone, kneeling or sitting depending on which position was least uncomfortable.

After a June bid, the NA-62 was evaluated during July against competing proposals from Douglas, Martin and Stearman. Martin was selected the winner in August with a design that became the B-26. However, Martin would not commit to the entire 385-aircraft procurement in the time-span desired by the Air Corps. Consequently, second-place (and low bidder) North American was also given a contract for what became the B-25. Signed on 20 September, the $11,771,000 order was for 184 aircraft and a static test article.¶ These

¶ A static test article is the bare structure of the aircraft for ground tests representing loads (stress and strains) expected in service extremes. Testing might reveal design deficiencies or additional load capability.

§ A slot between the flap and the bottom of the wing allows high pressure air below to flow over the top of the flap, enhancing the lift increment contributed by the flap.

Right: Bomb bay tanks and the safety factor of twin engines made the early B-25s useful during the initial frenetic period of anti-submarine patrols after American was drawn into the war. This B-25C has an ASV nose Yagi antenna. The fixed and flex nose guns, and Bendix dorsal turret are evident. *National Museum of the United States Air Force*

would be built in three progressively improved variants so that the aircraft could be fielded at the earliest possible date. A wooden mockup was approved on 9 November and the static test airframe delivered to Wright Field on 4 July 1940. A nose gear failure during taxi testing required remedy, but the maiden flight from Inglewood was accomplished on 19 August. By that time, the war in Europe was making clear the aircraft required changes to be survivable and effective.

The first B-25-NA grossed 27,310lb (12,388kg) and initial testing uncovered issues that required further work.** Directional stability was deficient, affecting bombing accuracy. Changes addressing this included enlarging the vertical tails and flattening dihedral in the outer wing panels.†† The successful wing configuration was flown on 25 February 1941 and five vertical tail designs were tested. Only 24 of the B-25-NAs were delivered from February to May 1941, the first nine without the dihedral change.

The 40 B-25As introduced armour and the four main wing tanks were given self-sealing cells. With no commensurate increase in engine power and a loss of 222gal (840lit), range was decremented by 650-750mi (1,046-1,207km). A 418gal (1,582lit) bomb bay auxiliary tank was developed to compensate where practical.

Like the B-25-NAs, the As were kept Stateside and devoted to coastal patrol duties with early ASV radar. The bay tank was most useful in this role but made under-wings racks necessary for bombs and depth charges.[4]

The next model introduced electrically powered dorsal and ventral turrets with twin .50s. The 525lb (238kg) Bendix A4 top turret (400 rounds per gun, rpg) was manned while the 497lb (225kg) Bendix A5 belly turret (350rpg) was remote and retractable. The latter was operated by a kneeling gunner using a periscopic sight. As these turrets

Above: The B-25C and D models were the most common Mitchells in the early war years, establishing its reputation for ruggedness and reliability. They soon found their element in the Asia-Pacific theaters. Although well armed, the ventral turret proved troublesome, and the tail plus waist stations were sorely missed. *Ray Wagner Collection*

were considered adequate and balance issues had become critical, the tail and waist gunner stations were eliminated, the side hatches reduced to scanning windows. A plexiglass tail cone remained for scanning, but many crews added two poles projecting from the fairing to appear like gun barrels and discourage rear attack. A 12.6ft (3.8m) propeller was adopted that would persist throughout the remainder of production. However, weight increase again impacted performance. These 120 B-25Bs filled out the original contract, the first delivered in August 1941.

The ventral gunner quickly discovered it was very difficult to locate and track targets, even with the addition of scanning windows beside him. This was apart from being uncomfortable from the hunching over the sight. Not moving in concert with the periscope head (lacking a swivel seat), his vestibular cues did not coincide with the visual as the sight slewed about, with vertigo and nausea resulting. The narrow field-of-view alone made the value of the turret marginal. Additionally, the optics would often be obscured by dust or mud thrown up on takeoff, or by oil collecting during flight. Ammunition feed was unreliable and sometimes an electrical micro-switch would fail, leaving the turret stuck down, greatly increasing drag for the reminder of the flight. The turret was considered

of so little value by October 1941 that it was often removed by operational units who, in the Pacific theatre, generally flew low enough that an attack from below was unlikely.

There were 130 B-25s by the time the US entered the war. A new contract had been signed on 28 September 1940 for 863 B-25C Mitchells (NA-82). The Netherlands government in exile had placed a 30 June 1941 order for 162 Cs (NA-90, later B-25C Block 5) to supply the Dutch East Indies. The C model substituted the R-2600-13 with different carburetor. Fuel capacity was increased to 974gal (3,687lit) by the addition of 152gal (575lit) self-sealing cells in each wing. Also featured were self-sealing oil tanks, autopilot, high-pressure brakes, 24V electrical system, electrical releases for bomb racks and the bay could accommodate a wider assortment of weapons. Empty weight rose nearly 1,500lb (680kg) and gross by over 7,250lb (3,289kg), losing 16mph (26km/h) off the top speed and 2,300ft (701m) off ceiling.

Considered worthy of frontline combat, the B-25C was produced in

** W Many early war American bombers had the first model identified without suffix letter in the designation. To differentiate these from general references with type designation alone, the post-suffix manufacturer code will be employed as done here: B-25-NA for the first model and B-25.

†† Dihedral is a positive or upward spanwise angle on otherwise-level wings or tails. Anhedral is a negative or downward angle.

North American B-25C-10 (D-10 similar) characteristics:

span	67.6ft	weight empty	20,300lb
length	52.9ft	gross	33,500lb
height	15.8ft	max.	34,900lb
wing area	610ft²	bomb load, max. (int.+ext.)	3,200+2,000lb
fuel	974gal	normal	2,000lb
service ceiling	21,500ft	speed, max. (15,000ft)	284mph
initial climb rate	1,375fpm	cruise	233mph
take off distance*	4,000ft	range, 3,200lb bombs	1,525mi
(32,000lb)		5,200lb bombs	1,225mi
landing distance*	2,800ft	ferry	2,750mi
*over 50ft obstacle			

markedly greater numbers. To meet this demand, a new facility was built in Kansas City, Kansas. The General Motors' Fisher Body Division in Cleveland, Ohio, would provide a substantial portion of the aircraft as subcontractor. The new plant got a 1,200-unit order on 24 February 1941 for the B-25D (NA-87), essentially the same as the Cs from California.

The first B-25C took flight on 9 November 1941, the D in December and initial deliveries were in January and February 1942 respectively. The advent of Lend-Lease brought further orders. These were 14 January 1942 contracts for 150 to China as NA-93s and 150 Mitchell IIs to Britain (NA-94s, eventually Block 10s). The Air Forces placed its own order for 300 more Cs (NA-96, Block 15s) on 28 March 1942. In the event, the Americans chose where the aircraft went, so the allotment by contract proved meaningless. Another order for 1,090 B-25Ds (NA-100) was placed on 26 June 1942. Production ran through May 1943 with 1,625 B-25Cs and 2,290 Ds through March 1944.

By March 1942, the 100 B-25Cs on hand were urgently needed. Most were passed along to the Soviets and Dutch. The 42 sent to Australia enroute to the Dutch was instead seized by the USAAF in-country and they first saw action in early April. Of course, the Mitchell was made famous by the Doolittle Raid in which 16 B-25Bs, specially modified with additional fuel capacity and low-level bombsight, flew off the carrier USS *Hornet* on 18 April 1942 to strike Tokyo and other Japanese targets. At 31,000lb (14,061kg) gross, these were the heaviest aircraft launched off a ship at the time. All aircraft were lost and nine airmen killed seeking the recovery site in Asia, but the legendary raid was fantastically successful. The morale boost at home was enormous and the Japanese were compelled to keep fighters at home for defence.

Production of Cs and Ds saw numerous changes introduced as block upgrades. The earliest appearance was wing hardpoints for two racks each and a total eight 250lb (113kg) bombs, raising payload capacity to 5,200lb (2,359kg). A 2,000lb (907kg) torpedo could be mounted under the bay in lieu of bombs. Removable de-icing

boots were fitted and 'Finger' exhausts under the cowl flaps provided flame damping. This was later revised as a Clayton S-type ejector exhaust for each cylinder, protruding around the cowling. A flex-mounted .50cal gun was added in the middle of the nose and another fixed in the starboard side of the compartment, each with 300 rounds (1,350 rounds total). Turrets were upgraded, but the ventral unit omitted from some blocks. Bay 'aux' tanks were devised, along with small ferry tanks for the waist stations. The C-25s returned to tail and waist stations with a .50 each and feed chutes.

Field modifications began appearing during fall 1942 which improvised waist stations and a tail weapon for a prone gunner, usually with .30cal weapons. Added tankage included a unit in the radio operator's station and another replacing the ventral turret. The few examples of radar in USAAF Mitchells were installed in extendable radomes replacing the ventral turret. Of the many variations, the most noteworthy were enhancements to strafing potency. The most successful was first tested in December and deployed in February 1943 in the Southwest Pacific Area (SWPA). The bombardier/navigator station was replaced with four fixed .50s and feeds to two pairs attached on either side of the nose within blister fairings. With the top turret rotated to fire forward,

a 10-gun barrage was created. The side 'package' or 'pack' guns had to be moved aft and the ammunition fed from the bomb bay to assist CG issues. Although some fuselage skin deterioration and popped rivets resulted from the early installations, substituting higher gauge skin and installing internal braces solved these problems. Later, an aluminum sheet with felt or rubber backing was attached to the nose skin adjacent to barrels.

The strafer modifications offered an alternative to attacking shipping with skip bombing. The concentrated stream of large calibre slugs could chop the superstructure of a freighter to scrap and sink smaller vessels. The first strafers were used to good effect in the March 1943 Battle of Bismarck Sea, helping to prevent the landing of enemy infantry reinforcements. Combining the intense .50cal fire with bombing could wreak terrible havoc in airfield attacks. This came to use six 100lb (45kg) demolition or white phosphorous bombs and 60 parafrags.

A modification centre was established in Townsville, Australia, to introduce the pack guns to 175 C/Ds by September 1943. These proved so effective that the configuration was officially adopted in an example of field units directly affecting production. They employed individual blisters for the two guns per side instead of the unified blister. A tapered blast deflector at the end of the barrel direction muzzle gases up and down, reducing over-pressure on the skin. The B-25D-35s gave the operators waist stations in bulged windows and a tail position under a greenhouse for headroom.

To add even greater striking power for ground attack and leveraging off B-18

Left: The Mitchell became the subject of possibly more field modifications than any other American type. The addition of forward-firing .50cal machine guns, like those seen added in and on the sides of the nose of this C/D, enhanced the strafing potency that became more valuable than bombing as the war progressed. *National Museum of the United States Air Force*

Right: After years of experimentation, a large-bore cannon was finally introduced into a production aircraft with the B-25G. The 75mm gun was installed in the bombardier crawlway and serviced by the navigator with just 21 rounds onboard. The cannon did not prove very popular, and units frequently removed it. *Ray Wagner Collection, insert National Archives*

test work, a Colt 75mm M-4 field gun was added to the last B-25C-1 (41-13296) to become the XB-25G. This weapon weighed about 900lb (408kg) and was 9.5ft (2.9m) long with 1.8ft (0.5m) recoil. The gun was on a hydro-spring cradle to absorb recoil shock. The entire installation weighed 1,400lb (635kg) and required a 14.0ft (4.3m) long volume. It was mounted in the bombardier crawlway to the navigator compartment in the lower port nose with a tray of 21 shells above, each 26in (66cm) long and weighing 20lb (9kg). These were manually loaded by the navigator. Given the weight and confined space, this was a difficult task. The aircraft nose was shortened to match the barrel length and also fitted with two .50cal machine guns and 400rpg. This nose armament was aimed via an optical sight on the glareshield that also supported bomb delivery.

The XB-25G was first tested on 22 October 1942. Tests found muzzle blast damaged adjacent nose structure, so the barrel was lengthened 3.0in (7.6cm). The intent was for the MG tracers to help aim the cannon in addition to suppressing ground fire during a firing pass. A muzzle flash shield was added to the lower portion of the pilot's port quarter windscreen transparency. Armour was added for enhanced forward quarter protection and to the cockpit sides as external appliqué. Speed was, naturally, sacrificed by the changes. A drag-reducing barrel end cap that split to open as petals was not taken to production.

Five C-15s were completed as B-25G-1s (NA-93) as service test examples, the first flying on 16 March 1943. These were followed by 58 Cs modified to G standard and 400 B-25Gs (NA-96) manufactured in California and delivered during May through August 1943. These were the first American production aircraft sporting a large-bore cannon.

The cannon was met with mixed responses. Although accurate, only four

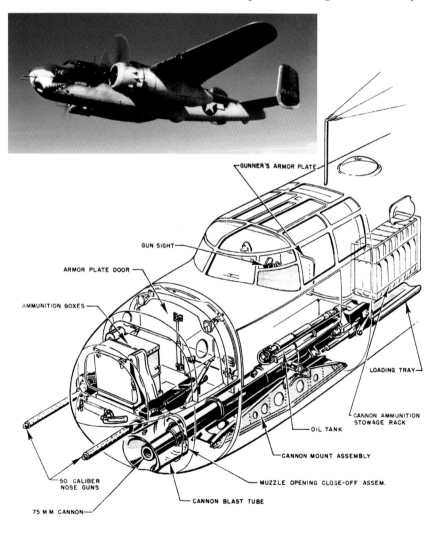

GUNNER'S ARMOR PLATE

GUN SIGHT

ARMOR PLATE DOOR

AMMUNITION BOXES

LOADING TRAY

CANNON AMMUNITION STOWAGE RACK

OIL TANK

CANNON MOUNT ASSEMBLY

MUZZLE OPENING CLOSE-OFF ASSEM.

.50 CALIBER NOSE GUNS

CANNON BLAST TUBE

75 M M CANNON

Left: The B-25H moved to a lighter version of the 75mm while also inserting many of the desirable features being installed via field modifications. These included tail guns, waist gunners, and deleting the unreliable ventral turret. The dorsal turret was moved forward for balance, and this Block 10 has package guns. *Air Force Flight Test Center*

shells could be fired effectively on a pass during which the aircraft had to be flown on an unwavering path that delighted enemy gunners. Further, gun gases in the cabin were annoying and the muzzle blast caused sheet metal damage over time. Some crews preferred lighter, faster firing weapons, especially as suitable targets for the 75mm became few. Consequently, Gs were modified with nose .50s replacing the cannon.

The B-25H (NA-98) split the difference, adopting the lighter Oldsmobile T-13E1 75mm and four .50s in the nose, another pair in individual blisters on the starboard nose with 400rpg. The tail gunner returned but in a larger space due

to deepening the aft fuselage volume by 7.0in (17.8cm) to allow seating in front of armour. He fired twin .50s with 600rpg in a Bell Aircraft M-7 electro-hydraulically powered mount. The dorsal turret (400rpg) was moved forwards to the navigator's station for CG considerations while also providing space for staggered waist gunner stations to avoid crowding. These had a .50 in window aft lower corners and 200rpg each, 3,000 rounds total onboard. The copilot station was omitted to save weight but a jump seat retained for the navigator/cannoneer, displaced by the turret relocation. However, the crew still grew to five. The B-25H, with its large-bore cannon and

14 machine guns, was the most heavily armed American production bomber.

The B-25C-10 42-32372 was converted as the XB-25H with 1,900hp (1,417kW) R-2600-20 and initially flown on 15 May 1943. A 20 June 1942 order for 1,000 of the model led to flight of a production example on 31 July 1943, although the -20 engine was set aside. First seeing combat in February 1944, these possessed up to 800gal (3,028lit) bay fuel, 3,200lb (1,452kg) weapons load, 869lb (394kg) of armour and late-model Hs had zero-length launchers for eight 5in HVAR rockets. The aircraft also introduced flush riveting in the forward third of the fuselage and all flying surfaces to reduce drag. The 300 H-5s had the side .50s reflect on the starboard nose. The cannon was removed in the field by many units.

Inglewood ceased B-25 production in July 1944 as the plant focused on fighters. Kansas City carried on with what would be the most numerous model, the B-25J (NA-108).‡‡ This was initially ordered on a 4,390-unit 14 April 1943 contract. The model had the same

‡‡ The model I designation was skipped, to avoid confusion with the numeral 1 when designations were written out. This was a common practice with all American military aircraft.

Left and above: The B-25J dropped the cannon and returned to the bombardier nose, but with armament layout of the H and built in the largest numbers. It also had a 4,000lb (1,814kg) payload not counting external stores. Shown is a B-25J-20 on 25 September 1944 and the eight-gun nose of a J-22. *San Diego Air & Space Museum, above Gerry Balzer Collection*

Right: Underwing rockets were added to the weapons suite for the Mitchell with the H model in 1944. These four 5inch HVAR projectiles are mounted on zero-length launch stubs of a B-25J. The added ground attack punch was a welcome compensation for departure of the 75mm cannon. *National Museum of the United States Air Force*

armament as the H but without the cannon. It restored the bombardier nose with a ball-mounted. 50 (300 rounds) and a fixed gun in the starboard side (300 rounds). The waists had 250rpg. Bomb bay capacity was raised to 4,000lb (1,814kg). With return of the bombardier and copilot (much missed by the over-burdened B-25H pilot), the crew became six.

The first B-25J took flight on 14 December 1943 with first delivery in the same month, and block changes soon introduced. The pack guns (400rpg) were restored in late production, but sometimes removed to avoid structural deterioration. Upgraded under-wing mounts accommodated up to six 350lb (159kg) depth charges and waist guns received computing gunsights. The bombardier station side guns were soon standardised (300rpg), but the flex gun reduced to 200 rounds. Armoured pilot seats were introduced, bombardier armour having been added previously for a total 944lb (428kg). The eight under-wing rocket launchers were also adopted upgrades. Aerial mining and glide bombing capabilities also appeared. By 1945, these alterations had raised loaded weight by nearly 1,000lb (454kg). Some aircraft had the nearly identical R-2600-29 substituted for the -13.

Again, field units sought a more lethal ground attack configuration. In August 1944, they introduced a 'solid' nose of eight .50s (400rpg) or they simply added a second pair of the internal side guns in the port side. The 18 MGs (7,300 rounds) were the most heavily armed aircraft of their class. Eventually, 510 bombers were so modified, mostly with the 1,000 8-gun nose kits manufacturer by NAA that could be mounted on any model Mitchell, accommodating 3,200 rounds.

Kansas produced 4,390 Js. Mitchell production was terminated abruptly on 17 August 1945, the last a B-25J finished on 15 October but, along with 72 others, broken up before delivery. Cancelled contracts including B-25Hs identified as NA-113, 1,050 B-25J as NA-114 and 2,400 NA-115s.[5] North American ultimately made 3,209 Mitchells in California and 6,725 in Kansas, with 706 of the latter United States Marine Corps (USMC) PBJs and 45 as photo ships, plus hundreds more in the form of spares and non-combat models. The peak months were May and June 1944 with an average 13 bombers per day.

North American B-25H-5 characteristics:

span	67.6ft	weight empty	19,925lb
length	51.0ft	gross	33,500lb
height	15.8 ft	max.	36,600lb
wing area	610ft²	bomb load, max. (int.+ext.)	3,200+2,000lb
fuel (int.+bay)	974+650gal	normal	2,000lb
service ceiling	23,800-24,300ft	speed, max. (13,000ft/33,500lb)	293mph
average climb rate	790fpm	cruise 230mph	
takeoff distance* (32,000lb)	4,000ft	range, 2,000lb/434gal	940mi
landing distance* *over 50ft obstacle	2,800ft	3,000lb/974gal	1,350mi
		ferry	2,700mi

North American B-25J-5 characteristics:

span	67.6ft	weight empty	19,480lb
length	53.5ft	gross	27,000lb
height	16.4ft	max.	33,400lb
wing area	610ft²	bomb load, max.	3,000lb
fuel (int.+bay)	974+650gal	normal	2,000lb
service ceiling	24,200ft	speed, max. (13,850ft)	293mph
average climb rate	790fpm	cruise	230mph
takeoff distance* (32,000lb)	4,000ft	range, 2,000lb/434gal	990mi
landing distance* *over 50ft obstacle	2,800ft	3,000lb/974gal	1,350mi
		ferry	2,700mi

After their initial combat debut in spring 1942, the Mitchells were soon flying in every theatre. It was rugged and comparatively easily maintained, and so suitable for forward basing in austere conditions. The USAAF did not initially use the B-25 from the UK. Since the B-25s did not require as long a field as the B-26 and had longer legs, it predominated in the East while the B-26 was concentrated in Western Europe. The B-25 excelled in the interdiction role.

Nearly 2,000 Mitchells were exported in nearly all models. The RAF eventually accepted 618 machines through April 1945. The largest foreign operator was the Union of Soviet Socialist Republics with 867 as the only American medium bomber going to that nation. Comparatively smaller numbers went to Canada, Australia, The Netherlands, China and Brazil.

The USAAF's B-25 inventory peaked at the end of July 1944 at 2,656 aircraft (some devoted to transport and reconnaissance). More than 500 were serving in the Pacific by autumn 1944 where they were in their element. At war's end the number was 1,865 B-25s in the Army. It was the most numerous, widely employed and best liked of the American twin-engine bombers, and regarded by many as the best well-rounded World War 2 bomber of its class from any nation. However, the Air Forces did not operate the type in a combat role beyond the war as the A-26 was then the preferred medium bomber.

Mitchell Oddments
(XB-25E, XB-25F, NA-98X)

An experimental hot air de-ice system in reworked wing leading edges typified the XB-25E (NA-94), a C-10 (42-32281) modified in Inglewood. It was principally characterised by revised cowls with a duct in the bottom leading edge of the lips to exhaust gas heat exchangers. The leading edge heat was great enough that water droplets were vaporised, preventing them to flow aft on the wing and freezing elsewhere. The modified aircraft was initially flown on 4 February 1944 and extensively tested. While the system was successful, it was too costly and complex to insert into production lines for an aircraft not typically operating in icing conditions. Testing continued from July 1944 with NACA and the ship was also seen with paddle-blade propellers. The XB-25F was to be another modified C using electrical anti-ice heating, but never materialised.

A B-25C (43-32732) conducted experiments with a 1,570lb (712kg) flamethrower using a 210gal (795lit) tank secured in a unique bomb-bay rack. Flight testing was considered so hazardous it was apparently never conducted.[6] Another C (41-12800) with H nose was fitted with two 37mm cannon in a fairing beneath the bomb bay from which shells were fed. The modifications by NAA were completed in February 1943. Testing revealed cannon firing damaging the lower fuselage and would require more extensive redesign than considered practical.[7] An external drop tank under each wing graced a B-25J (44-295359) for tests in Inglewood, but this configuration was not taken to production. After introduction of the Clayton ejector exhaust stacks, it was suspected additional horsepower might result for which four-blade propellers would exploit for additional thrust. One ship was fitted with the propellers for flight testing, but with no marked benefit.[8]

Responding to an Air Forces request in early 1944, prompted by their impatience with the Douglas A-26 programme and NAA suggestions, North American

Right: This B-25H was modified to test a rocket launch system seen as tubes in the cannon tunnel and under the port side of the fuselage. The folding-fin rockets could be reloaded in flight as shown by the hatch cut into the sealed bomb bay doors and the tube breech. *National Museum of the United States Air Force*

submitted three proposals to enhance Mitchell attack potency. These were to mount Pratt & Whitney R-2800s on the B-25, and NAA offered versions with 10 or 12 forward-firing guns and a J-configured option. It was hoped the powerplants would offer a substantial increase in speed. The bomber option would weigh in at 33,390lb (15,145kg). The attacker with 10 guns forward (an eight-gun nose and turret) would be 34,822lb (15,795kg). The last, called the Super Strafer, would add twin pack guns on both sides for a projected 35,522lb (16,113kg) gross weight. This combination was expected to achieve 300mph (483km/h) and 1,800fpm (9.1m/s) climb at sea level in military power, and touch 325mph (523km/h) in emergency power.

A B-25H-5 (43-4406) was fitted with R-2800-51 engines offering 2,000hp (1,491kW), with 15min water injection, in A-26 cowlings and spinners. The test aircraft had only the typical H nose

Below: The earliest B-26s had .30cal defence with a gun in the nose, one in the tail, two in low waist stations, and two in a power turret developed by Martin. The early operational history of the Marauder was marred by accidents like this nose strut collapse, earning it a bad reputation. *National Museum of the United States Air Force*

without packs. Square wingtips allowed the ailerons to be extended outboard 1.0ft (0.3m) for greater roll rate. These surfaces were internally balanced and the gap between its leading edge and cove sealed with fabric. Control system changes were made to lighten stick forces, a computing gunsight included for the pilot and the turret canopy revised for lower drag. Without strengthening the wing for intended dives to 400mph (644km/h) and high-g pull-outs, the test aircraft had to be limited to 340mph (547km/h) and 2.67g, but this was still well above a standard H.

The aircraft (NA-98X) first flew on 31 March 1944. This and subsequent flights showed the potential of the configuration, reportedly flying to 350mph (563km/h) and climbing at around 2,000fpm (10mps). Unfortunately, on 24 April, a USAAF test pilot performed a high-speed pull-up beyond the placard limits. The outer wing panels shed and removed the tail, the avoidable mishap claiming the life of pilot and crewman. The Super Strafer died with them.

A separate proposal for a Double Wasp Mitchell was a B-25J fitted with R-2800s and 18 MGs. Known as the NA-108X Strafer Bomber, this was to have a single vertical tail. However, the eight-gun nose kits for the Js was apparently judged adequate.[9]

Another H was modified at Wright Field with rocket guns. Two of these were fitted in the cannon tunnel, the barrels projecting beyond the tip of the nose, and another mounted under the port side of the nose. They fired rocket projectiles like a bazooka and were reloadable in flight. The tube under the fuselage made the bomb bay inoperable and rounds were fed from within the bay through a small opening, presumably by hand. Photos show bullet-like end caps on the tubes to reduce drag before engaging the enemy. The concept was not taken beyond the experimental stage.

Left: In early years, twins like this B-26 in Alaska on 5 November 1942 were to deliver a torpedo. This was challenging because of the weapon's size, plus special integration and delivery needs. The requirement was set aside because the Mk. 13 torpedo was initially ineffective and other maritime attack means were devised. *National Museum of the United States Air Force*

Martin B-26-MA characteristics:

span	65.0ft	weight empty	21,375lb
length	56.0ft	gross	27,200lb
height	19.8ft	max.	32,000lb
wing area	602ft²	bomb load, max.	4,000lb
fuel (int.+bay)	700+250gal	normal	3,000lb
service ceiling	25,000ft	speed, max. (15,000ft)	315mph
average climb rate	1,200fpm	cruise	265mph
takeoff distance*	2,500ft	range, 3,000lb bombs	1,000mi
landing distance*	1,900ft	ferry	2,200mi
*over 50ft obstacle			

Demanding Respect (B-26)

The Glenn L. Martin Company's Model 179 was the original winner of the AC 39-640 competition that spawned the B-25. The 'off the shelf procurement' appeared reasonable given the Baltimore, Maryland, company's long history of supplying bombers to the Army and building multi-engine flying boats for the Navy. Although the initial intent was to procure 385 B-26s within 24 months of contract award, Martin would commit to just 201 in a 10 September 1939 order. The $15,815,685 USAAC contract was still the largest to that time. Martin then acceded to adding 139 more aircraft in a 16 September order for B-26As with crew station armour and Goodyear self-sealing tanks, bringing the contract to $16,029,750.

The B-26 mockup was inspected in the later half of November 1939. Among the recommended changes was the addition of waist guns and a molded perspex nose that complemented other use of plastics and alternative materials. An unusual aspect of the March 1939 invitation for bids had been its silence as to take-off distance and landing speed, emphasising instead maximum airspeed, range and payload. The designer exploited this with the highest wing loading of any American bomber at the time (51psf/10kg/m²), the small area supporting high speed.§§ Although this would extend landing speed and takeoff distance, the mandated tricycle landing gear would help make this tolerable.

§§ Wing loading is the aircraft gross weight divided by wing area.

Power was to be provided by R-2800s at 1,850hp (1,380kW) as first use of the new Double Wasp. Martin had sought a turbosupercharged variant, but this was substantially delayed. They had to press on with the single-stage/single-speed R-2800-5, losing over 50mph (81km/h) off the hoped-for top speed. The B-26 was also among the first employing large-diameter (13.5ft/4.1m) four-blade propellers with root cuffs.

The Model 179 employed extensive electrical and hydraulic subsystems, plus pneumatic backup braking, for one of the most sophisticated American warplanes at that time. The tricycle undercarriage was still atypical as was the metal-skinned elevator.¶¶ Martin's Mareng Cells rubber self-sealing, 350gal (1,325lit) wing tanks, another first in the US, were grouped inboard of the engines. The bombardier occupied the nose while the navigator sat behind the two pilots and a gunner was in the rear. Bomb bay door arrangement was unusual in that it had bi-fold units for a forward bay and simply hinged units for a aft bay. Carrying up to 2,000lb (907kg) in the forward bay and 2,800lb (1,270kg) in the rear, the electric bomb releases were another first for the US. The flex-mounted .30cal guns were distributed with one in the nose and tail, and two in the waist (all 400rpg). The 1,200 rounds of .30cal ammunition were in 200-round cans. The low position of the beam stations meant gunners would have to squat and the guns could not be raised above horizontal. The tail gunner sat upright in another first.

A 600lb (272kg) electrical dorsal turret with a pair of .50cal guns (400rpg)

¶¶ W The light weight of control surfaces was important for low control forces and simplified balancing to dynamic instabilities. Even the advanced XB-36 would have fabric covered control surfaces. However, fabric was easily damaged and had to be replaced periodically. It also 'ballooned' under airloads to alter aerodynamic characteristics. Powered controls answered the forces issue while refined balancing techniques answered the dynamics issue. Yet, metal-covered surfaces remained rare on American bombers throughout the war.

was requested by the Air Corps as the B-26 was in design to become the first production American aircraft with a power turret. It was developed by Martin in just 21 days as the A-3 (Navy 250CE). This turret would prove so successful it was adopted by other aircraft programs and also manufactured by Emerson with total output of approximately 56,000.

The B-26 design supported the expected high production rate with unusually large alloy forgings, large stretched sheets of aluminum and spot welding eliminating time-consuming jigging and riveting. As ever seeking reduced drag, it possessed flush riveting and an unusual circular cross-section. It was also the first to employ butted sheet metal skin seams, the skin of unusually high gauge to reduce distortion under airloads. An astrodome above the navigator/radio operator's compartment was retractable. The bubble nose eliminated bracing and construction time, but was an exceptionally large bit of heavy plexiglass, pushing the state-of-the-art.

In May 1940, the B-26 contract was renegotiated in the face of the new European war and insight into early combat experience. Deliveries were slipped four months so that armour and tank protection could be incorporated into the initial 201 machines, and the turret made fully rather than partially powered. The President's 50,000-plane plan spurred a second order for 791 B-26Bs on 28 September 1940 before the aircraft had flown. A new Baltimore plant was also constructed by the government at Middle River for a second production line.

The first B-26 was taken up for its maiden flight on 25 November 1940.[10] Only an aerodynamic overbalance condition of the rudder was a major complaint. The specified 26,625lb (12,077kg) gross and 323mph (520km/h) peak speed had, with the combat changes, become 27,200lb (12,338kg) and 315mph (507km/h). Yet, the performance remained tremendous and roll rate fighter-like. With 1,131 by then on order and the RAF seeking 459,

the design appeared a winner.

Deliveries of the new B-26-MA Marauder occurred between 22 February and October 1941. The tail guns were uprated to .50s almost immediately. Some serious teething problems, to include collapsed nose gear, propeller pitch issues and troubles with the new P&Ws were soon overcome. Hydraulic leaks and electrical problems were additional headaches, earning criticism the aircraft was too complex. More frustrating, some aircraft were delivered without the turrets as these were still in development, and during late 1941, a grave delay in the propellers occurred. Propellers were removed from delivered aircraft and shipped back to Martin to permit accumulated bombers to be ferried.

As it already had a turret, tail gun and self-sealing tanks, the B-26 was one of the first deploy to the Pacific during spring 1942. A 250gal (946lit) auxiliary tank was created to fit the rear bomb bay. The added range of the bomber was beneficial, supporting 2,600mi (4,184km) flights, although sacrificing payload. The inadequacy of the defensive armament became evident. Tail gunners would discard their transparency and sometimes use a 100-round magazine from a B-17 to replace their 25-round .50 cans. Units also added a second nose .30 via a socket near the base of the plex on the port side. The small

clearance between propeller and ground (9in/22cm) on dirt surfaces resulted in pitted blades and battered fuselage from thrown stones. The Marauder was to concentrate in the western hemisphere from 1943 on.

The B-26A model, accepted between 31 October 1941 and April 1942, saw about 1,000lb (454kg) added to gross weight. Included was a total 555lb (252kg) of armour, two 250gal (946lit) optional bomb bay fuel tanks that would reduce bomb load to 2,000lb (907kg), electrical system upgraded from 12- to 24-volts and a low-pressure crew oxygen system. At Army insistence, the rear bay doors each had a window and socket for a .30cal, although these proved worthless. Shackles for a torpedo were added under the keel running through the bomb bay. The torpedo delivery capability was actually employed during 1942, the only American bomber to do so, although with negative results.*** 30 B-26As were followed by 109 B-26A-1 machines with R-2800-39s converted from S1A4G commercial powerplants with different carburetor owing to short supply of the R-2800-5. The As were not committed to combat.

The B-26-MAs and the As were soon modified with .50cal guns replacing all the .30s, the flex-mounted nose weapon with 270 rounds. Another .50 with 200

*** This excludes A-20s operated by the Soviets with torpedoes.

rounds was mounted in the starboard corner of the nose floor, angled slightly downward for ground attack.

Britain had placed a 26 June 1941 Lend-Lease order for 459 of planned B-26B-1s, but the Americans delayed this as an emergency measure. However, the situation in North Africa in spring 1942 and delays in Martin Baltimore deliveries demanded immediate action, so 52 B-26A-1s with minor revisions were provided to the British as Marauder Is. The first arrived in-country on 2 September 1942. They also took 19 B-26As, denoted Marauder IAs.

With the A-model Marauder, gross had reached 28,367lb (12,867kg). The high landing speed deriving from the heightened wing-loading, as much as 130mph (209km/h), was a challenge during training. Inexperienced pilots and mechanics flooding into the expanding USAAF had difficulty with the advanced B-26.[11] Takeoff and landing distance was uncomfortable, stall speed comparatively high, and engine-out handling unfortunate owing to poor directional stability. The high training accident rate of the Marauder, 162 per 100,000 flying hours in 1942 (although only three were lost the previous year), drew national attention and recommendations that production be terminated. Some aircrew refused to fly the aircraft. A radical solution to the B-26's problems was requested in September 1941 as adoption of a larger wing. This, however, would require many months to implement. Review boards

and further threats of cancellation came and went. Adjustments to training and maintenance were instituted. Efforts at weight reduction saw some creature comforts and such gear as the astrodome and camera mount ordered removed in February 1943.

The B model finally emerged in May 1942 reflecting experience with the type and lessons of the war. It still went through many significant changes during its run. The B began with improved armour of 1,094lb (496kg) that included armoured pilot seats, 121gal (458lit) auxiliary tanks outboard of each engine, fuel lines made self-sealing, and spinners deleted. Weapons load could be as much as 5,200lb (2,359kg). Greater protection came with twin .50s on a hydraulically boosted mount in a revised tail station with 1,500rpg employing feed chutes with electric boosters for the first time in the USAAF. A .30 was placed in a ventral tunnel position created from an entry hatch. There were 1,200 rounds of .30cal ammunition and 3,800 of .50cal. All this brought gross to 36,500lb (16,556kg).

The USAAF needed B-26Bs for the North Africa campaign in late 1942, but these required rework to be suitable. With deliveries beginning 5 April 1942, the aircraft were passed through the Martin Modification Center at Offutt AB in Omaha, Nebraska, and the machines were denoted B-26B-1s. Among the changes was enlargement of the two carburetor intakes atop each cowling to permit use of sand filters and provisions for two 250gal

(946lit) ferry tanks in the bays. The nose was enforced to support a .50cal gun with ammunition fed from a floor box of 135 rounds (later 270), another .50 fixed to the floor to fire out the starboard side (200 rounds) The B-1s went into action during late December 1942.

An effort to recover performance and other improvements were made during the B-model run. The 1,920hp (1,432kW) R-2800-41 was introduced with Block 2s, these converted 2SB-G powerplants intended for the RAF order. The Block 3 went to the 2,000hp (1,491kW) R-2800-43 engines, retained for all subsequent Marauders. The R-2800-43 was little changed except for Ford manufacture at a new plant in Dearborn, Michigan. Later, the nose gear strut was lengthened to increase wing incidence on the ground for a shorter takeoff, winterising equipment was adopted and 1,041lb (472kg) of armour installed. The waist guns were replaced with .50s (240rpg) and the ineffectual ventral .30 deleted. Field modifications saw a fairing added under the tail to collect spent shells and links. Low-level bombing, 500-2,000ft (152-610m) with the Estoppey D-8 bombsight, so successful in the Pacific, proved exceedingly hazardous in Europe, and their earliest experience was discouraging. However, the team moved to medium altitude of 8,000-12,000ft (2,348-3,658m) that summer with the Norden M-7.

The enlarged wing finally appeared with 150 Block 10s in January 1943 after 641 earlier Bs, seeking to make it easier for new pilots to transition to the Marauder. These had wingspan extended 6.0ft (1.8m) for nine per cent increase in area and the wing granted a slight dihedral and slotted flaps. Addressing directional stability, the vertical tail height was upped 0.97ft (0.30m) and the rudder enlarged. Larger main gear tires allowed better flotation on sod, but this entailed bulged gear doors. The beam gunner openings were moved aft one fuselage frame, enlarged, blast deflectors

Left: This B-26B-55, photographed on 16 February 1945, shows the powered Martin-Bell tail turret and the enlarged waist station openings characteristic of late-production Bs and Cs. Slotted flaps helped reduce landing speeds and more engine power compensated for added weight. Most Marauder production reflected these features. *National Museum of the United States Air Force*

Below: The B-26G was the final Marauder model and included the F's wing incidence increase (up-angle on engine nacelle noticeable) for improved takeoff characteristics. It also simplified the Martin-Bell tail turret and installed a shell collector fairing under the aft fuselage. These French B-26G-10s also show the slotted flaps. *National Museum of the United States Air Force*

added and ammunition fed via flexible chutes from boxes above. Two .50s were added in fixed 'packages' on both side of the nose with 250rpg for the top weapons and 200rpg for the bottom, all inclined slightly down. This reflected a growing low-altitude attack role for the aircraft, but the packs could be removed as missions dictated. With 12 .50s and 4,250 rounds, crew had risen to seven. All these changes and additional tactical gear had gross elevated again to 37,000-38,200lb (16,783-17,327kg) by mid-1943, so wing loading was not reduced for high gross weight (GW) landings. Top speed was also sacrificed, going to 282mph (502 to 454km/h).

Martin moved into a government plant in Omaha (Fort Crook), Nebraska, during early 1941 to build wings. Martin-Nebraska soon moved to building complete aircraft with a 28 June 1941, $162,475,685 contract for 1,200 B-26Cs (-MO suffix). The plant relied upon subcontract work that had the forward and mid fuselage segments built by Chrysler, wings by Goodyear and rear fuselage by the Hudson Motor Car Company. This consortium encountered delays such that initial deliveries were in August 1942. These were essentially late-model Bs, the B-26C-5s preceding the B-10s.

Further changes ensued in later Bs and Cs. The 60 B-26C-6s were intended for ground attack and so eliminated the copilot station and some armour. However, the machines were employed

Martin B-26B/C characteristics (late model):			
span	71.0ft	weight empty	24,000lb
length	58.3ft	gross	37,000lb
height	21.5ft	max.	38,200lb
wing area	658ft²	bomb load, max: (inc. torp.)	6,000lb
fuel (int.+bay)	962+1,000gal	normal	3,000lb
service ceiling	21,700ft	speed, max. (15,000ft)	282mph
average climb rate	612fpm	cruise	214mph
takeoff distance* (37,000lb)	3,500ft	range, 3,000lb bombs	1,150mi
landing distance*	2,900ft	ferry	2,850mi
*over 50ft obstacle			

in the usual medium bombardment role, and dislike of the changes saw an end to the configuration. The hand-swung guns in the tail gave way to a Bell M-6 electro-hydraulically powered unit (800rpg). This was under an extended plex covering for the gunner blessed with a reflector sight and armour. Appliqué armour was added beside the pilot. The torpedo capability was eliminated and the seldom-used aft bomb bay sealed with racks removed to save weight. This last help avoid overloading but reduced bomb capacity to 3,000lb (1,361kg). On the downside was another 4,300lb (1,950kg) added weight, landing speed going to 135mph (217km/h).

The 1,883 Bs were produced through February 1944 as the most numerous Marauder model. The similar 1,210 Cs were rolled out until 4 April 1944, an additional 615 examples cancelled on 12 August 1943. Both sites built 700 unarmed trainers. Servicing British Lend-Lease continued with 104 B-26Cs of various blocks during 1943 as Marauder IIs.

The Army had continued pondering B-26 production cessation as focus shifted from medium altitude, level bombing. However, the reputable combat value of such warplanes were being demonstrated daily and the B-26 had outstanding bombing accuracy. In addition, the production rate of other types alone could not meet combat requirements. A definite decision was made in summer 1943 to slow B-26 production to 150 per month toward the earliest halt. That would allow quick conversion of the Nebraska line to B-29 production and Baltimore to planned B-35 work. However, A-26 development,

meant to replace the B-26, was lagging and it was desirable to ensure continuity of resources until B-35 manufacturing began. The Marauder's accident rate had fallen to 65 per 100,000 flying hours in 1943. The bad reputation was balanced by a respectable combat record, and the aircraft proved more survivable in flak than others of its ilk. These factors and a September 1943 demonstration of potential Marauder upgrades led to an additional 450 bombers being ordered to sustain production into 1944 at Middle River while Omaha left the B-26 behind.

An increase in wing incidence by 3.5° introduced in the B-26F was yet another effort at improving takeoff performance, reducing takeoff distance and lowering deck angle in cruise with elevated engine thrust line. Landing speed was down to 110mph (177km/h) and 300ft (91m) cut from takeoff distance. While handling was improved, performance suffered again with 277mph (446km/h) top speed. Other changes were an increase to 4,000lb (1,814kg) in the single remaining bay and provisions for two droppable 250gal (946lit) bay tanks. The most obvious change was replacement of the clear dome in the aft turret with a canvas boot as the M-6A. Total .50 ammunition onboard was then 4,400 rounds. Ordered in September 1943, the F entered action during June 1944. Of the 300, 200 went to the RAF as Marauder IIIs.

Production was extended again to cover 893 Gs introducing further refinement and standardisation that included the C-1 autopilot. The final example flew on 18 April 1945, one of 57 unarmed trainers G. The British received 150 Gs as Marauder IIIs.

The B-26 contributed in all theatres to the end of the conflict. Medium altitude became its domain in Europe, generally against tactical targets. However, in the waning days of the war the Marauder returned to low level in some instances to attack trains and the like. Pathfinder B-26s (leader equipped for precision

Martin B-26F/G characteristics:			
span	71.0ft	weight empty	23,700lb
length	58.1ft	gross	37,200lb
height	20.35ft	max.	38,200lb
wing area	658ft²	bomb load, max.	4,000lb
fuel (int.+bay)	1,002+500gal	normal	3,000lb
service ceiling	19,800ft	speed, max. (10,000ft)	277mph
average climb rate	612fpm	cruise	216mph
takeoff distance* (36,000lb)	3,200ft*	range, 3,000lb bombs	1,300mi
landing distance	3,200ft*	ferry	2,100mi
*over 50ft obstacle			

Right: The MX-241 project sought to introduce recoilless rocket projectiles to aircraft for air-to-ground attack. Such a "rocket gun" is shown installed under the bomb bay of a B-26 on 29 May 1944, apparently without inflight reload capability. The XB-26E with the 37mm cannon was also known to have this installation. *National Archives*

navigation) were also employed, using Britain's Oboe navigation beacon system of 250mi (402km) range, supporting blind bombing and even night work.[†††]

At peak strength in the end of March 1944, there were 1,931 B-26s in the USAAF inventory. The Air Forces lost 911 Marauders during 129,943 sorties. At the end of the war there were 731 aircraft. The RAF took 525 in total, operating them mostly in North Africa and the Mediterranean with SAAF and Free French Air Forces units. With few exceptions, the American inventory was purged of B-26s within months of the war's end.

Even in its earliest forms, experienced crews operated the Marauder with only typical attrition. The multiple changes over time made the type easier for inexperienced men, but also significantly cut into performance. The accident rate to 37 per 100,000 flying hours in 1944, or an average 55 during 1942-1945 compared adequately with 33 for the B-25, 131 for the A-20 and 53 for the new A-26s. The Marauder ultimately enjoyed the lowest combat loss rate (0.3 per cent) of any US bomber. One B-26B-25 (41-31773) flew 202 missions – more than any other Allied bomber of the war. Dozens exceeding 100 missions.

Its early reputation and a move away from this class of bomber left the B-26 with comparatively small production of 5,266 aircraft. Addressing the type's perceived deficiencies and a persistent threat of cancellation, combined with a sense that medium bombers had

a limited future, meant a lack of the aggressive improvements seen in other American bombers. At the peak, the two plants turned out 120 Marauders in a month. During 1943 alone, they manufactured 1,215 Bs and 1,149 Cs. Unit cost had gone from $261,062 in 1941 to $192,427 in 1944. Man hours to complete an aircraft also dropped, from an initial 28,873 in late 1941 to 18,104 in June 1943 at Middle River. These figures, too, were more than many similar bomber types and another inducement to drop the Marauder.

Marauding (XB-26D, XB-26E)

The missing B-26 letter designations were a mix of modifications for different purposes. Wing de-ice experiments were performed with a converted B-26-MA (40-1380), the singular XB-26D, during 1942. This ducted hot air from the engine into a heat exchanger through which passed ram air, porting the warmed volume to the wing and tail leading edges. Martin offered a wealth of other ideas for improving the Marauder, but few were accepted. Proposed were B-26s with all manner of guns and turrets (including nacelles), cannon, radar, various engines and even four engines. Pack guns were placed in a belly installation under the bays of B-26B-10 41-17571, but this was not carried forward.[12]

Four XB-26Es were created from existing Marauders by introducing various experimental modifications. Aircraft 42-43459, a B-26B-40, tested the wing incidence increase of 3.5° as the official XB-26E. However, Martin took such work further with three machines

unofficially referred to as XB-26Es. There was 41-31672, a B-26B-15 intended for enhanced ground attack. This was given a 'solid' nose with two 37mm cannon and two .50 machine guns, the usual four package guns, four more .50s added as pairs in each wing outboard of the propeller arcs and armour relocated for greater protection to the front. The waist gun ports were moved up on the fuselage, rocket launchers (MX-241 'rocket gun') installed under the rear of the bomb bay and a rudder with balance extending forward at the top.[‡‡‡] Beginning in January 1943, B-26C-5 41-34680 entered a weight-reduction programme that eventually yielded 2,600lb (1,179kg) savings by stripping out equipment not supporting the low/medium altitude mission, including eliminating the copilot station. The dorsal turret was moved to the navigator's station in the forward fuselage as a balancing measure. This machine was tested at Wright Field during March 1943. A B-26B-40 (42-43319) incorporated extended engine nacelles, rudder with revised balance, the turret moved to above the aft bomb bay, the two .50 nose guns moved to opposing sides plus the four wing guns. One of the E quartet probably also had 'shark-nosed' aileron seals.

The 'XB-26E' modifications were undertaken at Martin instigation. Three of the machines were demonstrated in Washington, D.C., to General Arnold and other officials in September 1943. The 'Old Man' was known to have been swayed by promising proposals and to make snap programs decisions. Martin's gamble paid of, as previously explained, helping win further Marauder orders. As programme officials were then trying to shutdown B-26 production, they were furious. However, only the wing incidence and revised aileron seals were carried to production.

[†††] Oboe employed intersecting radio beams from two ground stations.

[‡‡‡] From early 1941, secret Army technology development projects were routinely given such code numbers; MX meaning Materiel, Experimental.

Chapter Three

Attackers cum Bombers

Distinction Without a Difference

Prewar, Army attack aircraft were intended for close support of ground forces. This was the most important mission of the Air Corps from the perspective of ground force commanders. However, airmen felt interdiction and strategic bombing were the best use of airpower. Consequently, there was a constant pull in both directions and attack aviation was somewhat neglected. The aircraft had matured as powerful single-engine monoplanes for low-level bombing and strafing. Some had weapons bays and typically two or three crewman. Twin-engine attackers were resisted because of cost and complexity. However, Japanese conquests and the Spanish Civil War demonstrated value in such machines in the face of intense ground fire. This emphasised the need for armour and the safety of two engines. Low-altitude engagement also demanded a different selection of equipment than medium-altitude bombardment, including defensive weapons and bombsight. The cannon was also receiving attention as a potentially effective ground attack weapon. These considerations and the desire to extend range and endurance meant heavier aircraft that inevitably paved the road to twins. This class of combat aircraft was clearly required and so they were developed in the immediate prewar period, and then matured during the conflict.

The sudden emphasis on dive-bombing engendered by the depredations of the Ju-87 Stuka and Japanese attackers was generally resisted by the Air Corps leadership and had little influence on bombers. Further, they felt fighters could perform the attack mission suitably, with or without the vertical dive, as an ancillary mission. Likewise, twin

attackers could serve as light, medium-altitude bombers, as circumstances dictated. Despite the mixed signals, Air Corps and foreign interest in twin-engine attack bombers was not lost on the nation's aircraft manufacturers.

Simultaneous development of twin-engine attack bombers and medium bombers produced a blurring of the lines between the two classes. That only two USAAF twins denoted as attackers were fielded during the war, one developed from a type initially ordered by foreign operators and the other as a replacement, illustrates sustained antipathy toward this distinction. The allies continued to value to the class, with attackers produced in the US solely for those nations. In terms of combat mission assignments, any distinction became meaningless for the Air Forces. Attackers were generally operated by light bombardment units and the medium bombers took on more attack roles.

By summer 1944, fighters were taking on a growing share of the ground attack mission as newly incarnated 'fighter-bombers'. This offered multi-role potential and, assuming single-engine/single-pilot machines, greater efficiency than the multi-engine/multi-place attackers that evolution and the lack of firm high-level support contributed to an intention to eliminate the attack category by the war's end.

Principal Performers

Ready and Able
(DB-7, Boston, A-20)

The Air Corps' new twin-engine attacker was on order when war dawned. The initial attempt at acquiring such an aircraft was expressed in a December 1937 specification that called for a twin carrying 1,200lb (544kg) for 1,200mi (1,931km) at 200mph (322km/h).

A 20,000ft (6,096m) service ceiling was required and 25,000ft (7,620m) desired. Top speed was to beat 250mph (402km/h) at 5,000ft (8,047m), with 280mph (451km/h) desired. The rear gunner's station was to have minimal flight controls and instruments for emergency recovery of the aircraft Although proceeding with a March 1939 competition, the service recognised by then its requirements would yield an aircraft already unable to compete suitably in evolving air combat Revised specifications, C-130, were issued in September 1938 and results of the fly-off set aside.

Douglas had developed the 7B for the initial competition. They immediately began a substantial redesign to meet C-130 that called for 350mph (563km/h) top speed, 14,000-20,000ft (4,267-6,096m) optimal altitude and three-man crew. France placed a February 1939 order for 100 of these DB-7s off the drawing board plus a static test airframe.

The DB-7 proposal was submitted to Wright Field in April 1939 along with other C-130 entrants. The Douglas submission stood out as the best predicted performer and at a competitive price. In May, the Air Corps ordered 63 A-20-DOs with 1,700hp (1,268kW) R-2600-7 Cyclones and General Electric (GE) turbosuperchargers, and 123 A-20A with 1,600hp (1,193kW) R-2600-3 and single-stage/one-speed gear-driven supercharger. They were to carry 2,000lb (907kg) of bombs and 4,700 rounds of ammunition. Aside from two flex-mounted .30s for defensive fire, another pair were fixed in the nose and optionally augmented by a gun in a blister on each side of the nose.

In spring 1939, Douglas was simultaneously developing aircraft for two customers from a common design.

The DB-7 engineering and manufacturing work was performed in El Segundo. The fuselage had a raised top deck enclosing the cockpit in front and dorsal gunner in back. The flush-riveted fuselage was notably narrow, negating crew interchangeability during flight. The mid-wing and under-slung nacelles reduced landing gear strut length. Horizontal tail dihedral improved handling by raising it above the wing downwash. Control surfaces remained fabric covered but the tricycle landing gear, without nose wheel steering, was carried over from the 7B. Douglas adopted the Pratt & Whitney 1,050hp (783kW) R-1830-SC3-G Twin Wasp (military equivalent R-1830-45) for the French model, fitted with a single-speed mechanical supercharger and 11.3ft (3.4m) props. The 87 octane fuel was distributed between two 163gal (617lit) integral tanks in the inboard wing segments. Hydraulics powered were landing gear, flaps, cowl flaps and bomb bay doors. A pneumatic bottle provided emergency pressure to the hydraulic wheel brakes. Fluid anti-ice was provided for the propeller, windscreen and carburetor intake.

The DB-7's bay could accommodate up to 2,000lb (907kg). Four 7.5mm MGs (500rpg) were fixed in the nose (two per side) and two flex-mounted in the aft fuselage. The dorsal opening was created by sliding the aft transparent fairing forward and deploying the gun through the opening. The ventral 'tunnel' station had two panels that were raised and the gun deployed into the opening. The crew comprised pilot, bombardier and gunner/radio operator.

The DB-7 first flew in August 1939. Landing speed was 7mph (11km/h) faster than specified, giving a longer landing rollout. Lateral stability was deficient and rudder area inadequate for single engine-out or low-speed operation. Range was also less than required. However, the French chose not to hold up production to correct these issues, even ordering an additional 170

Douglas DB-7 characteristics:

span	61.3ft	weight empty	11,400lb
length	47.0ft	gross	15,150lb
height	15.8ft	max. gross	17,031lb
wing area	463.9ft²	bomb load, max.	2,080lb
fuel	325gal	normal	1,000lb
service ceiling	25,800ft	speed, max. (9,650ft)	305mph
initial climb rate	2,440fpm	cruise	270mph
takeoff distance*	1,180ft	range, 2,080lb bombs	462mi
*over 50ft obstacle		1,760lb bombs	869mi
		max. combat	996mi

examples from Douglas on 14 October 1939. Although France desired that all DB-7s be equipped with 1,200hp (895kW) R-1830-S3C4-Gs (R-1830-90C) with two-speed supercharger and 100 octane fuel for a slight performance improvement, these were not immediately available.* Consequently, vital production continued apace until the new engine could be introduced.

Initial production acceptance of a DB-7 was on 30 October 1939. However, the delay of shipments spawned by the outbreak of war and imposition of Neutrality Act terms meant the first machines did not arrive until 25 December. It was then March before operational units began taking them on strength. The last of the initial 100 machines was delivered on 1 April 1940 and the first of the second batch shipped on 27 May. All this seriously set back the

*The Allies adopted 100-octane fuel by 1942 and 100/130 in mid-1944. This permitted greater intake manifold pressures and provided significant performance advantage for the remainder of the war.

French schedule for assembly, checkout, training and fielding.

On the day of the German offensive, 10 May 1940, 64 DB-7s had been assembled. Of these, just 33 were active in squadrons still working up on the type. They joined the fray on the 31st where they were employed as light bombers. The nose guns were seldom used because firing generated strong vibrations in the plex transparencies.[1] By the capitulation, they had flown some 70 combat sorties with eight or nine lost to enemy action.[2] Of those that remained at the surrender, some were flown to Britain while many became Vichy assets. A few DB-7s continued in Free French service until 1945.

The A-20-DOs and A-20As were built entirely in the large new Santa Monica plant, with an additional 20 of the latter ordered in early summer 1940. The more powerful engines and more than 3,500lb (1,588kg) higher gross weight demanded a stronger airframe and larger tail than the DB-7, with altered landing gear. They had

an integral 87gal (329lit) auxiliary fuel tank outboard of each nacelle for a total capacity of 500gal (1,893lit). The minimum flight controls and instruments in the DB-7s and A-20-DOs for the gunner, whose lack of forward vision made them superfluous, were dropped from the A-20A and all subsequent models. The two .30 nose blister guns were seldom installed.

The maiden flight of the first A-20A was on 6 September 1940. It was found necessary to introduce 11 holes in the cowling perimeter to ensure adequate engine cooling, although later eliminated. Deliveries began on 30 November 1940. As the first aircraft were coming together, the lessons of war emphasised the importance of self-sealing fuel tanks and armour. Seventeen A-20As were completed before the switch to protected cells that cut capacity to 388gal (1,514lit). Deliveries of the revised aircraft were from 7 February 1940 through 29 August 1941. Early in the production run, in February 1940, the R-2600-11 replaced the -3 model, although the differences were slight. The A-20A Havoc was the first of the USAAF models to see action with American crews.

The exhaust-driven turbos on the A-20-DOs' R-2600-7s were mounted on the outboard side of the nacelles in a bulky assembly that included the intercooler. Only one A-20-DO for test was fully configured. This was first taken aloft on 11 November 1940 and proved the fastest model of the Havoc at nearly 390mph (628km/h). However, over the next few flights the team learned they would also have considerable trouble with engine overheating during turbo operation. The addition of louvres and holes in the cowlings were not sufficiently curative. These difficulties and evolving tactics

made the turbos more trouble than they were worth. The original intent for the Havoc and short-supply of the Norden bombsight focused the aircraft's mission initially to low altitude attack. Consequently, in spring 1941, 60 of the A-20-DO order were re-engined and diverted to non-bomber roles.

By mutual agreement with the Free French government, the British assumed responsibility for outstanding French military orders in America on 17 June 1940. The UK took up all remaining DB-7s after the 194th aircraft, and these arrived during August through 3 September. To these 75 machines were added, some flown to the UK by escaping French crews. The RAF dubbed the original machines Boston Is (perhaps 30) and those with the two-speed superchargers Havoc Is (perhaps 131). English weapons (.303cal), radios and other unique gear changed as necessary for interoperability. The Bostons remained primarily as trainers while the Havocs worked at night on 'Intruder' missions with large exhaust flame dampers that cost 20mph (32km/h). However, the Havocs were comparatively poor as bombers originating from Britain owing to their shorter range and smaller payload. Consequently, these were soon diverted to other roles.

France had ordered 100 DB-7A aircraft (DB-71 to the French) on 20 October 1939, promising 16 to the Belgians. These moved towards the A-20A by adopting the more powerful 1,600hp (1,193kW) GR-2600-A5B with two-speed supercharger, larger fin and rudder, improved landing gear and added armour. A 7.5mm gun was fixed to fire out the back of each nacelle, lengthened to matching the A-20, as additional discouragement to fighters. The

gun was activated by the dorsal gunner using a foot switch. The second batch of DB-7s and the DB-7As was built solely in Santa Monica, although DB-7 fuselages continued to be assembled in El Segundo.

As none of the DB-7As were completed prior to the French capitulation, the RAF adopted them as Boston IIs. The RAF directed changes that included substituting .303 guns in the aft fuselage and nacelles, and in the nose as well for the final 69 machines. While the French bombsights emerged through the bottom of the nose, the British required the more typical flat optical window. With GW increased over 2,000lb (907kg) and no fuel capacity increase, range was halved. The first DB-7A flew on 30 July 1940. Like the A-20A, engine cooling challenges led to holes being added in the cowlings. The bulk of the DB-7As were accepted from 20 November to 25 February 1941. They became Havoc II intruders and night fighters.

The British had initially shunned the DB-7 owing to its lack of turret and crew interchangeability during flight. However, the advent of war compelled the RAF to order 150 of their own model of the bomber on 20 February 1940 as the DB-7B or Boston I (later III). The design largely reflected the A-20A development, including comparable GW and performance. It adopted the GR-2600-A5B engine plus British bombsight and racks. Bomb capacity was 2,000lb (907kg) and the bay had to be extended by about a 1.0ft (0.3m) to accommodate larger British weapons. Fuel tanks were self-sealing with 136gal (515lit) inboard and 64gal (242lit) outboard of the nacelles with a practical 395gal (1,495lit) total. However, the enlarged bomb bay allowed the addition of a 100gal (379lit) tank at the top of the bay. Some 450lb (204kg) of armour was incorporated. Two additional nose guns were introduced in blister packs with .303s. The British desired a four-gun Boulton-Paul turret be installed at the dorsal gunner's station and this was mocked-up on the 34th DB-7A and flown in spring 1941. A shortage of the turrets caused pairs of .303s to be substituted.

The Boston IIIs were built in Santa Monica. The first was taken aloft on 10 January 1941 and initial shipment followed on 4 April. After the earliest DB-7s, and with the DB-7B and A-20s, Douglas began building the fuselages in halves for more efficient equipment installation. A contract option for 150 more Boston IIIs was exercised on 17 April. The last of the 300 were completed in early September 1941.

A DB-7C (DB-73) configuration was developed for the French against an April 1940 order. To accelerate production, the customer encouraged Douglas to license Boeing to build half the aircraft in Seattle, Washington, or 240 from each manufacturer on 18 May contracts. Unlike the DB-7A, the C was to be more like the original aircraft in that it retained the R-1830-S3C4-G two-speed powerplants with ejector stacks exhausts. Also substituted was a 'solid' nose containing two .50cal MGs and four 7.5mm. The nacelle 'morale' guns were not included in this or any A-20 models. Armour was to be introduced for the wing tanks and crew stations.

The DB-7C did not go into production before France fell. Instead, the RAF directed they be built to the Boston III specification. Their initial Boeing example was flown on 10 July 1941 and first delivered in 30 October, the last on 26 January 1942. These featured carburetor intakes extended forward for a tropical air filter. Douglas began delivery of its machines on 8 September 1941. The Boston IIIs were employed in classical light bombing and attack roles.

American entry into the war and urgent need for warplanes, plus Lend-Lease commitments, caused a great many Boston IIIs to be diverted. Only 163 DB-7Bs were actually delivered to Britain. The USAAF appropriated 317 aircraft. Of these, 77 were exported to the USSR

beginning in November 1941. As early as the end of September 1939, the Soviets had been negotiating with Douglas for a commercial sale of ten DB-7s and license production of the airframe and R-2600. Their aggression against Finland halted this with an American embargo. The German offensive against the USSR induced a reversal and the Americans promised 3,125 of the light bombers at a rate of 100 per month.[3] Also, 32 intended for the Chinese were instead rushed to the Dutch East Indies. In the event, only six of the Dutch aircraft arrived in Java before the area was overrun by Japanese forces. The remaining 26 were transferred to the USAAF between 9 May and 14 July 1942. Of these, 22 were passed to the Australians.

On 16 October 1940, the Dutch had ordered 48 DB-7Cs for the Netherlands Naval Air Service with delivery to begin May 1942. Not to be confused with the aborted French DB-7C model, these were DB-7Bs altered to deliver American Mk.13 torpedoes. This would have had the bay doors removed and the weapon partially extending below the bottom mold line. The customer also had Douglas explore a belly tank and an interchangeable 'solid' nose with four 20mm cannon and four .303 MGs.[4] Ground tests were performed with such a nose configuration. As the Dutch territories had been overrun, the aircraft went to the USAAF that moved some along to the USSR.

On 11 October 1940, with the war overseas taking an ominous turn and revealing new combat requirements, the US Army ordered hundreds of a

new model Havoc. These A-20Bs had the structural 'beef-up' of the A airframe for glide bombing and used .50cals throughout except for the tunnel gun. This required the nose to be lengthened some 0.8ft (0.3m) for the forward .50s. Blister packs were never developed for .50cals. The aircraft was also to have the nacelle aft-pointing guns with .30s canted for fire to converge 300ft (91m) behind and cover a 5° 'blind spot' to the rear. However, this GE development was deleted before assembly. The B employed R-2600-11s with ejector stacks and provisions to carry a 200gal (757lit) ferry tank in the bomb bay. The Douglas ejector design, with exhausts from each cylinder routed to individual squeezed pipes, added 15mph (24km/h).

All A-20Bs were assembled in Douglas' new government plant at Long Beach, but with most elements built elsewhere. The A-20B eventually amounted to 999 aircraft, the first delivered on 24 February 1942 and running through February 1943, but with 665 going to the USSR. The lack of sufficient armour was the principal detractor for the Americans. Another was the B's relative scarcity as so many were sent to allies. Indeed, the Havoc was not deployed in large numbers with the USAAF until well into 1943.

The USAAF continued production with 948 A-20Cs that reflected many of the best features of the Boston III. It was manufactured in Santa Monica, henceforth the home for all Douglas production. These returned to .30cal MGs throughout but adopted 1,600hp

Above: The A-20C was almost entirely shipped to allies. The was the first model to be produced in several production blocks but, although evincing suitable armour, the return to .30cal guns ensured inadequate defence. This example from 4 April 1942 has the belly drop tank, secured with releasable straps to the bomb bay exterior. *Ray Wagner Collection*

(1,193kW) R-2600-23s with ejectors and added armour for 415lb (188kg) total. Gross rose to 21,000lb (9,525kg) or 1,000lb (454kg) over the A-20-DO. Whereas previously the A-20s had used vertical racking of fragmentation bombs and horizontal for demolition weapons, all were now hung horizontally. This permitted a 140gal (530lit) self-sealing tank to be introduced in the upper volume of the revised bomb bay, bringing capacity to 540gal (2,044lit). The Block 5s featured provisions for torpedo carriage, added electrical gunsights for fixed guns and introduced the bullet-proof windshield.

The initial A-20C production was for allies, explaining the return to .30cal MGs. A further UK order for the DB-7B fell under Lend-Lease as A-20Cs (Boston IIIAs) with military engines, effectively ending the DB-7 lineage. They added a drum-fed Vickers K flex gun in the tunnel. This saw 140 built at Boeing with R-2600-11 engines but lacking ejectors, the first flying on 24 July 1941 and deliveries through 31 March 1942. Concurrently, 375 were built by Douglas

with -23 engines and ejectors through 19 November 1941. Aircraft on the USAAF A-20C contract were delivered from late August 1942 through January 1943.

The USAAF took over 108 of the Lend-Lease warplanes and shipped the remaining 407 to the Soviets, none reaching Britain. To make up for the diversions, the Air Forces kept just 85 of the machines produced under its order while sending 200 to the UK as Boston IIIAs and 148 to the Soviet Union. However, 56 of the USSR assigned aircraft were instead passed to Britain between December 1942 and September 1943, and thence to the SAAF.

Douglas was tasked with removing self-sealing tanks from A-20 models and possibly substituting the

turbosupercharged R-2600-7s to create A-20Ds. This may have been intended to increase fuel capacity and reduce weight by 2,000lb (907kg) for improved performance as a survivability compromise. One aircraft, but more likely none, were so modified before the plan was dropped.† The 17 A-20As completed without the leak-proof tanks and armour were ordered redesignated A-20Es, but this was apparently ignored.

Modification shops in Australia created a critical mass of these A-20A strafers for SWPA during summer 1942. This effectively supplanted the bombardier station with guns and cannons to create a powerful 'gunship' strafer. Depending

† That turbos on the Havoc was explored beyond the A-20-DO debacle would seem unlikely.

Douglas A-20C/Boston IIIA characteristics:

span	61.3ft	weight empty	15,625lb
length	47.3ft	gross	21,000lb
height	17.6ft	max. gross	24,500lb
wing area	463.9ft²	bomb load, max.	2,000lb
fuel (int. + bay/ext.)	540+540gal	normal	1,000lb
service ceiling	25,320ft	speed, max. (13,000ft)	342mph
average climb rate	1,587fpm	cruise (14,000ft)	280mph
takeoff distance*	2,250ft	range, 1,000lb bombs	800mi
landing distance*	2,250ft	2,000lb bombs	1,050mi
*over 50ft obstacle		ferry	2,300mi

upon model, the most prominent modification added four .50cal MGs to the four .30s or two .50s in the nose. Two bomb bay tanks totaling 450gal (1,703lit) proved valuable in the far-flung theatre. Parafrags were also introduced on special bay racks holding 40 or more.

Another modification configuration had two clusters of three bazooka-like rocket tubes under outboard wing panels. These fired 4.5in T-30 high-explosive, fin-stabilised rockets. With the rockets generating no recoil, the mounting hardware was very light. However, the installation generated high drag, and weapons were quite heavy. They were unpopular and seldom employed.

The distinctive A-20 model was the G with 'solid' strafer nose, -23 engines and approximately 400lb (181kg) of armour. Initially, the nose had four 20mm cannon with 60rpg and two .50cal MGs in the lower corners of the nose sides (some early examples with .30s) and in the dorsal and ventral stations as well. However, the cannons had a tendency to jam and, with low rate of fire, were less desirable than MGs. After 250 baseline A-20G-1s (most passed to the Soviets), the Block 5s substituted four .50 MGs with 350rpg for the cannons, giving

the six-gun nose that became common. The Block 1 through 15 aircraft also had provisions for up to four bomb bay ferry tanks (displacing bombs) of a total 676gal (2,559lit) capacity. A torpedo could also be carried in the bay. All this added another 2,000lb (907kg) to GW and performance was again decremented. Ordered on 1 June 1942, the first A-20G was delivered in February 1943.

Through 1943, the DB-7/A-20 series stood out as retaining the anachronistic manual gunner stations. The British and Soviets had made attempts at resolving

Above: A rather unsuccessful attempt by USAAF personnel to enhance the ground-attack potency of the Havoc was wing-mount rocket launch tubes. The 4.5 inch T-30 rockets were fin-stabilized and produced no recoil, allowing the light mounting hardware. This installation was photographed on 27 June 1944 at Hollandia, New Guinea. *National Museum of the United States Air Force*

Below: Responding to theatre requests, and reflecting field modifications, the A-20G adopted a "solid" nose with fixed weapons. The initial blocks were fitted with four 20mm cannon in addition to the existing two .50cal machine guns. The cannons did not prove popular and were replaced in later blocks with machine guns. *Ray Wagner Collection*

Above: The A-20G and H swapped reliable .50cal machine guns for the 20mm cannon in the nose, adopted the Martin dorsal turret with twin .50s, and added external store stations on later blocks. This A-20G-35 models the six nose guns, Army ejector exhaust, and external weapons. *National Archives*

the deficiency. The Americans finally found a solution when the A-20G-20 was introduced in August 1943. This had the Martin 250CE-10 electrical turret with twin .50s and 400rpg (3,300 rounds total onboard). A third crewman was added to operate the .50 with 400 rounds in the tunnel. However, depending upon the mission and perceived threat, only one gunner might be on the crew.

The Block 20s also got external racks under the outer wing panels for 500lb (227kg) each, raising total bomb load to 4,000lb (1,814kg). Bay tankage was also increased to 325gal (1,230lit) for 725gal (2,744lit) total internal capacity. These machines introduced a belly drop tank as a production installation (it was seen on earlier models, possibly as a retrofit). The 374gal (1,416lit) unit was carried flush under the bomb bay, held by three quick-release straps. The torpedo option was deleted with the A-20G-40s. The ejector exhausts were altered (Army design) to individual stubs around the periphery of the cowling, mid-chord. Added armour plus improved navigational and bombing gear aided mission effectiveness.

There were 2,850 A-20Gs built in Santa Monica, more than half sent to the Soviet Union. Valuable features of the late-model Gs came with a weight penalty of more than 3,000lb (1,361kg) over the A-20C, giving another performance decrement. The 412 A-20Hs were essentially Gs

with 1,700hp (1,268kW) R-2600-29 engines featuring emergency power and recovering about 15mph (24km/h) on top speed.

Having responded to SWPA requirements by turning the Havoc into a strafer, the ETO demanded a return to level bombing from 8,000-12,000ft (2,438-3,658m); low-level work was too costly owing to intense flak. As the A-20Gs progressed through manufacturing, a revised bombardier nose was adopted for the A-20J. This had a frameless 'blown' forward plex for the Norden and with two .50s in the nose sides. The total five .50 MGs were provided with 1,900 rounds. The four-place Js could serve as lead for Havocs fitted with a solid nose in formations as large as 36 machines who dropped-on-the-lead. With a gross of around 24,000lb (10,886kg), the J's top speed achieved a new low of 317mph (510km/h) at 10,700ft (3,261m).

The J production was interspersed with the G, the first accepted in October

1943, initially with intent that every tenth aircraft would have the glass nose. The noses were essentially interchangeable, requiring two men and no more than 6hr work, although this appears to have been seldom performed. There were 450 A-20Js built from March 1943 to 14 June 1944, some 169 were provided to the RAF as the Boston IV and many also provided to the USSR.

The A-20Hs were also built as Ks with a 'glass' nose like the J. The 377 A-20Ks came out of Santa Monica jointly with the Hs and G/J run from 29 February through 1 November 1944; Of the Ks, the Soviets got 140, the British 90 (Boston Vs), the Brazilians 30 Ks and the balance to USAAF outfits.

The DB-7/A-20 production ended on 20 September 1944 and delivery in October, with 7,098 units from Douglas and 380 from Boeing. Unit costs had been cut from $94,080 for an A-20A to $79,055 for a G. With 1,199 manufactured on foreign contracts and thousands

Douglas A-20G Block 20 characteristics:

span	61.3ft	weight empty	16,993lb
length	48.0ft	gross	24,127lb
height	17.6ft	max. gross	26,200lb
wing area	463.9ft²	bomb load (int.+ext.)	2,000+2,000lb
fuel (int.+bay/ext.)	725+374gal	normal	2,000lb
service ceiling	23,700ft	speed, max. (10,700ft)	317mph
average climb rate (26,000lb)	1,136fpm	cruise	256mph
takeoff distance* (26,000lb)	5,400ft	range, combat	945mi
landing distance*	3,000ft	2,000lb	1,150mi
*over 50ft obstacle		ferry	2,100mi

provided as Lend-Lease, 56 per cent of the aircraft were exported. The RAF alone took on about 1,250. Britain gave some of its aircraft to Australia, South Africa and Free French forces. Canada received a single Boston III, IIIA and IV, but that nation only flew the Douglas bomber in combat as elements of the RAF. The Soviets remained the primary operator with 2,908 A-20s and Bostons – these and the B-25s making up a substantial portion of the approximately 14,000 American warplanes supplied to the USSR. Brazil received a Boston III in November 1941 and 30 A-20Ks in summer 1944.

America was the second largest user of the Havoc in all its guises, with 2,804 taken up of which about 1,900 were deployed to combat theatres and roughly 300 diverted to non-bomber or non-combat roles. Because of the heavy contribution to supplying Allied forces, the initial deployment of USAAF A-20 groups was comparatively small until 1944 despite the aircraft being well ahead of its contemporaries in established mass production.

In USAAF and RAF service, the different circumstances of the Asia/Pacific, Mediterranean and West European theatres dictated configurations and usage. Desert operations required sand filters be installed on the carburetor intake. In its heyday, the type was versatile, reliable, rugged, comparatively easy to fly and vitally needed. However, in later years, the design was dated and improvements had essentially run to the limits of the airframe. Hence, the A-26 was developed to replace it with the Americans.

American A-20s did not operate over Western Europe in significant numbers before March 1944. Still, their contribution there, as measured by number of sorties and tonnage dropped, was substantially less than the B-25 and B-26. In the Pacific, they continued to be used primarily in attacks by a few aircraft at a time while in Europe they were more often employed as medium

bombers in large formations. Compared with the USAAF's medium bombers, the A-20 was some 30mph (48km/h) faster, carried 1,000lb (454kg) less bomb loads, but over 100mi (161km) more range than the B-26 but about 60mi (97km) less than the B-25. All could deliver essentially the same strafing punch. Additionally, the A-20's non-interchangeable aircrew remained a concern throughout – an incapacitated pilot meaning the end for all and a bombardier unable to leave the nose compartment during takeoff and landings when a nose-over could prove fatal. By virtue of its origins as a light attack bomber, the A-20 had less growth potential than others. Adding a ventral turret or tail gun was simply impractical, and it never received de-ice gear. Nonetheless, it had a place in the fight to the last year of the conflict. At the end of 1944, many A-20 units were converting to A-26s, and their service was essentially ended before the war wrapped up.

Experimental Havoc (XA-20B, XA-20F)

With the added engine power to be introduced with the DB-7A, directional stability concerns were raised. While the enlarged vertical tail and rudder of the A-20/A-20A appeared a sound solution, another avenue was explored that might also yield an improvement in the dorsal gunner's field of fire. After initial production testing, the first of the DB-7s with the two-speed supercharger, the 131st aircraft, was fitted for testing commencing on 26 July. This amounted to vertical stabilisers at the tips of the horizontal with its notable dihedral. However, stability was

only slightly improved at the cost of a speed decrement and added buffeting, and field-of-fire obstruction directly aft traded for two to the sides. Although the modified machine was delivered to the British, they were uninterested in pursuing this option.

A tail gun installation was explored for the A-20 early in its life. This was likely a .30cal with a prone gunner. It may have been mocked-up or actually built as a modification. General Electric received a $50,000 June 1940 contract from the USAAC to developed a fire control system for A-20 remote nacelle and tail guns. It was soon evident the weight and balance implications of such equipment would be prohibitive. Consequently, the tail gun was dropped and the project refocused in July on remote electrical dorsal and ventral turrets plus the nacelle guns, all commanded from a single gunner and central fire control system via a bifurcated sighting periscope. The nacelle guns were discarded in August and by then the remaining aspects of the effort were behind schedule. However, a $60,000 contract was promulgated in December 1940 for a production design for the A-20A. An A-20A may have been modified in mid-1941 with these powered gun stations and continuous ammunition feed as the sole XA-20B with a three-man crew. Whether an X-plane was actually created or not, the remote gun installation was not pursued to production.

While remote turrets remained a desirable addition to the Havoc, the technology did not mature fast enough to meet the production schedule. The system was aimed instead at the A-26. Douglas desired to gain experience with

the equipment and so worked with GE to create a trial installation on an A-20A. This XA-20F was the last A-20A, 39-725, and delivered on 21 April 1941. It was modified in El Segundo, finished that July, with dorsal and ventral turrets, each having a pair of .50cals. The domes of the electrically driven turrets were installed opposite the wing trailing edges. The gunner station, with transparencies, was behind the top turret with a bifurcated periscopic sight, the prisms emerging above and below the fuselage.

The XA-20F was tested alternately at Eglin Field and Wright Field for several years beginning in September 1941. The addition of a T-20-E-1 37-mm cannon in the nose further enhanced its experimental value. The aircraft was retired in March 1945 after providing useful data for the A-26 development.

An A-20G was reportedly fitted with an experimental installation of twin 37mm cannon along with the normal pair of .50s. Mention is also found of an A-20C converted with a bombardier's station just aft of the bomb bay as originally intended for the A-20G and H. This required modification of the aft portion of the bay and the gunner's station.[5]

Late Arrival (A-26)

With the European war providing insight into desired bomber and attacker attributes, and in examining experience with American models operated by all combatants, room for improvement became evident during 1940. Additionally,

the fast pace of aeronautical science and aircraft development in the few years since design of the earlier aircraft offered potential for greater capabilities. Douglas began exploring advanced design options in autumn 1940. Their A-20 was criticised for inadequate defensive firepower, insufficient growth potential to meet demands for greater airspeed, especially at medium altitudes, insufficient structural strength for dive bombing, excessive takeoff and landing distance, and no interchangeability of crewmembers.‡ The Army was also interested in fitting a 75mm cannon to an attack ship for 'tank busting', but the A-20 fuselage appeared too narrow for such a weapon.

The service discussed these subjects with Douglas during winter 1940 and encouraged a study of possible solutions. The associated specification was released on 21 January 1941 and the firm presented a proposal on the 27th. Given the company's experience and saturation of the industry

‡ The Havoc's 6g manoeuvering limit, reduced to 5.25g at elevated weights, appeared too low.

with ongoing work, only Douglas was invited to participate.§ They proceeded into preliminary design and mockup as contract negotiations continued.

The team focused on then-advanced features like tricycle undercarriage, electrically operated remote turrets, 75S aluminum for high strength without weight penalty, laminar-flow wing, electrically operated double-slotted flaps and 2,000hp (1,291kW) R-2800 engines. The weapons suite was to be easily altered to meet mission requirements. Self-sealing tanks and armour were incorporated from the start.

The Air Corps examined the mockup during April 1941. Although requesting changes to the canopy and raising the seats to ensure pilots could see past the large nacelles, the personnel came away sufficiently impressed to recommend Douglas be placed on contract. Two XA-26 Invader prototypes were duly ordered on a contract approved 2 June for an estimated $2,208,385.79. A third was added on 9 June for $541,773.05 and delivery in October 1942.

After a 23 February 1941 Douglas proposal to build 500 A-26s in Santa Monica, and following protracted negotiations, a $78,834,950 production

§ Normal terms of acquisition statues were suspended during the war.

Right: The XA-20F was photographed near the end of its test career on 26 January 1945. It was originally modified with remote dorsal and ventral turrets evident here, and a gunner station (out of view aft). The later addition of the 37mm nose cannon earned the airplane the Porcupine I moniker. *National Museum of the United States Air Force*

Above: The two remote turrets of the A-26 Invader are seen on this A-26B-20. The upper optical head of the bifurcated periscope(inset) is seen above the gunmens compartment. The dorsal turret could be locked to fire forward at pilot command and the ventral was occasionally removed. A six-gun nose is fitted. *San Diego Air & Space Museum;* insert *National Museum of the United States Air Force*

contract for the aircraft was awarded on 31 October 1941. First delivery was to be in January 1943. This was before the XA-26 design had reached any substantial hardware stage. Another 500 were ordered on 17 March 1943 for $109,164,900. More were sure to follow, and the Army was contemplating an A-26 peak production rate of 500 per month.

The XA-26 development and assembly work was undertaken in El Segundo. More innovations were introduced during detailed design. Douglas sought an empty weight of 20,450lb (9276kg) and maximum gross of 26,000lb (11,793kg). The R-2800-27 had a single-stage/two-speed supercharger and turned a 12.6ft (3.8m), three-blade propeller. The tremendous power was one key to achieving the objective top speed of 372mph (599km/h) at 17,000ft (5,182m). Combat range was to be 683mi (1,099km). Instead of the typical steel tube engine mount, a simpler and lighter sheet steel dome and forgings assembly with shock mounting points was substituted. This attached to the firewall with six bolts. The 'power pack' was designed to be removed and installed in 2hr and interchangeable side-to-side. The bottom cowling, when lowered, served as a work stand. The cowling featured the latest designs for reduced drag but improved engine cooling. The engine exhaust was collected into nine 'fishtail'

stacks around the cowl exit plane for the ejector while also providing a measure of flame damping. Ease of maintenance was a particular design consideration.

The laminar-flow objective demanded an exceptionally smooth wing finish. There were provisions for leading edge de-icing boots, but these were not fitted during the war. The squared-off fuselage cross-section simplified integration of the cannon with no more aerodynamic penalty than a larger circular cross-section. The long bomb bay accommodated two semi-recessed Mk. 13 torpedoes. Bomb load was 3,000lb (1,361kg) in the bay and 2,000lb (907kg) on under-wing mounts outboard of the engines. The twin-gun General Electric turrets (500rpg) were arranged above the mid-fuselage and below the aft. The gunner was in a compartment just behind the bomb bay and sat on a seat that revolved around a bifurcated periscope sight. This avoided the disorientation of the earlier static position and the sight had greater field of view. An indicator in the cockpit revealed the orientation of the guns so the pilot could manoeuver the aircraft for optimal defensive fire. The upper turret could be locked in forward azimuth and zero elevation for firing to the front by the pilot.

The aircraft was envisioned as being alternately fitted with a bomber nose, a nose with a 75mm cannon or multiple

other weapons like .50cal MGs for ground attack. The noses were to be interchangeable, the swap performed within 24hr. For the cannon-equipped aircraft, the navigator would service the 75mm with its 20 racked shells. The shells would be manually fed into the breach and, after firing, the casing ejected into a chute and out the bottom of the aircraft. The cannon was 11.0ft (3.4m) long with 1.8ft (0.6m) recoil, the entire installation weighing 1,296lb (4,906kg). Via such ready changes in equipment to match various missions, the USAAF intended for the A-26 to replace A-20s, B-25s and B-26s.¶

The crew would consist of the pilot, bombardier/navigator and gunner. The pilot sat to the port side of the cockpit. The heavy forward-firing weapons made a gunsight necessary, a reflector type selected although a ring-and-bead was retained as backup. A jump seat on the starboard side of the cockpit was

¶ This demonstrated the growing lack of differentiation between Attack and Bomber categories, and the progressing impression that medium bombardment would be unnecessary given sufficient numbers of heavy bombers.

Left: Much vacillation in nose weapons plagued the A-26. An initial 75mm cannon installation in the XB-26B is shown with translating/opening muzzle cover. This and the wooden nose were not adopted. The insert right shows an experimental dual-37mm installation, possessing advantages of high rate of fire and automatic shell feed. *Jay Miller Collection*

employed by the bombardier for takeoff and landings. A crawlway ahead of this seat accessed the nose and the Norden bombsight. The gunner could gain the cockpit via small doors and carefully working his way across the bomb bay, provided the weapons load did not preclude this.

The first XA-26 (41-19504) prototype was built with a bomber nose. The second machine, designated XA-26A (41-19505), was a night fighter prototype that was not produced. The third was the XA-26B (41-19588) with a 75mm installation.

Work on the A-26 was slowed by the US entry into the war, the pressures of other priority programs and late delivery of scarce materials and government furnished equipment (GFE) like landing gear struts, fuel tanks, propellers and turrets. The expected first flight date of 15 January 1942 proved unattainable. On the bright side, the aircraft came in 700lb (318kg) underweight. The XA-26 finally took flight on 10 July at Mines Field (Los Angeles Municipal Airport). The first XA-26B flew in March 1943. As testing progressed, engine cooling issues prompted cowl revisions and removal of the propeller spinners. The dorsal turret installation had to be revised to eliminate tail buffet. These and numerous minor issues caused work to drag on.

A large number of nose armament combinations were explored, offering options but also reflecting USAAF indecision. Douglas drew, mocked up and flew various combinations that included a manually loaded starboard

75mm mated with a port 37mm, 75mm with two port .50s, two and four 37s, a 37 (75 rounds, 140rpm) with two or four .50s (400rpg), plus all-MG noses with 12, 8 or 6 .50cals. One 75mm installation had the cannon mounted such that the barrel could be depressed 15°, this evidenced by the oblong barrel opening in the nose. Another effort was begun to create removable twin-gun pods on the two under-wing hardpoints on each side, the .50cal ammunition fed from within the wing (300rpg).

A XA-26C model with four 37mm in the nose was explored as a tank destroyer beginning in January 1943.[6] Douglas began designing an 'all-purpose' or 'universal' nose, secured to the forward fuselage with six bolts, in which seven combinations of 75mm, 37mm and .50cal weapons could be installed to meet individual combat requirements. An A-26B fitted with 105mm cannon was ground tested in 1945.

Consideration of employing the 37mm in any form was dropped in August 1943. Instead, the decision had been made on 22 February 1943 to produce the XA-26 with transparent nose as the A-26C, and the XA-26C was cancelled in August. Two .50cal MGs (400rpg) were placed in the starboard side of the 'glass nose'. The 'solid nose' configuration remained undecided.

After much government vacillation, plans evolved for manufacture on the first order in the Long Beach plant (suffix -DL) and the second order in a new Tulsa, Oklahoma (-DT) facility.** Soon the

decision was made to concentrate on Bs in California and Cs in Oklahoma.

The A-26 was shaping up to be everything the Air Forces wanted and Douglas promised, except timeliness. Test wing structures failed in static test about ten per cent below the specified load. To keep the programme moving quickly, only modifications and retest could be done to approach required strength. A dearth of production engineering manpower, machine tools, insufficient milling machine capacity to make the tapered wing spars, late deliveries from suppliers and government, indecision on the B nose weaponry, and just getting the new plants operating, all combined to delay production substantially. The service kept up a steady stream of change requests, most minor and generally advisable but a few very significant like addition of the C-1 autopilot.

By fall 1942, first deliveries had slipped six months to summer 1943. Once begun, manufacturing was then slow coming up to speed. All this earned the ire of General Arnold and put great pressure on all concerned, with special measures taken. With the initial intent that no other medium bomber/attack contracts would be let after the A-26 entered production, it was necessary to order additional A-20s as a stopgap.

The military had decided in summer 1942 to build 1,000 aircraft with 75mm cannon in a wooden nose but would also have 200 six-gun noses (400rpg) and 126 bombardier noses constructed for field swaps. By edict, no further work on nose armament or wing pods were to be undertaken until the 75mm production design was completed. Yet, USAAF changes continued, including a request that two .50s (400rpg) be placed in the nose with the 75mm and discussion of accommodating 150 to 180 parafrags.[7] They then considered building bomber and MG noses at various ratios with cannon noses while employing the

** Beech Aircraft would build the wings for the Tulsa plant.

all-purpose assembly, the twin 37mm installation again rising to the surface.

Owing to the slow rate of fire and added logistics burden, the 75mm were eliminated. Near the end of 1944, and after much lost time, the service settled on six-gun noses for the A-26B. The cannon, with two MGs, made it into 35 aircraft, that apparently were never deployed, after which the universal nose was substituted. Then, the AAF chose to include an eight-gun installation (360rpg) in production using the universal nose beginning with the A-26B-10s. Other than the interchangeable nose, the B and C models were identical. Once a nose was swapped, the original designation became meaningless, although in practice such swaps were rare.

The under-wing provisions for two 500lb (227kg) bombs or the twin-gun 'gondolas', the ammunition within the wing, was introduced with the A-26B-15 aircraft beginning in February 1944. Later still, two 'wet' wing stations were added to which 165gal (625lit) drop tanks (although limited to 155gal/587lit) could be mounted. The bay capacity was also increased by 1,000lb (453kg) for a total aircraft bomb load of 6,000lb (2,722kg). Ultimately, the aircraft was not intended for dive bombing, only shallow dive releases being practised.

It was 10 September 1943 before the A-26Bs began to roll off the California line, nine months late, and January 1944 for Oklahoma. However, by 13 March, only 21 aircraft had been delivered. It would be approximately a year after initial delivery before the type could be in combat. Nonetheless, orders were placed on 29 March 1944 for an additional 1,100 Bs and 1,600 Cs for $308,454,619, followed by a further 2,400 on 30 November 1944 on contracts valued at $231,999,989. A $106,211,313 contract supplement adding 1,250 aircraft of unspecified models was signed on 5 April 1945. This brought the total A-26s ordered to 7,350.

Four A-26B-5s, fitted with early universal

noses and under-wing gun pods, were flown to New Guinea for combat tests in July 1944. The team noted high elevator control forces during low-altitude pull-out. Particular criticism was directed at poor lateral visibility from the cockpit, given the canopy design and long engine nacelles, and the starboard seating of the pilot that compromised vision to port, making line-abreast formation flying hazardous. Finding the wing guns reducing the airspeed to that of the B-25, their removal left forward firepower less than the A-20. While the team ignored the 75mm completely, they were interested in the 37mm installation but were provided with no shells. Range was barely suitable for the theatre and the combat summary suggested removing the bottom turret to improve this measure. Word was passed back to the States that the A-26 was unwelcome because of its unsuitability for theatre tactics.

Operation of 18 of A-26s (six glass-nose, 12 6-gun nose) from England in late summer yielded more positive comments, the crews appreciative of the performance advantages. Single-engine characteristics were particularly outstanding. There were still plenty of deficiencies noted and many crews who saw no need to give up their A-20s or B-26s.

The first production aircraft went to the ETO and Mediterranean Theatre of Operations (MTO) in fall 1944, about 600 reaching the theatre and seeing steady action. The Pacific and CBI theatres began receiving Invaders in spring 1945 with only about 250 arriving before the

end and so had little opportunity for combat. Hence, the A-26 fought in only the last 10 months of the war.

The new aircraft still had systems problems that were slowly corrected through production block upgrades, but enhancements were also introduced. The oil cooler inlets in the leading edge, outboard of each nacelle, were enlarged and given protruding lips for improved effectiveness and reduced contribution to tail buffet. A weak nose gear that tended to collapse with minor abuse was quickly addressed. Retractable spoilers were added ahead of the bomb bay doors to reduce buffet and allow maximum speed dives.

The C aircraft were usually fitted with dual controls and proper copilot seat, the control column and rudder pedals being removable to permit passage into the nose compartment. The twin nose guns were occasionally removed in the field. The initial A-26s had R-2800-27s from Pratt & Whitney or -71s manufactured by Ford with a new ignition system. The Ford R-2800-79 eventually became standard. This featured water injection for a WE spurt to 2,370hp (1,771kW, sea level), boosting peak speed to 372mph (599km/h). The aircraft had 1,600gal (6,057lit) of fuel and provisions for a 125gal (473lit) self-sealing auxiliary tank in the forward bomb bay. A 675gal (2,555lit) tank could also be installed in the bay, although limited to ferry because it was not self-sealing and consumed all volume. Since the bottom turret was

Right: The dual .50cal pods, ammunition fed from within the wing, are seen on a A-26B-1-DL. While addressing an early criticism of inadequate forward firepower, the "tubs" imposed a discouraging drag penalty and took up stations that could be used for bombs and fuel tanks. They were seldom mounted. *National Museum of the United States Air Force*

found superfluous in the circumstance of the final year of the war, it was omitted for aircraft bound for the Pacific and a 125gal (473lit) auxiliary tank installed in its place.

The heavy canopy on the initial aircraft, the hatch over the starboard side of the cockpit and hinged at the front, was disliked by crews because emergency egress was difficult and the wide framing impaired visibility. This and restricted vision past the nacelles required years to remedy in production. This involved raising the cockpit floor and creating a clamshell canopy arrangement, hinged to the side. The higher moldline meant the ventral turret could no longer be fired forward by the pilot. The canopy was initially provided as a retrofit item before being introduced to production in fall 1944. With the under-wing gun tubs widely condemned, production shifted to three guns internal to each wing, the eight-gun noses introduced concurrently. Also added were zero-length launchers in the outboard wings, seven per side, for 5in HVARs or earlier rail-launched rockets.

The RAF evaluated three A-26Bs and Cs beginning in July 1944 and placed an initial order for 140 C examples as Invader Is. They requested minor changes plus flame dampers. The USAAF was loath to offer up any A-26s for Lend-Lease, but acquiesced. However, in early April 1945, the British decided the war situation made introduction of a new type unnecessary.

Peak A-26 production was 318 aircraft from both plants in May 1945 against a goal of 400. By that time the aircraft was being used more as an attacker than level bomber, so the production ratio of 2/3rds gun noses to 1/3rd glass noses was established on 15 April. The surrender of Germany was cause to slow production to 150 aircraft per month, contracts being cancelled and long term engineering changes dropped. All Tulsa contracts were terminated on 13 August and Long Beach followed on the 27th. Some aircraft were allowed to proceed to completion, the last delivered on the 31st. This left 1,359 A-26Bs manufactured and 1,114 Cs, of which 2,452 were actually delivered, almost all in the final 20 months of the war about 5,200 were cancelled.

The Invader was generally superior to all other American production medium bombers and attackers – rugged, versatile, capable, easier to handle and maintain, of standout performance – and stood at least toe-to-toe with the best of any other nation. Although with issues typical of wartime projects, it would have replaced all that came before if arriving sooner. However, the long period from inception to combat reduced its contribution to near insignificance. Instead, it went on to establish a long and worldwide postwar service.

Mongrel Invaders
(A-26D, A-26E, A-26G, A-26H, A-26Z)

Pursuing a further boost in speed, the 2,100hp (1,566kW) Chevrolet-built R-2800-83 engines with four-blade, 12.7ft (3.9m) propellers were contemplated. These delivered 2,400hp (1,790kW) with water injection, had large spinners and revised carburetor air scoop. Under the surface were revised engine mounts, generators, carburetors and improved supercharger. These would power solid-nose A-26Ds and glass-nose A-26Es.

Douglas created flight test examples via modification beginning in January 1945. The first A-26D was from A-26B-71-DL 44-34110 and second an A-26B-40-DL 41-39543. The A-26E prototype was derived from A-26C-40-DT 44-35563 and flown in 1945.[8] Empty weight rose to 22,550lb (10,229kg) and normal maximum to 35,000lb (15,876kg), speed topped 403mph (649km/h) at 15,000ft (4,572m),

Douglas A-26B-5 or -10 characteristics:			
span	70.0ft	weight empty	22,370lb
length	50.0ft	design gross	27,600lb
height	18.5ft	max. gross	35,000lb
wing area	540.5ft²	bomb load, max.	6,000lb
fuel (built-in–max.)	924-2,025gal	normal	4,000lb
service ceiling	22,100ft	speed, max. (15,000ft)	355mph
climb rate, 35,000lb	1,235fpm	cruise	284mph
takeoff distance* (35,000lb)	6,000ft	range, 4,000lb bombs	1,400mi
landing distance*	3,000ft	ferry	3,200mi
*over 50ft obstacle			

Above: Seeking greater speed for one of the fastest bombers, R-2800-83 engines were mounted on a A-26B to become the XA-26D. These saw return to the large spinners of earlier prototypes and introduction of four-blade propellers. Coming late (14 July 1945 image at El Segundo with XB-42 beyond) the configuration was not produced. *Jay Miller Collection*

while climb rate was 2,326fpm (12mps) and service ceiling 31,200ft (9,510m). A typical range was given as 1,480mi (2,382km). The USAAF ordered 750 Ds on 13 April 1945 from Long Beach and it has been said the 5 April order for 1,250 aircraft was expected to be built as Es from Tulsa. These contracts were cancelled after VJ-Day with none finished.

As production wound down into summer 1945, the Tulsa plant took on more modification work. One such project was converting Cs to night pathfinders with an AN/APQ-13 radar in the forward bomb bay, a spherical radome projecting below the door line. The turrets and sighting periscope were removed. Another effort was converting 96 A-26Bs to a night intruder variant. These were to be fitted with a large, self-sealing, bomb bay tank to bring range to 2,500mi (4,023km), add flame dampers to the engine exhausts and flash suppressors to the guns, put a taxi light on the nose strut and install LORAN. All these projects were cancelled at the end of the war. At least one pathfinder (A-26C-55-DT, 44-35946) was completed by special request after all work was to have ceased.[9]

In summer 1945, Douglas proposed various other changes to the Invader to improve the type progressively. Offered

as the A-26G (solid nose) and H (glass nose), or lumped together as the A-26Z, these had such features as jettisonable tip tanks and expanded bomb bay tank capacity to 200gal (757lit), strengthened wing structure, more powerful R-2800s, cockpit raised and canopy sealed with a one-piece transparency with crew entrance and egress through a nose gear well hatch. Although it was clear these would be produced postwar, the Air Forces showed interest and discussions continued. However, the drastically reduced budgets and advent of jets meant the programme was not funded.

Supporting Roles

Loose End (XA-21)

Another contender in the 1939 attack bomber competition that begat the A-20 was a 'dark horse' from The Stearman Company. The X-100 was the company's first twin, first all-metal structure with flush riveting, first monoplane and initial use of Fowler flaps.[††*] This major step began design in 1938 and was completed after the firm became a division of The Boeing Company. The aircraft first flew in March 1939. All told, it came in last for

†† Fowler flaps slide aft and down, both enhancing low-speed lift and effectively increasing wing area.

performance during the competition. It was evaluated later against the B-23, B-25 and B-26 in a bomber competition, but with the same outcome.

The X-100 had a normal crew of pilot, bombardier and radio operator/gunner, but with accommodations for another gunner. The electrically actuated landing gear (not fully enclosed) and integral fuel tanks were then still rare. It was powered by the new Pratt & Whitney R-2180-7 Twin Hornet (commercial -S1A1-G). This was a 14-cylinder, twin-row engine of 1,400hp (1,044kW), spinning three-blade props and would find no subsequent application. Sealed compartments in the wing, fuselage and tail assisted flotation during ditching. The streamlined nose with vast greenhouse was the most unusual feature, but the conventional undercarriage was becoming anachronistic. Five .30cal MGs were distributed as one in the nose, one on an aft ventral position, two in the aft sides and another in a dorsal turret.

Above: After modification to a stepped canopy, the Army bought the solitary X-100 and dubbed it XA-21. It served test purposes for a time and had paint smeared on in an airpower lineup for President Roosevelt on 19-20 January 1940, at Bolling Field. Note the added under-wing stations with smoke tanks mounted. *National Archives*

Left: The Boeing-Stearman X-100 competitor for the Air Corps' 1938-1939 attack bomber competition evinced all the most modern features except fully retracted tricycle landing gear. The squared fuselage cross-section was somewhat retrograde while the streamlined nose was eye-catching. The numerous gun placements were harbingers of things to come. *Jay Miller Collection*

Boeing XA-21 characteristics:			
span	65.0ft	weight empty	12,760lb
length	53.1ft	gross	18,230lb
height	14.2ft	max.	20,200lb
wing area	607ft^2	bomb load, max.	2,700lb
fuel, max.	450-520gal	normal	1,200lb
service ceiling	20,000ft	speed, max. (5,000ft)	257mph
takeoff distance*	1,575ft	cruise	200mph
landing distance*	1,675ft	range, (1,200lb/230mph/5,000ft)	725mi
*over 50ft obstacle		max (200mph/5,000ft)	1,200mi
		ferry (190mph/5,000ft)	1,500mi

Four additional .30s could be installed in fixed wing mounts for strafing.[10]

After the initial part of the competition, the aircraft was flown back to Wichita in April 1939 and modified with a more common stepped canopy and isolated bombardier station. Flying resumed in August and the Army took delivery on 1 September, having bought the aircraft. Designated the XA-21 (40-191), it was employed at Eglin Field in developing low-altitude, high-speed bombing techniques. No one saw any future in the type once war broke out and demonstrated that such designs were inadequate.

Not for Domestic Consumption

Many American bomber types found their way into the hands of foreign operators during the war. A few were only adopted by United States forces after being first sold abroad. However, even given the marginal state of readiness and tremendous force expansion underway, there were two types never taken up by the US military. Yet, the Marylands and Baltimores from Martin were noteworthy aircraft and played interesting roles early in the conflict.

Finding a Home (Martin 167, XA-22, Maryland)

Martin's Model 167 twin was conceived as another contender for the Air Corps' 1938 twin-engine attack bomber competition. The aircraft first flew in February 1939.

The elegant Model 167W prototype was unusual in being a low-wing bomber and eschewed the latest engines for the proven 1,200hp (895kW) R-1830-37 turning 10.3ft (3.1m), three-blade props. All leading edges were fitted with de-icing boots and the wing trailing edges with slotted flaps. The single pilot was accompanied by a bombardier/navigator and radioman/gunner in a fuselage so narrow the men could not move between stations. The bombardier had fold-aside flight controls as a safety measure should

the pilot be incapacitated. The enclosed bomb bay accommodated four 300lb (136kg) or 60 30lb (14kg) fragmentation bombs. A manually retractable top turret, covered with a sliding panel when stowed, was fitted with a single .30cal machine gun. Another such gun covered the lower aft quarter on a mount within a fuselage ventral inflexion. A pair of .30s were fixed in each wing to fire forward. There were 3,000 rounds onboard.

The Martin design was neither the fastest (200mph/322km/h at 5,000ft/1,524m) nor the heaviest of the competition, but performed best at low altitude. However, a second round of competition was called for that emphasised medium altitude, where the DB-7 excelled. Martin protested bitterly when the production contract was awarded to Douglas. This was only enough to gain a consolation prize of $505,390 when the USAAC purchased the test aircraft on 26 September to become the sole XA-22 (40-706).

Further remuneration came as French orders for the type. Even after advent of the WE, the Martin aircraft was just more of the same to the Americans; slow, underpowered, under-armed and with too little growth potential. If allies found them useful, all the better. Martin conceived various upgrades and major changes to the design for improved performance, including swept wings with pusher engines, tricycle undercarriage

and heavier weapons. These stirred no interest in America.

The French had decided in January 1939, prior to first flight of the 167, to place a substantial order. The contract, signed on 6 February 1939, was for 115 machines (Model 167-F1) with another hundred (167-F2) ordered in March. The first batch was to be delivered in just eight months. Facilitating this, France funded a $2,400,000 expansion of the Middle River facilities. Built in less than three months, nearly doubling the floor space, this marked Martin (briefly) as the largest American aircraft plant and first to work at three-shift wartime pace. Rapid assembly was assisted by the fuselage being constructed in halves, permitting easier parts installation.

The French naturally required changes to the design they designated 167-A3.‡‡* This substituted the commercial 1,050hp (783kW) R-1830-SC3-G supercharged engines burning 87-octane fuel, Belgian 7.5mm FN machine guns, French bomb racks, metric instruments and a throttle quadrant in which aft advanced power.

‡‡ The 'A3' meant Army support 3-seater.

Below: The Martin 167 performed well, albeit unsuccessfully, in an Air Corps attack bomber competition. The one example of this medium twin was bought and became the XA-22 seen here at Wright Field during 1939 in civil markings. The sliding hatch over the centre fuselage enclosed a retracted turret. *National Museum of the United States Air Force*

Above: French Navy 167s in Vichy markings fly formation. Like so much of the equipment acquired just prior to the calamity, the "Glenns" could not be used to their full potential. Yet, they had valuable roles to play in French hands to the end of the conflict. *Ray Wagner Collection*

Martin 167-B3/B4 Maryland II:			
span	61.3ft	weight empty	11,213lb
length	48.7ft	gross	16,808lb
height	10.0ft	bomb load, max.	2,000lb
wing area	538.5ft²	normal	1,250lb
fuel, max.	433-528gal	speed, max. (13,000ft)	316mph
service ceiling	31,000ft	cruise	187mph
average climb rate	2,400fpm	range, (1,250lb bombs)	1,300mi
takeoff distance*	1,760ft		
landing distance*	1,500ft	*over 50ft obstacle	

They dispensed with the sliding panel over the turret as this was only partially retractable (and still manual) with the change in guns. Weapons load was upped to 1,760lb (798kg). Being approximately 1,000lb (454kg) lighter than the XA-22, the 167F had a 9,000ft (2,743m) ceiling advantage. The first of the new type flew on 8 August 1939. The aircraft handled nicely and the 71mph (114km/h) landing speed was most welcome. Top speed and range were respectable.

The first machines were shipped two months late on 2 September 1939. With war declared the following day, there was a further two-month suspension in deliveries. Aircraft collected in Canada while awaiting resolution of the Neutrality impasse. Not waiting, the customer ordered a further 280 of the bombers in October. The 130 F3s introduced 1,300lb (590kg) of armour at crew stations and over fuel tanks. The 150 F4s were to have self-sealing fuel cells, improved engines, lighter armour and display greater airspeed.

The first 93 bombers the French called 'Glenns' were delivered by 25 December 1939. However, the attack mission was new to the Armée de l'Air and Aèronavale. This and slow assembly of the aircraft lengthened the training of crews such that only a portion of force was ready when battle was joined. By the armistice on 25 June, 189 of the F1s and F2s had been assembled.[11] Still, they acquitted themselves well against the German and Italian invaders despite 18 being shot down and many more lost in accidents. Those remaining were taken up by Vichy forces and then employed against British elements seeking to unseat the collaborators. This fighting claimed many more bombers. For a time, Free French and Vichy forces both flew 167s on opposing sides.

The undelivered 167s were transferred to the British who claimed 62 complete or nearly complete aircraft yet to leave the States and 19-22 others on the high seas or brought to them by fleeing Frenchmen. The RAF dubbed the type the Maryland I and had 43 reworked before entry into service. Instruments, radios, throttle quadrants, bomb racks and guns were replaced with English equivalents. Only 95 F3s were completed, Martin finishing 35 to the British standard (Model 167-B3). British shops converted another 50. A notional Dutch order for two - place 167-H1s and three-place 167-H2s disappeared with their capitulation to Germany

The 150 F4 machines became Maryland IIs (167-B4). These mounted the 1,000hp (746kW) R-1830-S3C4-G with two-speed gear-driven supercharger burning 100-octane from self-sealing tanks. Weapons load was increased to 2,000lb (907kg) and armour plating added. A pair of Vickers K or Browning .303 MGs was placed in the turret and two more fixed in the belly to fire aft as 'scare' guns. These alterations raised empty weight by 627lb (284kg). Deliveries ran from December 1940 through April 1941.[12]

The Maryland Is and IIs performed useful duties in North Africa, operated in light bomber and armed reconnaissance roles during which they downed 10 Italian aircraft. However, even in this theatre the slow speed and light bomb load of the Martins made them a marginal asset. All were replaced in frontline service during 1942 but continued to fly behind the lines and on reconnaissance missions throughout the conflict, including by Free French units.

With 495 Martin 167s built between fall 1939 and spring 1941, it was an important American bomber contributing early in the war. It demonstrated the ability of the American aircraft industry to manufacture quality aircraft at a wartime pace while introducing required upgrades.

All Grown Up (XA-23, Baltimore, A-30)

Foreign interest in the Model 167 did not end Martin's desire to sell the aircraft at home. Conceptual design of a growth version of the Maryland as the Model 187 was shown to the Air Corps and garnered enough interest to earn an XA-23 designation in 1940. This was envisioned as using Wright R-3350-11 Cyclone 18 engines at 2,000hp (1,491kW) with four-blade propellers to achieve 380mph (483km/h). The Army soon passed on the project, but Martin again attracted foreign investment.

As the Model 167s rolled off the Martin production line, the joint Anglo-French Purchasing Commission sought a more capable model that possessed more growth potential and so less likely to become obsolete in a year or so. Consequently, the 187 was taken to full design and development to meet this requirement. The 18 May 1940 order for 400 aircraft, including 166 machines for France as Model 187-F1s, was based solely on preliminary design data. The Dutch expressed an interest in participating as well and a 187-H1 model was conceived. This evaporated when The Netherlands succumbed to the Nazi blitzkrieg. The $44,000,000 Anglo-French deal required US government approval, especially as it would impact some B-26 work. As was the practice at the time, the export windfall was approved with the proviso Martin give something to the US government in return. This was introduction of power turrets, armour and self-sealing tanks to the Marauder at no charge.

By the end of June 1940, the order was assumed *in toto* by the UK as the Model 187B Baltimore and they became active participants in development. After the B-26 emerged, the British considered dropping the Baltimore in favour of the newer aircraft. However, the 187 could be had sooner and at lower price, so the programme proceeded.

The new aircraft built upon the best qualities of the 167. The deeper fuselage

Below: South African Maryland IIs operate in the dusty northern Africa desert, a pair of Vickers K guns visible in a modified turret. Throughout the war, the British and French forces made effective use of the light bomber in the margins of the conflict despite it not measuring up to frontline requirements. *National Archives*

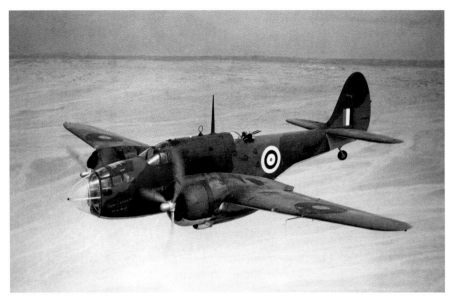

Above: This Baltimore IIIA models the tall Boulton-Paul turret, but without the four .303 guns. The large intakes atop the cowlings enclose sand filters required for operations in North Africa. The ventral gun station for two .30cals is evident in the fuselage bottom inflexion. Note the extended flaps. *National Museum of the United States Air Force*

and more powerful engines permitted more weapons in an aircraft a third heavier. The wings were 'beefed up' but otherwise largely unchanged while a revised tail was necessary. Each had GR-2600-A5B engines (military R-2600-19) of 1,600hp (1,193kW) with two-speed supercharger. These had 12.1ft (3.8m), three-blade propellers and were to be fitted with a large air filter supporting

desert operations. Self-sealing tanks cost some fuel volume, but that and 211lb (96kg) of armour were most welcome. A hydraulic British turret with four .303s was planned, this complementing a bevy of .30cals including four in the wings and two in the ventral position that was activated by raising a panel and sliding the guns aft into the opening. The rear-firing 'scare' guns increased to four, while weapons load was 2,000lb (907kg). Crew complement rose to four.

The increasingly heavy workload at Martin lengthened 187 development. Instead of delivery in early 1941, the first example only flew on 12 June. Empennage changes were found

necessary and other problem areas addressed. To fill the delivery gap, the Americans agreed to supply B-26A-1s. In addition, the turret and air filters were deferred to the 151st aircraft. The first 50 machines, Baltimore Is, had a single .30cal MG mounted in the turret opening with a sliding plexiglass hood. The 100 Baltimore IIs added a second Browning. Upon entering service, it was found these guns were unsuitable.[13] The RAF replaced them with their own .303s. The 610lb (277kg) Boulton-Paul turret finally appeared in the 250 Baltimore IIIs with sand filters. Deliveries began in October 1941 and numbered 146 by year end, the type first seeing action in May 1942. The balance of the 400-aircraft order was delivered by that June.

With advent of Lend-Lease, a further 575 Baltimores were ordered on 17 June 1941, followed by another 600 on 23 September 1942. Since the programme was supposed to cover supply of American equipment with US funds to foreign combatants, it was necessary that the Martins be identified as American military assets. They were designated A-30s and given some US equipment.

The first 281 A-30s (187-B2) were like the Baltimore IIIs except with military R-2600-19 engines, provisions for a bomb bay ferry tank and lighter, lower-profile 250CE turret. These were accepted as Baltimore IIIAs, the first in August 1942. The Air Forces also sought other changes, although the aircraft were bound for someone with more insight into combat requirements. They wished to replace the forward firing MGs with .50cals, delete two of the 'scatter' guns and place a 37mm cannon in the nose in lieu of the bombardier. The British welcomed the .50s but saw little compelling need for changes and emphatically rejected the cannon. Some IIIs and IIIAs were taken up by the Americans as RA-30s in the emergency following Pearl Harbor. The remaining

294 machines of the first order had minor instrument and radio changes as A-30As/Baltimore IVs. These were delivered in two blocks as 187-B3s beginning in January 1943.

The 600-aircraft order became Baltimore Vs with 1,700hp (1,268kW) R-2600-29 engines, earning another 15mph (24km/h) in top speed and 1,700ft (518m) in ceiling but losing roughly 120mi (193km) off range. All guns became .50s. Initially shipping in July 1943, these were delivered at a peak 60-aircraft per month.

The Baltimores served well in Egypt as a daylight level. After the Germans were pushed out of North Africa and the type was displaced by B-26s in frontline units, the Baltimore continued to serve in the Mediterranean theatre in such roles as night intruder, reconnaissance, maritime patrols, liaison and target tow. They were ultimately operated by British, South African, Australian, Free Greek, Free French, Turkish and Italian Co-Belligerent units. The aircraft continued the Maryland's reputation of reliability and ruggedness. One loud complaint was the care required in power management during takeoff and landings as uneven application of power

Above: The more powerful engines on the Baltimore Vs aided performance gains. The Martin powered turret with twin .50cal machine guns had earlier replaced the heavier and taller British four-gun unit. Although appearing as the type moved to second tier status, it was still a fine example of American bomber technology. *Ray Wagner Collection*

on the two engines resulted in a strong swing leading to a discouraging number of crackups and casualties.

All told, Martin built 1,575 Baltimores through May 1944. The aircraft compared favourably with early-war medium bombers from all nations. Delivered quickly at a reasonable $104,000-120,000 per aircraft, they were economical.

A USAAF order for a planned A-30B variant, A-30A-1s with 1,700hp (1,268kW) R-2600-13, was cancelled on 10 March 1943. Likewise, a 900-aircraft British order for the Model 187-B4, Baltimore VI G.R., (A-30C), proposed in July 1943, was also dropped. These were intended as a maritime reconnaissance version of the V with ASW radar. Martin modified two Baltimore Vs in early 1944 as examples, each with nose radome and fittings for a belly-mounted long-range fuel tank. Martin also conceived several other variants in seeking to prolong production, but to no avail.

Martin 187 Baltimore V characteristics:			
span	61.3ft	weight empty	15,991lb
length	48.5ft	gross	23,185lb
height	14.2ft	max.	27,800lb
wing area	538.5ft²	bomb load, normal	1,000lb
fuel, max.	490-1,440gal	max.	2,000lb
service ceiling	25,000ft	speed, max. (15,000ft)	320mph
average climb rate	2,083fpm	cruise	224mph
takeoff distance*	2,050ft	range, (2,000lb bomb load)	720mi
landing distance*	1,875ft	(1,000lb bomb load)	980mi
*over 50ft obstacle		ferry	2,500mi

Chapter Four

Off-Colour and Sidebar Twins

Puffed-Up Twins

The Air Corps' interest turned to bomber cabin pressurisation very early in the war, before any other nation gave it much attention. Prior research showed a 'supercharged cabin' was practical and of potential tactical value as, it was believed, the bomber could operate above flak, fighters and weather. The service issued specification XC-214 for a pressurised medium bomber in August 1939. Only North American and Martin submitted proposals. Design studies were funded for both offerings, but only the NAA product was taken to prototype as the XB-28.

Although B-28 production was contemplated, nothing firm issued forth. By 1943, medium bombers were finding their most productive work as low- or medium-altitude interdiction. Only heavy bombers need dwell at such heights where pressurisation was advisable, and they were far from invulnerable. Interrupting ongoing production lines

to begin manufacturing a new model or type without compelling mission need was actively discouraged. Additionally, the unpressurised A-26 promised much the same performance as the XB-28.

Other twins were explored in concept or hardware seeking dramatic advances in performance. Again, some were set aside before 'metal was cut' while others advanced to the prototype stage. These efforts highlight the breadth of work undertaken by the United States during the war.

Paper Aircraft (XB-27)

Martin proposed its Model 182 in August 1939 for the Army's high-altitude medium bomber specification. This appeared much like a B-26 but with turbosuperchargers on 2,100hp (1,566kW) R-2800-9s and 4-blade propellers. These were expected to give 33,500ft (10,211m) service ceiling. Bomb capacity was to be 4,000lb (1,814kg). The aircraft appeared much like the B-26 but more sleek with extended nose and

low-profile cockpit bulge, all supporting pressurisation. All but the bomb bay was to be pressurised to 'shirt-sleeve' environment, with movement between the forward and aft compartments by crawling across the wing box. The main landing gear retracted outboard into the wing and left partially exposed, probably because the engine nacelles were consumed with supercharger hardware. There was to have been one .50cal tail machine gun, with prone gunner and 200 rounds, and three .30s with 1800 rounds. The small calibre weapons were to be in the nose, top amidships, and a movable weapon firing through two side port or bottom aperture, these envisioned as ball-in-window to maintain pressure seal. As many as seven were envisioned for aircrew, with a single pilot but jump seat beside him. A span of 84.0ft (25.6m) with 750.0ft² (69.7m²) area, and length of 60.8ft (18.5m), supported a 23,125lb (10,489kg) empty weight and 32,970lb (14,955kg) gross. Martin expected

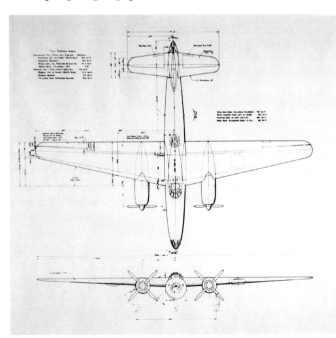

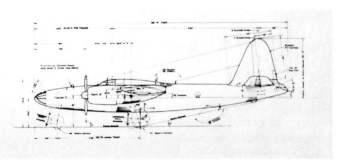

4-1 Having got the B-26 to production, Martin moved on with design of a similar aircraft meeting the Army's desire for a medium bomber to operate at high altitude. The sleek XB-27 (period drawing) was to have been pressurised and the engines fitted with turbosuperchargers, but was not chosen for development. *Glenn L. Martin Maryland Aviation Museum*

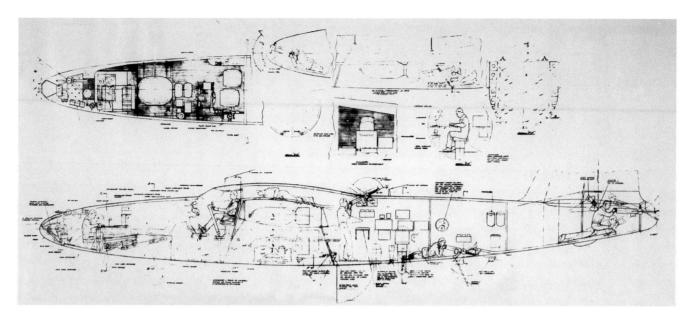

376mph (605km/h) at 25,000ft (7,620m) and 259mph (417km/h) cruise for 2,900mi (4,667km) range.

The USAAF funded a more detailed design effort into 1940 as the XB-27. Considering the understanding of pressurised aircraft construction at the time, the Martin conceptual design was overly simplistic and armament would not have met combat needs by time of production. In any event, North American won the development contract.

Passed Over (XB-28)

On 15 November 1939, just two months after contracting for the B-25, the Air Corps struck a deal with North American for initial design of a pressurised version of that medium bomber. The initial design concept for the XB-28 (NA-63) was essentially a B-25 with a circular fuselage and substituting Double Wasp engines in extended nacelles for turbosuperchargers. Design work had already begun in Inglewood during August. The original design retained the twin tails, but this soon gave way to a cruciform arrangement. Many other departures eventually left almost no commonality with the Mitchell. A contract for three prototypes (40-3056/8) was signed on 13 February 1940.

Each 2,000hp (1,491kW) R-2800-11 was augmented by a General Electric C-2 exhaust-driven turbosupercharger. A single engine-driven 'Roots blower' supercharger provided cabin pressurisation while gasoline-fired heaters in the pressurisation ducting heated this air. Intercoolers were fed air through inlets in the wing leading edges outboard of the nacelles and exhausted out the upper surface of the wing ahead of the outboard flaps. Supercharger exhaust, out the rear of the nacelles, added a minor quantity of thrust. The P&Ws drove counter-rotating, four-blade, 14.2ft (4.3m) props. North American experimented with propeller cuffs to augment cowl flaps for engine cooling. A CO_2 engine fire extinguishing system was adopted. Fuel tanks were integral with the structure.

All leading edges were fitted with de-icing boots and propellers with de-icing fluid. Nose wheel steering was featured, the pilot pushing a lever down and then rotating it forward or aft to affect right or left steering, respectively. Releasing the lever centred the wheel. As a novel aid to night flying, the primary instrument markings used fluorescent paint illuminated with ultraviolet lights on the control columns.

Only the forward portion of the fuselage was pressurised, this to be maintained at 8,000ft (2,438m) up to 33,000ft (10,058m). To prevent air leaks, rudder and packing strips were sandwiched in all riveted cabin joints and the interior was sprayed with a plastic sealant after assembly. The crew of five sat cheek-to-jowl in the narrow fuselage. They included pilot, copilot, bombardier/navigator, primary gunner and radio operator/gunner. For the bombardier to access the nose compartment, the copilot had to fold up his rudder pedal and lower a floor panel,

then slide his seat aft so the bombardier could squeeze past under the instrument panel. The navigator and gunner stations were in a space just aft of the flight deck.

Initially, the hydraulic remote turrets were to be designed and built by NAA. These included dorsal, ventral, and tail units, each with two .50cal guns and 1,200 rounds total. A planned nose gun was dropped as the anticipated high speed of the aircraft was to make frontal attack impractical. Bifurcated periscopes for two gunners were coupled to a Sperry fire control system, but this and the turrets were programmed to be GE equipment for production.[1] The periscope optical heads projected above and below the fuselage, just forward of the wing. The gunners also had 'fisheye' scanner windows. As this was among the first aircraft to fly with such a fire control system, the data gleaned was of much value. Four hydraulically operated doors enclosed the bomb bay of 4,000lb (1,814kg) capacity and provisions for long-range ferry tank.

Work on the XB-28 was slowed somewhat by the US entry into the war and emphasis on production types. Maiden flight of the first prototype was on 24 April 1942 from Mines Field. The

Above: The XB-28 won the battle but lost the war. North American created a fine machine that met requirements handsomely, advanced features like pressurisation and remote turrets were handled expertly. However, the Army had decided high altitude operations for medium bombers was no longer necessary and the XB-28 was passed over. *San Diego Air & Space Museum*

testing demonstrated the unusually high performance at altitude, flying as fast as a fighter above 24,000ft (7,315m). Following fight tests with a full crew, the USAAF took delivery of the XB-28 in December. It was subsequently ferried to Wright Field for service trials.

The decision was made soon after contract award to build the third machine as a reconnaissance/photo mapping aircraft. However, the B designation and guns were retained. The second XB-28 was subsequently set aside to focus on the XB-28A (NA-67) and never completed. Alterations were introduced during construction to reduce weight. Turrets were switched to GE units, cameras installed in the aft fuselage and R-2800-27s mounted. These changes may have been carried into the production bomber design.

Right: The North American XB-28 had sleek lines commensurate with its mission of high-speed medium bombardment. First flying in spring 1942, it was the fastest medium bomber of its class, and the only one with cabin pressurisation for sustained high altitude flight. A XB-28A had reduced weight for even greater performance. *Gerald Balzer Collection*

North American XB-28 characteristics:

span	72.6ft	weight empty	25,575lb, 23,500lb A
length (excluding guns)	56.3ft	gross	35,763lb 34,297lb A
height	22.0ft	max.	39,135lb, 38,079lb A
wing area	675.9ft²	bomb load, normal	2,000lb
fuel, max.	1,170-1,508gal	max.	4,000lb
service ceiling	34,800ft	speed, max. (25,000ft)	372mph, 353mph A
average climb rate	1,111fpm	cruise	255mph
takeoff distance*	2,600ft	range, (600lb bomb load)	2,040mi
landing distance*	2,250ft		
*over 50ft obstacle			

The XB-28A was flown the first time exactly one year after its mate. However, it was lost in a tail flutter mishap during a dive on 4 August 1943, the crew parachuting to safety.*

The XB-28 was already doomed by the time of the XB-28A accident. The type performed superbly and production design was well underway (NA-89). The only known changes in that model were addition of scanning windows in the floor of the bombardier and gunner stations. After the decision not to pursue production, the outboard wings were shorn off the XB-28 at Wright Field and the aircraft employed in cabin pressurisation tests and demonstrations.

Busy Work (XB-33)

Martin tried again with another medium bomber design in the same vein as the XB-27 at a time the USAAC was looking ahead to a programme occupying Martin after the B-26. The effort began in September 1940 when the Army suggested the company develop a twin 'larger than the B-17 and B-24 but smaller than the B-29 and B-32'.[2] This would seem to contradict the definition of 'medium' and the desired performance is unclear. The associated specification was signed on 15 October. Martin immediately commenced concept design as the Model 189, suggesting a performance guarantee of 342mph (550km/h) at 25,000ft (7,620m). Apart from the figures falling short of specification, the Air Corps made clear its desire to keep the aircraft 'fairly orthodox' to control technical risk and hasten the path to production.[3] Although the R-2800 engine was considered, the R-3350 was selected 'as it had considerable leeway'.[4]

The conceptual design was submitted for company approval on 5 December 1940. Martin intimated the prototype could be flying within 12 months, as the Army wished, and production begun by October 1942. An extensive series of wind tunnel tests would likely be impossible under this schedule. Consequently, discussion with the service, NACA Langley Memorial Aeronautical Laboratory, Langley Field, Virginia, and

* Flutter is the oscillatory motion of an aircraft component in the presence of an unstable coupling of aerodynamic forces, inertia and structural elasticity. The oscillations can rapidly grow to destructive amplitudes.

other labs were held to review and offer advice as the design matured.

A Letter of Intent was signed on 7 February 1941 to procure a single prototype, by then referred to as the XB-33. Martin responded on 8 March with a proposal to build two 'Super Marauders' for $3,000,000, the first delivered in 14 months and the second two months later. Discussion still suggested production commencing in October 1942.[5] The pressurised aircraft was to have twin vertical tails, basics including a span of 100.0ft (30.5m), length of 71.0ft (21.6m) and height 22.6ft (6.9m). It would gross 42,125lb (19,108kg) and be powered by two turbosupercharged R-3350s delivering 2,200hp (1,641kW) each. Peak speed was to be 340mph (547km/h), range 2,000mi (3,218km) and ceiling 30,000ft (9,144m). Remote controlled gun turrets would be integrated via a fire control system.

Arranging funding and other issues contributed delays. To help things along, Martin provided draft specifications on 26 March as supplement to their proposal. A draft contract was finally

Above: The twin-engine XB-33 proved a short-lived affair. Factors included growing weight that threatened desired performance, a focus on heavies, and a feeling that mediums should dwell at lower altitudes where pressurisation was superfluous. However, the work was not wasted as the design transitioned to a four-engine requirement. *Glenn L. Martin Maryland Aviation Museum*

provided on 7 April for two XB-33s (41-28407/8).

Another sticking point became how soon Martin could move to production. The pressurisation, turbos and fire control system were all new to them. Martin first expressed concern with the planned pace in late March 1941. They wished to wait until four months after the start of flight testing before commencing production design. This suggested first production articles would

Below: No images of the XB-28A have emerged, and none of the type in flight. Here the XB-28 performs an engine run at Mines Field, the Los Angeles Municipal Airport, showing off many features of the advanced, pressurised medium bomber. The counter-rotating propellers and fish-eye scanner windows were rare on bombers. *National Museum of the United States Airforce.*

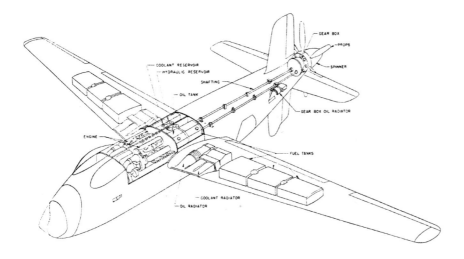

not be available before December 1943, much later than the Army desired. Faced with multiple delays, Martin suggested further B-26C production with the R-3350 would serve as a suitable stopgap. This raised no enthusiasm from within Materiel Division.[6]

During discussions, the Air Corps suggested greater interchangeability of fuel and bombs, and an increase in range. These and other inputs increased projected weight by 1,223lb (555kg) above the 652lb (296kg) Martin had found necessary as it refined the design. All would bring the medium bomber from 48,125 to 50,000lb (21,829 to 22,680kg) GW. As a high altitude medium type was by then losing appeal, it was an easy decision by service leadership on 28 April 1941 to refocus on a four-engine B-33. The twin fell by the wayside.

Worthy But Late (XA-42, XB-42)
In examining the impediments to markedly improving bomber performance, Douglas developed a concept in early 1943 with the goal of matching B-29 performance with a less costly tactical aircraft, smaller and lighter. This called for an aircraft carrying 2,000lb (907kg) of bombs more than 5,000mi (8,046km) faster than 400mph (644km/h) and maximum 8,000lb (3,629kg) bomb capacity. The challenge was avoiding the added weight and drag of ever larger engines. Two liquid-cooled inline engines would be buried in the fuselage, leaving a relatively thin wing free of nacelles. The powerplants could drive coaxial pusher propellers at the end of the fuselage, eliminating drag generating propwash over the aircraft exterior.

This configuration was estimated to yield 30 per cent improvement in aerodynamic efficiency. Speed would rival that of opposing fighters, making numerous turrets and gun ports unnecessary and reducing crew size. The Douglas arrangement naturally meant a tricycle landing gear with nose wheel steering, main gear retracting into the fuselage. The design could deliver performance of a heavy bomber on two engines, promised lower maintenance effort and greater in-service rate. It could be produced in half the time at two-thirds the cost. The dual-rotation propellers would also eliminate takeoff and landing torque and critical engine-out issues for safer operation.†

† For a multi-engine aircraft with the engines placed on the wings, the critical engine is that, which having failed, permits the most yawing moment to develop about the CG from the remaining operating engine(s). For American engines turning propellers clockwise, this is generally the port engine, or most outboard port engine. Placing all thrust producing devices on the aircraft centreline eliminates such concerns.

The concept was presented to the USAAF in April 1943 as an unsolicited proposal. Although plenty of bombers designs had recently been finalised and placed into production, with ongoing improvement efforts, the Douglas design promised so much that it appeared worth pursuing. A letter contract for two XA-42s (43-50224/5, MX-392), static article, mockup and engineering data was approved on 25 June. The first example was to be ready for flight in 12 months and the second four months later. The definitised $3,103,686.56 contract followed on 11 February 1944. To help meet the ambitious timeline, Materiel Division agreed to give Douglas free rein, resisting redirection that could delay progress. It was acknowledged the project was experimental with no overt intention to place the design in production. The aircraft was to be versatile, moving from strategic to tactical roles as the circumstances

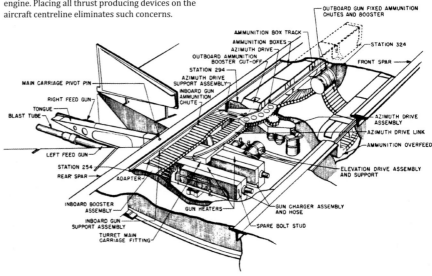

dictated, possibly accounting for the unusual Attack designation.

Design and fabrication of the XA-42s (Model 459) was undertaken in Santa Monica. From the beginning, detailed design placed aerodynamics paramount. The relative positions of the laminar-flow wing, tail, and propellers were worked out first to minimised drag of their interactions and yielding ideal stability and control. Hydraulic double-slotted flaps enhanced low-speed lift. The aft-mounted propellers were significant stabilising influences. However, this effect was reduced with power off, limiting aft CG travel. The small CG range and unusually far aft position of the main landing gear would challenge the ability to get early nose rotation on lift off, potentially extending takeoff roll.

The Allison V-1710-103 V-12 inline delivered 1,325hp (988kW), 1,820hp (1,119kW) in WE (water injection). They were fitted with 'Auxiliary Stage Superchargers' – effectively a gear-driven unit with carburetor located between two stages. These were placed side-by-side just behind the flight deck and readily accessible by via stressed and hinged top panels. Canting the engines 20° inboard at the top reduced their profile, and toeing in a few degrees at the rear aligned them with the propeller gearbox at the aft end of the fuselage. The two very long power shafts combined in the gearbox. These were each made up of six shafts, from Bell P-39 fighters, joined end-to-end, allowing for airframe flexure.

The engines drove coaxial Curtiss, three-blade pusher propellers that gave the aircraft its unofficial 'Mixmaster' moniker.[‡] The right hand engine drove the 13.0ft (4.0m) diameter aft propeller counterclockwise and the left the 13.2ft (4.0m) forward propeller clockwise. The propellers were independently governed, separately controlled and automatically synchronised. This meant that, unlike contra-props powered by a single engine, the individual propellers would be stopped and feathered should an engine fail or be shutdown. These initial propellers were a 'stop-gap' supporting the schedule for first flight while an 'ultimate' product, with better performance and the reversing feature, continued to be

‡ Mixmaster was a familiar kitchen appliance.

Above: This view of aircraft 43-50224 shows well the twin "bug eye" canopies, typical bombardier nose, wing leading edge cooling inlets, flush carburetor intakes, V-1710 exhaust stacks, two-piece bomb bay doors, slotted flaps, and steerable nose wheel. Writing on the nose stencil identifies this event as a taxi test on 5 May 1944. *Jay Miller Collection*

developed. Reversing would permit rapid deceleration on landing and would limit dive speed to 400mph (644km/h) without speedbrakes. To ensure safe bailout of the crew without passing through the 'meat grinder', a length of cordite charge was passed through the gearbox mounting frame to blow off the gearbox and props on command.

The engine coolant and oil radiators were in the wings, fed via leading edge inlets and exhausted out top openings with inward opening, electrically actuated doors. Since there was no propwash to force air through the inlets during ground operations, a 17in (43cm) electric fan was placed aft of each coolant and oil radiator to draw air through the heat exchangers. In another possible 'first', air to the carburetors was fed via flush intakes with boundary layer bleed slots on each side of the forward fuselage.

A typical bombardier nose was matched with a twin 'bug eye' canopy arrangement. Wing leading edge heating for de-ice was featured. Hydraulically retracting and stowing the main gear in the fuselage proved one of the more difficult aspects of the design. Ultimately, the posts were at the wing roots, stowed in 'arm pit' fairings, and the wheels fully enclosed in aft fuselage cavities. This required the posts to rotate as well as pivot during the actuator cycle.

A wheel tread of 12.5ft (3.8m) was achieved, hopefully sufficient for ground stability. To protect the propellers from a strike with over-rotation (9in/23cm clearance), a ventral fin had an integral oleopneumatic shock strut skid.

Up to 8,000lb (3,629kg) of weapons with the bay long enough to accommodate two Mk. 13 torpedoes. The two bomb bay doors were each made up of two elements that folded together and were of 'snap action', reducing adverse flow into the propellers. Four 275gal (1,041lit) long-rang tanks could be installed in the bay and there were provisions for two 300gal (1,136lit) under-wing drop tanks.

Two .50cal MGs (500rpg) in the lower nose were fixed to fire forward. Douglas had all manner of other weapon installations in interchangeable noses on the drawing board reflecting A-26 work. Two GE twin-gun, rear-firing turrets were conceived for installation in the trailing edge of the wings. Initially, discrete and bulky turrets were envisioned protruding from the trailing edges. However, this

evolved to the guns pivoted for vertical motion on a "tongue" with lateral rotation, all integrated within the wing structure. The twin .50cals (350rpg) were placed between the flaps, ammunition trays running outboard within the wing. Doors covered the turret for a clean wing when not in use, snapping out vertically when commanded. The copilot acted as gunner, rotating his seat to sight rearward.

Ongoing engineering supporting combat types had priority and caused delays, but Douglas still moved quickly with the Mixmaster. The mockup was inspected on 13 September 1943 and approved with several recommended changes. On 25 November, the USAAF changed the designation to XB-42 as holding to a distinct Attack mission had fallen from favour.[7]

Aircraft 43-50224 was completed, disassembled and moved to Palm Springs Army Air Base (AAB) for its maiden flight on 6 May 1944. This was just ten months after contract award – a remarkable feat and redeeming Douglas' performance on the A-26. Unfortunately, the quick work apparently did not permit rigorous weight control measures as the aircraft came in more than ten per cent heavy. Refinements were introduced with 43-50225, especially in an effort to reduce weight that included lighter propeller blades. Slightly larger vertical tail and rudder were introduced.[8] This machine was moved from El Segundo to Mines Field when completed for first flight on 1 August 1944. This was the only XB-42 with the guns and snap-action bay

doors installed, and also had V-1710-129 engines.

The Air Forces did not care for the dual canopies, despite the reduced drag and improving all-around visibility. While the two men could technically see each other and communicate via the intercom, there is much more to crew coordination that was made difficult by the arrangement. The pilots would tend to lean forward into the cockpit to communicate clearly, briefly leaving no one scanning outside and risking vertigo. The canopies also did not provide emergency egress in flight and proved to be hot in summer and noisy from air rushing past. Anticipating all this, a conventional windscreen arrangement was mocked up, like that seen on some models of the British Mosquito fighter. Although 43-50225 was initially built and made at least the first flight with the twin canopies, it was soon modified with the 'Mosquito' canopy. As the new canopy appeared to complicate the previous plan to have the copilot sight the rear-firing guns, there were plans to sight these via radar.[9]

After six flights, 43-50224 was ferried to Inglewood for changes and rework. The first months of flying suffered from hardware issues common to all new aircraft, not necessarily indicative of problems with the fundamental design. Generally, flying was trouble-free and continued at a good clip, completing about 150 flights and 125hr by the end of the war. The first USAAF pilot was exposed to

Above: The Douglas XB-42 was among the most innovative and promising bombers to appear during the war. Built as an experimental aircraft, the effort to take it to a production design was not seen as essential by the time it was showing its capabilities, especially with jets just on the horizon. *Gerald Balzer Collection*

the aircraft in October 1944, coming away impressed by the performance.

The aircraft flew quite well, although there were certainly areas for improvement. Ground handling and visibility from the cockpit was praised. Harmonising of controls remained to be accomplished as some axes were too heavy and some too light. A dutch-roll oscillation (combined yaw and pitch) was annoying and potentially detrimental to stable bomb delivery. Aileron buzz (high frequency, low amplitude oscillation) was encountered at 0.716 Mach, mandating a 0.7 Mach placard. Air Forces testers also reported a rudder shake and elevator buzz that produced a slight porpoising oscillation. Flow off the leading edge radiator inlets contributed disconcerting elevator buffeting during tight turns and approach to stall.[10]

Some more serious discoveries were addressed or potential solutions identified. As feared, keeping engine temperatures under redline during ground operation and during run-up was difficult. To improve cooling, radiator inlets were modified with wider opening while the interior ducts were given greater camber and a venturi shape. The propellers suffered disturbing vibrations from the asymmetrical airflow produced by combinations of

Above: The first XB-42 is seen at Palm Springs AAB on 10 May 1944, days after first flight. Wing root doors for the main gear are open while the fuselage doors are closed. The base of the ventral stabilizer is a compressible skid to protect the propellers from ground strike. *Air Force Flight Test Center*

Left: XB-42 aircraft 43-50225 models the gear retraction during a takeoff. This aircraft has the single "Mosquito" canopy but also shows the nose guns ports and the wing pairs of .50cals at the trailing edge are evident. The clean wing contributed to the outstanding performance of the bomber, as did the pusher propellers. *San Diego Air & Space Museum*

Douglas XB-42 characteristics:

span	70.5ft	weight empty	20,888lb
length	53.6ft	design gross	33,208lb
height	20.8ft	max.	35,702lb
wing area	554.63ft²	bomb load, normal	2,000lb
fuel, max.	652-1,750gal	max.	8,000lb
service ceiling	29,400ft	speed, max. (23,440ft)	410mph
sea level climb rate	1,050fpm	cruise	312mph
takeoff dist* (35,700lb)	6,415ft	range, combat (2,000lb bomb load)	1,800mi
landing dist* (35,700lb)	2,130ft	ferry	2,200mi
*over 50ft obstacle			

undercarriage down, coolant doors open and especially flaps extended and bay doors open. The lighter blades on 43-50225 made matters worse. Apart from pilot objections, these vibrations were transmitted to the engines and airframe with objectionable stresses. The problem had been anticipated and the engineers were looking to isolation mounting of the engine, shafts and gearbox.

While the XB-42's performance appeared impressive on the surface, the over-weight airframe could not meet many of the most important guarantees accepted by Douglas. Aircraft 43-50224's top speed of 410mph (660km/h) fell short of the guarantee and well below the originally expected 440mph (708km/h). The initially predicted service ceiling was 33,600ft (10,241m) and the aircraft was well under that, although reportedly meeting the guarantee. Speed, range and ceiling values could only be satisfied with

half the payload removed. The original predicted takeoff distance of 3,000ft (914m) was more than double in reality. Other values were exceeded, including rate of climb, landing distance and sea level airspeed. The armament systems were never tested.

Discussion in early 1944 explored acquiring a 'small quantity' of service test examples and Douglas was asked to provide an estimate. Later in the year there was consideration of a photo reconnaissance version. Nothing came of these tentative explorations. It was clear considerable additional work would be required to cut the large over-weight fraction and the propeller vibration remained worrying. Although all engineering issues with the aircraft

Below: Late-model P-38s carried an impressive weapons load (six 500 'pounders' in insert), so use as level bombers was natural. Finding the target and bombing accurately required a lead aircraft with navigator and bombsight, bringing forth the rare 'Droop Snoot' P-38J with bombardier and Norden sight in the extended nose. *National Museum of the United States Air Force*, insert *National Archives*

could likely have been corrected given time and money, both were nearly exhausted. The programme had already run over-budget by $4,500,000. Although all agreed the XB-42 was possessed of great potential, there was no compelling reason to polish the design further. It was very unlikely to contribute to the present war and jets appeared to be the way of the future. In fact, a jet version of the XB-42 was in work before the first aircraft flew. The follow-on 'ultimate' propeller was cancelled in March 1945.

The XB-42 was an intriguing design with promising features. Had piston powered, propeller-driven bombers remained the focus, the aircraft might have had a future. Testing continued after the war, highlighted by 43-50225 setting a transcontinental speed record. This aircraft was subsequently lost in an accident in which two of the men bailed out successfully before the pilot remembered to jettison the propeller (although likely feathered and stopped), which separated as designed.

Fighter cum Bomber (P-38)

Another little-known adjunct to the Army bomber story is adaptation of the P-38 twin-engine fighter for the role. It was noted late-model Lockheed Lightnings could carry up to 4,000lb (1,814kg) of external stores, equivalent to most medium bombers (although those went to greater range). They might be especially helpful when bombing special targets, once unburdened of bombs, for which a running fight might result.

Following a recommendation from two officers in 8th AF Headquarters to facilitate level bombing from a formation of P-38s, several Lightnings were modified by Lockheed with a bombardier station in place of nose guns. The extended nose structure with plexiglass tip contained a Norden bombsight, oxygen, intercom, navigation gear, seat and armour. It would act as Pathfinder for a formation of heavily loaded Lightnings which would 'drop on the lead'.

This 'Droop Snoot' project began with P-38H 42-67086 fitted with a wooden form of the proposed nose shape. Testing demonstrated acceptable flying qualities. A new P-38J-10 was then given the actual nose, engineered by Lockheed

Overseas Corporation at Langford Lodge, near Belfast, Northern Ireland. The initial flight was made during late February 1944. The modification was then applied to a total of 23 P-38Js at Langford Lodge and, reportedly, in India by Hindustan Aircraft. Lockheed prepared 100 kits for field modifications, but these were apparently never used. The 'Snooty' saw action through the end of the war in Europe.

The Droop Snoot may have inspired another P-38 Pathfinder with BTO radar. Grafted onto the front of a P-38J was an extended nose with blunt plexiglass tip and AN/APS-15, the radar operator seated behind the unit. This Pathfinder modification was created in 35 days, mostly in May 1944, and deliveries

Above: With a BTO radar and operator in a new nose of the P-38, the Pathfinder leads a formation of bombers to hit targets otherwise hidden by clouds. The first such modification, P-38J-15 44-23138, is seen here at Burbank on 6 June 1944. The rest were P-38Ls modified in Dallas. *National Archives*

began in June. The first was a P-38J-15 (44-23139) converted in Burbank. The quantity of Ls modified is said to have been 'small numbers'. Possibly designated P-38L-3, they were reworked at the Dallas Modification Center. Most were employed in the Mediterranean and Western Europe, but some in the CBI theatre. These 'Mickeys' would lead formations of any bombers yet make a quick, fighting escape if necessary.

Lockheed P-38J Droop Snoot characteristics:

span	52.0ft	weight empty	12,780lb
length	37.0ft	gross	17,500lb
height	9.8ft	max.	21,600lb
wing area	327.5ft²	bomb load, max.	3,200lb
fuel (int.+ext.)	410+600gal	normal	0lb
service ceiling	44,000ft	speed, max. (25,000ft)	414mph
average climb rate	2,857fpm	cruise	290mph
takeoff distance*	1,500ft	range, 3,200lb bombs	450mi
landing distance*	1,800ft	410-740gal fuel	1,220-1,780mi
*over 50ft obstacle		ferry	2,600mi

Chapter Five

Heavies

The Striving

The USAAF's four-engine heavy bombers were decidedly the apple in the leadership's eyes. The strategic bombing campaign was considered the main event of the war for the Air Forces. The President also saw this as vital, on 4 May 1941 urging expansion of production to 500 bombers per month.[1] Consequently, tremendous resources were expended in developing and fielding these warplanes that were built in enormous numbers.

The success of the heavy bomber was a major accomplishment in the aeronautical field. The USAAC had sought such capabilities long before the war, but had been limited to experimental types. Yet, the Air Corps remained devoted to the bomber; perhaps more so than any other air force. Only the B-17 was in production, although sporadically and in low numbers when war dawned. This soon changed, also permitting a second source to be sired as the B-24.

As with other bombers, the deficiencies of these aircraft were evident in light of early war experience. Initial production models were wisely kept to modest numbers as each evinced progressive improvements before large scale production was initiated. That, then, entailed a great industrial undertaking with several major aeronautical manufacturers collaborating in an unprecedented way. Even the initial large-production models were found wanting as the Americans committed them to battle. Corrective actions required additional effort under the daunting strain of combat losses and operational tempo.

Evolution of these aircraft followed the same theme as with other categories of American bombers. Weight rose dramatically as additional armour, defence weapons and electronic systems were added and means of carrying more bombs were introduced. The impact on climb rate, speed and range were very evident but not debilitating. More engine power chased these factors in an effort to recover lost performance. In the final year of the war, with enemy interceptors becoming few and friendly escorts many, some defence systems were off-loaded in another measure to carry more payload farther.

Lingering On (XB-15)

During the 1930s, the Army planned a calculated series of one-off experimental aircraft programs supporting progressive advancement of aeronautical science and heavy bomber development, ensuring means were available to build a war-winning force. Execution was frustrated by the grave financial conditions of the country and isolationist tendencies, but some notable results were initiated. Among these were bombers sized by wing span and gross weight to enormous dimensions. Such an experimental bomber available to America at the beginning of World War 2 was the XB-15.

The planned 150ft (46m) span, 60,000lb (27,215kg) GW experimental bomber was to carry 10 tons of bombs. When defined as a procurement programme in 1933, range was emphasised. Identified as Project A, it set the goal of developing a four-engine bomber flying 5,000mi (8046km) at 200mph (322km/h) with a ton of weapons. Boeing was contracted in 1934 to develop the XBLR-1 (Bomber, Long Range) that became the XB-15 (35-277, Model 294). The competing Martin XB-16 was not funded beyond conceptual design. The Boeing was the USAAC's first four-engine monoplane and, when it flew in 1937, introduced innovations that would become common during the war. For several years it remained the world's heaviest and largest bomber.

For exceptionally long missions, the XB-15 had a crew of 10 that included a relief team. They enjoyed heated and sound-proofed spaces that included kitchen, bunks and lavatory facilities. The crew included the Air Corps' first flight engineer at his own flight deck station. The aircraft had the first 110V AC electrical system with alternators driven by two gasoline-powered auxiliary engines in the fuselage as another first. A Sperry autopilot was also featured. The leading edge de-icing boots and fire protection systems were notable. There was a pair of ailerons on each wing, one serving as a servo control for the other to reduce pilot control forces. The 11.5ft (3.5m) diameter, three-blade, metal, constant-speed, full-feathering propellers were noteworthy at the time. The bomb capacity was 8,000lb (3,629kg), and the fuselage bomb bay was augmented by two 'wing stub' bays (near the roots). The six manual turrets included a nose, amidships dorsal, two aft fuselage beam, plus front-facing forward and rear-facing aft fuselage ventral stations. The teardrop side blisters had elements that rotated in elevation while the gun was swung in azimuth within a slot. The gunner had similar capabilities for the nose gun within a dome. However, the dome was attached to the transparent nose cone that revolved to bring the dome to the bottom for better engagement of threats from below. While .50cal guns (600rpg) could be fitted to some stations, the .30s (1,800rpg) were common. All this was considered formidable at the time, but lack of a tail gun would be considered a fatal flaw within the first months of World War 2.

With all its advances, the XB-15 displayed much dated engineering by

1940 as the Air Corps was intentionally cautious to avoid failure that would embolden heavy bomber opponents.[2] Although considered 'all-metal', the wing skin aft of the spar was fabric. Basic split flaps were adopted, although the aircraft had a docile 70mph (113km/h) landing speed. The wing root was of exceptionally broad chord and thickness. Although this allowed personnel to crawl within the leading edge to service engines in flight, the drag and lift characteristics were not up to 1940s standards. The dual-wheel main landing gear was unusual at the time. The vertical struts were a V-truss and shock absorbing coming from a trailing drag strut – a heavy arrangement. Braking was pneumatic. The undercarriage was only partially retractable.

Most disappointing was engine power. Even though Boeing used the most powerful radials then available, the R-1830-11 of 1,000hp (746kW), these were still new and maturing powerplants lacking superchargers. Consequently, the aircraft was underpowered.

Although the XB-15 flew well enough and set world records for payload to altitude and distance, overall performance fell substantially short of programme objectives. Its range was still impressive, but the associated payload seemed meager for the effort of dragging it across thousands of miles at excruciatingly slow speed. The true value of the aircraft was as a testbed for systems via numerous small modifications. Two follow-on Y1B-20 service test examples competed with the Douglas DB-4 for planned 1938 procurement. These were to have a high wing, tricycle undercarriage and 1,400hp (1,044kW) Pratt & Whitney R-2180-5s reaching for 240mph (386km/h). However, political calculations that there were no Air Corps missions for bombers larger than the B-17, left the project unfunded. Nonetheless, lessons from the

Above: Production of US Army heavy bombers was a national priority supporting the strategic bombing strategy. The B-17 Flying Fortress, like these G-models flying over Britain, dominated in western Europe but was second place in numbers built to the B-24 Liberator. Such aircraft came to incorporate some leading aeronautical design and equipment. *National Archives*

XB-15 benefited bombers that followed. These allowed sound specifications to be cast with high probability of supporting rapid development of successful aircraft that could be expeditiously placed into production and service.

The sole XB-15 was still being flown when war broke out. More modern bombers were already in development and the XB-15 was not the basis for a truly useful combat aircraft. Much more powerful engines were required, but these remained just beyond reach. With so few long-range aircraft, the XB-15 continued to be operated as a patrol and transport aircraft.

via semi-submerged stacks. Induction air flowed to the system via leading edge inlet and ducting. Charged air then flowed up into the nacelle aft of the engine, mixing with air from another leading edge inlet and ducting to the intercooler and hence to the downdraft carburetor. Each nacelle had intercooler and carburetor intakes on one side, oil cooler intake on the other. Hot air from the intercooler and oil cooler was exhausted through slots atop the wing ahead of the flap hingelines.

Air Corps persistence and emergence of threats abroad finally brought funding for additional B-17s. The first production examples, 39 B-17Bs (Model 299M) with 1,000hp (746kW) R-1820-51 engines, were built at Boeing Field (King County Airport). Apart from B-3 turbos, this model had enlarged rudder and flaps, metal-skinned flaps and hydraulics replacing pneumatics for wheel braking. The two droppable bomb bay tanks totaled 820gal (3,104lit). Normal bay capacity was 4,000lb (1,814kg) of bombs. An additional 4,000lb could be installed on optional external racks. The crew was eight men

Legend (B-17)

At the beginning of World War 2, the USAAC had a modest number of Boeing B-17 heavy bombers. The Air Corps leadership had high hopes for the aircraft meeting its ambitions for strategic bombing, but acquisitions remained few owing to the high cost of the four-engine aircraft (about $250,000 each) and resistance from isolationists and the Navy that saw it as a threat to its maritime defence mission. Nonetheless, the type had already reached maturaity since first appearing years before. It was the largest and best performing fleet bomber in the world.

The B-17 had servo tabs in all three-axis and split flaps. The undercarriage possessed multi-disk wheel brakes and steerable tail wheel, and was electrically retractable but all wheels left partially exposed. The bomb bay doors and flaps were also electrically actuated. De-icing boots graced wing and tail. More unique were the two spars of tubular Warren truss with corrugated inner skin stiffening between replacing stringers. There were manual gun blisters like the XB-15's with five .30cal MGs and 2,000

rounds in the classical dorsal, ventral, waist and nose positions with a few hundred rounds each (.50s and 1,000 rounds optional), earning the bomber the name Flying Fortress.

Each R-1820 turned a 11.5ft (3.5m) three-blade propeller and was fed by 1,700gal (6,435lit) of fuel in four wing tanks and optional ferry tanks for the bomb bay. Turbosuperchargers lent outstanding high-altitude performance. One was in the bottom of each nacelle to which engine exhaust was ducted

Boeing XB-15 characteristics:

span	149.0ft	weight empty	37,709lb
length	87.6ft	gross	65,068lb
height	19.5ft	max.	70,706lb
wing area	2,781ft²	bomb load, max.	12,000lb
fuel, max.	3,350-4,260gal	normal	2,511lb
service ceiling	18,850ft	speed, max. (5,000ft)	197mph
best climb rate	700fpm	cruise (6,000ft)	152mph
takeoff distance*	3,250ft	range, 2,500lb bomb load	3,400mi
landing distance*	2,450ft	maximum (152mph)	4,000mi
*over 50ft obstacle			

with pilot, copilot, navigator, bombardier/ gunner, radio operator/gunner and three gunners. The 'glass' nose had an off-centre ball-and-socket mounting for the .30 MG (500 rounds). Delayed by turbosupercharger failure issues, the first B was finally flown in June 1939 and delivered from 20 October to 30 March 1940. A B-17B was the first American 'Fort' to engage in combat, bombing a U-boat during October 1941.

The long period between B-17 orders, and these of small quantity, left Boeing struggling financially. The next contract, placed just before the war, was little better. The 38 B-17Cs (299H) had 1,200hp (746kW) R-1820-65s with B-2 turbos and leak-proof fuel tanks. Boost pumps and transfer pumps permitted fuel from any tank to feed any engine. A manifold oxygen system replaced individual bottles for the crew of nine. The Norden bombsight was introduced to the B-17s during 1940.

Armament changes with the C sought to address requirements gathered from recent combat experience abroad. Gun blisters were jettisoned, the waist stations becoming windowed hatches. The window was opened and forward air deflector deployed to permit the pedestal-mounted gun to be fired. The dorsal station, above the radioman's position, became a stepped, windowed hatch, slid forward to allow the gun to be extended out, a deployable blast deflector just forward. The ventral station became a gondola, the gun emerging from the rear behind an air deflector and the gunner kneeling to fire. The nose got three sockets, including side 'cheek' windows to which the .30cal (500 rounds) could be moved. This, however, was a very difficult task even with the lighter .30, especially if the aircraft was manoeuvering. A .50 could not be moved in such a manner and, in fact, would have to be braced to avoid the firing shock shattering the window. The waist stations had .50cal guns, but a .30 remained the preference for the radioman (200 rounds) and only a .30 was practical in the tunnel. Some 800lb (363kg) of armour was included. Empty weight rose more than 3,000lb (1,361kg) and range lost 400mi (644km), but maximum speed gained over 30mph (48km/h) – fastest of any Fortress incarnation.

Above: The B-17 Flying Fortress dated from 1935, but only modest numbers were purchased through 1940. Improvements had yielded the B-17C just after war broke out, and most went to Britain. It lacked a tail turret and had poor bottom defense via the tunnel tub, but the turbosuperchargers supported excellent performance.
Ray Wagner Collection

The first B-17C flew on 21 July 1940 and the last was delivered by 29 November. Nineteen Bs were upgraded to C-standard. The first 20 B-17Cs went to the RAF as Fortress Is in exchange for combat experience information. The aircraft required retrofit work (Model 299T or 299U) to include more effective leak-proof tanks and replacing the Norden with Sperry bombsight. With this and crew training, the Cs did not begin arriving in the UK until spring 1941. The Americans expected the aircraft to be employed as four-engine trainers preparatory to a larger supply of later-model B-17s. However, the hard-pressed Brits tried them in their identified utility of high-altitude, daylight, precision bombing. The 30,000ft (9,144m) bombing capability of the aircraft held a promise of success. However, the light armour and defensive weapons left them too vulnerable, although the Americans criticised lack of suitable formation. Although the bombers could fly quite high, some systems like machine guns did not cope well with the extreme cold and stability was also degraded. Rearward defence was woefully inadequate, they scored few hits with the immature Sperry bombsight and the aircraft left condensation trails that help give away their position to enemy interceptors.* The aircraft were soon devoted to Coastal Command and plans to acquire more Fortresses were initially dropped. However, the experience gave the Americans keen insight into needed evolution of the type they had previously considered a decisive if not invincible weapon.

Seeing the need for changes even as the B-17C entered production, a 17 April 1940 order for 42 more was rewritten on 6 September, shifting to D models (299H again). This also required tough negotiations on price as Boeing was still losing money and threatened to cease production. These introduced cowl flaps for improved engine cooling during laboring climbs, self-sealing bladder-type fuel tanks, more armour, revised bomb racks and release mechanisms

* Water vapour produced as a product of combustion freezes at high altitude, or passage of the aircraft causes water to condense out of the air. RAF pilots aborted missions if they discovered their machines generating heavy contrails. Since the Germans tracked aircraft and vectored fighters via radar, the contrails were eventually accepted as tolerable, if unavoidable.

Boeing B-17C characteristics (early production):

span	103.8ft	weight empty	30,600lb
length	67.9ft	gross	39,065lb
height	15.4ft	max.	47,242lb
wing area	1,420ft²	bomb load, max.	4,800lb
fuel, max. (wings+bay)	1,799+792gal	normal	4,000lb
service ceiling	37,000ft	speed, max. (25,000ft)	323mph
average climb rate	1,333fpm	cruise (15,000ft)	227mph
takeoff distance*	1,850ft	range, typical (4,000lb/25mph/25,000ft)	2,000mi
landing distance*	2,700ft	maximum (180mph/10,000ft)	3,400mi
*over 50ft obstacle			

Boeing B-17E characteristics (early production):

span	103.8ft	weight empty	32,251lb
length	73.8ft	gross	40,260lb
height	19.2ft	max.	53,000lb
wing area	1,420ft²	bomb load, max.	4,000lb
fuel, max. (wings+bay)	1,700+792gal	normal	2,000lb
service ceiling	36,600ft	speed, max. (25,000ft)	317mph
average climb rate	1,333fpm	cruise (15,000ft)	226mph
takeoff distance*	2,150ft	range, typical (224mph/15,000ft/4000lb)	2,000mi
landing distance*	2,700ft	maximum (180mph/10,000ft)	3,200mi
*over 50ft obstacle			

to prevent freezing at altitude, a low-pressure oxygen system, a 24-volt versus 12-volt electrical system and twin .30s in dorsal and ventral stations, and the nose got more gun sockets for a total of seven. Crew was now ten.

The initial B-17D was flown on 3 February 1941 and the last rolled out on 29 April. Seventeen B-17Cs were upgraded to D standard (except for the cowl flaps). The Ds were the first to be deployed, most sent into the Pacific during 1941 as a show of force. Many would be destroyed in the initial Japanese onslaught, but also executed the first offensive bombing operations of the war by Americans. The B-17s subsequently became rare in the region as they were concentrated in Europe.

After the collapse of France and the President's call for heavy bomber expansion, the service had told Boeing in July 1940 to expect orders for 512 more B-17s. Engineering leadership had been working with Boeing since May of that year to define upgrades

meeting emerging requirements. The B-17E (299O) addressed many lessons from earlier models and made it more suitable for mass production. Pilot side windows were enlarged and overhead eyebrow windows added. The tail wheel was made fully retractable, although without doors. The major change was enlarging the aft fuselage diameter for a tail gunner. A much-enlarged tail had a dorsal extension and horizontal stabiliser span extended 9.3ft (2.8m) for enhanced stability at altitude and better bombing platform.

Considerable attention was given to E defensive armament. In the tail was a Bell manually operated twin .50s mount (565rpg) with a ring-and-post sight articulated to match gun motion. In the cramped station under the rudder, the gunner half sat/knelt, the ammunition feeding from boxes on either side. The accommodations were so cramped he could not wear a parachute and flak vest simultaneously. Each waist gunners' stations got larger openings

with rectangular hatches that permitted greater traverse of his .50. The containers of ammunition hung on the guns (a very heavy 100 rounds) were soon eliminated. Each was then fed from a wall-mounted and later floor-mounted box containing all 500 rounds. The ventral tub was replaced with the periscope-directed, powered Bendix remote turret (500rpg) described previously, the periscope optical head projecting below the skin aft of the turret, under a transparent blister. The radioman's dorsal station had the gun mount for a belt-fed .50 moved to the centre in a ball-and-socket. This gun was the least effective on the aircraft and so was frequently left off. An aircraft commander's scanning bubble was replaced with a 650lb (295kg) Sperry A-1, electrically powered, dorsal turret with twin .50s (400rpg) and computing gunsight. The flight engineer operated the turret while seated on a canvas sling or standing on a rotating platform with adjustable feet pad height. Employing two hand grips, twisting the right grip adjusted the sight range. The aircraft nose had six MG ball-and-sockets, with two in the cheeks, one in the lower starboard front, two above and on ether side of the bombardier, and one overhead. These took either .30 or .50 MGs, although only a single of the former was common.

An initial order was to be 150 B-17Es. The dribs-and-drabs production of Fortresses had ended and Boeing dutifully ordered requisite materials. However, contract approval was delayed and the firm, having lost money previously on the B-17, cancelled the orders. After difficult negotiations over price, a new contract was approved on 30 August 1940 for 277 machines, increased by 235 on 16 September. Despite the large order and airmen clamouring for the bomber, the company then had considerable difficulty obtaining materials and a break in B-17 production ensued. The project fell five months behind schedule. It took decisive action by the government to break the logjam and the first B-17E finally flew on 5 September 1941.

The E rapidly displaced the earlier 'Forts' in combat service. The 2,000lb (907kg) added weight and increased drag naturally impacted performance. The loudest complaint arose over the Bendix turret. As with the B-25, gunner discomfort and the narrow field of view rendered the turret of marginal value. It was occasionally removed in the field and replaced with a simple gun mount in the opening.

After 112 B-17Es, through January 1942, the ventral turret was replaced with the electrically powered, 500lb (227kg) Sperry (built by Briggs and Emerson) A-2 3.7ft (1.1m) diameter ball turret containing two .50s (500-575rpg). A gunner, without parachute, entered the ball while pointed straight down. Turret motion and triggers were commanded with handgrips, sight range adjustment with a left foot pedal and interphone switch with the right foot.

The B-17Es numbered 512 built through 28 May 1942, some fitted with R-1820-91 engines that were the same as the -65 except for a special diffuser and two-speed supercharger. There were about 50 Es on hand when America went to war, a third of the total Flying Fortress force that also included Ds plus upgraded Bs and Cs that were deployable. The E was the first truly effective American heavy bomber in the Asia-Pacific theatres, the Japanese surprised by the tail guns.[†] They equipped the first USAAF combat team to reach England and to bomb the continent on 17 August 1942. The RAF got 45 Es under Lend-Lease between March and July 1942, diverted from a USAAF order, as Fortress IIAs. To puzzlement of the Americans, the ally again assessed the bomber as ineffective and assigned them to Coastal Command. British heavies, devoted to night and area bombing, required less defensive armament, armour, and speed, and so generally enjoyed heavier payload and longer range by comparison. During RAF night operations the ball turret was almost impossible to sight, the gunner becoming disoriented in the bargain. These turrets were removed.

Boeing alone could not meet Air Forces demand for high volume production, so Lockheed's Vega division and Douglas' plant in Long Beach tooled-up to produce the Flying Fortress. This team became known as the Boeing-Vega-Douglas pool, or BVD.[3] These plans also presented the opportunity to further refine the

† Crews of earlier models would occasionally affix a black pole protruding from the tail cone to create uncertainty for fighter pilots.

bomber for all three producers as the B-17F (299P), with existing 300-aircraft B-17E contracts converted to this model and block designations introduced. The first B-17F from Seattle (suffix -BO) was delivered on 30 May 1942. Vega (-VE) put out its first example on 4 May 1942, six months ahead of schedule.[‡] Douglas (-DL) began deliveries in June 1942.

A subsequent contract had Boeing turning out Fs through 2 September 1943, ultimately manufacturing 2,300. Vega turned out 500 against a 13 September 1941 contract and Douglas 605 on a 28 August order. Originally planned to meet a 300-aircraft RAF lend-lease order from June 1941, British lack of enthusiasm for the type left most for the USAAF. The RAF would take 19 B-17Fs from 19 October 1942 as Fortress IIs.

The B-17F incorporated more than 400 changes to the E. More armour enhanced crew and systems protection. Engine power was upped with the R-1820-97 at 1,200hp (895kW) and forged cylinder heads, carburetors fitted with dust filters and aromatic fuels permitted. Self-sealing oil tanks, additional electrical power sources (provisions for a auxiliary power unit) and an improved communication system were introduced. Cowlings lips were reshaped and shortened to permit use of a new propeller. With broader, 11.6ft (3.5m) 'paddle' blades that were more efficient at altitude, additional clearance was required from the lips at full feather.[4] The C-1 autopilot was introduced and coupled to the Norden. A single-piece, molded nose transparency reduced obstructing frames and time

‡ Vega Aircraft company...November 1943.

Above: Addressing vital requirements, the Fortress was greatly altered as the B-17E. Obvious was the expanded fuselage to accommodate a tail gun and enlarged tail surfaces, revised waist gun stations, and a remote ventral turret. This formed the basis for the B-17F that was built in large numbers by three manufacturers. *National Museum of the United States Air Force*

in assembly. This nose possessed four sockets (including cheeks), although only a single .30cal MG (500 rounds) near the centre of the transparency was common. Waist guns went to .50cals (300rpg).

Further improvements were introduced with block upgrades and changes at modification centres. The radioman's .50, previously optional, eventually became standard (although still usually left at base). The last of the .30cal guns were also eventually replaced. Crew complement reached ten. Early on, external bomb racks could be installed under the inboard wing segments for a 4,000lb (1,814kg) weapon each. With internal capacity now 9,600lb (4,355kg), these allowed an overload to 17,600lb (7,983kg). Such loads were seldom carried owing to range demands and the wing racks were finally deleted. A typical 1,400mi (2,253km) mission into Germany would usually have 4,000lb to drop.

The bay tanks soon became leak proof, bladders replacing metallic wing tanks. Fuel cells totaling 1,100gal (4,164lit) were added in the outer wing panels, referred to as 'Tokyo Tanks', 2,820gal (10,675lit) internal and 820gal (3,104lit) in bomb bay. This gave late-model Fs the greatest range of the Fortress family. Top speed was notably impacted, requiring over 25min to reach 20,000ft (6,096m) and landing was up to 90mph (145km/h)

compared with 80mph (129km/h) for the B-17B. However, a water injection system added in 1944 yielded 1,380hp (1,029kW) for 5min of WE power. This could temporarily boost speed 15mph (24km/h) at maximum gross weight.

Field shops sometimes made unique changes. Most important among these were nose gun installations addressing forward quarter defence as enemy fighters exploited the inadequate fire and armour. The weight and hammering fire of a .50 required bracing. The production nose weapon became .50cal in August 1942. However, with addition of mounts for .50cals (575rpg) in the cheeks, gunners were interfering with each other. The windows were then enlarged, the guns staggered and finally placed in bulged fairings to allow increased field of fire forward. The dorsal turret also underwent changes, first with more transparency area and then to a model with fewer metal frames and 6.0in (15.2cm) taller. The 11 .50s had 4,430 rounds. More extensive field unit modifications included placing two guns side-by-side in the nose position and even mounting a 20mm cannon in the nose of a B-17F in August 1943.[§]

The 412lb (187kg) Bendix remote turret, found lacking in the ventral application, found new use under the

§ This is not to be confused with a test imstallation of two 20mm cannon in the nose of B-17C 40-2046 for evaluation of the Sperry central fire control system at Eglin during spring 1942. The fixed installation made the weapons unsuitable for air-to-air gunnery.

B-17's 'chin' (365rpg). This was first installed on Douglas' Block 75 Fs and subsequently added to other Fs in depot. It initially employed the same indirect sight that combat again demonstrated as wholly unsatisfactory.[5] This was quickly replaced with direct aiming, a control and trigger yoke folding aside to avoid obstructing the bombsight. The turret installation had been matured on a B-17F testbed since 1942 and proven on the XB-40 'escort bomber' that was not carried to production (and did not carry bombs). Although a substantial weight addition, the forward shift in CG was beneficial.

The B-17G made the chin turret standard and returned to the small cheek windows without sockets. A 'formation stick' had electrical boost at the control

column for smoother operation.[6] Boeing and Douglas began manufacturing Gs off existing F contracts and later on new documents. The first production example flew on 23 May 1943 and followed by initial delivery on 4 September, although only reaching the ETO in February 1944. Some early Gs lacked the chin turret owing to short supply and so were delivered as Fs or had the turrets installed later.

Waist gunner hatches quickly transitioned to sealed windows with the guns in a rotating element with elevation ball, increasing comfort for the gunners. These were initially three-pane affairs with the gun (500-600rpg) mounted on a swivel atop a post, but transitioned to a single-pane with the gun mounted on the sill. The waist stations were also eventually staggered (starboard moved forward three fuselage frames), reducing mutual interference between the gunners. Shell casings began to be collected in bags beneath the guns rather than littering the deck. Improved turbos ensured no degradation in ceiling with added drag and weight. These introduced high speed turbines with Honeywell electric regulators, eliminating prior hydraulic control to reduce failures and pilot workload.

Experience soon showed that cheek guns were still required. The bulged fairings were installed at 'mod'

Boeing B-17F characteristics (early blocks):			
span	103.8ft	weight empty	34,000lb
length	74.7ft	gross	40,260lb
height	19.2ft	max.	56,500lb
wing area	1,420ft²	bomb load, max.	8,000lb
fuel, max. (wings+bay)	1730+820gal	normal	6,000lb
service ceiling	37,500ft	speed, max. (25,000ft)	299mph
			(314 WE)
average climb rate	778fpm	cruise (5,000ft)	160mph
takeoff distance* (55,000lb)	3,400ft	range, typical (200mph/10,000ft/6000lb)	1,300mi
		ferry (152mph/10,000ft)	2,880mi
landing distance*	2,900ft	*over 50ft obstacle	

Boeing B-17G characteristics (late blocks):			
span	103.8ft	weight empty	36,134lb
length	74.3ft	gross	55,000lb
height	19.2ft	max.	65,500lb
wing area	1,420ft^2	bomb load, normal	6,000lb
fuel, max. (wing+bay)	2,810+820gal	max. (int.+ext.)	12,800+8,000lb
service ceiling	35,600ft	speed, max. (25,000ft)	287mph (302 WE)
average climb rate	541fpm	cruise	160mph
takeoff distance*	3,400ft	range, typical	
(55,000lb)		(182mph/10,000ft/6,000lb)	2,000mi
landing distance*	2,900ft	ferry (180mph/10,000ft)	3,400mi
*over 50ft obstacle			

centres before being reintroduced to production. The radioman's gun port was altered to allow firing without opening the transparency. The gun mount was changed to a rotating bevel with internal elevation pivot at the rear of the enclosed transparency. This supposedly permitted greater traverse, although many gunners disagreed, and the gun (275 rounds) also received an optical sight. However, the radio compartment gun remained little-used and was finally dropped. Weaponry was then 13 .50s with 6,380 rounds.

At some point the Bell tail turret got power boost, but was still cramped and with archaic sighting. Late in G production a powered tail turret with 500rpg was introduced with enlarged gunner station possessing more comfortable seating, a reflector gunsight and increased firing arcs. Developed by the United Air Lines Modification Center, in Cheyenne, Wyoming, this became known as the Cheyenne or 'pumpkin' turret. It was retrofitted to earlier aircraft at other centres and sometimes had appliqué armour on adjoining fuselage sides. The abrupt end of the fuselage with this turret caused buffeting so, in September 1944, small, fixed spoilers were added ahead of the turret on both sides of the fuselage. Several Gs were given a 20mm cannon in the tail by a mod shop.[7]

Right: The B-17 was among the first bombers in late 1943 to employ Bombing Through Overcast radar to allow attack without visual targeting. The AN/APS-15 H2X in retractable radome replacing the ventral turret on Pathfinders, as on these B-17Gs. Insert is a B-17F with a British H2S within a chin radome. *National Museum of the United States Air Force,* insert *Air Force Flight Test Center*

A fully equipped late-model B-17G was a ton heavier than an F and so roughly 10mph (16km/h) slower, although with more range and payload. Maximum gross was increased to 72,000lb (32,659kg), requiring strengthened landing gear and adopting heavy duty brakes.

The first radar installation on a Fortress was a British H2S set under the nose of a B-17F in a tub radome during mid-1943. The first B-17 Pathfinder Forces aircraft mission was as a lead ship on 27 September 1943. However, the H2S was troublesome, but the MIT lab was already working with the H2X set. This first appeared on B-17s as partially retractable radomes under the noses of a dozen Fs modified at the Rome Air Depot, New York. The H2X was much more successful, yielding Pathfinders in-theatre during November 1943. The location of

the set was moved to the ventral station for aircraft provided in January 1944. These American sets were soon available in quantity and B-17G's ball turrets were replaced with the Mickey radar in a retractable radome on more than 260 examples. Many pathfinders were also eventually equipped with Oboe.[8] Also, at the end of 1943, B-17s were all being fitted with the British Carpet transmitters to jam flak radar.[9]

The B-17G appeared the penultimate Fortress and so was built to the end of the war in numbers reaching 8,680 (4,035 from Boeing, 2,395 Douglas, 2,250 Vega). Boeing production peaked in April 1944 at 16 per day but 12 average, or just shy of 19 per day from all three sources in March.¶ The RAF took 85 Gs from March 1944 as Fortress IIIs where they were employed in maritime patrol as G.R. IIIs, plus radio countermeasures (dispensing Window) and pathfinders as B IIIs. Twenty-six of the British aircraft were retained by or returned to the USAAF and 12 others operated in Canada. Fourteen more Gs were received as Fortress IIIAs.

The B-17 found its home in European where it flew 98 per cent of its combat sorties and the most of any other bomber in the theatre. It outnumbered the B-24s there by more than 2:1, but the numbers were reversed in the MTO, and the B-24 was the pre-eminent heavy almost everywhere else.

At its peak the USAAF had 4,574 B-17s

¶ Averaged from a monthly 578.

Above: The B-17G was the final model of this capable bomber, benefiting from all the improvements to date. Shown are the new tail gunner's station, enclosed waist guns, revised dorsal turret, ventral and nose turrets, cheek guns, and even the radio station gun, for a total 13 .50cal guns. *National Museum of the United States Air Force*

during August 1944. On a single day, Christmas Eve 1944, the USAAF put up 1,400 B-17 sorties to counter the final German offensive. It lost 4,750 'Forts' in combat, 3,219 operating from the UK alone. These were higher than any other type, or about 60 per week during spring 1944 against the peak production rate of about 130.

There were many ideas for extending the Fortress' potency further. However, at that late stage of the war, with R-1820s plentiful and the B-17G emerging, Arnold ordered the nascent projects cancelled. The 10 year old design had reached its pinnacle.

With the end of the war in sight, Boeing ceased B-17 production on 13 April 1945. Aircraft remaining on contract were cancelled, including 600 from Douglas and 100 from Vega. Dozens of B-17s were diverted to non-bombing roles. The Vega line was last to close on 29 July 1945 as the final B-17 was completed. Total production had reached 12,731 (6,981 from Boeing with 41 delivered prewar, 2,750 Vega and 3,000 Douglas) with average unit cost falling from $357,655

to as low as $187,742. This improvement in efficiency was evident in manhours as well, requiring 54,800hr to complete a B-17E but only 18,600 for the B-17G. Hundreds remained in American service beyond the war as bombers, but for only a few years. Foreign nations kept them up longer.

Fortress Spin-offs

An effort to quickly improve B-17 defensive firepower saw a B-17E (41-9112) modified in September 1943. It featured a hydraulically powered Consolidated turret from the B-24 nose installed front and back. A new bombardier station had to be created as a gondola under the nose. The nose gunner duties were divorced from the bombardier, who then took on navigator responsibilities as well. Above the tail turret the rudder had to be cut back, sacrificing approximately half the trim tab. The radio compartment gun was replaced with an external twin .50 powered mount aft of a bubble enclosure for the gunner (radio operator station relocated to the nose). The waist gun stations could be eliminated, allowing a crew of eight. The Sperry dorsal turret was replaced with the 120lb (54kg) lighter and shallower Martin turret that also provided the gunner a proper seat. The ball turret was modified to allow external

ammunition feed, giving more room and allowing the gunner to wear a parachute. The bomb bay doors were replaced with bi-fold units for less drag and improved ball gunner visibility.

Astonishingly, this extensive work was undertaken by a bombardment group shop. Although the aircraft was 1,000lb (454kg) lighter with improved handling (better CG location) than a standard B-17E, the drag was so great that there was no speed advantage. Evaluated during 1943 in Europe and at Wright Field, there is no indication the aircraft saw combat. The B-17G was already in production.

A B-17F (42-29729) got a Sperry spherical ball turret in a clean nose installation, although displacing the bombardier aft to a recessed bombsight window. Nothing more came of the modification.[10] Reducing the size of the bay doors would make it more difficult for enemy fighter pilots to see when they were opened, indicating the bomber was least likely to take evasive action if attacked. A shop in the UK created doors that slid forward and aft along the fuselage to reduce drag and evidence of opening. Eglin tested doors with snap action, opening just ten seconds before bomb drop. Although some were tested in combat, none of these designs was adapted to production.[11]

The NACA got one B-17F-27-BO (41-24613) they labeled the 'XB-17F' for performance testing. They also operated B-17F 42-5474 during 1942-1943 for icing trials and referred to it as 'XB-17F' as well.[12] The B-17G-1-VE 42-39840 was held back for testing as the XB-17G.

Task Oriented
(B-24, SB-24D, LB-30)

In 1938, the USAAC approached Consolidated Aircraft Corporation (Consolidated-Vultee, or Convair, after 17 March 1943) with a recommendation that they manufacture the B-17 to accelerate production. A team from the firm visited Boeing, but came away with ideas for a bomber of superior performance, designed and built in the same time it would take to set up B-17 production. Consolidated had preliminary specifications and a mockup completed in January 1939. In February, they presented their Model 32 proposal at Wright Field, suggesting they could move very quickly.

The four-engine Model 32 used features of their XP4Y-1 twin, to include the same twin tails and new Davis wing with leading edge slots ahead of the ailerons, hydraulic Fowler flaps, and remarkably large aspect ratio (11.55).**

The very efficient 'Fluid Foil' airfoil promised high lift with greatly lowered induced drag for a 20 per cent increase in efficiency compared with a conventional NACA airfoil. Wing root tanks held 2,400gal (9,085lit) or 41 per cent more fuel than the B-17 for greater range. This was the first US military aircraft with wet wing integral tanks, allowing more fuel as a function of volume and at reduced system weight. Tanks fed individual engines but had transfer pumps. As on Consolidated PB2Y, four 1,200hp

** A slot between the bottom and top of a wing allows high pressure air to flow to the top, energising the airflow downstream to keep it attached longer and delay stall. Aspect ratio is the square of the wingspan divided by the area of the wing, normally seen as a normalised, non-dimensional value. A high aspect ratio wing is comparatively long and narrow.

(895kW) R-1830-33 engines turned three-blade, 12.0ft (3.6m) propellers and fitted with single-stage/two-speed mechanical superchargers. The tricycle undercarriage with steerable nose wheel would also be a first for a production American bomber. It facilitated the greater takeoff and landing speeds associated with high wing loading than previously considered practical. The main gear retracted outboard into the wing but was not fully enclosed, a fairing placed at the rear of each partially exposed wheel.

The deep fuselage was optimised for carriage of weapons distributed between two bays with a capacity of 8,800lb (3,992kg), twice that of the Fortress. The roller-shutter bay doors were unique, seeking to avoid buffeting that commonly accompanied side opening doors. These dural sheets with corrugated backing that covered the bays simply rolled up on tracks like a roll-top desk. The fuselage depth continued to the empennage for a tail gunner. Three manually swung .50cal MGs were distributed in dorsal, ventral and tail stations (the last a simple mount behind sliding windows) while .30s were in two nose sockets and in two waist stations

with closing panels, all without turrets. With a crew of seven, there were too few gunners at three.

The USAAC was suitably impressed with the Model 32, the prospect of a second heavy bomber type being appealing. They issued an associated type specification in February 1939. This called for a bomber with a top speed of 300mph (483km/h), 220mi (354km) cruise, 3,000mi (4,828km) range, flying to 35,000ft (10,668m) service ceiling and carrying 8,000lb (3,629kg) payload. In the interest of competition, the service solicited proposals from Martin and Sikorsky, but with only three weeks to respond this was clearly gratuitous. Consequently, a March contract to Consolidated sought a single XB-24 by 30 December. Almost immediately, the Air Corps decided not to wait for the prototype and ordered seven YB-24s in April for a total programme investment of $2,800,000. This was followed on 20 September by a contract for 38 B-25As.

The USAAC permitted Consolidated fairly free rein and the company did not disappoint. Wing/fuselage join of the prototype was on 26 October 1939 and it began flying on 29 December. This began an aggressive flight test programme in San Diego and Dayton. To resolve issues, the horizontal stabiliser was extended 2.0ft (0.6m). The 38,350lb (17,350kg) GW Liberator definitely had range and payload exceeding the B-17, but fell

short of specification top speed by more than 25mph (40km/h). Consolidated had refinements to the quick design on the drawing boards and in wind tunnels, including fully retractable gear, but the press of world events compelled a rapid transition to production.

In April 1940, France had begun negotiating for 175 export Liberators, the LB-30MF (Land Bomber, Mission Français, Model 32B7). The 4 June contract was taken up by the UK on the 17th.[13] These 165 LB-30s were to have commercial R-1830-S3C4G powerplants (military -61s), armour, leak-proof tanks, and powered dorsal and tail turrets. However, to acquire Liberators as early as possible, they traded 26 LB-30 production slots to the US Army for 6 YB-24s (LB-30A Liberator) and 20 B-24As (LB-30B Liberator I).

The LB-30As were similar to the XB-24 but for different propellers for a maximum 290mph (467km/h) and 27,000ft (8,230m) service ceiling. They lacked the wing slots that were found unnecessary, the pitot probe was moved from the starboard wing leading edge to both sides of the nose, projecting like insect antennas, used a Sperry bombsight and possessed de-icing boots. Initially flying on 17 January 1941, the RAF took its first in 14 March. The lack of tank protection and exhaust flame dampers left the LB-30As devoted to unarmed ferry. The Air Corps' sole YB-24 (40-702)

Above: The B-24 heavy bomber was developed by Consolidated in a very short time by using elements from other designs. Perhaps inelegant, it none-the-less possessed considerable payload and range as a worthy companion to the B-17. The XB-24 prototype is seen at Lindberg Field, San Diego, on 24 January 1940. *San Diego Air & Space Museum*

was delivered on 7 April and was soon known simply as B-24 then RB-24. It had R-1830-33 engines, self-sealing tanks, de-icing boots, 637lb (289kg) of armour, with manually swung .30cal guns in the nose (upper and bottom sockets) and six .50s at the other stations.

The LB-30Bs, delivered from 29 March through 26 May 1941, were considered more suitable than the As as they had self-sealing tanks. Most were modified for ASW as Very Long Range (VLR) assets and were in action by June. The USAAC collected its B-24As between 16 June and 10 July 1941. They were nearly identical to the YB-24 but for 519lb (235kg) of armour and grossing 41,000lb (18,597kg). They were of little use as combat aircraft, instead employed in test and transport tasks. Only nine B-24As were completed as such, soon redesignated RB-24s, the balance built as later models.

The original LB-30s, reduced to 139, were built as Liberator IIs with tank protection, S3C4Gs and delivered from August through 31 December 1941.[††]

†† 140 LB-30s were actually built, including one as a loss replacement.

The crew of eight was blessed with 850lb (386kg) power turrets of four .303cal guns each. These Boulton-Paul units were at the aft end of the bomb bays and in the rear. The waists had twin .303 mounts firing from enclosed ports, one gun was in the aft bottom hatch employed as a tunnel station, and another in the nose, for a total 14 MGs. The LB-30 also had a nose lengthened 2.6ft (0.8m) by order of Consolidated's president, Reuben Fleet, to improve appearance. Most of the LB-30s were operated in the Far East and Mediterranean, but also by Coastal Command. They were never considered suitable for RAF strategic bombing for reasons stated previously, although range was impressive.

The USAAC insisted on 26 July 1940 that turbosuperchargers be adopted for the Liberator to help make up the speed deficiency and compensate for the addition of self-sealing fuel tanks and armour. The Consolidated design had oil coolers in one side of the nacelle and intercooler plus turbo air induction intakes in the other side, giving the B-24 its characteristic horizontal elliptical cowling. The engine was given electric primers and the propellers a quick feathering feature and anti-ice fluid system. A safety addition allowed at least 60 per cent engine power even if control from the cockpit had been severed. An APU in the nose wheel compartment also became standard.

The prototype was reworked with 1,200hp (895kW) R-1830-41s possessing exhaust-turned General Electric B-2 turbosuperchargers (135lb/61kg weight penalty each). It then became the XB-24B when resuming flight testing on 1 February 1941. Although turbos raised critical altitude to 25,000ft (7,620m) and top speed to over 310mph (499 515km/h), disappointment with the R-1830-41 led to the -43 being adopted for production.

When America entered the war, there were still no USAAF Liberators suitable

for combat. Consequently, the service commandeered 75 LB-30s between 10 December 1941 and 6 January 1942, identified by RAF serials and the same designation. A Tucson, Arizona, modification centre undertook to 'Americanise' these aircraft. A Martin A-3C replaced British turrets and a simple opening in the tail had two .50cals (400rpg) as no suitable substitute turret was then available. Single .50s were placed in all other positions, including a magazine-fed nose gun. Additional armour plate was installed. These were the first Liberators flown into combat by the US during January 1942. Later in the year, 23 of the machines were relinquished to the RAF.

The need for powered turrets, leak-proof tanks and armour was evident even before RAF requests and they were mandated in a 24 June 1940 change to the B-24A contract for B-24Cs. These were to have -41 engines, self-sealing tanks with 2,364gal (8,949lit) capacity and longer nose. The radio operator was moved from a compartment aft of the bomb bay to a station behind the copilot while the navigator was moved into the nose to also operate the bombsight. The C also had dorsal and tail turrets, each with two .50cal MGs. The Martin unit was placed just aft of the flight deck and operated by the flight engineer. Consolidated developed the 954lb (433kg) A-6 hydraulically powered and armoured turret for the tail, also with twin .50s (825rpg) and illuminated sight and motion controlled by hand grips. Bottom protection came

as the Bendix remote, retractable turret aft of the bomb bay with periscopic sight. The nose .50 (200 rounds) was in the centre of the 'glass', but an alternate mount was provided at the base of the nose that did not interfere with bombsight operation – although it also did not elevate above level and so was of little value. This brought a total of seven 50cals with 2,900 rounds. Gross weight was 54,000lb (24,494kg) compared with 41,000lb (18,597kg) for the B-24A.

Initially flown on 14 October 1941, only nine B-24Cs were delivered from December to February 1942 as the balance of the original B-24A contract. They served as 'production breakdown aircraft' to prove-out tooling for more suitable follow-on models. The rare Cs were fated to spend their days in test and training.

The B-24D was the first Liberator model placed in large-scale production. Given the Air Corps' heavy bomber ambitions and a 12 May 1941 British lend-lease order for 700, demand exceeded Consolidated's plant resources. Consequently, a group of manufacturers was formed in February 1941 as the Liberator Production Pool Program and the block system adopted. The government built new plants for Consolidated at Lindberg Field, San Diego (-CO designation suffix) and in Fort Worth, Texas (-CF), in time for a 19 February 1942 contract covering 1,200 B-24Ds. The Fort Worth factory floor was the longest in the industry at nearly a mile and built to apply production line methodology to large aircraft

Right: The first models of the B-24 were built in comparatively small numbers as the design was undergoing rapid evolution in response to the war overseas. Among the early models was the LB-30 Liberator II provided to Britain. Note the extended nose and circular cowlings without turbosuperchargers, like the YB-24s and B-24As.
Ray Wagner Collection

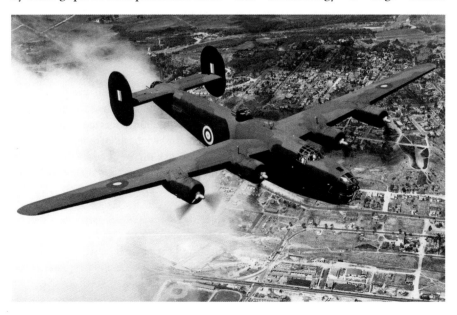

Above: Learning quickly the essential value of powered turrets on bombers, the USAAF allowed Consolidated to develop their own articles for the B-24. The hydraulically powered A-6 tail turret on the B-24D was a good start, but required refinement over time. The armoured turret had 825 rounds for each .50cal gun. *National Archives*

construction. The entire factory complex and adjacent airfield was the largest aircraft plant in the world. The California facility had a moving production line, advancing at 8.5in (21.6cm) per minute. Other manufacturers were brought in to build the bomber in new government furnished facilities. Douglas had the duty in Tulsa, Oklahoma (-DT). The Ford Motor Company was asked to retool and retrain from automobile to aircraft production at an enormous plant in Willow Run, Michigan (-FO). They were to manufacture major assemblies ('Knock-Down' or KD kits) for the Fort Worth and Tulsa lines at a rate of 100 aircraft per month, later 150. In time, Ford got its own contract for aircraft production but was designated the primary source for B-24 spares, building 1,893 KD kits. North American was added in January 1942 with a contract to built 750 bombers (Model NA-95) in Dallas, Texas (-NT). In January 1943, the Fort Worth facility cut the tether to Ford and was manufacturing the entire bomber on-site. Likewise, production of the R-1830 was stepped up with addition of Buick and Chevrolet, turned from automobile

engine manufacture to building the P&W powerplant. This team ultimately produced about 178,000 Twin Wasps, more than any other piston aero engine.

The first D, from San Diego, was initially flown on 12 January 1942 and handed over on the 23nd. Ultimately, 2,696 B-24Ds were rolled out through 22 July 1943. Ford B-24Ds were designated B-24Es owing to different assembly techniques and variations in the interest of production line efficiency. They were slow coming up to speed because Henry Ford insisted on reworking the production process for greater efficiency and redoing 30,000 Consolidated drawings. The plant used giant presses to stamp parts with punched rivet holes rather than drilled and employed spot welds in some locations. They delivered 490 Es from 30 September 1942, four months late and so riddled with varying production quality that they were judged not combat worthy and largely employed in training. Ford also sent 311 B-24E KD kits to Fort Worth and Tulsa in 1943. Likewise, Dallas B-24Ds had Sperry's S-1 bombsight and A-5 autopilot and so were designated B-24Gs. The first of 430 was delivered in March 1943, although, as will be seen, only the first 25 were similar to Ds. Their output was slow and it was January 1944 before the goal of one aircraft per day was achieved.

The B-24Ds were the first USAAF Liberators to enter large-scale operations.

They began European operations in June 1942 and participated in many notable firsts. Their complex and long-range missions helped grow Air Force's capabilities, while also revealing areas for improvement. Gains in combat effectiveness were partially facilitated by improvements in the aircraft. Changes were introduced incrementally as block upgrades during the prodigious production. Variability was also engendered by individual producer preferences or availability of equipment from vendors. These changes reached such complexity that they will only be generalised herein with just the most combat-relevant revisions.

The B-24Ds initially had the R-1830-43 engines turning 11.6ft (3.5m) propellers. However, the 1830-65 with a different carburetor was fitted to many blocks. Also soon introduced was a shorter ring cowling for more propeller blade clearance at full feather, permitting a broader blade replacing the 'toothpick' or 'spider' blade. Although supposedly more efficient, aircrew swore performance suffered with the 'paddle blade' prop. Cowl flap length and opening angles were also changed in an effort to reduce tail buffet while maintaining adequate engine cooling. Auxiliary fuel cells totaling 450gal (1,703lit) were installed adjacent to the outboard engines early in the production runs to bring the load to 3,614gal (13,680lit) and provisions were added for two forward bay tanks totaling 780gal (2,953lit). These additions required a new fuel transfer system.

Payload rose early in the runs to 12,800lb (5,806kg) with the ability to carry 1,600lb (726kg) armour-piercing bombs, although the bay doors could not be closed over the bottom weapons and this limited top speed to 275mph (433km/h). With these and the fuel changes, GW climbed again to 56,000lb (25,401kg), top speed dropping to just above 300mph (483km/h).

Crew had increased to nine men with seven .50cals, armour summing to 901lb (409kg). The Bendix ventral turret only appeared on a small number of the bombers before being eliminated. The opening was faired over and an impromptu tunnel station reinstated with a gun (300 rounds) added in a ventral camera port, later adopted for

production. Formal mounting of two cheek guns and the bottom nose gun became standard in December 1942, all 300rpg. The normal armament then became 10 weapons with 4,800 rounds. Fortunately, late production blocks were given the Sperry/Briggs ball turret like the B-17, but the 850lb (386kg) A-13 model made retractable owing to the low ground clearance of the B-24. If battle damage or system failures

prevented retracting and rotating the turret, landing with the ball extended represented an extreme hazard for the gunner. If unoccupied, the turret could be jettisoned.

Consolidated moved to the A-6A tail turret possessing more plex panels along the sides for greater gunner visibility. At some point, the lighter A-6B was introduced, this built by Motor Products Corporation (MPC) and weighing 564lb (226kg).

Above: The B-24D was the first model of the Liberator considered combat-worthy and built in large numbers by the group of five manufacturers. Like the C, it featured a tail turret and dorsal power turret, nose and waists guns, with all .50cals. This model also introduced Block upgrades to the Liberator. *National Museum of the United States Air Force*

As with other bombers, factory-delivered Liberators were frequently sent to other facilities for modification or installation of supplemental production equipment. Other work was undertaken in the field. Appliqué armour, especially in the neighborhood of the flight deck and blister transparencies in the pilots' sliding side windows were some of the modest modifications introduced in the field. Navigator visibility from the Liberator nose was so dismal that squadrons would sometimes add a second to the already crowded compartment. Larger and bulged windows for the navigator were sometimes added as an answer.

Some Ds were fitted with radar for the ASW mission while others used BTO units as Pathfinders. The latter began first with a chin 'Dumbo' configuration

Consolidated B-24D characteristics (late model):			
span	110.0ft	weight empty	32,605lb
length	66.3ft	gross	56,000lb
height	17.9ft	max.	63,500lb
wing area	1,048ft²	bomb load, normal	5,000lb
fuel, max. (int.+bay)	3,614+780gal	max.	12,800lb
service ceiling	32,000ft	speed, max. (25,000ft)	303mph
average climb rate	909fpm	cruise	200mph
takeoff distance* (56,000lb)	3,800ft	range, 5,000lb bomb load	2,300mi
landing distance*	2,700ft	maximum	3,500mi
*over 50ft obstacle			

Above: With the enemy exploiting weak nose defence of the Liberator, an urgent programme yielded a power turret for this quarter with the B-24H and more numerous J. An upgraded dorsal turret and the ventral ball unit had been introduced in an earlier block. The Liberator had reached its full potential. *National Archives*

as with British installations, but later replaced the belly turret, as on the B-17, with the retractable AN/APS-15. Ten Ds were modified for low altitude blind bombing missions and worked in the Pacific from August 1943. These SB-24D 'Snoopers' had exhaust flame dampers, SCR-717B search and navigation radar with scanner replacing the ball turret, AN/APQ-5 Low Level Radar Bombsight that providing data for blind bombing, and radar altimetre. Another blind bombing system was Gee-H, derived from a British system, which employed a navigation homing beacon with 200mi (322km) range to assist in locating targets. This was first employed in January 1944 against Japanese targets in the Pacific.[14] The APQ-9 jammer was installed in some machines and chaff dispensed from bomb bays. Two additional crewman were carried to support such work. Over Europe, waist gunners would dump

Window out of their hatches.

Lend-Lease B-24Ds went to the UK as 164 Liberator B.IIIs and GR.IIIs and 205 GR.Vs. Many had .303s replacing the hand-swung .50s and the Martin turret was replaced with a Boulton-Paul unit.[15] Ventral ball turrets were often removed as unnecessary and because, during night operation, engine exhaust glow disrupted the gunner's night vision. The first were 11 Ds, Liberators IIIAs, provided in April-May 1942 with some urgency, still carrying standard USAAF armament. Nearly all IIIs and IIIAs were fitted with American ASV Mk.V radar for ASW work. The RAF's night operations with the Liberator continued to be frustrated by the turbosupercharger glow. The GR.Vs ocean patrol machines began arriving in March 1943 and benefited from the outboard fuel cells and generally had APS-15 radar in either the chin or ventral 'dustbin' radome installations. With bay tanks and depth charges, such machines could fly roughly 15hr or 3,500mi (5,633km) missions. A dozen B-24Ds went to Australia during 1944 while Canada got 15 of Britain's GR.Vs from April 1943 to replace the Digby. The latter had US defensive suite

and a different autopilot, and designated were GR.V(Can).

Added B-24 nose armament soon received urgent attention. In seeking greater firepower, field modifications added a .50cal in a ball mount (300 rounds) on both side of the plex nose assembly. This 'cheek gun' configuration was adopted as a factory installation in December 1942 for a total 11 guns and 3,800 rounds, requiring the pitot probes to be moved up and aft on the nose away from gun pressures and gases. While beneficial, the field of fire for the weapons were too limited with inability to fire directly forward and the compartment too cramped for them to be used ideally. Other one-off field 'mod' saw twin .50s in the nose or guns added under the bombardier's floor, as turrets or makeshift mounts, and the ability to fix the forward oriented gun for pilot firing.

A more extensive field modification by personnel in Australia during July 1942 had an A-6 tail turret installed in a greatly reworked nose of a B-24D. This was already seen back home as the shortest path to adding a nose turret. The design was taken up by Ford who developed a standardised kit, the turret modified with wind baffles, and a glassed bombardier's station created in a chin beneath. This proved successful and depots began making similar changes to aircraft. The first installation was performed at the Hawaiian Air Depot and tested in November 1942. Additional kits were sent off, Hawaii ultimately performed over 200 mods during spring and summer 1943. States-side installations were undertaken at the Oklahoma City Modification Center.[16] The Hawaii depot and Ok' City mods had two distinctly different chin designs. Even with the turret, some units continued to mount cheek guns with .30s in the navigator windows.

At a USAAF request, Emerson had been developing a cylindrical, electric tail turret with two .50s (600rpg) to replace the Consolidated unit owing to design deficiencies. With the urgent scramble to find a suitable forward turret, Emerson were directed to turn their unit instead to nose installation in a 'crash' programme of just 3.5 months. This decision was made on 25 February 1943, selecting the B-24 to get the 1,006lb (456kg) manned unit, twice as heavy as the Bendix chin unit for the B-17 to ensure immediate and adequate supply to both programs. The added 190lb (86kg) to the B-24 gave a forward shift in CG that was beneficial, allowing the aircraft to trim-out at lower angle-of-attack for less drag.

The armoured Emerson A-15 turret (500rpg) with optical sight was first made standard in June 1943 with delivery of a new model: the B-24H. These Liberators also featured Sperry balls, A-6B tail turret and A-3D dorsal unit with taller 'top hat' or 'high hat' plex for greater visibility and more suitable for the computing gunsight. The total 10 guns were supplied 4,700 rounds. Crew reached 11 that includes two pilots, bombardier, navigator, flight engineer/ radioman and gunners. Instead of the open-port waist stations with retractable air deflector ahead, each gun was on a new swivel mount on the sill for firing through an enclosing hatch with windows, improving crew comfort. The waist stations soon became staggered and the guns got computing gunsights during this period. The Hs were initially powered by -43 engine but later got the -65s. The S-1 bombsight and A-5 autopilot was also common.

Three plants eventually delivered 3,100 Hs, Ford delivering the first on 30 June 1943 and they began reaching theatres in September. Dallas adopted the Emerson nose turret for B-24G production after the 25th example, the first delivered on 3 November 1943. Despite the similarity to Hs, they continued to be designated Gs. The Emerson nose turret was also introduced in some late-model Ds in the Pacific theatre.

Since Emerson could not meet full Liberator production demand for their nose turret, Convair adopted the MPC A-6B for nose installation of what became the B-24J. The J had 5,200 rounds of ammunition for the 10 guns. The A-3D dorsal turret and staggered windows were introduced later in the CO run of Js. Instead, the guns were mounted staggered in the windows. Internal system improvements included fuel transfer system refinements complementing the -65 engines, electrical turbosupercharger regulators for smoother control reducing pilot workload, a new M-9 series Norden bombsight and better C-1 autopilot. Earlier Gs and Hs were modified with the Norden and C-1 but not redesignated.

Contracts for an additional 6,004 Hs were cancelled or converted to the new model. The B-24J was initially produced in San Diego, the first on 13 August 1943. Beginning in January 1944, the MPC nose turret was adapted to the CO line. By spring 1944, Emerson had caught up with the orders and those nose turrets were installed in place of the Convair beginning in September 1944. With the 90-COs, the -65 engines got the new B-22 turbos for higher critical altitude. In April 1944, the bombsight and autopilot

changes were fully adopted such that all five Liberator plants were pushing out Js of essentially identical configuration. The de-icing boots gave way to a Thermal Ice Preventative System (TIPS) during the latter half of 1944. Ram air was heated through exhaust heat exchangers and circulated in the leading edges.

The B-24J became the most numerous model produced at 6,678. There were variations in the J run. The 122 Block 165-CO machines substituted a hand-swung, hydraulically assisted twin .50cal mount, the M-6A 'Stinger', in the tail. This weighed 200lb (91kg) less than the A-6B turret. Others had BTO radar modification. Shops in the Pacific modified bomb racks of some aircraft to accommodate smaller bombs for up to 40 weapons.

By July 1944, deliveries were running well ahead of aircrew training and unit formation, with aircraft being stored while awaiting rework. Three lines were closed, the associated contracts cancelled. Tulsa completed its last B-24J in July 1944 as it shifted to A-26s, Dallas in November with a move to P-51s and Fort Worth on 17 December as they focused on B-32s work.

The weight growth of the Liberator was most apparent in the J with longer takeoff rolls, slow climbs, degraded handling (particularly with ball turret extended) and higher trim deck angles that deteriorated forward vision. All this drove wider distances in formation to prevent collisions, lower combat altitude and higher landing speed. Although starting with many performance advantages on the B-17, a combat-equipped B-24J had little on a comparable B-17. Still, it was difficult to plan operations employing

Consolidated B-24J characteristics (B-24H similar):

span	110.0ft	weight empty	36,500lb
length	67.2ft	gross	56,000lb
height	18.0ft	max.	65,000lb
wing area	1048ft²	bomb load, normal	5,000lb
fuel, max. (int.+bay)	3,614+780gal	max.	12,800lb
service ceiling	28,000ft	speed, max. (30,000ft)	300mph
average climb rate	800fpm	cruise	215mph
takeoff distance* (56,000lb)	3,800ft	range, 5,000lb bomb load	2,100mi
landing distance	2,700ft	maximum	3,300mi
*over 50ft obstacle			

both bombers because of performance differences, and the UK-based force moved toward a predominantly B-17 force. With the drop-off in number of enemy fighters and the increase in escort, the opportunity to reduce Liberator defensive armament to regain lost performance appeared practical. Field units began removing ball turrets, instead mounting a pair of hand-swung .50s to fire out of the hole with a floor hatch. The tail turret was sometimes removed to leave guns firing from the resulting opening.

Convair followed these trends with the lightweight B-24L that used the M-6A tail guns and reflected the field's preference for ventral armament. These changes, elimination of 240lb (109kg) or armour, and other weight-saving measures exceeded 1,000lb (454kg), yet ammunition onboard peaked for the type at 5,500 rounds. The 1,667 Ls were finished from July 1944 through January 1945. On 10 July 1944, the USAAF requested B-24Ls be delivered without tail armament, leaving it to modification centres to install the preferred 'theatre armament'.

The B-24M model that followed had an A-6B tail turret or lighter Southern Aircraft SAC-7 (or A-6C) unit, total 5,300 rounds, plus revised 'knife-edge' canopy for improved visibility by reducing the number of braces. These 2,593 machines appeared from October 1944 through

June 1945. A turbo deflector hood, turning the exhaust aft for some 6.0mph (9.7km/h) thrust contribution, appeared about the time of the M. Combat units typically took up any weight savings with fuel and ordnance such that performance of these lightweight models were little different from predecessors.

Beginning in November 1943, the RAF took 1,213 Liberator B.VIs (1,049 Js and 164 Ls from December 1943), 287 GR.VIs (Js from March 1944), 110 B.VIIIs (38 Js and 72 Ls from late 1944) and 312 GR.VIIIs (182 Js and 130 Ls).[‡‡]

‡‡ The Liberator IV was not acquired as such, although it may have been intended as B-24Es. Instead, some Liberator VIs were converted to IV in an unclear configuration. The Mk.VIIs were transports.

Above: As fighter opposition waned and escort increased, defensive armament of the heavy bombers could be reduced to allow more fuel for longer range or more bombs. Lightweight turrets, sometimes with less capabilities, were adopted, as on the B-24L. This image shows the simplified M-6A tail turret. *National Museum of the United States Air Force, insert San Diego Air & Space Museum*

Right: The XB-24F was employed in inflight icing trials by NACA, along with a few other Army bombers on loan. A number of test installations are visible on the aircraft, including sensors on the forebody and above the flight deck, and a tall fin to collect ice, observed via added blisters. *NASA*

Consolidated B-24M characteristics (B-24L very similar):

span	110.0ft	weight empty	36,000lb
length	67.2ft	gross	56,000lb
height	18.0ft	max.	64,500lb
wing area	1048ft²	bomb load, normal	5,000lb
fuel, max. (int.+bay)	3,614+780gal	max.	12,800lb
service ceiling	28,000ft	speed, max. (30,000ft)	300mph
average climb rate	800fpm	cruise	215mph
takeoff distance* (56,000lb)	3,800ft	range, 5,000lb bomb load	2,100mi
landing distance*	2,700ft	maximum	3,300mi
*over 50ft obstacle			

The patrol aircraft had SCR-517 radar while some of the bombers had radar for Pathfinder duties. Deployments to the Mediterranean and Southeast Asia included night operations. Canada received some 49 Liberators, including 15 GR.VIs in May 1943 with APS-15, 40 Liberator VIs borrowed from the RAF in 1944, 16 VIIIs, and in 1945 4 B-24Ds, 38 Js, 16 Ls and 4 Ms. Australia got 145 Liberators between February 1944 and August 1945 to include 83 VIIIs (Js) and 47 Ms. China received 37 B-24Ms in 1945, but they did not see World War 2 combat. The USSR seized B-24s and B-17s that made emergency landings in its territory, enough to equip a single squadron each. In April 1944, it sought 540 Lend-Lease Liberators or Fortresses, but the USAAF countered with an offer to mount strategic raids from Soviet bases. Neither approach was fruitful.

The rundown of the war made the M the final Liberator model produced 'in 'bulk'. Outstanding contracts were cancelled in June 1945, included some for the RAF, and the last was delivered on the 25th. Liberator production peaked at 985 in May 1944 and unit costs dropped from $304,391 to $215,516. By March 1944, Ford was completing a new B-24H every 100min. This plant could have produced 600 aircraft per month and so never reached full capacity because the USAAF could not absorb the aircraft so quickly. The 18,284 Liberators surpassed all other American combat aircraft or any bomber in the world. The design easily accommodated modifications for improvements or ancillary missions. Counting PB4Ys, related trainers and hundreds of camera ships, transports, tankers, and spares 20,322 airframes were produced. Contracts for thousands more were cancelled. It was all not without quality control problems, however. Parts were not always interchangeable despite aircraft from different lines having the same designation, causing a great deal of extra work for the supply chain. The largest

foreign operator was Britain with 2,181.

The Liberator operations did not reach full strength until fall 1943, and the end of that year saw the USAAF with 649 arrayed against Japan and 576 against Germany. By that point, they had displaced the B-17s in the Pacific where the B-24s long range would be welcome and frustrating handling in formation was less troublesome. The longest B-24 mission was on 13 August 1943, nine bombers flying 1,280mi (2,060km) from Darwin to Borneo in 17hr at a maximum 68,000lb (30,844kg) gross with 2,500lb (1,134kg) of bombs and 3,590gal (12,590lit) fuel. The farthest was a 2,700mi (4,345km), 15.5hr mission in June 1945 against shipping near the Japanese home islands. Teams would work to extend range by moving crewman about during certain portions of a flight to change aircraft trim for lower drag, and firing off remaining ammunition once off the target to reduce weight.[16]

The American B-24 inventory topped out at 6,043 in September 1944, while

Above: The Emerson 128 manned nose turret was initially tested in a Liberator installation on this modified B-24G. The clean design is evident, cutting drag and improving aircraft handling – plus reducing the cold draft from around the older turrets – while also answering persistent complaints about visibility from the Liberator nose. *Jay Miller Collection*

Right: The nose of the single-tail XB-24K was modified with a Bell twin-.50cal turret beneath a blown plexiglass nose. Turret control appears to be at the top of the nose compartment, above the bombsight and flat window. This work was apparently waylaid by the looming end of the war. *San Diego Air & Space Museum*

highest unit strength had been achieved in June. At the end of the war the USAAF had 4,986 B-24s and 400 brand new Liberators were stored. Although derided as the "flying boxcar" it got the job done as well as any others. Purpose-built for the war, they were all disposed of almost immediately thereafter.

Liberating Modifications (XB-24F, XB-24J, B-24ST, XB-24K, B-24N, XB-24P)

A B-24D (41-11678) was modified in March 1943 as the XB-24F with treated-surface thermal de-icing, and tested in May at NACA Ames Aeronautical Laboratory, Moffett Field, California. This was to have replaced the de-icing boots, but TIPS was ultimately adopted. The unpainted aircraft was characterised by a fairing, 3.0ft (0.9m) high and 5.0ft (1.5m) long, extending atop the mid fuselage.

Seeking the ideal nose configuration, a team in England modified a B-24H (42-7580) during the first half of 1944 by installing a Bell boosted ball turret with twin .50s from a B-26 in the upper portion of a B-24D nose. This looked so promising that it was flown to the States for evaluation during the latter half of the year. There was also a B-24D that had the turret installed in the middle of the nose during early 1944, leaving a bombardier station below. The H installation was replicated at the end of 1944 by Convair, in Tucson, on the single-tail XB-24K but with blown plexiglass nose and 5,300 rounds onboard. The aircraft was to go to the UK on 1 March 1945 for a look by theatre personnel, but it is unclear if this occurred.

Another nose configuration employed the new Emerson Model 128 manned turret initially tested on a B-24G (42-78399). This ball nestled in a smoothly contoured nose with generous clear areas and 210lb (95kg) weight savings. The turret could be centred and fired by the copilot. Eglin reporting on their testing in August 1944 verified the spherical shape reduced drag, improved handling, enhanced crew visibility, and had the advantage of spent shells being collected instead of expelled as a hazard to other formation aircraft. Although some quarters favoured the Bell configuration, the Emerson could be introduced to production sooner.

A B-24E-15-FO (42-7127), brought up to H standard, was given remote control side gun barbettes replacing the waist guns and controlled by a sight at each station. One of the rare B-24Cs (40-2384) was employed at Eglin for other armament trials. Apart from testing turrets that appeared later in production, flights were performed with an experimental pressurised ventral Emerson Model 110 ball unit. This 3.8ft (1.2m) diameter unit had the guns in fairings outside the sphere with 2,000 rounds. More startling was a field mod with a Bendix remote turret grafted under a B-24G's nose, replicating a rework in the UK employing a B-25 ventral turret. Eglin tested a B-24J with this configuration in a nose like a D.

Eglin's J was employed to thoroughly test wing external bomb racks, one mounted just outboard of the fuselage on each side, rejected in 1943 following flights on a B-24D. These could each accommodate up to a 4,000lb (1,814kg) bomb, but with substantial drag penalty, and so were again rejected.

An H sent to Willow Run as a pattern

Above: In seeking improved visibility from the nose with less crowding, this Liberator had a B-17 nose grafted onto the forward fuselage. This also gave more effective cheek guns in addition to the chin turret. However, there were less radical means to this end, and nothing more came of the XB-24J. National Archives (top), *National Museum of the United States Air Force* (bottom)

aircraft was designated XB-24J. Another XB-24J was B-24J-25 42-77130 built with a B-17 nose for improved visibility and easier operation of cheek guns than the narrow Liberator nose. Three flights of this hybrid found performance to be poor, with excessive weight and degraded stability and ceiling. The "Libfort" went no further.[18]

The Liberator was known for having poor lateral stability, especially on landing approach, and a single central tail was thought superior for a scenario of dual-engine out on one side. However, changes to the tail were held back in the interest of high production rate. The first single-tail Liberator was B-24D 42-40058 converted by Consolidated with a B-23 tail. This "B-24ST" (Single Tail) was first flown on 6 March 1943. The tail

was later changed to a new vertical and rudder with C-54 horizontal unit before the aft fuselage from the ST was simply removed and grafted onto another B-24D (42-40234) with A-6A nose turret. Ford did the work in Michigan, substituting 1,350hp (1,007kW) -75 engines with hooded B-31 turbos. The resulting XB-24K was initially taken aloft on 9 September 1943. The advantages were explored at Eglin and reported in April 1944. They verified improved handling and better field of fire for all aft- and beam-firing gunners.

With a recommendation to configure future Liberators with single tails and the Emerson turret, the XB-24N (44-48753, an airframe off the J line) was ordered on 28 January 1944. Assembly began in April at Ford. It had -75 engines in longer nacelles for larger oil tanks and a Quick Engine Change feature by which the entire nacelle, from the mount at the firewall forward, could be removed and another installed in a short time. Servo tabs offered lighter control forces, the horizontal tail had mild dihedral, and a new canopy was included. The Emerson 128 turret was mounted on the nose, waist stations enclosed and staggered, and A-13A ball in the belly. Under the tail was a lightweight turret reduced to a hemispherical cover, like that on late-model B-26s, with bubble

gunner station above.

The XB-24N was delivered to Wright Field on 5 November 1944, went on to

Eglin for operational suitability trials, and then to the UK for assessment by theatre actors. It is uncertain if this last

Above: The B-24 was notorious for poor lateral stability. Among the first examples of a Liberator with a single tail to cure this problem was the XB-24K, a B-24D with the aft fuselage of an earlier single-tail incarnation. Results were encouraging enough to pursue a production design. *National Archives*

Right: The XB-24N was the prototype for a proposed single-tail production model of the Liberator. Apart from the tail, changes included a smoothly contoured nose ending with a ball turret, and a ball tail turret under a gunners bubble window. Testing of the XB-24N began at the end of 1944. *National Archives*

5-23 With the XB-24N appearing promising, service test examples were ordered for field trials The YB-24Ns, including that shown here, replaced the tail turret with a lighter-weight unit. The field trials never occurred as the pending end of the war rendered further B-24 evolution and production unnecessary. *Air Force Flight Test Center*

Consolidated XB-24N characteristics:

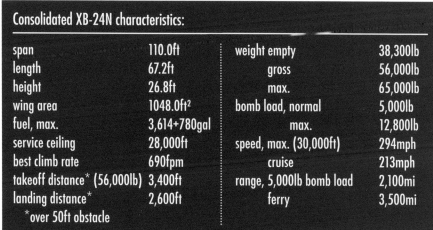

span	110.0ft	weight empty	38,300lb
length	67.2ft	gross	56,000lb
height	26.8ft	max.	65,000lb
wing area	1048.0ft^2	bomb load, normal	5,000lb
fuel, max.	3,614+780gal	max.	12,800lb
service ceiling	28,000ft	speed, max. (30,000ft)	294mph
best climb rate	690fpm	cruise	213mph
takeoff distance* (56,000lb)	3,400ft	range, 5,000lb bomb load	2,100mi
landing distance*	2,600ft	ferry	3,500mi
*over 50ft obstacle			

actually occurred, the aircraft only being accepted by the USAAF in May 1945. The USAAF wanted to be sure they had the design and configuration correct before going further to production because depots and modification centres were already saturated with work.

The X-plane was followed in May-June 1945 by seven Ford YB-24Ns (44-52053/9). These differed in having SAC A-6D 413.5lb (187.6kg) tail turrets. There were also plans to include a remote twin-.50 barbette submerged by each waist and directed by the gunner via a gunsight in each window. However, an order for 5,168 B-24Ns from Ford was cancelled on 31 May, waylaid by the approaching end of the war. The Y-planes never left the States.

Other B-24 oddballs included a B-24D-CO 42-40344 converted in July 1945 by Sperry as a fire control system research testbed, the XB-24P. A B-24J-20-FO (44-48802) was fitted with the B-32's nose

Left: This B-24J-20-FO has been modified to test the Sperry ball turrets in nose and tail installation. This supported the B-32 heavy bomber programme before any of those aircraft were available. The installation was clean and probably cut drag, but may have been heavier than standard J armament. *San Diego Air and Space Museum*

Chapter Six

Flying Boat Bombers

Heydays

As war threatened, the Navy had come to focus on the twin-engine PBY Catalina as its pre-eminent flying boat patrol bomber. Other designs were fielded to strengthen this force. The Martin PBM twin had advantages over the Catalina and was bought in respectable numbers. Although these were superior to the 'Cat' in many respects, PBY production was ramped up and the design evolved during the war to include becoming amphibious. Other twins were developed that showed promise and production plans were laid. However, these programs were set aside for other priorities. The big, four-engine flying boats had appeal, especially in light of prewar commercial operations. Several were evaluated before and during the war but only the Consolidated PB2Y was bought, albeit in comparatively small quantity. However, it was evident that more costly large aircraft were no more effective at patrolling the sea than twins. Radar, electronic navigation aids, heavier armament, and other technological innovations were introduced to the force to aid the all-weather, day-night, multi-faceted mission of these flying boat bombers.

Flying boats patrol mission were typically 10-14hr, low-altitude and slow-speed affairs from dawn to dusk. It was also a low-yield endeavor, with engagement of enemy vessels very infrequent. Surface ships could be attacked with bombs and machine guns, submarines with depth charges, or mines laid. Torpedo drops were very rare. The flying boat might be optimised for ASW and so equipped with searchlights and special electronic equipment, particularly radar. The advent of radar also made practical safe and effective hunter-killer missions

at night to locate enemy vessels running coastlines to resupply isolated garrisons. It also permitted final navigation to a land target for night bombing. However, pure bombing missions against land targets, even in daylight, were uncommon. Non-bombing missions for the P-boats were numerous as their range and freedom from prepared-surface runways lent them great utility.

Although Navy land-based bombers were challenging dominance of the flying boats by the end of the conflict, as late as 1945 the Saipan campaign was beyond effective patrol range of land-based PBs to help protect the invasion fleet. This highlights the great importance of the US Navy flying boat bombers during the war.*

* Besides the large flying boats reviewed herein, there were other seaplane twins that carried a few bombs and performed coastal patrol duties. These included the Grumman JRF Goose and J4F-1 Widgeon with a mount under each inboard wing segment for a 250lb (113kg) bomb or 325lb (147kg) depth charge. However, these were not intentionally built as bombers and so are not included herein. Likewise, blimps (airships, lighter-than-air) performed patrol and anti-submarine warfare missions, to include use of radar and bombs, but were certainly never regarded as bombers.

Hard Work

Operating from water drives many unique design features of flying boats. These include high-placed wings, engines, and tails to keep them from spray, and bomb carriage without the benefit of belly bays. A boat hull has to permit efficient movement and stability on the water yet without excessive aerodynamic drag in flight, while wing floats give lateral support while static on the water.

Flying such aircraft require skill to operate safely and efficiently, especially in moderate sea states. Given the drag and suction of the water and typically less-than-desired thrust:weight ratio, takeoff could require miles and more than a minute to get to flying speed and 'unstuck' from the water. The ideal attitude and speed to liftoff ("on the

Below: This PBM rests on its beaching gear on Saipan sometime in 1945 while seamen perform engine maintenance. Such activity would be much more difficult with the aircraft afloat, indicating the measures and resources required to maintain and operate a large flying boat. Note the open nacelle bomb bay doors. *National Museum of Naval Aviation*

step") required judicious handling to achieve. Landing required orientation with respect to waves and wind, with only these factors and idle power determining landing distance. Judging height over the water was difficult, especially at night, mandating a careful descent. Too high and the aircraft bounced with jarring impacts and too steep the nose dug in and risked flipping the craft or causing a breakup.

The boats were best operated from waters near a shore where the swells are of modest height. If the water was rough, a takeoff might have to be postponed. Open sea takeoffs and landings were nerve-wracking because of the higher waves. Swells of more than a few feet could be intolerable. Impacting such a wave at the wrong angle could cause damage and flood the boat, or catching a wing float on a wave could cause the aircraft to swing about violently ("water loop"). Floats were snapped off and other structures buckled as waves washed over the boat.[1]

Lacking water rudders, manoeuvring on the surface required the pilot to use the tail rudder and differential engine thrust, or powering down and using only the starter for brief bursts of thrust. Those with reversing propellers had

considerable advantages that included backing up. Additional control was affected by judicious use of sea anchors thrown out either side of the boat, fore or aft.[†] Manoeuvring in close proximity to vessels, other seaplanes, and buoys took considerable skill and time. A seaman at the bow snagged the buoy with a boat hook and tied the line.

The boats had autopilots to reduce the strain and tedium of long patrols. They also had unique features that added deleterious weight and drag. These included anchor, mooring ropes and line attach points, poles and hooks to snag mooring buoys, compartments with water-tight hatches, bilge pumps, strakes and vanes redirecting water spray away from critical components, stepped boat hull, wing floats, etc.[‡] The aircraft usually carried flare and smoke dispensers in the back to mark objects on the water. The boat and internal components had to be occasionally washed down with fresh water to prevent salt residue accumulation and accelerated

† A sea anchor is a fabric funnel with a hole at the apex. It creates drag, like a paddle in the water, for directional control.

‡ One or more steps in the hull help break the capillary or suction properties of the water and allow the aircraft to rise to a hydroplaning height where liftoff and climb-out is possible.

Above: A PBY-5 Catalina is poised to be towed ashore during late 1942. The tail wheel beaching gear may already been installed by the waders while the main gear rests on the boat ramp awaiting action. The considerable manpower for this operation highlights the labor-intensive nature of flying boat operations. *National Museum of Naval Aviation*

deterioration. Operators also had to control barnacle build-up on the hull.

The aircraft could not be run up on the beach except in unusual circumstances, so work on the aircraft was typically performed afloat. For such maintenance, work platforms were attached. For work ashore, beaching gear was attached and the aircraft pulled up a boat ramp via winch or tractor – the process requiring more than an hour. The beaching gear typically consisted of struts and wheels attached on each side of the fuselage and under the aft fuselage. The gear had floats to assist handling in the water and keep them at an ideal orientation.[§] The brakes on the main posts had to be applied by a seaman walking beside the aircraft or reaching out from within the aircraft. Ground personnel also steered the tail wheel by hand.

A seaplane tender provided aircraft and crew support during operations at

§ The PB2Y's beaching gear weighed approximately 1,000lb (454kg) each.

Locomotive Works, one or two 250ft (76m) long catapults would be central features of the barge (lighter). After being drawn up a slip and inclined rails, the aircraft would be mounted on the catapult using a large crane or hydraulic jacks. The flying boat would require structural reinforcement and catapult attachment points.

The catapult project was complex and required several years beyond the original schedule to complete. A single catapult weighing 450 tons was installed on the Catapult Lighter (AVC-1), 424ft (129m) long and weighing 5,860 tons. This was launched on 17 August 1940 and placed in service on 17 December 1941 following installation of the XH Mark 3 catapult. The device would accelerate a 100,000lb (45,359kg) aircraft to 130mph (209km/h).

Following launch of a 60,000lb (27,216kg) dead weight, a XPBM-2 was successfully launched on 19 May 1942. Plans had been laid for initially six larger production lighters to be built in 1943 with hydro-pneumatic XH-VII catapult to launch 120,00lb (54,431kg) PBB-1 flying boats, built as catapult-capable. However, the project was shelved in summer 1942. Resources were more productively expended elsewhere, and rocket boosters offered a suitable alternative.

The Jet-Assisted Take-Off (JATO) booster rockets offered an answer to the continuing thrust:weight challenge of flying boats, assisting over-weight takeoff or a normal-weight takeoff in shorter distance. With some initial Army developmental funds, production began in early 1942 by AeroJet Engineering Corporation of Azusa, California. The standard unit was the solid propellant 12AS-1000 D-1 unit; a steel bottle

forward locations. The tender chose an area, marking a seadrome 'runway' with lines of buoys, and placing mooring buoys. Fuel was passed via hoses to the floating aircraft or brought in a bowser boat. Some of the tenders had a crane to lift seaplanes onto an aft deck accommodating up to three large flying boats, and perhaps a hangar for an aircraft with its outboard wings removed.¶

¶ Removing the outboard wing panels was a common

Extreme Measures

Since 1937, the USN had been developing an enormous barge with catapult to launch overweight flying boats. This would save the fuel of an excessively long takeoff run and permit doubled or tripled payload. Designed and built by the Naval Aircraft Factory and Baldwin

feature of USN flying boats.

approximately 0.8ft (0.3m) in diameter, 3.0ft (0.9m) long, and weighing 205lb (113kg). It operated for about 12sec delivering 1,000lbf (4,448N) of thrust, or about the equivalent of 330hp (247kW) at 90mph (145km/h). Several bottles could be attached externally and ignited electrically. The fittings could be made to drop the empty motor after exhaustion.

The first JATO tests with a seaplane were with two 1,500lbf (6,672N) thrust, 200lb (91kg) bottles on a PBM-3 flown off California's Salton Sea on 16-17 July 1944. Burning for 11sec, the added boost reduced takeoff time by 44-60 per cent. Mariners were the first Navy aircraft to use JATO in combat, this in February 1945 at Iwo Jima, although it was used earlier for getting off from open-sea landings.

Mainstays

Legendary
(PBY, PBN, PB2B, PBV, OA-10, GST)
The famous twin-engine Consolidated

PBY Catalina (Model 28) began as the first Navy monoplane flying boat devoid of most struts and wires, but also with twin-row engine and possessed of phenomenal range. The war made it the most widely employed and longest-lived flying boat in history. It was built in larger numbers than all other flying boats combined, and over the longest period. It was slow but reliable, and its contributions during the war were considerable.

The PBY began with a 1932 USN requirement and a 1935 prototype labeled XP3Y-1. Delivery of 60 production PBY-1s (Model 28-1) began in 1936. These were powered by two R-1830-64 of 900hp (671kW) each with supercharging and three-blade propellers. The 50 PBY-2s (28-2) went into production in 1937, the principal change being revised elevators and stabiliser, altered exhausts, and a rudder cutout was made for the extended stabiliser. The 66 PBY-3s (28-3) were also introduced during 1937 with the 1,000hp (746kW) -66 engines and

Above: The 424ft (129m) Catapult Lighter AVC-1 is seen at the Philadelphia Navy Yard on 9 April 1941 while still being completed. This contained an enormous hydraulic catapult to launch flying boats. The bottom image shows the XPBM-2 at the release point of the catapult launch car on 2 June 1942. *National Archives* via Steve Roberts

their down-draft carburetors requiring intake scoops moved from below to atop the nacelles. The 1,050hp (783kW) -72s and spinners came with the 33 PBY-4 model (28-4) that began entering service in 1938. Some were fitted with leading edge de-icing boots.

The PBY-4 typified the models to follow. The wing was mounted high on a central pylon and supported by external struts. The integral fuel tanks were then still innovative. The wing floats folded up to become the wingtips for reduced drag. There was three-axis trim and an autopilot eased workload (high due to heavy control forces) during patrol. An auxiliary power unit was a secondary source of electrical power. Bunks and a

kitchenette were contrasted with lack of insulation and soundproofing, or heaters and air conditioning. The eight-man crew consisted of two pilots, flight engineer (stationed in the wing pylon), bombardier/bow gunner, navigator, radioman, and two waist gunners.

A hardpoint outboard of each strut pair took up to two 1,000lb (454kg) bombs or a torpedo each. The weapons were raised into position for attachment via a hand-cranked winch attached atop the wing, the cables passing through the structure. The window for the Norden bombsight was normally covered by a Venetian blind-type cover to prevent accumulation of water drops and salt spray. Defence was via four .30cal machine guns with one each in a manual nose turret and two waist positions (1,000rpg), and a ventral "tunnel" gun (500 rounds). The waist guns could be replaced with .50cals (956 rounds). These guns were deployed out of forward-sliding roof hatches that also raised at the aft edge to serve as an air deflector for the exposed gunners. The bow gunner fired from within the shallow turret but

could also allow his head to extend out of an open roof hatch. The ventral gun deployed out of a hatch, the door raised for engagement. All guns were normally stowed, moved into position only when engagement was imminent.

Although with 190 PBYs in service as the war dawned, the type was essentially considered obsolete and replacements were already under test. The Consolidated production line was idle. However, with great need to expand its airpower rapidly, and the PBY well-established and more quickly built than four-engine P-boats, the USN resumed procurement. A $20,000,000, 20 December 1939 order for 200 PBY-5s (Model 28-5), to meet Neutrality Patrol requirements, was the largest single order for Navy aircraft since World War 1. A flurry of foreign orders were also placed for export PBY-5s. These were 30 for France, 30 to Britain as Catalina Is, 36 for The Netherlands and bound for the Dutch East Indies, 50 for Canada, and 18 Catalina Is for Australia. The export boats had 1,050hp (783kW) R-1830-S1C3G burning 90-octane.

Above: The chronically underpowered Mariner made good use of Jet Assisted Take-Off (JATO) during the last year of war. Four JATO bottles (insert) mounted on the waist hatches (here under the wings of a PBM-3R), could greatly assist a heavy boat getting off quickly or from rough seas. *Naval Aviation Archives*, insert *Air Force Flight Test Center*

The PBY-5 was given 1,200hp (895kW) R-1830-82 and introducing 100-octane fuel. Although the Twin Wasps retained the down-draft carburetor, the scoop was moved to inside the front face of the cowling. The oil cooler was moved from the wing leading edge to a cowl bottom fairing and the empennage further redesigned. Many had a fairing over the exhaust atop the cowling to support leading edge de-icing. The model also adopted large waist blister fairings with .50cal guns and 840 rounds. The bottom half of the blister rotated up to clear a path for the gun that was afforded an improved field of fire. These were a better environment for the gunner and improved long duration ocean scanning. During the production run, the Navy had armour and self-sealing tanks added, bringing 2,217lb (1,006kg) more weight.

The new cells also reduced capacity from 1,750gal (6,624lit) to 1,478gal (5,595lit).**

Deliveries resumed on 18 September 1940 with the first PBY-5s, and the British began receiving their boats in November. The RAF had bought a single PBY-4 for evaluation with R-1830-S1C3C engines, delivered in July 1939 as the first trans-Atlantic delivery of a military aircraft. Although not immediately impressed with the type, the UK found itself desperately in need of aircraft and soon reconsidered. Its January 1940 order was subsequently increased to 109, and the French boats went to Britain. The RAF aircraft employed Vickers .303cal guns paired in the blisters. The USN also passed seven new PBY-5s to the UK to become Catalina IIs. Australia began receiving its boats in January 1941, among with the first trans-Pacific deliveries. The Dutch began taking their airplanes in August 1941.

**External tanks of uncertain capacity were eventually devised to be carried on the hardpoints, but were very seldom seen.

The Russians obtained a license for Gidro Samolyet Transportnyi (GST, Hydro Aircraft Transport) to build 27 PBYs under license in Taganrog, on the Sea of Azov, with more powerful local engines. Delays meant production did not commence until 1940, but they went on to build about 150 machines. Variants included those known as GST, MP-7, and KM-2.[2]

A PBY-4 demonstrated a hydraulically powered, retractable, tricycle undercarriage that consisted of a fully enclosed nose gear and main gear. The ability to operate from paved strips allowed the PBY to continue contributing even in wintry conditions in the North Atlantic when seaplane operations were prohibitive. The Navy then requested the final 33 PBY-5s Catalinas be built in this PBY-5A (Model 28-5A) configuration, the first taken up in October 1941. They followed with a 25 November 1940 order for 134 -5As, adding 30 in June 1941 and 22 more in October. Some of the foreign customers

requested the amphibian gear be installed on their aircraft when built (Catalina IIIs for the RAF). However, as the amphibian feature added approximately 2,500lb (1,134kg) to the aircraft, the performance impact was not always welcome and some operators preferred the original flying boat. The aircraft were also built with 1,200hp (895kW) R-1830-92 engines and radar.

A further USN order for 90 machines was signed on 15 September 1941. By the time of Pearl Harbor, the PBY-1s were being relegated to training and transport duties. The -2s remained in patrol use through spring 1942, and the -3s were

Below: The PBY Catalina hailed from years before the war and so was already dated when it was called to combat. However, it yielded to updating and served with distinction throughout. This PBY-2, photographed on 29 October 1941, shows the original configuration with sliding dorsal hatches through which defensive guns would be deployed. *Naval Aviation Archives*

Above: The PBY-5 emerged in fall 1940, reflecting many of the features desired to meet the exigencies of World War II combat. Most obvious are the large blister fairing for the beam gunners that also aided ocean visual scan. Less obvious is the uprated engine, self-sealing fuel tanks, and added armour. *National Museum of Naval Aviation*

removed from frontline service in early 1943. The -4s operated a bit longer.

Early combat operations showed the Catalina to be vulnerable to AAA and fighters. The lack of self-sealing tanks and armour on early models was particularly felt. The waist gunners, their guns fed from 50-round cans, had to frequently reload in an activity readily visible to circling fighter pilots. The tunnel gun was too light and the field of fire too restrictive. Two additional waist guns were sometimes added as makeshift socket mounts in the tunnel gun compartment side windows. Tactics also had to be adjusted. Despite heavy losses in the first months, the situation improved and the Catalinas were welcome assets where airfields were scarce, crowded, or subject to attack.

Combat brought production changes to address deficiencies. The single .30 "peashooter" in the bow was much too light, especially if used against submarines. Opening the top hatch and placing the gun into position was a difficult task. Late production -5As got a eyeball mount for twin .30s in the bow (2,100 rounds) and domed fairing on top for the gunner's head. This bow installation became standard by 1943 and was retrofitted to earlier machines. Late models -5As and other models from the same or later period had continuous ammunition feed for all guns. The nearly 500lb (227kg) of additional armour would eventually come to include plate at fuel sumps and armoured pilot seats. Such changes contributed to an average weight increase of around 2,500lb (1,134kg).

The PBY-5 and -5A became the predominant model in USN service, with additional orders for the USN totalling to 426 and 583 procured for the service, respectively. The USAAF got 54 PBY-5As transferred from the Navy in 1942-1943 for air-sea rescue (ASR) of downed aircrew as OA-10s. However, several served in North Africa in a bombing

capacity. The US Coast Guard (USCG) also received some of the USN PBY-5s and operations included ASW and ASR work.[3] Twelve -5s went to a Dutch squadron in Ceylon. Brazil and Chile would receive Catalinas while Free French squadrons also operated -5As. An additional 225 boats were ordered on 30 June 1941 for Lend-Lease, these rolling off the San Diego line by May 1942. Among these were PBY-5B (Catalina IB) with de-icing gear and 361lb (164kg) or armour bound for the UK. The USN retained 60 of these machines. A contract for 496 PBY-5s (among these Catalina IVAs) and 430 PBY-5As had boats delivered through 31 March 1944.

A PBY-2 (0456) was the first USN aircraft equipped with airborne radar, this in early 1941. This was initially referred to as STURBA Curtain and had "ladder" aerials along the sides of the forward fuselage and above the aft fuselage. Factory installations of the ASV began in the spring and by summer it was being installed in one PBY-5 for each squadron, mandating another crewman. In its full installation, this consisted of

the homing transmitter "comb" array near the wingtip, the homing receiver arrays farther inboard, Yagi broadside transmitter arrays off the fuselage, and broadside receiving arrays along the forward fuselage. The first intercept and attack of an enemy submarine by radar-equipped PBY was in April 1942 (at night). By late 1942 the radar installation was becoming common. In 1944, a hydraulically rotated radar antenna array off the side of the forward fuselage provided homing capability. The ASD-1

(AN/APS-3) appeared in 1944.

Although the San Diego production capacity was increased, it could not meet demand. Consequently, a Boeing Aircraft of Canada factory in Vancouver, British Columbia, began manufacturing PBYs under license, the first delivered in October 1942. They began by building 55 PBY-5As from assemblies provided by Consolidated and delivered through July 1943, and then 240 entirely in-house, the first of these flying in May 1943. They included PBY-5s known in Canada

Above: The amphibious PBY-5A became the definitive Catalina model of the war, the retractable landing gear lending the flying boat tremendous versatility. It served in all theatres and with numerous foreign air arms. This example also displays the new bow turret and radar above the flight deck. *San Diego Air & Space Museum*

as Canso (Catalina IVB), PB2B-1 to the USN (165), and amphibians known as Canso A (55). Others were built under Lend-Lease contracts for Britain, Australia, and New Zealand, although perhaps five were taken up by the USN

Consolidated PBY-5 characteristics, A in parenthesis, all late production:

span	104.0ft	weight empty	17,526lb (20,910lb)
length	63.8ft	gross	31,813lb (33,975lb)
height	18.5ft (20.2ft)	max.	34,000lb (35,420lb)
wing area	1,400ft²	weapon load, max.	4,000lb
fuel, max.	1,570-1,750gal (785-1,463gal)	speed, max. (7,000ft)	195mph (179.6mph)
service ceiling	18,000ft (14,700ft)	cruise	110mph (117 mph)
best climb rate	660fpm (518fpm)	range (2,000lb bombs)	2,645mi (1,820mi)
		patrol	2,850mi (2,545mi)
		ferry	2,980mi (2,800mi)

between 6 September and 4 October 1944. Generally, only minor equipment and radio changes differentiated these machines. A Canadian Vickers plant (Canadair after December 1944) at St. Hubert (later Cartierville) near Montreal, Quebec, built Catalinas with the first delivered on 3 April 1943. Their 369 PBY-5As were built as 139 Canso As (Catalina IIA), with initial delivery in April 1943, and 230 PBV-1A through 19 May 1945, the latter the USN designation although all were handed to USAAF as OA-10As.

The Navy explored major improvements in the Catalina, but disrupting the production lines running flat-out was unpalatable. Consequently, production of the revised aircraft was undertaken at the Naval Aircraft Factory (NAF) in Philadelphia as the PBN-1 Nomad.[4] The research and engineering design began in 1940, and an order for 156 machines was placed on 16 July 1941 with the first to be delivered in one year.

Production preparation was slowed by BuAer indecision on the design alterations, and difficulty getting suitable drawings and specifications from Con-

Above: The PBN-1 was an upgraded Catalina developed by the Naval Aircraft Factory through a frustratingly long process. Evident in the image is the "clipper" nose, revised nose turret, angled main step and aft breakstep, plus tall tail. It was manufactured in small numbers and passed to the Soviets. *National Museum of Naval Aviation*

Below: This Royal Air Force PBY-5, shown before delivery, is equipped with ASV radar seen as the Yagi "comb" antennas under the wing and another projecting from the fuselage. Such equipment, undergoing continual evolution during the war, greatly aided the maritime warfare mission. *San Diego Air & Space Museum*

solidated who had failed to keep the data up to date with production changes.[5] Initial plans to produce 25 aircraft per month were more reasonably reduced to 16, and even this with subcontract work like Brewster Aeronautical manufacturing the outer wing panels. The revised schedule in December 1941 sought first delivery in November 1942.

An extended "clipper" bow was adopted with a semi-retractable, hydraulically power turret holding a .50cal, sliding shutters for the lowered bombsight window, and 426lb (193kg) of armour. The upper segments of the turret collapsed down fore and aft to reduce drag. Hydrodynamics were improved with a 20° diagonal and tapered step instead of straight, the hull afterbody (rear planning surface) extended 5ft (1.5m), adding a shallow breakstep just forward of the tail and complete redesign of the wingtip floats. Empennage changes included control surfaces altered for overhanging balance weights and seeking to finally resolve lateral stability problems. Strengthened outer wing panels accommodated 3,360lb (1,524kg) additional fuel and 36,353lb (16,489kg) maximum gross. Overload weight could be as high as 38,000lb (17,237kg), an 11 per cent increase over the PBY-5, although the PBN-1 was expected to be just 9mph (15km/h) slower. The total 2,085gal (7,893lit) of fuel would extend range to 2,590mi (4,168km). Other changes included an uprated electrical system, thermal de-ice system, new Sperry autopilot, provisions for a more advanced radar, strengthened ailerons, and an oil dilution system for improved cold weather starting of the R-1830-92s.

The PBN (Catalina V, but not delivered to the RAF) was a disappointment. Although the production line was established in 1941, developing the design changes delayed flight of the first aircraft until October 1942. The hull changes caused the aircraft to plane with a lower nose attitude and generate unacceptable spray. Anti-spray fairings had to be designed. Remedying these deficiencies required considerable time and it was February 1943 before the first aircraft was delivered to Anacostia for comprehensive trials. The testers came away discouraged. They found the weight

Above: This PBY-5A flies past a blimp, both major anti-submarine forces elements. This is an example of a "Mad Cat" as it has the Magnetic Anomaly Detector (MAD) probe protruding from the aft fuselage and retrobombs under the wings. It also has a Yagi broadside transmitter array on the forward fuselage. *San Diego Air & Space Museum*

increase degraded stability further and control forces were heavier. After considering terminating the programme, BuAer instead agreed to add 2.2ft (0.7m) to the height of the vertical stabiliser and rudder, the rudder and elevator balance weights also altered. This cured the stability problem admirably, but contributed to greater non-commonality with other Catalinas.

Despite the engineering success, the fleet remained sceptical of the Nomad. Furthermore, production defied efforts at acceleration such that only 16 had been completed by September 1943 and costs were running well beyond expectations. Consequently, that same month, an 18 November 1942 contract for an additional 124 units was cancelled. The last PBN was taken up on 15 March 1945, but only 17 were operated by the US Navy. The balance went to the USSR as Lend-Lease. The taller tail of the PBN, eyeball bow turret, dorsal radome, and thermal de-ice system were adopted for Canadian production as 67 PB2B-2s (Model 28-6, Catalina VI), delivered from 7 November 1944 to May 1945. The USN operated 4 of these, with 16 going to the USAAF and 47 to Australia.

Consolidated-Vultee production caught up with the Nomad changes in the PBY-6A amphibian. These featured the empennage alterations, twin .50s in the eyeball turret (1,156 rounds), tunnel compartment window sockets for the .30, APS-3 radar in a dorsal teardrop fairing, and 455lb (206kg) of armour. The PBY-6As were also faster at 196mph (315km/h). The aircraft were built in a Lake Pontchartrain, Louisiana, plant acquired by the government from Vought-Sikorsky and transferred to Consolidated in January 1943. It was turned to Catalina production in July 1943 and rolled out the first example in April 1944.[††] They began by producing a single PBY-5 then 59 PBY-5As, while San Diego wound down its PBY work the same month. The PBY-6As (Model 28-6A) followed, the first flying in January 1945. Although 900 -6As were ordered, the facility would turn out just 175 of the amphibians, the last in September 1945, after the balance was canceled in April. Of these, 75 were taken up by the Air Forces as OA-10Bs and 48 went to the Soviet Union.

The highly versatile Catalina served in all theatres with adjacent oceans. Anti-submarine patrols in the Atlantic used depth charges and were augmented

††Some 119 hulls and 172 wing centre-sections were provided to New Orleans by Vickers.

in mid-1943 with the Mk. 24 acoustic homing torpedoes that could engage submerged boats.[6] This was a top secret weapon called a "mine" for security reasons and Fido by crews. Torpedo attacks in the Pacific almost vanished after 1943 as other, more capable, platforms became numerous. Night operations, assisted by radar, were conducted, with entire units devoted to these Black Cat missions. Typical targets were Japanese resupply shipping or advanced bases. The aircraft would descend from 'up moon' with engines idle (low noise) for an attack at about 100ft (31m) or less. The low-level attacks employed delayed-action bombs and the machines, apart from being painted black, had exhaust damping shrouds atop the cowlings. Several boats were fitted with four .50s in place of the bombardier window that was useless in these missions as bombs were released by "seaman's eye".[7] JATO installations were also standard by war's end, with two bottles per side on the forward fuselage.

Further assisting the ASW mission was Magnetic Anomaly Detector gear and retro-bombs combined with sonobuoys and float lights dropped from the tunnel hatch to mark contacts

and so the submarine's course. A dozen retrobombs were carried under each wing. A squadron of PBY-5s were fitted with MAD and rockets, operating over the Mediterranean from July 1943. A MAD Bird system was designed to detect mines. It was a sensing unit in a bomb-like shape, lowered and trailed beneath the aircraft on a wire from the ventral gun opening. This may have been purely experimental.[8]

Despite the age of the design and the advent of more advanced patrol bomber flying boats, the PBY remained the most numerous and widely used, and hence most important of these types in service during World War 2. Catalina war production had seen 3,074 total (excluding the uncertain Soviet numbers), with just under half as amphibians. These included 1,952 from San Diego, 362 from Vancouver, 369 from Montreal, 235 from Louisiana, and 156 from the NAF. The USCG operated 114 Catalinas and 375 by the USAAF. Some 602 went to the UK (only 12 amphibians), and perhaps two dozen passed through them to other Commonwealth forces. Canada operated 274 Catalinas. The PBYs rapidly faded from Navy service after the war but had a long life elsewhere.

A Step Up (PBM)
Feeling a need to respond to the PBY's success and the potential inherent in powerful new engines then emerging, Martin offered the Navy the Model 162 in 1937. This promised speed and payload

advantages on the PBY, more room and accommodations for personnel, better sea-keeping attributes to ride out rougher seas, but costing much less than the developmental four-engine PBs. The proposal won the firm a prototype contract for the XPBM-1. Unusually, a $5,300,000 production order for 21 PBM-1 Mariners was also placed in 1937, well before first flight.

Martin chose the 1,600hp (1,193kW) R-2600-6 with 15.0ft (4.6m) three-blade propellers for the 32,000lb (14,515kg) aircraft. Most of the fuel was in the bottom of the hull. The gull wing was a more aerodynamic solution than a parasol arrangement. It had retractable floats, folding inboard and up against the wing, and electrically operated flaps – then a rarity on seaplanes. Outer wing panels were removable. The "pilot house" had the two pilots, flight engineer, radio operator, and navigator. The Norden bombsight window in the bow was shielded by sliding shutters. The usual bunks, lavatory, and galley were provided. A bomb bay was in the aft portion of each engine nacelle accommodating 2,000lb each.

The X-aircraft first flew in February 1939. Flight testing found a porpoising tendency on the water for which the step was lengthened and judicious fuel loading for an ideal CG location also helped.[9] A tail oscillation was addressed by adding dihedral. Otherwise, the aircraft was most promising and production proceeded in Middle River, deliveries occurring between September 1940 and April 1941. The PBM-1s were immediately put to work in the Neutrality Patrol. They were essentially identical to the X-plane, with a crew of seven. There were single .50s in electro-hydraulically power nose and dorsal turrets, and waist .50s were in socket mounts surrounded by sighting windows. A hand-swung .30 in the tail and a .30 in a tunnel station were fired from prone positions.

The rapid build-up of American airpower saw an order for 379 PBM-3s (Model 162B) on 1 November 1940, the first accepted in April 1942. These were built in a new government plant at Middle River. These machines employed the 1,700hp (1,268kW) R-2600-12 with two-speed supercharger, had larger and fixed floats, revised aft fuselage, armour, and the bomb bays lengthened beyond

Below: The 21 Martin PBM-1 Mariners were promptly put to work in the Atlantic on Neutrality Patrol as they were delivered beginning in late 1940. Lacking heavy armour, weapons, and self-sealing tanks, it had admirable performance However, absence of these features also limited employment as the US moved to war. *Ray Wagner Collection*

the wing trailing edge for 8,000lb (3,629kg) weapons capacity. A pair of torpedoes could be mounted under the inboard wing racks, but were rarely carried. A new twin-gun dorsal turret was adopted and the beam .50s were now deployable through hatches with extendable air shield. The ventral position was deleted. However, the deepened aft fuselage permitted a proper turret with single .50 gun. The crew was increased to 7-10, including a relief pilot commonly carried. The nacelles were also extended forward to improved CG for better water handling, although porpoising remained a chronic challenge. Four small vortex generating airfoils added at the base of the verticals were further cure for the tail dynamics issues. All this added more than 6,300lb (2,858kg) to the aircraft at the expense of 10mph (16km/h) on peak speed and a few hundred miles on range. Four-blade props were substituted late in production and some creature comforts (refrigerator, stove, etc.) began to be deleted to save weight.

As matters developed, only 32 standard PBM-3s were completed before variants began to be introduced. The

first to be completed were unarmed transport versions, converted as 31 PBM-3Rs (also PBM-1B) and 18 built new in this configuration, illustrating the most urgent Navy requirements. The 250 boats built as PBM-3Cs (Model 162C), with 24 added on another contract, were the common combat model, the first commencing service in October 1942. These had self-sealing tanks, 1,178lb (534kg) of armour, two-gun bow and tail turrets, and 4,840 rounds for the eight .50s. De-icing boots also appeared, complementing prop fluid de-icing. These changes added another 2,000lb (907kg) to the empty weight with further decrement to performance.

As early as 1940-1941, the PBM-1s began to be fitted with British search radar sets to assist the ASW mission. The earliest brought "ladder" aerials along the fuselage of some PBM-1s. The units had an effective range of just 15mi (24km) from a typical 1,200ft (366m) patrol altitude. The second PBM-3 (6456) was modified with the AN/APS-15, employed as a search radar, to become the PBM-3E. This radar had an antenna with a pencil beam used in low altitude and high seas

Above: This PBM-3C is typical of hundreds of Mariners operated during the war. Twin .50cal machine guns grace the three powered turrets, with additional guns deployable from two waist hatches. Bomb bays were located in the aft portion of the nacelles. The search radar above the flight deck greatly aided patrol. *Ray Wagner Collection*

detection, and an antenna emitting a larger beam for high altitude work. These could ideally detect a large ship at 81mi (130km), a cargo vessel at 69mi (11km), and a surfaced submarine at 12mi (22km). Most of the PBM-3Cs were delivered with radomes above the flight deck for the APS-15, and room was found on the flight deck for the radar operator.‡‡ Later, the type would begin being fitted with the ASG centimetric search radar (AN/APS-2 "George") and the APQ-5 radar bombing system. The former was a 10cm S-band unit capable of detecting a large vessel at 69mi (111km), 58mi (93km) typical for a destroyer-sized target, and a submarine at 3.5mi (5.6km). An APQ-5 model with preset release parametres was complemented by another integrated with the Norden.[11]

‡‡ With radar becoming so prevalent, the typical suffix E in designation was not used.

109

Above: The PBM-3S was optimized for anti-submarine warfare and so dispensed with the heavy turrets and armour to focus on fuel for range. Visible in this image are the fans in the face of the cowling to assist cooling engines that were heavily taxed to get heavy airplanes off the water.
National Museum of Naval Aviation

Martin PBM-3D characteristics:			
span	118.0ft	weight empty	33,175lb
length	79.8ft	gross	51,608lb
height	27.5ft	max.	58,000lb
wing area	1,408ft²	weapon load, maximum	12,800lb
fuel (int.+aux.)	2,102+786gal	speed, max. (15,900ft)	202mph
service ceiling	20,800ft	cruise (1,500ft)	127mph
best climb rate	740fpm	range, patrol	2,260mi
takeoff time (51,600lb)	41sec	1,300lb bombs	2,580mi
		ferry	3,140mi

Seeking a boat optimised for Atlantic ASW, the PBM-3S was conceived. This began with the XPBM-3S, PBM-3C 6693 converted in May 1943, and was followed by 94 production PBM-3S (also Model 162C), delivered from July through October 1943. As enemy fighters were less likely to be encountered, turrets were deleted to leave just hand-operated twin .50s in the nose (400 rounds) one in the tail (250 rounds), and the port beam gun (350 rounds, the starboard side taken up by the relocated navigator station), and armour was reduced to just 261lb (118kg) in the bow. Fuel capacity was increased to 2,350gal (8,896lit) internal, 788gal (2,983lit) in jettisonable bomb bay auxiliary tanks, to extend range by a quarter more than the C. These alterations shaved nearly 2,500lb (1,134kg) off the empty weight and yielded performance resembling the original PBM-1s. More Ss were created at Navy depots by conversion of Cs for a total of 156. Some had cooling fans installed in the forward opening of the nacelle.

The opposite approach was taken with the PBM-3D. Intended for Pacific combat, it had fuel in self-sealing tanks, 1,058lb (480kg) of armour, and mounted 1,900hp (1,417kW) R-2600-22s with four-blade props. Droppable auxiliary fuel cells of 393gal (1,488lit) capacity could be installed in the bomb bays. Two 1,935lb (878kg) Mk. 13-2 torpedoes could be mounted under the inboard wings, and weapon capacity rose to 12,800lb (5,806kg). A more capable tail turret was fitted. The eight .50s had 4,840 rounds total. This made the model about 500lb (227kg) heavier than the PBM-3C. The XPBM-3D (Model 162D) was converted from -3C 6656 in March 1943 and production models followed. Delivery

of the -3Ds began in fall 1943 and they found more use against surface shipping than submarines. Added horsepower did not compensate for the greater weight and the -22 powerplant was more troublesome. Consequently, 259 Ds were built before moving on.

The UK had sought 150 PBM-3 in 1940, but the USN held onto all Mariner production until 1943. As it happened, only 27 radar-equipped Cs were actually transferred between August and December 1943 as Mariner G.R.1s.[10] These were no longer so eagerly desired and did not find a ready home. Being returned in December 1943 through March 1944, they became USN assets. A dozen Lend-Lease -3Rs were provided to Australia beginning in late

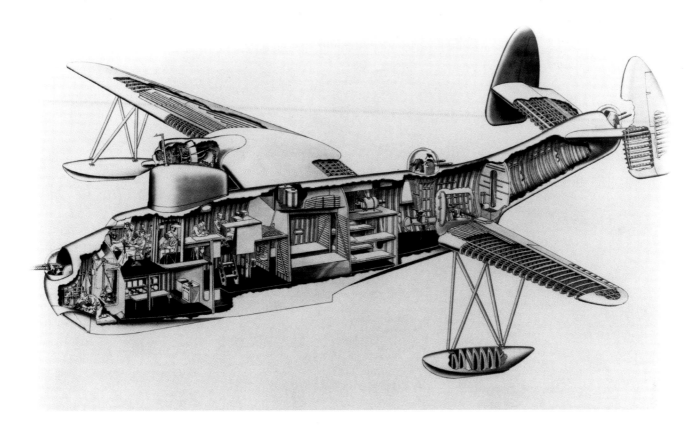

1943. The USCG also got 27 PBM-3S in the latter half of 1943.

Seeking more power than the R-2600 family could offer, two XPBM-5s were created from D production (45275 and 45276), the first flying in May 1943. One had R-2800-34s engines and the other -22s. The 2,100hp (1,566kW) R-2800-22, with three-blade aluminum propellers, was selected for production and an order dated 3 January 1944 led to PBM-5 (Model 162F) delivery in August of that year. A four-blade steel propeller was substituted late in the run. Some aircraft also had nacelle fans. The -5s had range and airspeed advantages on the earlier boats. The aircraft also could carry four 1,000lb (454kg) torpedoes, had updated turrets,

and more current radios. The usual eight .50s were retained with 1,067lb (484kg) of armour. The APS-15 was standard from the beginning. The USCG received 41 PBM-5s in 1945. Production continued to 589 during the war, with 460 cancelled and many of the last going directly to storage. They served more than a decade beyond the conflict.

The PBM-5 was built originally with fittings for up to 11 JATO bottles installed on the aft fuselage and under the inboard wing segments. Fittings were retrofitted to many -3s to help reduce the effects of low engine power. The usual installation was two bottles on each waist hatch, or a racked mounted in the hatch opening, affording the ability to open the hatch

Above: This cutaway drawing of a Martin PBM-5 Mariner illustrates the considerable room and relative comfort afforded aircraft that were to remain on patrol for a day. Note the bombardier kneeling before the bombsight, and the air deflectors ahead of the beam gun, galley, and bunks. Most compartments were separated by watertight hatches.
San Diego Air & Space Museum

and install fresh bottles from stowage racks inside the aircraft. These were especially helpful in getting off from the open-sea, greatly reducing the takeoff run and pounding from the swells.

The 1,287 Mariners built during the war were valuable assets, although not without flaws. The PBM-3 was intended to replace the PBY in the core PB mission, especially in the Atlantic, but early service was plagued by mechanical problems, with several groundings for fleet-wide engine issues. All variants of the PBM-3 were considered quite under-powered, complicating the crews' job. Fortunately, these issues were overcome, and there was plenty of work for both types.[§§] It was only in early 1944 that the number of operational PBM squadrons equaled PBY counterparts, and summer before the Mariner dominated as USN flying boats reached their pinnacle. Along with PBYs, Mariners did yeoman service as a patrol bomber in all waters, becoming

Martin PBM-5 characteristics

span	118.0ft	weight empty	33,200lb
length	79.8ft	gross	55,968lb
height	27.5ft	max.	58,000lb
wing area	1,408ft²	weapon load, maximum	12,800lb
fuel (+bomb bay tanks)	2,702+786gal	speed, max. (9,700ft)	215mph
service ceiling (typ.)	15,800ft	cruise	138mph
best climb rate (typ.)	550fpm	range, patrol (5,200lb bombs)	2,100mi
takeoff time (typ.)	56sec	(1,300lb bombs)	2,760mi
		maximum	3,463mi

§§ Only one wartime PBY squadron converted to PBMs.

the first American seaplane of the war to sink an enemy submarine. Mariners also made the first bombing attacks in the Japanese home islands by American flying boats. Also, coastal anti-shipping missions like Black Cats were executed, although sometimes called Nightmares. The greater weapon capacity and comfort of the PBM made it a desirable aircraft for such missions. Radar played a big role, run-in on targets often based solely on radar returns. Bomb releases became too low to use the bombsight.

Mariner One-Offs (XPBM-1A, XPBM-2, XPBM-4)

A 20mm cannon had been an optional Mariner armament installation from the beginning. It was added as an experimental installation in the nose turret of the prototype Mariner, to become the XPBM-1A. This was tested at the Aircraft Armament Unit at Norfolk NAS, but was not introduced to production.

A PBM-1 (1247) was converted to the sole XPBM-2, accepted in April 1942, for heavy-weight launch from the AVC-1 catapult barge. This had a strengthened hull and additional fuel capacity to 2,115gal (8,006lit) for 4,000mi (6,437km) range, and was intended to be launched at 51,000lb (23,133kg). Although flown from the barge, the project was shelved.

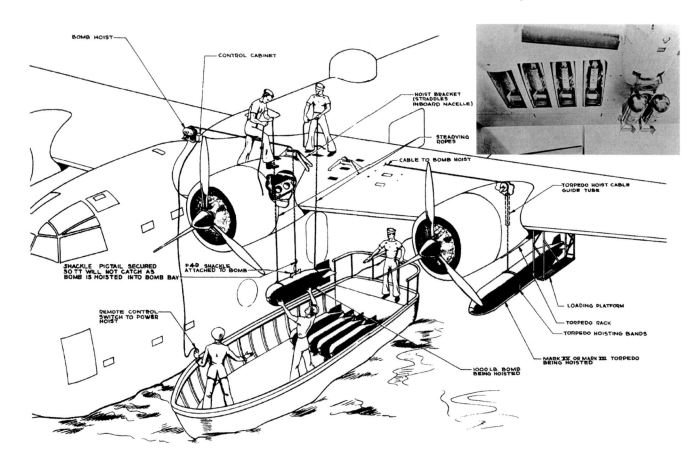

Left: An image of the XPB2Y-4, shot on 27 December 1943 at the Naval Air Test Center, shows the Convair tail turret and four-blade props on all R-2600-10 Double Cyclone engines. A mocked-up dorsal turret appears to be in place. The configuration remained a one-off prototype. *National Museum of Naval Aviation*

Before the R-2800 was selected for the PBM-5, a PBM-4 with R-3350-8 engines was envisioned. The XPBM-4 (6456) and 180 production Model 160Es were ordered on 20 August 1941, the order eventually rising to 230. These never left the drawing boards as the B-29 consumed nearly all production of this powerplant. An amphibious version of the PBM-5 was proposed in April 1944, but this did not come to fruition until after the war.

Reconsidered (PB2Y)

Having observed the growth of large, long-range flying boats in commercial transoceanic service, the USN sought to explore their potential in military service. A 1935 competition for four-engine types yielded 1936 prototype contracts to Sikorsky and Consolidated. Such aircraft might achieve speed and carry sufficient armament for mission success despite enemy fighter opposition.

While Consolidated's XPB2Y-1 (Model 29) showed promise, it underwent considerable prewar metamorphosis. Production offered the opportunity to permanently correct deficiencies and expand its potential. Money was short and the boat cost approximately three times that of a PBY, so the March 1939 production order encompassed just six PB2Y-2s.

The redesign included a more voluminous fuselage and crew of nine, larger, and dorsal scanner bubble. Retained were the floats retracting to the wingtip. Bomb capacity was 8,000lb (3,629kg) carried within eight wing bays and four more 1,000lb (454kg) bombs or two torpedoes on racks beneath the outboard nacelles. The stores were loaded via a hoist atop the wing and cables passing through the structure. The bays were each covered by two doors that opened to the side as they slide up into the wing. Armament was six .50cals that included a powered bow ball turret, hand-swung tail mount, gun in a dorsal blister, waist guns, and tunnel. The 1,200hp (895kW) R-1830-78 engine had two-stage centrifugal supercharger with intercooler between the stages, and the primary stage gear-driven. There were three-blade propellers outboard and four-blade inboard. The propulsion changes helped compensate for the nearly 7,500lb (3,402kg) increase in empty weight and over 10,500lb (4,763kg) in maximum gross. Yet, the PB2Y-2 was the fastest of the type at 255mph (410km/h) peak speed.

Initially flown on 22 November 1940 and deliveries commencing on the last day of the year, the war overseas was already showing the model to be vulnerable as it lacked armour and self-sealing tanks. Hence, the half-dozen aircraft were primarily devoted to test.

The last of the -2s (1638) was altered as the XPB2Y-3, first flown on 11 November 1941 and delivered in December. The PB2Y-3 production order had been placed on 19 November 1940 for 200 examples at $311,000 apiece. The first of these flew on 29 April 1942 and delivery proceeded from 4 June through October 1943.

The PB2Y-3 was powered by 1,200hp R-1830-88 engines with automatic synchronising system for 12.5ft (3.8m) propellers. This eliminated the throbbing noise from propellers operating out of phase. These were three-blade aluminum propellers outboard and four-blade steel blades inboard with reversing. However, photographs frequently show three-blade propellers throughout on fleet aircraft. Featured were the requisite leak-proof tanks for the two wing main cells, the outboard cells remaining unprotected. A carbon-dioxide inerting system was employed to reduce the fire hazard of fumes in tank air spaces. Split flaps were electrically driven, as was wing float actuation that also had manual backup, and there was an APU onboard.

Consolidated PB2Y-3 characteristics:			
span	115.0ft	weight empty	40,935lb
length	79.3ft	gross	68,000lb
height (on beaching gear)	27.5ft	max.	72,500lb
wing area	1,780ft^2	weapon load, maximum	12,000lb
fuel	2,041-3,730gal	speed, max. (20,000ft)	223mph
service ceiling	20,500ft	cruise (1,500ft)	141mph
best climb rate	550fpm	range (12,000lb bombs)	1,550mi
		(1,000lb bombs)	2,540mi
		maximum	3,250mi

Above: The few late-war PB2Y-5s were created via modifications of PB2Y-3s, substituting more economical "low altitude" engines, added fuel capacity, and updated nose and dorsal turrets. Performance suffered, but use of JATO bottles assisted heavy takeoffs. This image shows use of the beaching gear and reveals the wing bomb bays.
Naval Aviation Archives

The removable outer wing panels had slotted ailerons. The aircraft had the usual three-axis trim with tabs and autopilot. A crank within the boat allowed the length of the beaching gear strut to be adjusted to keep the aircraft level. De-icing boots were employed initially, but thermal de-icing substituted in late production used exhaust heat exchangers to heat ram air.

The XPB2Y-3's three power turrets included an armoured bow unit from Martin for two .50s (400rpg), a Convair tail unit with paired .50s (2,000 rounds), and twin .50s (1,200 rounds) in a new dorsal turret. These and the waist positions with one gun (600rpg, tunnel position deleted) gave eight .50 guns with 4,840 rounds total. The bombsight window in the bow was usually covered by two doors. An ASV radar was added

above the flight deck to some -3s. Some 2,000lb (907kg) of armour was introduced for the crew of ten. Of the crew, the flight deck accommodated the two pilots, commanding officer (seldom a separate individual), navigator, radio operator, and flight engineer. Below decks were the usual officer and enlisted accommodations.

The PB2Y-3 became the archetype Coronado. It took its name from the RAF who were to be sent 32 via Lend-Lease as PB2Y-1Bs or Coronado GR.1s. However, only 10 were transferred from April 1943. In early 1944, the British judged the type was less suited for PB work than transport duties, where they served out the war. Indeed, the comparatively small number of PB2Y-3s manufactured reflects the limited value of the type in combat. It was generally relegated to solitary patrol and transport duties, and 31 were disarmed and converted as PB3Y-3R transports in 1945. The aircraft flew very well but could be a handful on the water, with heavy controls plus swing and skip tendencies. The skipping was later largely cured with a "ventilated

step" on most examples. With another 5,350lb (2,425kg) addition in empty weight, the engine change had not made up for weight growth, making them eager users of JATO (three bottles per side).

The Coronado's only formation bombing experience was four consecutive missions in January and February 1944 from Midway against Truk. This was the Navy's first experience striking a distant land target (approximately 2,200mi/3,540km and 14hrs round trip) with a formation of multi-engine bombers, and at night. Up to 15 aircraft participated, each carrying 8,500lb (3,856kg) of bombs for approximately 71,000lb (32,205kg) takeoff weight, and bombing from 50ft (15m) to 8,000ft (2,438m). Two twilight mine-laying missions to Truk were flown in April, each with a few aircraft. Carrying two 2,000lb (907kg) weapons or four smaller mines hung externally, the over-loaded boats wallowed badly. Bombing missions in May 1945 employed only internal weapons and included releases based on radar returns if weather was

foul. A later, ill-conceived, formation night mission against Japanese vessels hugging a coastline employed torpedoes that badly degraded aircraft performance and handling. For such night missions the aircraft engine exhausts were fitted with flame dampers.

The XPB2Y-3 was modified again by fitting 1,700hp (1,268kW) R-2600-10s, four-blade propellers throughout, and Convair A-6 tail turret. This XPB2Y-4 flew initially on 27 April 1943 but did not progress beyond prototype. Proposed production of 400 was dropped. Instead, R-1830-92s "low-altitude engines" with four-blade props and single-stage blower in shorter cowling giving greater fuel efficiency were substituted on several PB2Y-3s. Also featured was SAC tail turret with feed chute (1,250rpg), feed chutes for beam guns (560rpg), larger floats, 1,123gal (4,251lit) expanded fuel capacity for 270mi (435km) more range, and JATO mounts (four per side). All this added another 1,500lb (680kg) to empty weight, cutting top speed to 211mph (340km/h) and cruise to 154mph (248km/h). These PB2Y-5s, delivered in late 1944, also received superior AN/APS-

2 radar and all tanks were self-sealing.[12] None of the Coronados survived in service beyond 1945.

Not to See Action

Transformed (P4Y)
Consolidated had developed the Model 31 fast flying boat in 1937-1938 to meet a commercial requirement and hopefully replace the PBY. The double-deck interior was to accommodate a crew of five and passengers. The PBY's broad "tumble home" keel was eschewed in favour of a long and narrow planing hull with less aerodynamic drag. Hydraulically retractable, fully enclosed, tricycle beaching gear was included, allowing the aircraft to run up a ramp under its own power. In an emergency the gear could allow a landing ashore, albeit with the potential for blown tires. The Model 31 was powered by two of the most powerful aero engines then available in the 2,300hp (1,715kW) R-3350-8 Duplex Cyclone with two-speed supercharger. These turned 15.5ft (4.7m) three-blade propellers.

Most notable was the new, high

Above: The Consolidated Model 31 was to be a fast commercial or military flying boat. The modified airplane, photographed on 3 July 1941, shows the clean exterior and amazing Davis wing that gave it a top speed of 250mph (402km/h). The original configuration (insert), reveals retractable beaching gear and stowed wing floats.
San Diego Air & Space Museum

efficiency Davis wing that would be adopted for the B-24. Consolidated included hydraulic Fowler flaps, leading edge slots ahead of the ailerons, and 5,400gal (20,441lit) wet wing capacity in the centre-section. Wing floats, also developed with Davis mathematical modeling, folded up and inboard against the bottom of the wing. Flush riveting throughout would further help further reduce drag.

Having licensed exclusive use of the Davis wing, Consolidated chose to build the Model 31 with $1,000,000 of company funds to demonstrate benefits of the design. Construction began in San Diego during 1938 and first flight followed in May 1939. Neither commercial nor military interior was fitted. Testing verified the Davis wing performance and the aircraft was shaping

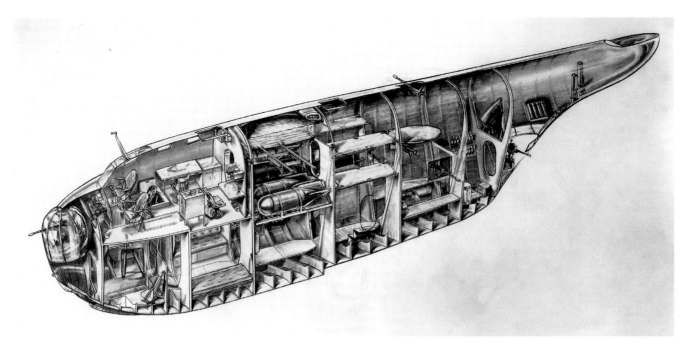

Above: This concept art of a military Model 31 shows bomb stowage under the wing center-section with carriage and rail mechanism for extending weapons out under the inboard wing section. A tail turret was not planned at this point, instead featuring a "tunnel" position, nose "birdcage" turret, waist and dorsal stations. *San Diego Air & Space Museum*

up to be the world's fastest flying boat. It reached 250mph (402km/h) at 15,000ft (4,572m) and 160mph (258km/h) cruise. Range exceeding 3,500mi (5,632km) was projected.

With war greatly reducing commercial sales prospects, Consolidated moved to interest the US Navy in the aircraft. An initial look in 1939 did not impress the service. Consolidated pressed on, modifying the Model 31 along military lines as a patrol machine. In demonstrating the boat to the Navy, beginning on 25 March 1940, they measured 258mph (415km/h) at 16,600ft (5,060m) and 46,620lb (21,146kg). However, the service was still unmoved. The aircraft tended to skip during heavy weight takeoff and landings.[¶¶] Besides finding fault in the planing hull, they were already working with Boeing on the XPBB-1. For another round of demonstrations in April 1941, Consolidated added a dorsal fairing to represent a turret, altering the nose lines to mock up a turret and bombardier station, and deepening the aft fuselage for another turret. The Navy

¶¶ Skipping is an unstable heaving action that could be dangerous with unskilled pilots.

did not react.

With the US drawn into the war, any USN hesitation fell away. The Model 31 was a potential alternative to the Mariner that was proving under-powered. With a 17 February 1942 decision to seek a militarised variant, the service appropriated the prototype (27852) on 13 April and a $433,000 contract was negotiated for further conversion. They requested full transformation into an eight-place patrol aircraft designated XP4Y-1 Corregidor. The USN placed an order for 200 of the boats (44705/904) on 8 July 1942 with a production rate of up to 45 per mount, the first to be delivered in July 1943. These would be built at the New Orleans facility.

The patrol modifications were carried to fruition, these adding more than 3,000lb (1,361kg) to the empty weight. The crew of seven was composed of two

pilots, navigator, flight engineer/radio operator, nose gunner/bombardier, tail gunner, and dorsal gunner. Some 869lb (394kg) of armour was added. New cowlings and 16.0ft (4.9m) propellers were substituted. The retractable beach gear was deleted in favour of detachable equipment to save weight. A bulged nose radome was added for an ASG search radar (not fitted). Mooring hatches were added on the sides of the nose. A flared skirted under the forward hull answered hydrodynamics criticisms. The aft fuselage was considerably modified to accommodate a tail turret, with the tail raised and the horizontal stabiliser widened 4.0ft (1.2m).

The M-1 hydraulically powered tail turret from United Shoe Machinery Corporation carried twin .50s (1,600 rounds) while a Engineering and Research Corporation (ERCO) electro-hydraulic

Consolidated XP4Y-1 characteristics:

span	110.0ft	weight empty	28,262lb
length	74.1ft	gross	46,000lb
height (beaching gear)	26.5ft	max. (catapult)	48,000lb
wing area	1,048ft²	weapon load, maximum	4,000lb
fuel	1,545-3,000gal	speed, max. (13,600ft)	247mph
service ceiling	21,400ft	cruise	136mph
best climb rate	1,230fpm	range (2 torpedoes)	1,745mi
takeoff time (no wind)	36sec	(2,600lb bombs)	2,300mi
	(46sec overload)	maximum	3,280mi

dorsal ball turret also sported twin .50s (1,200 rounds). The nose position had a 37mm cannon on a Bell hydraulic mount with 120 rounds in six-round clips. The gunner doubled as a bombardier. Defensive fire to the sides was clearly deficient, but the aircraft was expected to fly so low during combat as to make bottom attack unlikely. A means of adding bombing capability was adopted like that employed with the Shorts Sunderland flying boat. The weapons were stored within the fuselage, beneath the wing centre-section. These could include four 1,000lb (454kg) weapons or eight 325lb (147kg) depth charges. Two weapons were loaded on each of two carriages that ran electrically out on rails under each wing, along with the door covering the fuselage opening. These carriages could be reloaded in flight using hand winches, with weapons stored below them. A torpedo could be mounted separately under each wing, between the bomb carriage racks and engine nacelle.

The greatly altered aircraft flew again on 28 July 1943. The skipping tendency was not entirely cured. This and the inadequate defensive armament were factors in the termination decision.

The principal rationale was the Army's B-29 bomber demand on R-3350 production and the Navy's general move to landplane PBs. The programme was cancelled on 11 September 1943. The XP4Y-1 continued serving in a test role for a time longer.

Forsaken (PBB)

Despite the XPBM-1 having flown in February 1939, the Navy saw potential to greatly improve PB performance over this design concurrent with recent aeronautical advances. They issued a new VPB specification in March for another twin-engine boat employing the new R-3350 with 2,200hp (1,641kW). These powerful engines and aerodynamic efficiency would provide the performance of a four-engine design, permitting more fuel or payload in exchange for two fewer powerplants. The specification also had a requirement for "assisted takeoff" catapult launch from the AVC barge at maximum gross weight.

Boeing was invited to bid on the VPB, this company having just built the pinnacle of American commercial flying boats with the Model 314. Their competition was Vought-Sikorsky (V-S) with considerable

Above: This summer 1943 view of the XP4Y-1 reveals tail and dorsal turrets, both lacking their twin .50cals. The beaching gear, replacing the retractable hardware, lies on the ramp. Production plans came to grief over B-29 demand for the R-3350 powerplant and a general move to landplanes for the patrol mission. *National Archives*

flying boat expertise. The final Boeing concept featured a straight wing with Davis airfoil and floats retracting against its bottom surface, and bomb bay within the hull. Cabin pressurisation was planned. Top speed was estimated at 237mph (381km/h), GW projected at 52,500lb (23,814kg), and maximum 82,200lb (37,285kg) for catapult.

The Navy initially favoured the Vought-Sikorsky design over the Model 337, but V-S was too consumed by priority war production to take it through development. The service then asked Boeing on 24 February 1940 to consider developing the V-S aircraft.[13] Instead, Boeing quickly revised their concept and presented the larger and heavier design to their customer on 20 March. This Model 344 had a comparatively narrow hull consistent with latest research, fixed floats, wing bomb bays, and deletion of pressurisation that added marginal value

Left: The Boeing XPBB-1 flying boat bomber moves across what is likely Lake Washington during 1942. The relatively clean lines, including the fixed wing floats, assisted in achieving considerable range and impressive payload. Testing found few problems to rectify, and the boat was praised by the Navy evaluators. *Museum of Flight*

to the PB mission. A new straight wing, with outboard panel dihedral, replaced the Davis design after license negotiations had foundered. The Navy was impressed and ordered one prototype on 29 June 1940 as the XPBB-1 (3144).

A mockup of the XPBB-1 was ready in January 1941 and assembly of the prototype began in July in Seattle. An order for 57 PBB-1s (03745/801) was placed on 8 October 1941, well before first flight, with the first to be delivered on 8 April 1943. Plans were laid to expand this quantity to 500. A new government plant in Renton, on Lake Washington, was built to produce the aircraft.

The design had a notably large-span wing with a unique airfoil, Fowler flaps, and a clean wing float. The outer wing panels and horizontal stabilisers were very similar to those on the B-29. Each R-3350-8 with 2,300hp (1,715kW) had a single-stage supercharger and three-blade, hollow steel propellers of 16.5ft (5.0m) diameter. The planned counter-rotating propellers, to reduce takeoff yaw and engine-out issues, proved too much for the overwrought Wright Aeronautical. A wet wing eliminated the weight and complexity of fuel bladders. With the

enormous fuel capacity, the aircraft could conceivably fly a 72hr patrol. Empty tanks were purged for combustible vapors with CO_2 pumped from storage bottles.

The crew of ten included the bombardier in a typical nose position, with bombsight and sighting window with cover, but the man was seated instead of kneeling. The flight deck had stations for the two pilots, flight engineer, navigator, and radioman. Gunners made up the remainder of the team. A lower compartment had bunks. The PB was fitted with de-icing boots on all leading edges. Beaching gear included dual-wheel assemblies attached at four points in the side of the boat.

Each of ten bomb bays was covered by

a flexible door that rolled backwards, up aft the interior aft face and across the top of the bay. These lay within the inboard wing segments, essentially the cavities between the ribs and spars. They accommodated 20,000lb (9,072kg) of bombs with up to 1,000lb (454kg) individual weapons. With the maximum bomb capacity, the weapons projected below the wing and the doors could not be closed. Up to four torpedoes could be carried on pylons mounted below the bays. Eight .50cal MGs and 32,000 rounds of ammunition were in ERCO hydraulically powered and manned turrets with reflector sights, built from a Boeing design. The nose, tail and dorsal turrets, each with two guns (400 rounds), were all based on the same spherical design in which the gunner rode. The waist turrets, with single gun (400 rounds), were similar but a teardrop design. The gun swung through a horizontal slot and the pod rotated up and down as directed by the gunner.

The maiden flight of the XPBB-1, by then named Long Ranger, was conducted on 9 July 1942 from Renton. Initial trials found the usual minor issues with any new aircraft and Boeing moved promptly to correct them. For example, shallow spoiler flaps had to be added ahead of the bomb bays, deploying when the bay

Right: The Boeing XPBB-1 was the largest twin engine airplane and flying boat when it emerged in 1942. The size is evident in this image of the aircraft on flotation gear in Renton on 11 July 1942. The image reveals all the ERCO powered gun turrets but the dorsal and port position. *Naval Aviation Archives*

Boeing XPBB-1 characteristics:			
span	139.7ft	weight empty	37,383lb
length	94.8ft	gross	64,034lb
height (on beaching gear)	34.2ft	max. (catapult)	101,129lb
wing area	1,826.4ft²	weapon load, max.	20,000lb
fuel (protected - max.)	2,490-9,434gal	speed, max. (4,500ft)	219mph
service ceiling (61,500lb)	18,900ft	cruise	127mph
best climb rate (55,000lb)	980fpm	range (normal payload)	4,245mi
takeoff time (25,000lb, no wind)	0.7min	ferry (max. fuel)	7,300mi

Above: This image reveals all but one of the XPBB-1's ERCO gun turrets. Like other flying boats, the high-performance XPBB-1 employed several small bomb bays between wing ribs and external mounts for torpedoes as shown in the insert. Note the "roller top desk" doors rolled up into bays aft end. *Naval Aviation Archives*, insert *Museum of Flight*

doors were opened, to preclude adverse buffeting. The aircraft showed great potential when delivered on 12 January 1943 for Navy evaluation, also in the Puget Sound area. Boeing took it back later in the month for further tests and final changes.

Plans for PBB-1 production included employing an uprated R-3350 to 2,300hp (1,715kW), eliminating counter-rotation, bomb bays altered for 1,600lb (726kg) weapons, substituting Martin turrets, provisions for a search radar, and a 120V electrical system replacing the 24V. Self-sealing cells could be employed for the most commonly used tanks, augmented by additional fuel carried unprotected.[14]

During the XPBB-1's initial testing period, the B-29 began to dominate Boeing activities. It also became clear USN aviation priorities were moving away from large flying boats to land-based bombers. The Renton plant was traded to the USAAF for B-29 production in exchange for part of the B-25 and B-24 production. The XPBB-1 also used the same engines as the B-29 that had supreme national priority. Consequently, the flying boat was cancelled with a total

$2,185,697 expended.

All this graphically illustrates how the destiny of an aircraft programme is seldom determined solely by its technical merits, for the XPBB-1 was a fine aircraft. It was the heaviest and largest twin-engine flying boat ever built, and the heaviest American twin to that time. The Navy flew the machine to Patuxent River on 5 October 1943 where the official test results demonstrated the XPBB-1 was among the best flying boats ever developed for the service. Single-engine performance was especially praised. Therefore, although the Renton plant was gone, the Navy reconsidered and approached Martin about building PBBs in Baltimore as the Model 230.[15] The 2,500hp (1,864kW) Pratt & Whitney R-4360 was to be substituted and two jet "boost" engines added, the designation

changed to XP4M-1. Martin was likely not keen on this idea and their own landplane design eventually won production as the P4M with the customer's preferred hybrid engine arrangement.

Second Place (PBS)

In competition with the Consolidated XPB2Y-1, the Sikorsky XPBS-1 (9995) was ordered in 1936. The Sikorsky boat initially flew in 1937 and was accepted in 1938. It became the first USN flying boat with a tail turret, this and the nose turret

with a .50cal MG, and two waist .30s. The XPBS-1 spanned 124.0ft (37.8m), grossed 48,540lb (22,017kg), could carry 4,000lb (1,814kg) of bombs to 3,170mi (5,102km), and topped 227mph (365km/h) at 12,000ft (3,658m). The four R-1830-68 delivered 1,050hp (783kW) each. The design had the fuselage aft of the hull shallowed to reduce weight and exterior area. This would become a standard for boats to follow.

Although the Navy passed over the XPBS-1, the advent of war required

every aircraft. The boat continued to be operated in tests and special mission. The solitary example flew until 30 June 1942 when it suffered a landing accident. Vought-Sikorsky built three more of the aircraft as VS-44A commercial boats that were appropriated and operated in USN service as JR2S-1 transports. Any thoughts of reopening production as the PBS was not followed-up.

The Fewest (PB2M)

Even the XPB2Y-1 and XPBS-1 programs did not sate the Navy's desire for large flying boats in the mid 1930s. Martin felt certain it could prove bigger was better. It began preliminary design of their Model

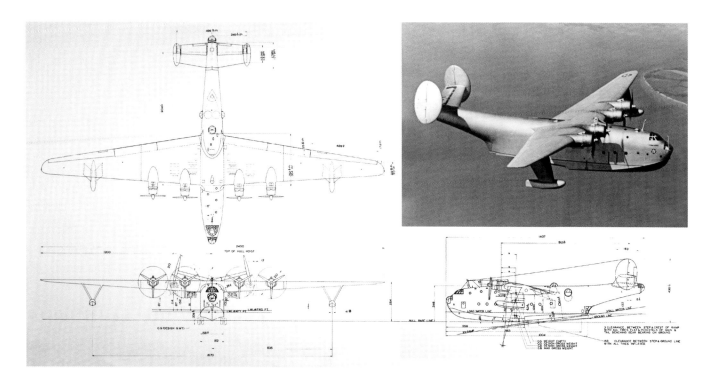

Martin XPB2M-1 characteristics:

span	200.0ft	weight empty	70,684lb
length	117.3ft	gross	140,000lb
height (on beaching gear)	38.4ft	weapon load, maximum	10,000lb
wing area	3,683ft²	speed, max. (4,500ft)	221mph
fuel	9,113gal	cruise	140mph
service ceiling	14,600ft	range (10,000lb bombs)	4,945mi
best climb rate	440fpm	(4,000lb bombs)	6,200mi

Above: These additional perspectives on the XPB2M-1 suggest the sensitive, and so rarely photographed, gun turrets. Soon to be considered 'archaic', the five identical ball turrets had a single .30cal machine gun each. The dorsal and beam turrets were retractable, hatches closing over the openings. *Glenn L. Martin Maryland Aviation Museum,* insert *National Museum of Naval Aviation*

170 in 1937, which was selected in 1938 and a contract signed in January 1939. Detailed design of the XPB2M-1 Mars (1520) commenced that September. It was to be the largest aircraft to that time with 200ft (61m) span and 140,000lb (63,503kg) gross weight.

Initial powerplants for the XPB2M-1 were 2,000hp (1,491kW) R-3350-4 with 17.0ft (5.2m) Schwartz laminated wood, three-blade, reversible propellers. The wing was thick enough to permit access to the engines in flight. Fuel was stored in the belly of the hull. A crew of 11 manned the double-deck interior. Accommodations included separate officer and enlisted berths and lavatories, two messes, wardroom, and state room for the commanding officer. On duty, the aircraft commander manned a desk behind the pilots. Bombs were stacked double on two racks, each with up to five

1,000lb (454kg) bombs or combinations of torpedoes and depth charges. For release, the racks extended, with the doors, on rails within the wing lower surface. Defensive armament was made up of five identical 4.5ft (1.4m) diameter, partially powered ball turrets, each with a single .30cal MG. These were placed in the nose, tail, dorsal, and two waist positions. The waist and dorsal turrets were retractable, the openings covered by moving panels. Another gun was flex-mounted in a tunnel station by the rear step.

Martin heralded the Mars as a flying dreadnought, and treated it as such. Construction began on 20 August 1940 with a formal "keel-laying" ceremony and was completed on 27 September 1941. The formal roll-out was like a battleship launching, with a champagne bottle broken on the bow and the aircraft

sliding backwards into Dark Head Cove on 5 November 1941.

Systems tests were conducted afloat on the Middle River in preparation for taxi tests. On 5 December, the Number 3 engine propeller went to flat pitch instead of reversing and shed a blade. This pierced the fuselage, barely missing the flight engineer, and the engine caught fire. In an effort to save the ship, the anchor was slipped and the aircraft run aground so firemen ashore could combat the flames. The blazing engine soon fell from the wing. The damage was repaired within 30 days, but the decision was made to mount uprated 2,200hp (1,641kW) R-3350-8 engines with 16.5ft (5.0m) Hamilton Standard propellers. This work required half a year such that the maiden flight was delayed until 23 June 1942.

The aircraft was demonstrated to the Navy on 3 July during operations from Chesapeake Bay. Test flights including flying the specified 30,000lb (13,608kg) payload. On 4-5 October, the Mars conducted a closed circuit 4,600mi (7,403km) course,

to other boats then in test and appeared too vulnerable. Further competition for R-3350 engines was unwelcome. Consequently, the decision was made to strip the solitary giant of weapons and modify it as a transport.

Flight test of the XPB2M-1 was suspended on 6 October 1942 so rework could begin. The aircraft, redesignated XPB2M-1R, returned to flight in May 1943 and served until March 1945, remaining the largest American military aircraft throughout the war. A production model followed, but none of the 20 JRM-1s entered service during the war.

Paper Colossus (XPB3Y-1)

Another giant American four-engine flying boat bomber was in development at the start of the war. Consolidated discussed their evolving Model 30 concept with the USN on several occasions, beginning in 1937. It was only after US entry into World War 2, on 2 April 1942, that the Navy reacted fiscally with a contract for a single prototype XPB3Y-1. A partial mockup was ready in October.

The XPB3Y-1 was to rival the largest boats flying anywhere. Empty weight was projected at 57,258lb (25,972kg) and maximum gross 124,700lb (56,563kg), with 3,350-8,400gal (12,681-31,797lit) of fuel. Four of the 2,000hp (1,491kW) R-3350-4 engines made such a monster a reasonable consideration. The wing

Above: This Consolidated concept art suggests the enormous dimensions of their proposed 100,000lb (45,359kg) plus XPB3Y-1 flying boat and the potential difficulties of supporting such a craft afloat. The numerous defensive gun stations are also evident, although the four bomb bays within the thick wings are not shown. *Ray Wagner Collection*

Below: This cutaway drawing shows the interior arrangement of the XPB3Y-1. Note that it was to carry its beaching gear with it in a belly bay. The long patrol missions could require a relief crew, besides the many gunners, and so bunks and kitchenette were featured. *Ray Wagner Collection*

32.3hr endurance flight, setting a new record for a flying boat.

The staggering loss of shipping to U-boats suggested giant aircraft like the Mars would have more value flying high-value, transoceanic freight. The resources required to manufacture a PB2M could produce two or more PBMs that offered more combat capability. The Mars would need to be redesigned with armour, self-sealing fuel tanks, radar, and heavier guns if it was to successfully perform the PB mission. It was also quite slow compared

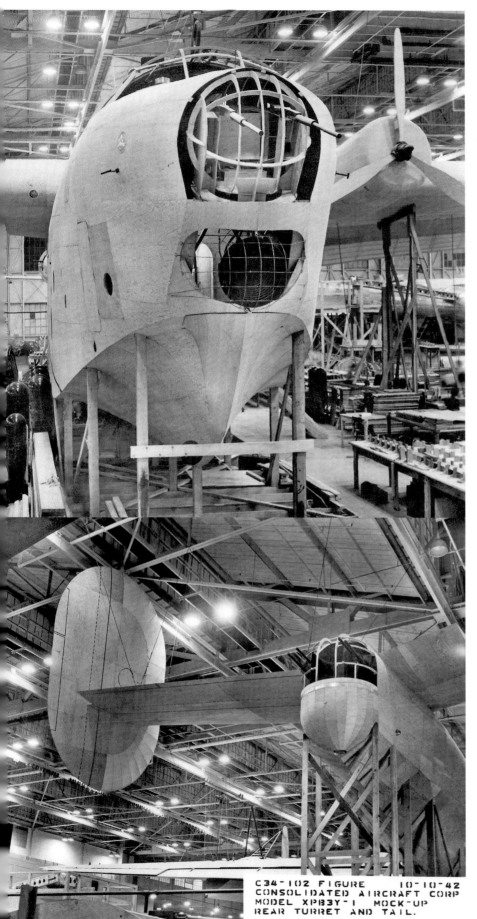

C34-102 FIGURE 10-10-42
CONSOLIDATED AIRCRAFT CORP
MODEL XPB3Y-1 MOCK-UP
REAR TURRET AND TAIL.

was to span 190ft (58m) with an area of 3,200ft² (297m²). Wing float supports would collapse to snug the floats against the bottom of the wing. A classical Consolidated twin tail was planned. Estimated peak speed was 246mph (396km/h) at 6,500ft (1,981m). Service ceiling was to be 21,750ft (6,629m) with best rate of climb 725fpm (4mps). A remarkable 8,200mi (13,197km) range was to be achieved with 4,000lb (1,814kg) of bombs.

Four bomb bays within the wings were to accommodate up to 36,000lb (16,329kg). Defensive weaponry was to be formidable with 11 gun positions consisting of powered nose and tail turrets, powered aft dorsal and forward dorsal turrets (the latter deleted in some drawings), a tunnel position, gunner stations in the root leading edge of each wing and in waist positions, and manned cupolas in the top and bottom of each wing. These last were one man in each wing with one gun to be transferred between top or bottom mounts inside broad ports. The ERCO hydraulic nose turret was to have twin 20mm cannon (400 rounds).[16] The Consolidated tail turret would have four .50 MGs. Much of the other armament was likely 20mm and .50cal. Consequently, the crew of 15 consisted mostly of gunners. As this description suggests, the wing was exceptionally thick, permitting passage to the gun station outboard of the engines. There was considerable space in the fuselage for bunks and a kitchenette.

In the event, the Navy turned away from such gigantic and costly solutions to its maritime bombing requirements. Convair actually encouraged them on 9 September to abandon the PB3Y for a land-based solution.[17] Development and production of the Wright engine was also proving slow and troubled, with the B-29 claiming the lion's share of those issuing forth. The XPB3Y-1 was cancelled on 4 November 1942.

Left: The XPB3Y-1 mockup was completed in fall 1942, but this did not help its prospects. The program was cancelled in November as the Navy turned away from big flying boats. A powered nose turret was to be armed with two 20mm cannon and the tail unit with four .50cal MGs. *National Archives*

Chapter Seven

Anti-Submarine Warfare Shuffle

Dispute

The experience of the Neutrality Patrol illustrated the difficulty of long-range anti-submarine warfare and patrols supporting merchant marine convoys. Even air warfare against surface combatants proved exceptionally challenging. Following the 11 December 1941 declaration of war against Germany and Italy, enemy submarines soon began ravaging shipping in American waters.

Given its other responsibilities, the US Navy simply did not have the resources to mount an adequate aerial patrol to answer the threat. Although maritime patrol was a Navy mission, coastal defence was an Army role that it saw as extending to attacks on vessels with hostile intent. However, both felt this entitled them to land-based bombers and the long-standing dispute endured to World War 2. The new war made clear it would take the combined resources of the Army and Navy to stem the immediate hostile tide. National leadership tasked the Army with supplementing Navy efforts while more aircraft were developed and procured, new technology applied, and personnel trained. This division of authority in performing the vital mission was not ideal, and it required resolution of the angst over command, tactics, and allocation of resources.

The USAAF carried the brunt of the work with ill-suited aircraft and crews learning as they went. The Army initially contributed converted B-18s, and some A-20s and B-25s for patrols while awaiting more effective B-17s and B-24s. The few B-17s that received ASV radar, with Yagi antenna on the nose and wings, were employed from Panama and Pacific coasts. The higher cruise speed and endurance of the four-engine bombers extended their range and

closed remaining gaps in convoy escort. The speed was also more suitable for submarine attack, flying boats carrying minimal bomb capacity and their slower speed giving the submarine too much time to crash dive to a safe depth. The four-engine bombers could also carry more crewmen for watch rotations. The Army soon began operating Hudson and Ventura twins for patrol duties, freeing up heavies for more aggressive missions. The USN had primarily the Catalina to assign the mission. The Army's Havoc was evaluated by the Navy and B-26s bought for training, but neither was adopted for the combat mission.

Navy projects to acquire land-based bombers more suitable to patrol and bombing roles were pursued even before US entry into the war, and this moved into high gear during 1942 after observing B-17 value in searching for the Japanese fleet at Midway. In February 1942, Rear Admiral John Towers, Chief of the Bureau of Aeronautics, requested that a portion of Army bombers be allotted to the Navy for the vital mission. He sought 200 B-24s, 900 B-25s and B-26s, with 200 Liberators and 200 Mitchells transferred by 1 July 1943. The Army proclaimed it would have no such aircraft for release to the sea service given the established war plans.

Countering in March 1942, General Arnold recommended to the Chief of Naval Operations, Admiral Ernest King that the USAAF take over the ASW role entirely. This would include close work with USN vessels. The Navy was disinclined to surrender a maritime mission to the Army. Furthermore, the USN insisted convoy protection was paramount while the Army urged offensive seek-and-destroy patrols.

It took the Chief of Staff, General George Marshall, to mediate a

compromise on 7 July 1942. As already related, the Navy gave up some established flying boat programs and production assets. In exchange, the Army gave the Navy responsibility for the Kansas City plant where North American built B-25s, dropping plans to have the facility transition to B-29 work. Further shuffling of plans and responsibilities ensued, with the encouragement of War Department leadership, until, by September 1942, the matter was settled. The Navy would receive a portion of B-24 and B-25 production, optimised to Navy requirements. The B-26 fell away as the Ventura was substituted.

In the meantime, the Army continued its ASW activities. As USN resources expanded, the service moved to assume full responsibility for the mission. The AAF disbanded its force on 24 August 1943, and some of the specially-configured aircraft, or those with little other utility for the Army, were passed along to the Navy. By the end of the conflict, Navy land-based patrol bombers were becoming the dominant force, the service pursuing 'clean-sheet' designs, and the age of the seaplane was waning.

Combat

The immediate combat requirement was defending shipping off American shores. Although the Germans were active in the east, fear of Japanese attacks on the west coast required action. By June 1942, the U-boats had been largely driven away from the eastern seaboard and the Japanese threat dissolved. Beyond that was the need to arrest the U-boat scourge in the North Atlantic, a struggle that was at its height with staggering losses of shipping and cargo. In that theatre, aircraft from the west and east performed

patrols and convoy cover missions, but range limitations left a 500mi (805km) gap. Introduction of B-24s to ASW in spring 1943, and fighters flying from new escort carriers, closed that void. By the end of May, the Germans refocused their U-boats' efforts and the Allies responded in kind. By summer 1943, the U-boat menace had been effectively muted, but only with application of enormous resources. Beyond countering submarines from all Axis powers, the same aircraft were employed against surface vessels worldwide, both warships and transports.

Advanced and evolving aircraft technology played a significant role in the Allies' success against submarines. Radar was paramount, making patrols more effective in locating the elusive boats. It also permitted ASW missions at night with the addition of searchlights. However, the Germans introduced radar detection systems aboard their submarines to provide adequate warning. The Allies responded with microwave

or centimetric radar that could not be detected by existing systems. The submariners also changed tactics, remaining on the surface to fight back with anti-aircraft deck guns. Weapons beyond bombs and depth charges were also introduced.

The adoption of searchlights followed the British example. Their lights were generally unavailable, so the Americans developed their own during 1942. The idea was to detect the submarine by radar and fly an intercept with intent to pass over the target at 100ft (31m). At 0.75-0.5mi (1.2-0.8km) from the target the light would be switched on and manually trained to illuminate the sub. This allowed the crew to bomb visually and also blinded gunners. Several searchlights were developed and fielded, most as podded systems to be mounted under wings. Some aircraft had a Mk. 23 sight for the searchlight that was coupled with the bombsight, and work was underway to couple the light with the radar. Despite these efforts and some

Above: The frightful toll taken by Axis submarines was addressed by redirecting Air Forces bombers to ASW patrol. The range and payload of the Army aircraft were most valuable in the role, although sorely needed elsewhere. This B-17E over Panama is fitted with ASV radar, aerials visible under nose and wing. *National Museum of the United States Air Force*

operational experience, photographic evidence and personal accounts indicate the searchlights were little used.

The airborne ASW consisted mostly of patrols and flying cover over a convoy. Patrols consisted of flying prescribed patterns over an assigned area in hopes of sighting a surfaced boat or periscope tail, or receiving a radar return worthy of investigation. Flying within a patrol sector required reliable and accurate navigation. LORAN was established to aid this requirement. It also allowed additional forces to be rapidly directed to an area where a target was sighted or had been left damaged.

Crews could fly more than a hundred hours without sighting a enemy vessel, and much more before engaging a target. The patrol was typically at just a few thousand feet altitude or less, and at under 150mph (241km/h). These parameters permitted a quick response to a sighting before the submarine dived below effective depth charge range. Aircraft made their pass at about 50-150ft (15-46m) dropping bombs by pilot judgement or basic timing. They dropped from two to six charges in a line while also firing their guns in the hope of crippling the boat and keeping gunners' heads down. Depth charges had to detonate within 20.0ft (6.1m) of the sub, and before it dived beyond about 25.0ft (7.6m), to achieve significant damage. If forced to the surface or when engaging a ship, the vessel could be attacked with conventional bombs.

When the submariners began firing on attacking aircraft, the bomber crew had to be resolute in their attack. Just forcing the submarine to remain submerged by the presence of the aircraft reduced its speed such that it could not keep up with surface vessels and might lose its quarry. It also prevented the crew from ventilating the boat and recharging batteries. The introduction of the acoustic homing torpedo during 1943 placed even submerged boats at risk.

Redirected

Gap Filler
(Hudson, A-28, A-29, PBO)

The Lockheed Model 14 Super Electra was a fast, twin-engine commercial transport offered to the British in spring 1938 when they came seeking America aircraft. The company recast the aircraft as a navigation trainer, but the Brits saw potential as a light bomber. The RAF purchased the type to replace the less-capable Avro Anson for coastal patrol bombing. The popular 14-passenger Lockheed was the first production aircraft with Fowler flaps, and also featured fixed leading edge slots, and integral fuel tanks. The flaps allowed a smaller wing with high loading for high speed.

In its new military guise, the aircraft's cockpit was optimised for single-pilot operation, but carried a crew of four. The bomber would have a Boulton-Paul electrically powered dorsal turret

Lockheed Hudson I characteristics:			
span	65.5ft	weight empty	11,630lb
length	41.3ft	gross	17,500lb
height (tail down)	11.8ft	weapon load, maximum	1,400lb
wing area	551ft²	speed, max. (6,500ft)	246mph
fuel	644gal	cruise	170mph
service ceiling	25,000ft	range, normal	1,020mi
best climb rate	1,200fpm	max.	1,960mi

with two .303cal MGs (the Americans then possessing no suitable substitute) complemented by two forward-firing .303s fixed in the nose upper deck. The nose also housed the navigator in a new transparent enclosure. A shallow bomb bay accommodating 1,400lb (635kg, typically only 1,000lb/454kg, carried) was created under the wing centresection. More powerful GR-1820-G102A of 1,100hp (820kW) were adopted to turn three-blade, two-position (coarse and fine pitch) propellers. Endurance reached 11hr. The bomber also featured a Sperry autopilot and de-icing boots. Hydraulics operated the undercarriage, flaps, and bay doors.

Lockheed's ability to deliver quickly weighed heavily in the contract decision. The initial document was signed in June 1938 for 200 aircraft at $25,000,000, and the customer would pay for up to 250 if delivered by December 1939. The first Model B14L (later Model 214) or Hudson Mk. I was flying by the end of 1938 with a mocked-up dorsal turret, and deliveries began in February. By expanding operations in Burbank and subcontracting, Lockheed succeeded in meeting the 250 aircraft goal. The 580lb (263kg) turrets was installed after delivery. It was large and draggy, looking incongruous protruding from the aircraft's tapered aft spine. The aircraft quickly proved exceptionally versatile, rugged, and useful. They did, however, require skill to land properly, especially in a crosswind. When invaluable Hudsons were lost to submarines while lashed to the decks of ships, ferry delivery began with these among the first to make the trek routine.

The RAF ordered an additional 100 machines and 28 were passed to the RCAF and 2 to South Africa. The Australians had already placed an order

for 50 machines as Model B14S powered by R-1830-SC3Gs at 1,050hp (783kW). These they called Hudson Mk. Is despite the engine change, but subsequently redesignated Hudson IVs. They initially had a flex-mounted gun in a dorsal hatch before adopting the turret. Delivery of these machines began on 9 February 1940 and was followed by another 50 with minor alterations, known as Mk. IIs to the RAAF but later Mk. IVs. The RAF also ordered 30 of these, with 7 going to Australia. They followed up with 20 Hudson Mk. IIs (Model 314) featuring constant-speed propellers and strengthened airframe elements.

The Mk. III (Model 414) was introduced in August 1940 with the GR-1820-G205A of 1,200hp (895kW), and additional .303 MG defensive armament in a retractable ventral station and two optional beam stations. Bomb capacity was upped to 1,600lb (726kg) and armour was added. A total 428 of the Mk. IIIs were delivered against a series of RAF orders. During the production run, additional wing tankage brought fuel to 1,020gal (3,861lit) from 644gal (2.438lit). These 241 aircraft were denoted Mk. III(LR) while the lower capacity machines were Mk. III(SR). Various methods for shielding and flame-damping the engine exhausts were introduced. The RAF's 409 Mk. Vs substituted the 1,200hp (895kW) R-1830-S3C4G with the two-position propellers. These had the Mk. III's armament and the initial 202 machines the smaller tank capacity as Mk. V(SR)s.

Further sales fell under Lend-Lease after March 1941 and so the Hudson was given American military designations, curiously as an attack aircraft. These began as 52 A-28s (Model 414-08) from a previous Australian Mk. IV order, equipped with military 1,050hp (783kW) R-1830-45s. These were delivered to

the RAAF beginning in December 1941 where they were known as Hudson IVAs. The 450 A-28A (or RA-28A) were Hudson Vs fitted with 1,200hp (895kW) R-1830-67s to become Hudson VIs with constant-speed propellers and alternate troop transport role

The 417 A-29s (also Model 414-56, the first 200 picked up from a commercial order) were built with military Cyclones, R-1820-87s at 1,200hp (895kW), as Hudson Mk. IIIAs. The first 396 of these had the Mk. II(LR) tank capacity. The 383 A-29As (also Hudson IIIAs) had optional troop transport accommodations.

The first RAF aircraft to engage a German aircraft in combat during World War 2 was a Hudson. The long patrols and convoy escort were mixed with some bombing raids against anchored vessels and coastal or inland targets, some missions at night. Its bombing and anti-shipping role in Western Europe was much reduced by summer 1942 as it concentrated on convoy escort and ASW. Detection was enhanced further with the ASV Mk. II coming in the Hudson Mk. III. Additional weapons also enhanced ASW effectiveness. As it became dated for this work by mid 1943, land bombing

and less aggressive missions continued. The RAF retired the type in May 1945.

The USAAF kept 153 RAF A-29s for its own use, almost immediately appending an R prefix. These had .50cal MGs installed in place of the British turret (unavailable) in the dorsal opening with an air deflector ahead. The A-29s were also employed in ASW as a stopgap awaiting more capable equipment, after which they were turned to training. The type claimed the first submarine kill for the USAAF in July 1942. The USAAF also placed its own orders for 217

machines built as AT-18 gunnery trainers and 83 as AT-18A navigational trainers. The former substituted the Martin low-profile, electric, twin-50s turret. The Americans also had a second pilot station added before the tunnel to the nose compartment.

Early US Navy experience with flying boats in the Neutrality Patrol showed their limited utility in the wretched weather and ice of the North Atlantic. Consequently, the service moved on 25 September 1941 to acquire 20 A-29s. These were the first Hudson IIIAs but requisitioned by emergency measure. The first was taken up on 29 October with its delivery from Burbank to Norfolk as PBO-1 Hudsons.[1]

The PBO-1s usually carried four 325lb (147kg) depth charges and were armed with the two .303cal fixed nose guns, two in the Boulton-Paul turret, and one in the ventral station. The guns appear to have been reduced over time, as they were excessive in the areas of operations lacking enemy fighter opposition. The turret was discarded almost immediately.

The USN squadron trained in great haste before deploying in January 1942. The Hudsons were easier to operate than seaplanes, and their speed advantage over the P-boats was immediately evident. Only the mission duration and weapons load were less. They sank the first U-boat for the Americans during March 1942. The PBO remained the sole USN landplane patrol squadron for nearly a year. As the PBY-5A amphibians and PV Venturas began to enter the force, the Hudsons were withdrawn.

Lockheed and its customers transitioned to more advanced types. The firm ultimately manufactured 2,941 Hudsons through May 1943 to include 1,338 direct-purchase, 1,302 Lend-Lease, and 300 trainers, plus a single civil variant. Britain, which received perhaps 2,418 Hudsons, liberally shared them with other Commonwealth forces that saw it deployed worldwide. The Canadians ultimately got 248 and operated them beyond the end of

Above: The US Army seized 153 Hudson IIIAs (A-29s), bound for the RAF, in the emergency following Pearl Harbor. Lacking access to the British dorsal turrets, an air deflector was placed ahead of the hole and a .50cal machine gun mounted in the opening. They also benefited from ASV radar. *National Museum of the United States Air Force*

Below: Still wearing RAF colors, the US Navy PBO-1 would soon dispense with turrets. The 20 Hudsons were diverted from British deliveries in fall 1941 to fill an urgent need for land-based anti-submarine patrol aircraft in the North Atlantic. They served for a year before more advanced types were fielded. *American Aviation Historical Society*

the war. The RNZAF received 100 aircraft of various models, Australia 100 of its own purchase plus an additional 165, and the SAAF two. The Americans also supplied 26 to China and more than 28 to Brazil after that nation declared war on the Axis on 22 August 1943.

Finding Purpose
(Ventura, B-34, B-37, PV)

On the strength of success with the Hudson, the British reacted favourably to Lockheed's September 1939 proposal to create a similar capability from their larger and faster Model 18 Lodestar civil transport. Like the Super Electra, this aircraft also had Fowler flaps and leading edge slots. From several options, the RAF selected the one with more powerful engines as a light bomber replacing the Bristol Blenheim. An initial contract was let in February 1940 for 25 aircraft that evolved into the Model 37. This was to be powered by 1,850hp (1,380kW) GR-2800-S1A4Gs combined with wide "paddle" blade propellers to compensate for inadequate ground clearance for more typical but higher diameter units. The order was expanded to 300 machines on 13 May and the name Ventura I adopted, adding another 375 aircraft ordered in September. Vega Aircraft was selected to manufacture the 675 Venturas in a new Burbank plant.

Detailed design improved on the Hudson's armament. The Boulton-Paul turret was moved forward on the fuselage, for improved field of fire. Initially with twin .303s, four were sported in late production. Two more of the guns were in the apex of the nose on flex mounts. Two forward-firing .50cals

Above: A successor to the Hudson was created from the successful Lockheed Lodestar passenger airplane. Double Wasp engines and a shallow bomb bay yielded the Ventura from Vega. This Ventura I shows to advantage the Boulton-Paul turret and twin .303s in the tunnel station, and possibly tail warning radar. *Naval Aviation Archives*

were fixed in the nose upper deck (1,190 rounds). Another pair of .303s were placed in a prone tunnel station in a fuselage inflexion. The shallow bomb bay accommodated 2,500lb (1,134kg). Gross weight rose 3,300lb (1,497kg) and fuel capacity was reduced by 79gal (299lit) compared with the Lodestar. However, the Wasps and the Fowler flaps ensured good field performance, and it was the first American bomber with metal-skinned control surfaces.

First flight was achieved on 31 July 1941 and deliveries to the RAF began in September, with 18 supplied by year-end. Deliveries by ship from Canada commenced in April 1942. From autumn 1943, some were reworked as Ventura G.R.Is for Coastal Command while others were passed to Commonwealth squadrons.

After 188 Ventura Is, the work turned to the Ventura II. This adopted military R-2800-31s with 2,000hp (1,491kW) and

single-stage/two-speed supercharger, mounting three-blade propellers of 10.6ft (3.2m) diameter. The bomb bay capacity was increased to 3,000lb (1,361kg) to include two 390gal (1,476lit) auxiliary tanks. Weapons of 1,000lb (454kg) or larger required the bay doors to be ajar. A crew of five was standard.

Only 224 Ventura IIs actually went abroad. In early 1942, the US Army began siphoning off Venturas for urgent American employment. This amounted to perhaps 23 Ventura Is and 239 IIs. As these retained an RAF configuration, they were denoted simply as Model 37s, and soon as R-Model 37s after September 1942.

With the advent of Lend-Lease, Vega was to build 200 Ventura IIAs or B-34s (Model 137) under a 13 August 1941 contract with Britain and then 550 from on an 8 August USAAF contract. The first was accepted in September 1941 and production ran through November 1942. These substituted the Martin turret with twin .50s (800 rounds) for the unavailable Boulton-Paul, American .30s (2,000 rounds) replaced the British .303s in the tunnel and nose apex, and standard US radios and bomb racks were installed. A .30cal would occasionally be installed on each side of the cabin as waist guns through field modifications.

Ultimately, the US Army carried away

Lockheed Hudson IIIA, A-29, PBO-1 characteristics:

span	65.5ft	weight empty	12,680lb
length	44.3ft	gross	18,837lb
height (tail down)	11.8ft	max.	20,203lb
wing area	551ft²	weapon load, maximum	1,600lb
fuel	644gal	speed, max. (15,300ft)	262mph
service ceiling	26,200ft	cruise	129mph
best climb rate	1,450fpm	range, patrol (1,300lb bombs)	1,750mi
takeoff distance*	1,800ft	max.	1,890mi
landing distance*	2,000ft		
*over 50ft obstacle			

most of the Ventura IIAs such that the RAF received just 25 as direct delivery. The first 20 USAAF examples retained their RAF configuration and became, in October 1942, RB-34s for non-combat missions and 13 became B-34B navigator trainers. The remainder would be denoted B-34A/RB-34A However, some 66 or so were subsequently sent to the RAF and Commonwealth forces. All the USAAF RB-34As were employed in non-combat roles.

Lockheed was to manufacture the 550 B-34s, replacing the R-2800s with 1,700hp (1,268kW) R-2600-13s, carrying single-stage/two-speed superchargers, as an armed reconnaissance and observation variant. These were initially to be designated O-56s and Ventura IIIs, then RB-34Bs (before that designation was applied to the 13 B-34B navigator trainers), finally becoming B-37 Lexingtons. These would carry 2,000lb (907kg) of bombs and two cabin fuel cells. The B-37 sported the two fixed .50cal bow guns, a third .50 flex gun in the nose and two in the turret, two .30cal MGs in the ventral station, and two .30s fitted in recessed waist stations.[2] Empty weight dropped to 18,615lb (8,444kg) while gross remained 22,500lb (10,206kg). Consequently, the power reduction cut top speed to 298mph (480km/h) from 312mph (502km/h). The first B-37

was taken aloft on 21 September 1942. However, the order was cancelled after just 18 machines, delivered in January-April 1943 to become quickly RB-37s, because plant capacity was required for higher priority work.

The USAAF had Vega study a ground attack variant of the Ventura as the Model V-142 featuring heavy forward-firing weapons, but this fell by the wayside.[3]

The USAAF Model 37s and B-34s served ocean patrol duties until withdrawn to non-combat functions. Some would have the turret removed and ASV radar installed across the fuselage top and beneath the wings. With the Navy assuming full responsibility for the anti-submarine patrol and assigned a share of land-based bombers, the Army ceased acquiring the type. The 7 July 1942 agreement had all outstanding Ventura procurement redirected to the Navy, and that service assumed oversight of the Vega plant at the end or the year.

The RAF was already losing interest in the Ventura. They were notably fast and with a pleasingly high climb rate. However, as bombers over Europe the RAF found them too vulnerable and so most were employed by Coastal Command. Consequently, all subsequent production went to the USN. The sea service had Vega begin work on a navalised Ventura IIA/B-34, to become the PV-1, while looking ahead to a more extensive alteration, the PV-2. In the meantime, the final 27 Ventura IIs on the RAF contract, taken up by the USAAF as Model 37s, were passed to the US Navy in September 1942 and designated PV-3.

The Navy carried on production with additional contracts. The PV-1 (Model 237) designation denoted a strictly ocean patrol and maritime attack role mission. It had fuel capacity expanded 262gal (992lit). This was distributed in 807gal (3,055lit) of wing and fuselage tanks, two drop tanks of 155gal (587lit) each, and two bomb bay auxiliary tanks of 210gal (795lit) forward and 280gal (1,060lit) aft (carrying both displaced all weapons). Self-sealing cells (excluding the bay tank) amounted to 1,055lb (478kg) and 763lb (346kg) of armour plate was distributed throughout the aircraft. At maximum fuel, the good field performance of the Ventura was finally impacted. The nose flex guns were deleted to accommodate

the AN/APS-3 installed in a 'solid' nose. At patrol altitude, detection range was about 80mi (129km). A bombardier station was retained farther aft in the nose, with bombsight window in the bottom. The bomb bay was adjusted to take six 325lb (147kg) depth charges or one Mk. 13-2 torpedo. Carrying the torpedo required the inner bay door segments to be removed so the weapon could protrude. A 1,000lb (454kg) bomb

or two 500lb (227kg) bombs could replace a drop tank. Late production PV-1s were augmented with eight zero-length stubs for 5in HVAR rockets under the wings and an optional trio of .50s (750 rounds) was installed as a chin pack under the nose. This covered the bombsight window as the bombardier station was eliminated. This allowed the crawlway to the nose to be eliminated and a second pilot station was added.

Maiden flight of the PV-1 on 3 November 1942 permitted deliveries to begin the following month. Vega ultimately manufactured 1,600 PV-1s through May 1944. Despite the original intent to direct all to the Navy, 387 PV-1s were taken up by the RAF as Ventura IVs and G.R.Vs for long-range reconnaissance and maritime patrol, many also equipping associated dominion squadrons. French and Brazilian units appear to have been supplied directly by the Americans.

With encouragement from the Navy, Vega undertook a more substantial alteration of the Ventura to meet more

optimally maritime missions while awaiting purpose-built aircraft still in conceptual design. The work yielded the PV-2 Harpoon (Model 15). To recover takeoff and landing performance while retaining the R-2800-31s, wingspan was extended with a new outer wing panel and the tail group entirely redesigned with enlarged surfaces for improved ground handling and single engine-out control. Fuel capacity was increased by 258gal (977lit) with integral tanks in the outer wing panels. The pack guns were made standard, complementing the two bow guns (250rpg). The Martin 250CE-13 turret (400rpg) was equipped with gyro-computing gunsight and could be locked forward for firing by the pilot. The two guns in the tunnel station became .50s. Internal bomb load increase to 4,000lb

(1,814kg) and the doors bulged for more volume and allowing the torpedo to be entirely enclosed. Added in the area of the hardpoints were zero-length rocket launchers for eight 3.5in or 5in HVARs. Two exhaust heat exchangers provided leading edges with anti-ice. An alcohol system gave anti-ice to the windscreen and propellers. Major components of the airframe could be disassembled for repair or replacement.

An order for 500 PV-2s was placed on 30 June 1943, and three subsequent contracts added up to 908 additional Harpoons. After a maiden flight on 3 December 1943 from the Lockheed Air Terminal, deliveries commenced in March 1944. The haste of getting the PV-2 into production was telling in several early problems. Initial testing

Above: Vega evolved the Ventura again into a navalized PV-1 with additional fuel and armour, bomb bay revisions, and ASD radar under a nose radome. This example, fitted with rocket launch stubs beside the external tanks, also shows the nose deck guns and bombardier nose windows. *National Museum of Naval Aviation*

found the landing gear drag struts deficient. The wing skins wrinkled and fuel leaked, prompting modifications that included a 6in (15cm) reduction in span. This proving inadequate, a redesign was necessary, requiring modifications to machines coming off the line. This was undertaken in Van Nuys, California, and slowed deliveries such that only 69 PV-2s were taken up by the Navy during 1944. The first 30 aircraft could not be suitably modified, so were accepted as PV-2Cs and relegated to training with

Lockheed-Vega PV-1 characteristics:

span	65.5ft	weight empty	19,190lb
length	51.8ft	gross	31,000lb
height (tail down, antenna top)	14.3ft	weapon load, int.+ext.	3,000+2,000lb
wing area	551ft²	speed, max. (15,200ft)	313mph
fuel (int.+bay & ext.)	823+790gal	cruise	170mph
service ceiling (26,500lb)	25,500ft	range, patrol (1,950lb bombs+tanks)	1,575mi
initial climb rate (26,500lb)1,665fpm		bombing (3,000lb bombs)	1,350mi
takeoff distance (calm, 26,500lb)	1,259ft	ferry	2,545mi

Right: The deeper bomb bay of the PV-2 permitted fully enclosed carriage of the Mk. 13-2 torpedo whereas previous models had to carry the weapon partially exposed with the inboard bay door segments removed. This PV-2 has zero-length rocket launchers and shows well the three .50cal guns in the under-nose pack. *National Archives*

permanent flight restrictions. These also suffered repeated leaks in the outboard integral tanks, having not been sealed properly by the Arizona subcontractor, and these tanks were bypassed. Self-sealing tanks were substituted for subsequent production. Consequently, the first squadron did not deploy until March 1945 where they saw some action in patrol, anti-shipping attacks, and shore bombing before the end of the war.

The aircraft ordered beyond the original 500 were to have eight forward-firing .50s as PV-2Ds. However, the end of the war prompted cancellation of these orders with only 35 delivered through September 1945, some passed to the Portuguese. Nine standard PV-2s were supplied to New Zealand and Brazil.

The Vega aircraft was in its element as a naval patrol bomber and found success with American units. The Venturas were active in the final year of the war, mostly in the Aleutians and Pacific theatres with operations that included long-range formation bombing missions. Retaining the R-2800-31, the added weight and drag

7-D Lockheed-Vega PV-2 characteristics:

span	74.9 ft	weight empty	21,028lb
length	52.1ft	gross	33,668lb
height (tail down, antenna top)	14.4ft	max.	36,000lb
wing area	686ft²	weapon load, int.+ext.	4,000+2,000lb
fuel (int.+bay & ext.)	1,150+557gal	speed, max. (13,700ft)	282mph
service ceiling	23,900ft	cruise	171mph
initial climb rate	1,630fpm	range (1,950lb bombs)	1,790mi
		ferry	2,930mi

Below and right: The evolution of wartime radar is evident in this image of the neat APS-3 mounted in the nose of a PV-2 with radome removed. The 18-inch parabolic antenna swept 180º. The radar operator station in the cabin is shown right. *National Archives*

were delivered from June 1943 through February 1944. These PBJ-1Ds were like the -1Cs but with a production tail gun graced with the raised gunner housing as on Hs and Js, waist gunner positions, four side "package" guns on the side of the nose, and 10 under-wing 5in HVAR stubs. As discussed previously, the D featured 1,000lb (454kg) capacity wing hardpoints for mounting bombs and a belly rack for a torpedo. Both models accommodated the standard 2,000lb (907kg) maximum internal bomb load.

The initial C and D models were equipped with AN/APS-2 radar. This was installed in place of the ventral turret that had a bad reputation and was perceived to have little value in the low-altitude missions of the PBJ. The radome provided 360° scan and was retractable. Many of the APS-2s were later replaced with AN/APS-3 in a protruding nose housing ("hose nose") for the 18in (46cm) parabolic antenna and possessed 145° sweep. Other gear fitted included LORAN receivers and radar altimeters.

degraded speed and climb by comparison to the PV-1, but the PV-2's range and other attributes earned it respect.

Vega produced 3,028 Venturas and Harpoons between July 1941 and September 1945. It offered the PV-2 to the USAAF in a Model V-147 configuration, unofficially designated XB-34B, but this was not pursued.[4] A proposed PV-4 (Model V-154) was to be a PV-2 with C-Series R-2800s delivering 2,100hp (1,566kW), revised armament, and beefed-up landing gear. However, the end of the war spelled the end of this effort.

Diversion (PBJ)

The June 1942 agreement with the Army gave the USN a share of B-25s from Kansas City. However, a mix of models were sought that also saw substantial numbers of aircraft delivered from Inglewood (C, G, and H) in addition to Kansas (D and J). The Navy took 188 aircraft delivered in 1943, 395 in 1944, and 123 in 1945, all diverted from Army orders. These were revised, as required, to carry depth charges, mines, and torpedoes in the bomb bay, or a 265gal (1,003lit) auxiliary tank, and Navy radios. These alterations were performed via modifications, delaying delivery. Martin performed the majority of such work at its modification centre in Kansas City while the Ds were modified at Convair's Elizabeth, New Jersey Modification Center.

By initial deliveries in February 1943, the U-boat threat in the Americas had receded. The bombers then appeared to have greater value for anti-shipping missions in the Pacific, supporting

landings, and interdiction during land campaigns that included striking enemy bases beyond the range of fighters. Hence, the aircraft equipped USMC medium bomber units. These became their first multi-engine combat aircraft, and with more than two seats, since the 1920s. The greater firepower in supporting ground forces, compared with USMC fighters, was most welcome.

The initial order was for a modest number of B-25Cs and Ds. These included 50 B-25Cs designated PBJ-1Cs and delivered from February-April 1943. (The model suffixes would parallel USAAF designations.) These featured a 'glass' bombardier nose with one flex-mounted .50cal machine gun and two fixed in the starboard side, and retained the dorsal turret. Some of the machines would later get a prone tail gun station as a field modification. The 152 B-25Ds

cannon was not popular owing to a dearth of suitable targets and the long lineup run. The eight-gun strafer nose was favoured to replace the cannon installation, but even this was relatively rare. The AN/APQ-5 low level radar bombsight was also installed in some aircraft.

The Mitchells found ready work in the Pacific during the "island hopping campaign" with a never-ending need for anti-shipping and general attack assets. Following a landing, the carriers would soon depart for other missions, taking away their fighters and attackers. The Marines were all-too-eager to fill the gap. The first USMC PBJ squadrons deployed to the South Pacific where their first action was in March 1944. Given their radar, night anti-shipping and intruder missions predominated early on, as well as bombing Japanese installations and bypassed garrisons ashore.

The Marines' use of depth charges as concussion bombs may have been unique.[5] Other important ordnance included HVARs and napalm. They also fired Tiny Tim rockets from the PBJs during the closing months of World War 2. This was a 1,290lb (585kg) projectile of 11.75in (29.85m) diameter and 10.25ft (3.12m) length with 500lb (227kg) warhead. It used the standard aerial bomb casing matched to steel oil well piping for rocket propellant. Developed by CalTech during 1944, it was first successfully air-launched in June. The tremendous motor blast on ignition could cause aircraft damage and much time was expended finding a suitable launch method. For the PBJ, this became a belly mount of two rockets, each dropped on dual lanyards for ignition at about 10ft (3m) from the aircraft that also used the APQ-5 bombsight. The two external weapons cut bomber speed by 12mph (19km/h). No radar targets presented themselves justifying night use of the rocket, and few visually acquired ships of any value were left. Of the few rockets fired, only one hit was scored.

Further acquisitions through June 1945 included 248 PBJ-1H and 255 PBJ-1J. The -1H retained the 75mm T13E1 cannon, joined by four .50s in the nose, four "pack" guns, waist gunners, dorsal turret, a Bell M-7 twin-gun tail turret, APS-3 on the starboard wingtip, plus radar altimeter. The PBJ-1J had the a glass nose containing one flex-mounted and one fixed gun, and dual cockpit controls. Alternatively, a "solid" four- or eight-gun nose could be fitted to serve as a strafer and ground attack machine. The wingtip radar installation gave about 125° coverage while complicating lateral balance and maintenance. Consequently, the nose mount was favoured and sometimes substituted in the field. One PBJ-1G was taken on.

Field modifications were common for the USMC Mitchells as combat requirements shifted in the final year. Waist stations with small window hatches were given "bay" windows, a tail gunner top housing, and guns and armour were added, particularly to acquire more effective strafers. Later, as the Japanese fighter threat slackened, units removed armour, guns and associated fairings to permit more bombs, rockets, or fuel. Sometimes reduced to just one tail gun, these were some of the lightest armed Mitchells of the war. As with the Army, the H's 75mm

Left: This series of photos record an April 1945 test shot of a Tiny Tim rocket from a PBJ-1H over Inyokern, California. The 1,290lb (585kg) weapon, with 500lb (227kg) warhead, swung down on twin lanyards before firing to reduce the motor ignition shock wave impact on the aircraft.
San Diego Air & Space Museum

Only half the USMC Mitchell squadrons saw combat before the end. In all, the Corps lost 99 of their PBJ-1s during the war, 59 to operational causes with 26 in combat. They discarded the Mitchell soon after.

Meaning Business (PB4Y)

Army B-24s diverted from the bombing offensive for ASW sacrificed some armour and defensive weapons, while fitting bay long-range tanks. Seventeen LB-30s were sent to the Panama Canal Zone in March-April 1942 to help hunt U-boats. They were fitted with ASV Mk. II radar units from Canada during the summer. Three more were posted to Alaska and six to Hawaii. In time, B-24Ds were committed to the task, still with early metric radar and Yagi antennas. Depth charges were introduced to the Liberator, usually as eight 650lb (295kg) weapons. In time, the Army equipped the bombers with the ASV-10 centimetric radar. Later still B-24Js had SCR-717 units for anti-shipping operations.[6] Also added were radar altimeter, sonobuoys, and LORAN.[7]

Liberators operated by Britain from Ireland and Iceland, and by the USAAF from Newfoundland and Greenland, helped fill the mid-Atlantic gap. Having

thus shown their value, some 77 of the B-24s were transferred to the Navy when that service assumed full responsibility for the ASW mission.* As a whole, with the 8,000lb (3,629kg) of ordnance, exceptional long range, and large crew complement, the Liberator was superior to flying boat PBs. The agreement with the Army ensured further supply of these warplanes.

Navy Liberators were initially B-24D line with few changes. Delivered as PB4Y-1s beginning in August 1942, the first seven were in hand by September. The flow slowly increased. This was fortunate because the need was so urgent in the

* The USAAF B-24s turned over to the Navy in August 1943 were in exchange for a like number of Liberators programmed for delivery to the Navy.

Pacific, the first squadron deploying there in January 1943 before having completed all planned training. Navy and Marine squadrons were soon flying in both oceans with notable success.

The Navy took on 278 B-24Ds, many of these passing through modification centres for installation of Navy-unique gear. The ERCO power nose turret from the XPBB-1 replaced the Convair or Emerson units beginning with the 112th example in May 1943, offering improved armour and field of fire. The USN Liberators were generally characterised by eight .50cal MGs paired in the nose, dorsal, and tail turrets, and one in each waist station, with a total 3,770 rounds. There was also 1,318lb (598kg) of armour and 2,110lb (957kg) devoted to fuel cell protection.[8] Many acquired ASV radar via modification, initially as 'comb' antennas under the wings. As with other patrol aircraft, the ventral turret was judged of little value, the APS-15 surface search radar substituted in its place on some of the aircraft.

The B-24Ds were followed by 368 B-24Js, 186 Ls, and 145 Ms, for a total 977 PB4Y-1s without separate suffix distinctions. The last was delivered in January 1945. All but one were manufactured in San Diego.

Dozens were devoted to non-PB missions. The PB4Y-1s served several years beyond the war.

Efforts to improve the anti-submarine punch of the B-24 included tests with a 37mm cannon but this was found to have little advantage over .50cal MGs. An attempt to introduce rockets to the Liberator was tried with B-24D (42-40830) during late 1943. Rails were attached within the bomb bay and on bay doors designed to open out. These were to fire 16 of the 60.0lb (27.2kg) Mk. XX Vertical Anti-Submarine Rockets. The first attempts, using surrogate rockets, nearly blew the forward doors off their tracks.[9] This USAAF work was carried on by the Navy. A PB4Y-1 (former B-24D) was given rocket rails on the forward fuselage; three on each side under the pilot side windows and a pair under each of these at the bottom of the nose. These were apparently for 0.5in HVAR projectiles and may have sought to reproduce success the British enjoyed with rocket rails under forward fuselage stub winglets on Liberators IIIs and Vs for 16 HVARs. No other information on the American modification has come to light.

Experience with the Liberator suggested changes that would make the type better suited to the PB role and also replace the PB2Y. (A proposed twin-engine Coronado variant, offered in 1942, was considered under the designation P5Y, but rejected.)[10] The service ordered three prototypes of a redesigned bomber (32086, 32095/6), the XPB4Y-2 Privateer (Model 40 then 100), in May 1943 via conversion from PB4Y-1s. A contract for 660 examples was placed on 15 October 1943 before a production-representative X-plane had flown.

Principal changes for the Privateer were a revised fuselage extending the forebody 7.0ft (2.1m) for a flight engineer station and RCM operator station. The flight engineer was considered essential for reducing pilot workload on long patrol missions. The poor lateral stability of the Liberator at low altitudes was addressed with a new single-fin empennage tested on the XB-24K. The lighter 1,350hp (1,007kW) R-1830-94 were adopted without turbos, sacrificing high altitude performance for low altitude speed. The installation was reworked to place the oil coolers above and below the engine.

Above: This PB4Y-1, former USAAF B-24D, has gained a nose turret and was subsequently employed in rocket trials, probably during 1944. The ten forward fuselage rails, most probably for HVAR projectiles, are nested beside the radar aerials. The installation bears some resemblance to an earlier RAF modification to ASW Liberators.
National Museum of Naval Aviation

The propellers were selected for efficient low-altitude cruise and given fluid de-ice. The engine accessories section was adopted from the Pratt & Whitney R-2000 (a revised R-1830) and a new electrical system was introduced. There were also mounts for eight JATO units.

The bomb bay was optimised for naval weapons and could also carry up to four 400gal (1,514lit) auxiliary tanks. Armour was reduced to 1,171lb (531kg) and armament expanded to a dozen .50cals in six power turrets. These were a ERCO hydraulic bow ball (800 rounds), Convair tail unit (1,000rpg), two Martin electric dorsal units (800 rounds), and protruding ERCO hydraulic side balls in teardrop fairings (500rpg). For downward firing, the rounds converged 30.0ft (9.1m) below the aircraft, so the ventral ball turret was eliminated.

The Navy standardised on the AN/APS-2 S-band search radar that could also be coupled to the AN/APQ-5 low level radar bombsight. For high-altitude work, there was the AN/APS-15B in an extendable fairing under the forward fuselage. Other navigation gear included LORAN, the radar altimeter, and IFF. Additional small fairings on the bottom of the fuselage contained radar and communications intercept receivers and jammer transmit antennas. Internal equipment allowed signals analysis and direction finding. Consequently, the typical crew of 11 included two radar and RCM operators.

The maiden flight of the first XPB4Y-2 was on 20 September 1943, although this aircraft still had the B-24 tail, turbos, and dummy turrets. The second example, flying on 30 October, was similar except with the planned turrets. This aircraft was then modified with the new tail and turned over on 2 February 1944. Both retained the original engine and nacelle configurations. The third prototype was supposed to be production-representative when flown on 15 December 1944, but stability deficiencies had been uncovered during tests earlier in the year at Patuxent River that required the vertical tail to be extended. Consequently, the machine was not accepted in its final configuration until 29 March 1944.

The initial production Privateer flew on 15 March 1944, but was not accepted until the 31st owing to required changes. Deliveries remained slow for the next few months as initial aircraft went through rework. Official deliveries of completed examples were in June and

squadrons began receiving them August. Only the 101st example, delivered on 23 September, and subsequent had the ERCO nose turret. Prior examples retained the Convair A6B unit and were referred to as PB4Y-2C.

Combat deployments began after the New Year. The Privateer first entered combat theatres on 6 January 1945, too late for the squadrons to leave much of a mark except anti-shipping operations during the Okinawa campaign.

Another Privateer contract for 710 aircraft was dated 19 October 1944, but only 79 were delivered from this order before the cessation of hostilities brought the end of production in October at a total 736 PB4Y-2s, all built in San Diego. Some 61 of the aircraft were expended during the conflict. The Privateer remained in service for more than a decade after the war. {7-E

Purpose-Built

Longevity (XP2V-1)
Observing how its light transports were being employed, Lockheed perceived the US Navy would desire purpose-built patrol bombers of markedly superior capabilities to the Hudsons

and Venturas. To this end, Vega began an internal design project in September 1941, anticipating a Navy requirement. The initial goal was a 25,000-35,000lb (11,340-15,876kg) aircraft with tricycle undercarriage equipped with power turrets and the required mix of ordnance. The effort was slowed by more pressing work after America entered the war.

As the conflict progressed, requirements for the latent design became clearer. The mission evolved from escort to search-and-engage, with the Pacific war demanding greater capabilities. The aircraft had to be fast, with tremendous range, but short

Above: The Navy took the B-24 in a different direction with their PB4Y-2 Privateer configuration. Most notable was the longer nose with radar radomes beneath, single tail, two dorsal turrets, ERCO beam turrets, lack of ventral ball turret, and reoriented nacelles without turbos. The model did not appear in-theatre until 1945. *National Museum of Naval Aviation*

field performance was also a primary consideration. The design, V-135 (later V-146), finally attracted Navy attention with a Letter of Intent issued 19 February 1943 to acquire two XP2V-1 prototypes (48237/8).†
Vega was subsumed within Lockheed in

† Although the aircraft had a considerable bomb bay and the mission included weapons delivery, the B was dropped from the designation as it had been for the PV series.

7-E Convair PB4Y-2 characteristics:

span	110.0ft	weight empty	37,405lb
length	74.6ft	gross	64,000lb
height	29.1ft	max.	70,231lb
wing area	1,048ft²	weapon load, maximum	8,000lb
fuel (int.+bay)	2,364+1,600gal	speed, max. (14,000ft)	248mph
service ceiling	19,500ft	cruise	158mph
best climb rate	1,090 fpm	range (4,000lb bombs)	2,630mi
		patrol	2,900mi
		ferry	3,530mi

November 1943. The design then became the Lockheed Model 26. A formal order for the aircraft was placed on 4 February 1944, the contract following on 4 April. An order for 15 pilot-production P2V-1s was placed ten days later, these for service trials.

The pace continued to be slow until summer 1944 when resources were finally freed up to move ahead smartly. The design changed a bit from initial conception. The wing was lowered and the tail altered. A retractable searchlight, within its own enclosed bay, and a ventral turret were deleted. An order for 151 machines was issued on 16 December 1944.

The P2V was designed for rapid wartime manufacturing but still incorporated advanced features. Engines were to be replaceable in just 30min and the airframe could be disassembled into major components. Steerable nose wheel and self-sealing fuel tanks were standard. A laminar-flow airfoil was rejected because of its sensitivity to roughness (low-flying sea patrol aircraft collecting salt on their surfaces). Instead, another low-drag design was developed. Sealed volumes within the wing ensured flotation in the event of ditching. Fowler flaps, augmented by ailerons drooped 10°, facilitated short takeoff. An extensive anti-ice system

supported the all-weather mission.

The noticeably large vertical tail gave good directional stability to reduce pilot workload in long, low-speed flight, in foul weather, and for single-engine operation. To provide similar qualities in the pitch axis while avoiding the excessive stability and drag influences of an overly large horizontal tail, and the need for boost, the engineers devised a clever elevator design. Called the Varicam (variable camber), this employed an electrically articulated aft portion of the horizontal stabiliser to which the manually actuated elevator was attached. It created a more pronounced camber change than the elevator alone for greater control effectiveness, and the elevator could be smaller for lighter forces.

The aircraft was powered by two 2,300hp (1,715kW) R-3350-8s, each with a two-stage supercharger. In front of these were four-blade props with reversing. The shallow bomb bay provided for a mix of weapons from two Mk. 13 torpedoes to depth charges and mines totaling 8,000lb (63,629kg). Four 250gal (946lit) tanks could also be installed in the bay. Manned turrets were planned for the nose (500rpg), tail (500rpg, a B-17G unit), and dorsal (400rpg) positions, all with

Above: This PB4Y-2 emphasizes the nose "warts". On the centerline is the partially retracted APS-15 radar radome, a retractable APS-2 radar fairing forward of this not seen. The antennas on the "corners" of the nose are for radio and radar intercept and countermeasures (jamming). This gear meant additions to the aircrew. *National Museum of Naval Aviation*

twin .50s. Armour and flak curtains were standard. A crew of seven was planned, with two pilots, navigator/bombardier/ nose gunner, radio operator, radar/RCM operator, and two gunners. The crew could move between the forward and aft compartments of the unpressurised aircraft by sliding across the top of the wing box beam. An APS-8 radar in a belly fairing was planned for production.

The first XP2V-1, the type by then named Neptune, flew on 17 May 1945 from the Lockheed Air Terminal in Burbank. A spring tab on the rudder was later deleted after it contributed to a mishap and was judged nonessential. The dorsal turret would be lowered for production to reduce drag, and the fin extension running to the turret would be deleted as its weight and drag did not balance its benefits. Aircraft handling in flight was uninspiring.

The production order backlog was

Above: The Lockheed XP2V-1 Neptune evinced many aspects of late-WWII bombers when it emerged in the final months of the war. All three turrets were fitted with twin .50 machine guns. The tricycle landing gear included a steerable nose gear. The Fowler flaps and drooped ailerons provided good short-field performance. *National Archives*

slashed by 48 aircraft after VJ-Day, and again by 52 to just 51 aircraft. However, the type went on to enjoy one of the longest production runs of any aircraft and evolved considerably beyond the initial design.

Navy's Own (XP4M-1)
As with the XP2V-1, a replacement for the PB4Y was also sought in 1944 for the land-based, long-range maritime patrol mission.

Another motivation was acquiring an aircraft to lay mines during the expected invasion of Japan.[11] Martin's Model 219 was selected for development, two XP4M-1s (02789/90) ordered on 6 July 1944. A mockup was ready in September.

The large aircraft might require four engines for takeoff and to deliver speed for escaping a threat, but most of a patrol mission was slow 'droning'. Hence, Martin conceived an aircraft with two powerful reciprocating engines for continuous use and a turbojet engine in each nacelle that would be used only when the additional thrust was required. This promised more economy than the PB4Y, allowing 16hr patrols, yet with similar heavy payload capacity but

reduced drag with just two nacelles. In the front of each nacelle was a 2,975hp (2,218kW) R-4360-4 Wasp Major with single-stage/variable-speed supercharger and 15.0ft (4.6m) diameter, four-blade, reversible pitch propeller. Behind each and beneath the wing was a 3,825lbf (17,014N) thrust Allison J33-A-17 jet engine with a hinged sugar scoop-like inlet "shutter" that closed when the engine was secured. This 4.2ft (1.3m) diameter turbojet had a centrifugal compressor with straight-through combustors. The four powerplants would all burn the same 100 octane fuel.

With nacelles fully consumed with powerplants, the main gear wheels folded outboard into the wing, although projecting below the surface and without enclosing doors. The inboard wing segments airfoil was optimised for high lift while the outboard segment was optimised for cruise.

The aircraft exceeded the Privateer in size and weight, with 114ft (35m) span, 1,311ft² (122m²) wing area, and a gross weight in the order of 75,000lb (34,019kg). There would be more than 650lb (295kg) of armour in the aircraft. Remarkably, a top speed with all four engines operating of 400mph (644km/h) and climb rate exceeding 2,000fpm

Lockheed XP2V-1 characteristics:			
span	100.0ft	weight empty	32,651lb
length	75.3ft	gross	54,527lb
height	28.5ft	max.	58,000lb
wing area	1,000ft²	weapon load, maximum	8,000lb
fuel, max.	2,350-3,350gal	speed, max. (15,600ft)	289mph
service ceiling	23,300ft	cruise	163mph
best climb rate	1,120fpm	range (2,600lb bombs)	2,879mi
takeoff over 50ft obs.	2,841ft	ferry (max. fuel)	4,210mi

(10mps) was anticipated. A service ceiling around 34,000ft (10,363m) was projected. Range with a modest payload and 170mph (274km/h) cruise was to be approximately 2,800mi (4,506km). This would rise to 4,000mi (6,437km) with bomb bay fuel cells.

The XP4M-1 was to have a crew of eight that included the two pilots, navigator/bombardier, radio/radar operator, RCM operator, and three gunners. It was planned from the beginning to have a radar in ventral radome. Three manned turrets included an Emerson turret in the bow with two .50cal MGs (400rpg), Martin 250CE-324 with twin .50s (400rpg), and Martin X220CH-2 tail with two 20mm cannon (300rpg). The bow turret was placed to permit a tremendous 180° of elevation and azimuth motion. A radome under the tail turret was evidence it was intended to be fired via radar means as well. As the mission did not require pressurisation, a flex-mounted .50cal (300rpg) was

Right: This drawing of the Martin XP4M-1 closely resembles the aircraft built except for lacking bomb bay door lines and nose guns. The inlets for the jet engine at the front of the nacelles are open, and the circular exhausts in the rear are evident. Note also the exposed main wheels.
Air Force Flight Test Center

placed in each of two waist ports. The bomb bay, enclosed by bi-fold doors, was long and shallow to permit any of a mix of weapons to be dropped as desired. It accommodated 12,000lb (5,443kg) of bombs, torpedoes, depth charges, and mines, or four fuel tanks adding 1,400gal (5,300lit). There was the requisite tube for sonobuoy deployment.

The XP4M-1 was still in construction at war's end, and did not fly for a year more. It proved a good aircraft, but several problems with the initial design were evident. Amongst these was the 2,000psi (13,790kPa) hydraulic system

Above: The purpose-built XP2V-1 was markedly superior to the ersatz twin-engine patrol aircraft that preceded it. It was built for rapid and simple construction, yet included enough advanced features to give it outstanding performance and utility. The R-3350 was tightly cowled but suitably cooled by clever flap design. Naval Aviation Archives

being found inadequate and uprated to 3,000psi (20,684kPa). It was discovered the outboard wing segments stalled first, contributing to unfortunate stall characteristics. A number of factor scontributed to only 19 much-altered P4Ms being procured.

141

Chapter Eight

The Very Heavy Race

Bulking Up

The Air Forces' four-engine heavy bombers were justified as required to destroy distant air bases under the concept of hemispheric defence. However, when Roosevelt asked in summer 1941 for the forces necessary to defeat potential enemies, even heavier and longer-range bombers were necessary. General Arnold had already been welcoming projects to develop a four-engine "super bomber" of 2,000-miles range, superior to the B-17, and continuing the developmental programs that had bred the XB-15. Studies were informally encouraged from manufacturers, with Boeing,

Consolidated, Douglas, and Sikorsky participating. However, isolationist sentiments in the country did not support such ambitions until 1939, so no formal requirement were released. The Very Heavy Bomber (VHB) was one of the weapons addressed by the Kilner Board. The XB-15 experience was weighed in an assessment of practicality. Concurrent with this goal came one of Very Long Range (VLR).

Prewar exploratory development yielded a VLR bomber coincident with the conflict as the XB-19. However, this was already judged impractical and other development programs had begun to develop VHB aircraft with suitable trans-oceanic range. These efforts yielded

results much later than originally desired. One, the B-29, played a decisive role in closing the conflict after strenuous effort to field a suitable bomber, but the B-32 was widely considered a failure.

Too Big (XB-19)

As another step in the planned evolution of American warplane development, the Air Corps had envisioned a 200ft (61m) span bomber of 150,000lb (68,039kg) GW. However, when begun in 1935, the primary objective became to create an experimental bomber with the greatest practical range using available technology under the 'hemisphere defence' concept. Douglas got the nod in fall 1936 to build the XB-19 (38-471).

Although the original schedule called for the prototype flying in spring 1938, engineering issues and funding delays greatly stretched out the effort. Construction only began in early 1938 in Santa Monica. With demands on its staff for other commercial, War Department, and foreign work, and the XB-19 design growing dated and weight escalating, Douglas recommended in August 1938 cancelling the programme. However, Materiel Division felt it required data from the aircraft to guide future large bomber development. The aircraft was completed in May 1941, Douglas spending nearly $4,000,000 above the $1,400,064 contract – another first as the costliest aircraft.

The XB-19 was replete with superlative firsts: largest, longest, heaviest, etc. The wing was built as a single unit in a seven-storey vertical jig, encompassing the centre fuselage as well, and then rotated horizontal. The assembly hangar (largest ever) had to be partially dismantled to get the aircraft outside. Each wing had two ailerons to preclude binding under flexure over the long span. The flaps were similarly segmented. Hydraulic boost assisted moving the large control surfaces very remote form the pilot. Two auxiliary

power units ensured uninterrupted electrical and hydraulic power.

As with the XB-15, the Allison X-3420 was originally programmed for the XB-19, but a radial engine had to be substituted. Four R-3350-5s of 2,000hp (1,491kW) turned three-blade propellers of 16.5ft (5.0m) diameter. Save for a single flap on the bottom, the cowling was sealed. Oil cooling ducts protruded beneath the wing leading edges, between the two engines on each side. Fuel was contained in integral tanks, with provisions for two bomb bay auxiliary tanks.

A nominal crew of 16 (including nine gunners) could be relieved by six for which seats, bunks, and kitchen was provided in a compartment above the bomb bay. The flight deck included stations for the pilot, copilot, plane commander, flight engineer, navigator, and radio operator. The aircraft was also fitted with an autopilot. The tricycle landing gear was a matter of concern when first proposed in 1935, but was more readily accepted when the XB-19 was built.

A maximum 18,700lb (8,482kg) of bombs could be carried internally, ten wing external racks offering an additional 18,400lb (8,346kg). The defensive suite was quite extensive because the bomber was expected to operate beyond support of escort fighters. The hydraulically powered nose turret and top forward turret both had a 37mm cannon (50rpg) with coaxial .30cal MG. The intent was that tracer fire from the machine gun could help sight the cannon, but the

Above: Tricycle landing gear greatly aided large aircraft ground movement while also raising and leveling the fuselage for easier weapons loading. The XB-19 is shown making a turn at Wright Field in August 1942 with its nose wheel steering evident. While this was innovative, the large and draggy turrets were not. *National Archives*

different ballistics of the rounds made this impractical at long ranges. The upper aft turret, ventral position, twin waist gunners, and tail gunner each had single .50 MGs (200rpg). Two .30s (600rpg) were on ball socket mounts to either side of the bombardier station and two more on either side of the aft fuselage, just forward of the empennage. The nose, two dorsal, and ventral turrets were all hydraulically powered, this last also retractable.

The long development and construction of the XB-19 meant few of its features were innovative by 1941, and some were dated. While it was interesting that the wing was so thick personnel could crawl through to the engines, this bespoke an old airfoil design with less than optimal characteristics. Armour and self-sealing fuel tanks were not included as these were not part of the original specifications. Adding such features would increase weight and sacrifice fuel volume. The flaps were simply hinged, but landing speed was still a sedate 70mph (113km/h). The nose and forward dorsal turrets were exceptionally tall and "draggy", and the rear dorsal was little better. The aircraft lacked the cabin pressurisation that was becoming important for long-range bombers.

Above: The enormous Douglas XB-19 suggested tremendous capabilities as a bomber, but its size also encompassed its limitations. It required equally enormous engines for suitable power, but these remained just out of reach. The size would also have complicated any potential series production and operational employment. *Author's Collection*

The main gear tyres were not fully enclosed upon retraction. Despite the enormous weight of the aircraft, single-wheel main landing gear was employed. The tyres were 8.0ft (2.4m) diameter and each wheel weighed over 2,400lb (1,089kg). The very high ground footprint that resulted was a concern, with all operating surfaces checked to ensure they were stressed for the high loads. Santa Monica's Clover Field runway was enlarged and reinforced for the aircraft's one and only takeoff from the site. During the XB-19's initial rollout, one of the tires sank 1.5ft (0.5m) into the asphalt surface, and this not even at loaded weight. The aircraft had to be pulled backwards out of its self-dug pit to avoid over-stressing the gear.

As feared, the XB-19 was greatly overweight and already obsolete when it was first flown. Taxi testing began on 6 May, but first flight was held up by brake problems. The 55min maiden flight finally occurred on 27 June 1941, alighting at nearby March Field.

Following 30hr of company tests, the XB-19 was taken up by the service in October who added another 40hr. It was flown to Wright Field on 23 January 1942. Improved brakes and other minor changes were made before the service formally accepted the machine in June.

As testing continued, cooling of the experimental engines proved problematic, requiring cowl flaps to be open even during cruise. The associated drag cut top speed from 224 to 204mph (361 to 328km/h) and range from a calculated 7,710mi (12,407km) to a practical 6,840mi (11,007km). Payload and range of the XB-19 were still impressive, but cruise speed was not. The maximum range would require 50hrs to fly. Climb rate was equally dismal.

Despite issues with the aircraft, valuable data were collected on structures and control of such enormous aircraft. It also served as an airborne laboratory for systems, such as new instruments, boosted controls, "flying" tabs, propeller synchronisation, and reversible inboard props.[1] It also served as a familiarisation trainer for pilots about to test other large aircraft. Notable was the time delay between control input and aircraft response, and inability to perform a full-stall landing owing to powerful ground effect.[2] Nonetheless,

the aircraft soon lost its value.

Supplanting the XB-15, the Douglas aircraft remained the largest American aircraft throughout the war years, and much heralded. The biggest bomber suggested great airpower prowess. However, the fact it was no longer shrouded in secrecy by the time of first flight underlined its marginal value. With many more bomber projects underway of more up-to-date characteristics, plus lacking armour and self-sealing fuel tanks, the XB-19 had little future. To be competitive the aircraft required the monster engines that remained elusive even late in the war. Its size was an impediment to fielding and mass production. There would be no operating from sod fields despite requirements for flexible basing demonstrated by the war. Even when the Pentagon was trying to conceive a means for bombing Japan in early 1942, the XB-19 was not seriously considered, although it could have performed the mission launching from Alaska. Perhaps the prospects of losing a symbol of America's aviation might was unacceptable.

With just 177hr logged, the XB-19 was modified during March 1943 to serve as a transport, and later as an engine testbed.

8-A Douglas XB-19 characteristics:			
span	212ft	weight empty	84,431lb
length	132.2ft	gross (loaded)	140,000lb
height	42.8ft	max.	162,000lb
wing area	4,285ft²	bomb load, normal	6,000lb
fuel, max. + aux.	10,350+824gal	max.	37,100lb
service ceiling	23,000ft	speed, max. (15,700ft)	204mph
best climb rate	545fpm	cruise	120mph
takeoff distance*	4,405ft	range, 37,100lb bomb load	1,000mi
landing distance*	1,785ft	2,500lb bomb load	6,840mi
*over 50ft obstacle		ferry (131mph)	7,710mi

Pressing On

The Kilner Board's report recommended procurement of the very heavy bomber with 5,000mi (8,047km) range and suitably powerful engines. Proposals from the aircraft industry and internal studies lent confidence in the capability of producing a bomber beyond anything built theretofore, leveraging off recent technological advances.

Chief of Staff Marshall proved receptive to Arnold's push for strategic bombers. With the outbreak of war in Europe and threats gathering around the world, the USAAC felt pressure to greatly expand its bombardment capabilities. Long range and heavy bomb loads appeared essential if the United States was denied bases in or close to the war zone, as appeared possible if the UK was defeated and necessary for a war against Japan in the vast Asia-Pacific area. Consequently, with the Kilner report in hand, Arnold sought permission on 10 November 1939 to begin a VHB programme. This was approved on 2 December.

The objective VHB performance proposed by the Kilner Board was reflected in Request for Data R-40-B released on 29 January 1940, soliciting proposals within a month. The requirements for this 'Hemisphere Defence Weapon' were 400mph (644km/h) peak speed, 5,333mi (5,583km) range, and delivery of 2,000lb (907kg) of ordnance at mission midpoint.[3] In some respects, these requirements were cautionary. Range was less than expected from the XB-19 that, although yet to fly, promised more than 7,000mi (11,264km) with

similar bomb load. In other ways the desired aircraft was cutting-edge. Cabin pressurisation was judged essential for crew comfort and efficiency during high altitude operations. The pressurisation would dictate remote gun turrets that were also low-profile for reduced drag. Tricycle landing gear was not called out but essentially assumed. The circular containing R-40B stated the acquisition was urgent, with a mockup expected by 5 August 1940 and first aircraft delivered by 1 July 1941.

Four firms submitted proposals against the VHB request, bids sought in February. However, a decision was delayed as the Army chose to inject lessons observed in the early stages of the war. Revised requirements emerged on 8 April as Type Specification XC-218-A. Adjusted proposals were to be submitted within 30 days. At minimum fuel, 16,000lb (7,258kg) of bombs were to be accommodated. Top speed of 300mph (483km/h) at 25,000ft (7,620m) and a 30,000ft (9,144m) service ceiling was stated, although 450mph (724km/h) at 40,000ft (12,192m) was desired. The specification also called for self-sealing fuel tanks, more armour, and additional defensive armament with more turrets with heavier weapons to include cannon. The contractors dutifully responded with revised proposals.

Contracts valued at $85,652 for collection and presentation of preliminary design data were issued in June 1940 to permit competitors to be whittled to two. On the 27th, the notional aircraft were designated the Boeing XB-29, Lockheed XB-30, Douglas XB-31, and Consolidated XB-32. However, Lockheed

and Douglas soon withdrew owing to the weight of other work. The subsequent contracts for XB-29 and XB-32 prototypes reflected the sense of urgency and confidence in these experienced manufacturers. Concurrently, there was a separate Martin programme for the four-engine XB-33 that reflected several of the desired attributes of the VHB. This would be an "intermediate type, between the B-17, B-24, and B-29, B-32, that could be produced rapidly".[4]

The national and military leadership soon committed to making the long-range bomber a principal aspect of the US military build-up. In spring 1940, President Roosevelt declared a goal of building 500 such bombers per month. Airwar plans through early 1944 included the VLR bomber, expressly the B-29, as an element of the planned combined bombing campaign against Germany.**

The VHB was the largest aircraft development programme and the largest aircraft produced during the war, consuming vast resources. By 1944, the B-29 was expected to facilitate strategic bombardment of Japan. The range and payload capacity of the bomber also made it the only choice to carry the large atomic bombs, should they be perfected in time. The VHB was an enormous gamble for the United States.

Feds Content

The VHB contractors had to rely on GFE developed separately, and with production and delivery managed by the Army. Most significant among these were the R-3350 engine and Sperry remote controlled turrets, both promoted by the Air Corps and adopted by the designers.[5] This was not always a harmonious exchange.

At 2,000hp (1,491kW), the R-3350 was the most powerful aero engine then in production, but many programs sought the powerplant. It had first run in early 1937 but had been built and flown only in small numbers, including first flight on the XB-19, when thousands were suddenly ordered. Each engine weighed around 2,670lb (1,211kg) and cost on

* Although VHB was the official programme title, the underlying goal was VLR. The acronyms were used interchangeably and no great distinction will be drawn within this text. However, B-29 and B-32 operational units were designated with a "(VH)" suffix for Very Heavy.

Above: The Wright R-3350 Duplex Cyclone was the most powerful aero engine available when the B-29 program was conceived. It made the very heavy bomber possible but was also its bane. Still maturing as production had to move into high gear, it had many 'teething' problems of which some proved lethal. *National Museum of the United States Air Force*

average about $13,000. Two General Electric B-11 gear-driven, two-speed turbosuperchargers were employed per engine, acting in parallel, sustaining sea level power up to 33,000ft (10,058m). Perfecting the powerplant and moving it to high-rate production had to occur in parallel with the bomber. This was fraught with problems and the engine was to prove one of the most significant impediments to VHB progressing to service.

Production of the R-3350 became as high a materiel procurement priority as the B-29 itself. Eventually Wright's Cincinnati, Ohio, factory was turned entirely to this product and a new plant in Woodbridge, New Jersey, was built to manufacture the R-3350. Production was also undertaken by the Dodge Motors Division of the Chrysler Corporation at a new facility in Chicago, Illinois. Some 32,221 R-3350s were delivered during the war despite a continuing evolution when the plants were still struggling to establish stable production lines and quality.

Service investment in RCT development was a boon for a pressurised bomber. When the VHB began, proposals for a remote gun systems were solicited on 20 March 1940 from Bendix, GE, Sperry, and Westinghouse. Sperry responded quickly and was given a development contract on 1 April 1940, followed by a production order in December 1940. This employed the bifurcated periscope with firing solutions coming from a Central Control Computer Station. The remote turrets were to be retractable and with self-contained hydraulic drives. The central control determined which of multiple periscope sighting stations controlled which guns. As with other computing gunsights, the gunner had to enter the estimated wingspan of the target.

Ultimate Victor (B-29)

When the R-40B specifications reached Boeing on 5 February 1940, the firm already had a solid basis for a proposal. A series of preliminary designs emerged via company studies beginning in March 1939 and discussed with the Air Corps to some level and detail. Several advanced features were adopted. Given the large bomb capacity and the need to distribute this load on either side of the CG, somewhere within the wing root chord, two bays were envisioned separated by the wing box. Faced with the need for pressurised personnel areas ahead and aft of the bomb bays, which itself was impractical to pressurise, Boeing conceived individual pressurised compartments joined by a crawlway

above the bays. A rounded aircraft nose, eliminating the familiar stepped windscreen, simplified structural design for pressurisation and cut drag. Cabin pressurisation represented a new engineering challenge, but Boeing had incorporated this in their Model 307 Stratoliner commercial transport in 1938 and so had experience. A mid-wing design was favoured as it eliminated the need for wing fillets at the fuselage because drag with this placement was already much reduced. Tricycle landing gear was also seen as necessary to improve ground handling and bomb loading, although there would be a weight penalty.

By the end of 1939 the Boeing design work had yielded the Model 334A for which the company constructed a partial mockup in December at their own expense. However, design work on a variation, the Model 341, had been progressing since August and employed a new Boeing high-lift, laminar-flow airfoil for a high aspect ratio planform.[†] This made for high wing loading that was desirable for extended range and lower drag. Fowler flaps were being designed to enhanced low-speed lift, answering the potential problems of a long takeoff roll and high landing speed associated with high wing loading.

The Model 341 was offered in Boeing's 5 March 1940 proposal. It was revised in response to XC-218-A, the Model 345 submitted on 11 May 1940. Maximum GW was then 112,300lb (50,938kg) with 5,140gal (19,457lit) fuel capacity for 6,950mi (11,185km) range, maximum speed 382mph (615km/h) with the R-3350. Wright Field insisted the bomb bays be lengthened to accommodate more bombs, contributing to an overall length increase of about 12.7ft (3.9m). Span was 141.2ft (43.0m), aspect ratio 11.5, and the gun complement rose with RCTs outside the pressure vessels. Originally, the B-29 was to employ counter-rotating propellers to reduce torque swing on takeoff. This unwelcome burden on the Wright team to develop a reverse gearcase was wisely dropped in favour of a revised rudder.[6]

The XB-29 study contract was issued on 17 June 1940 to continue concept

† Planform is the profile of the wing as seen from top or bottom, the plan view.

development and perform wind tunnel testing. This was amended on the 27th to fund preliminary design. A 24 August, $3,615,095 order covered two prototypes and two mockups. The first aircraft was to be delivered in April 1942. A third XB-29 and static test article was added in a 14 December contract change.

Despite its size, the XB-29 possessed essentially the same drag as the B-17. Boeing employed such techniques as flush riveting, panel butt joints, and even retractable tail skid. The thickest aluminum skin used to that date, 0.1875in (4.8mm), was employed.‡ Unlike most installations, the turbosuperchargers were enclosed within the nacelle. The size of the bomber's construction created new challenges. The wing spars, for example, were the heaviest and longest Duralumin extrusions then manufactured. At first, Boeing wanted to use the Davis wing, but Consolidated successfully defended its proprietary design. Fortunately, Boeing already had a wing under development as a fallback.

‡ This had the effect of eliminating skin "wrinkles" evident in most other aircraft from thermal or airload strain.

Two General Electric B-11 gear-driven, two-speed turbosuperchargers were employed per engine, acting in parallel, to sustain sea-level power up to 33,000ft (10,058m). The pressurisation system of early B-29s drew heated air from the two turbos in the inboard nacelles. The forward and aft compartments were joined by the 2.8ft (0.9m) diameter crawlway, 33.0ft (10.1m) long. The tail gunner was in an individually pressurised compartment under the tail.

The bomber had some redundancy designed in, to include flight controls, ensuring vital systems remained functional in the event of battle damage. Dual wheels on all three landing gear struts reduced runway contact pressure such that unusually high strength runways surfaces were not required. Additionally, a single tire blowout would not create as severe a yaw. Apart from basic aircraft systems, the flight engineer station had full engine controls and indicators while the pilots had basic instrument and "master throttles". The B-29 was the first in which the pilot lacked a full complement of systems instruments.

Above: The Boeing B-29 was the most advanced and capable bomber manufactured during the war. Its very long range and hefty payload made it ideal for a strategic bombing campaign against the Japanese Home Islands. However, the path to producing and fielding this complex weapon was long and arduous. *Air Force Flight Test Center*

The B-29 was the most advanced combat aircraft built in the United States during the war and the most sophisticated among all combatants. It was an "all-electric" aircraft with 129 electric motors for various functions that included landing gear and flap actuation. An auxiliary power unit in the aft fuselage provided electricity for engine start and augmented the six engine-driven generators per engine in high demand situations. These were the largest generators then installed on an aircraft and contributed to growing weight. Tabs were used to help move heavy controls versus more complex and maintenance-intensive hydraulic boost that had had a troubled history to that point. Pneumatics actuated the bomb bay doors so they could snap open and close quickly, reducing drag. An air deflector in the bays also

Above: The radome for the AN/APQ-13 radar bombsight is shown in the extended position between the two B-29 bomb bays. The radar aided navigation as well as locating targets through overcast. The radar was so prevalent and used relatively frequently, that the B-29 was occasionally referred to as the "radar bomber". *National Archives*

Below: The long-lived first XB-29 (41-002) had the short-lived installation of Sperry remote control turrets and periscope stations on the Superfortress. This is seen by the teardrop slighting blisters in the aft fuselage. The turrets do not appear to have been installed.
San Diego Air & Space Museum

deployed for flow more favourable to smooth store separation. The radio suite included transceivers, radio compass, navigation aids, IFF, and radar.§ De-icing equipment included boots on wing and horizontal tail leading edges and a propeller fluid system. However, the boots were eliminated early in production to save weight and based on combat experience.

The bomb bays had combined capacity up to 20,000lb (9,072kg) with weapon types up to 4,000lb (1,814kg) bombs. Two 640gal (2,243lit) fuel tanks

could be installed in each bomb bay for extended range. The bombardier employed a Norden sight through a nose sighting window or the radar operator directed bombing. As B-29 production began to ramp up, the AN/APQ-13 was introduced.[7] The unit was seen externally as a radome for the partially retractable 2.5ft (0.8m) diameter antenna, installed between the bomb bays. Later a more aerodynamic radome of teardrop cross-section was substituted that appears to have been only partially retractable.

Sighting the remote turrets was through four aft fuselage "teardrop" blisters for the periscope heads. However, the Sperry system was still developmental and faced an 'uphill climb' against problems. Worse, Eglin testers noted a small field-of-view through the periscopes that mandated one or more spotters to give verbal direction, distortion from the plastic cover on the periscope head, optical fogging, and complexity requiring additional training and support.[8] They came away declaring the system "useless". Sperry and its subcontractors were also having difficulty meeting delivery schedules.

In December 1941, the Army made a firm effort to have Boeing revert to manned turrets on the B-29. However, Boeing held fast that RCTs were essential to meeting altitude and speed requirements, and for gunner performance. They prevailed by

demonstrating how badly performance would be impacted and by switching to a General Electric system with direct sighting that had emerged in January 1942. The first and second XB-29s were initially equipped with Sperry blisters. The third XB-29 (41-18335) introduced the GE equipment.

The GE Central Fire Control (CFC) System operated from four computing, reflector gunsights, where the gunners visually tracked a target and manually adjusted for range with estimated wingspan. Electro-mechanical computers adjusted for lead, parallax, ballistics, and deflection angle from gunner inputs, flight condition, and other factors. There was also a manual backup capability. The sighting stations were within three hemisphere "blisters", one atop and two on either side of the aft fuselage, and a fourth at the bombardier's station. The GE system was first tested aloft aboard a modified B-24C during early 1942. Although, Eglin found the CFC to be unsuitable because of inaccuracy, vulnerability, excessive complexity, and inability to service the system in-flight, the USAAF was committed.

The CFC stations directed top and bottom, non-retracting, electrical turrets forward of the wing and another pair aft of the wing, each with two .50cal MGs. Typically, the bombardier sight directed the forward bottom turret, the top rear sight for both or either top turrets, and the side stations the bottom aft turret. However, secondary control could override these normal selections. The tail turret had an individually controlled gunsight for the two .50 guns and a 20mm cannon in a powered mounting. The turrets had 500 rounds per gun, later increased to 1,000, while the cannon had 110-125 rounds.

The cannon was the first such installation in a production bomber. However, feed mechanism problems and the different ballistics of the cannon and machine guns complicated firing. The CFC performed calculations just for the

Right: Production B-29s incorporated remote gun turrets aimed via computing, reflector gunsight at four sighting stations, a waist gunner station shown here in use. The General Electric Central Fire Control System was complex but proved practical in service.
National Museum of the United States Air Force

guns such that the cannon could only be used effectively against a target within 1,800ft (549m) where the ballistics of both types of rounds were similar. Hence, the cannon was often removed or occasionally replaced with another .50.

Normal B-29 crew complement and placement included two pilots, a bombardier/nose gunner, navigator and engineer in the forward compartment. Three scanner/gunners, the radioman, and radar operator were in the aft compartment and the tail gunner farther back. These 11 men could be augmented or reduced as mission dictated, such as adding an RCM crewman. This made for the largest crew complement of any bomber of the war. Armour plate, flak curtains, and individual flak suits provided crew protection.

The XB-29 Superfortress mockup was inspected in April 1941 and approval for prototype construction issued soon thereafter. This and other evidence of Boeing's progress, as well as the growing war overseas, was enough for the Army to move for B-29 manufacturing preparation well before first flight of what would be the largest production

aircraft of the war. General Arnold wanted to order 990 "paper aircraft" back in October 1940, but was stymied. The $20,000,000 order instead came on 17 May 1941 for 14 service test YB-29s. Added to this was an order for 250 production bombers, approved on 6 September. This move was met with astonishment by many considering its size, uncertainty surrounding the advanced project, and the fact America remained at peace. However, the order book was increased to 500 on 31 January 1942 following US entry into the war. The production quantity continued to be increased until, by first flight in fall 1942, there were 1,644 or 1,664 aircraft on order.[9]

Right: The B-29 initially featured a 20mm cannon with two machine guns in the tail, all indirectly aimed via an electronic gunsight. This first installation of a cannon as defensive armament in a bomber was not entirely successful. Shell feed was unreliable and the different ballistics were problematic. *Jay Miller Collection*

Weight of the XB-29 had gained nearly 12,000lb (5,443kg) over the Model 345 proposal, bringing range down to the 5,333mi (8,583km) requirement. With many other challenges designing and building a milestone aircraft under an ambitious schedule, detail design and prototype construction fell months behind schedule.

The high wing loading caused concern within Air Corps engineering circles as it was twice that of the B-17's 30psf (6.1kg/m²), theretofore considered a practical limit. However, Boeing convincingly defended this feature. Wing area increased 19 per cent with deployment of the large Fowler flaps, addressing takeoff and landing worries. Aerodynamics data were collected beyond wind tunnels through scale flight testing. A PT-19A trainer (41-20531) was bailed to Boeing for modification under project MX-220. Wing and tail surfaces intended for the bomber were sized to the trainer and installed through modification. These approximately quarter-scale surfaces could be readily altered or changed out entirely, and various configurations were flown. Other B-29 design elements and components were tested on B-17s.

Throughout 1941, plans for large-scale production of the B-29 were set in motion, with a goal of 50 aircraft per month by June 1943, and the programme became the USAAF's highest priority. Although the XB-29s were built in Seattle, a government plant in Wichita became a division of Boeing to manufacture the Superfortress (-BW suffix). The decision was made in February 1942 to seek additional manufacturers. Bell would contribute at a new government facility in Marietta, Georgia (-BA suffix). North American Aviation was to build B-29s in their Kansas City factory.

Soon there were shifts in the production plans. The USAAF traded the Kansas City facility to the Navy for the Boeing plant in Renton. The B-29s built in Renton were identified with a -BN suffix. Martin was also selected to build B-29s in its Omaha factory (-MO suffix) with Fisher supplying subassemblies. Wichita also began providing subassemblies in February 1945. This site led production initially as the Renton and Marietta assembly lines were completed. All had to rely on an unprecedented level of subcontracting to meet the Army's ambitious schedule, with thousands of firms contributing. All this added up to making the B-29 programme the most complex industrial undertaking for production of a single aircraft type.

The first XB-29 flight (41-002) was on 21 September 1942 from Boeing Field. Testing progressed slowed owing to numerous problems that cut flights short. Engine changes and alterations were discouragingly frequent. An engine fire on 28 December was followed by another on the 30th during the maiden flight of 41-003. The ninth flight of 003, 18 February 1943, ended in a crash when trying to return with a persistent wing fire following an engine fire. All 11 personnel onboard perished plus 19 individuals on the ground.

Flying of the B-29 and all Army aircraft equipped with R-3350s was suspended while an all-out effort was undertaken to make the engines minimally safe, although reliability remained unacceptable. Flying resumed on 29 May, and the Army took over responsibility for the testing with its pilots performing much of the flying that was concentrated at the new Wichita production facility.

Development was comparatively rapid after that despite numerous issues to be resolved. The airframe was fundamentally sound, but correcting the systems problems seemed endless. There were also wing modifications because production had started before ground structural tests of the structure had been completed. During these static tests, the structure suffered failures at as low as 60 per cent of design limit load. These and myriad other "mods" had to be incorporated into production examples already in work owing to the relentless pressure to ramp up deliveries.

The R-3350 continued to suffer grave problems. Engine changes were initially every few flights, or about 35hr.[10] This improved to 150hr by the time of initial service and growing to 400hr by war's end, consistent with other aero engines.[11] Overheating was exacerbated by Boeing's low-drag cowling that did not permit sufficient cooling airflow for takeoff and initial climb, but fires were made worse by the lightweight magnesium gearcase. Baffle alterations, propeller cuffs, and hundreds of small changes were required in seeking safety and reliability. The R-3350-13s used in the first B-29s gave way to the -23 "war engines". Even these required careful monitoring and special procedures to control temperatures.

The B-29 schedule was grueling as the Army sought to deploy the bomber as soon as possible. In early 1943, production was behind schedule and particularly Bell was struggling to get their plant operating. All faced materials and manpower shortages while Boeing worked to create production drawings, data, and templates for an aircraft that was still evolving. The aircraft was exceedingly complex, each requiring 15 times the manhours expended on a B-17. These problems, the crash, development issues, and engine fires made the programme appear to some close to failure. Arnold's firm defence of the Superfortress ensured its survival.

The B-29 had moved to the highest priority aviation programme in the United States, and the tight secrecy surrounding it was eased in an effort to move resources faster. In April 1943, the AAF wanted to restrict further design changes so as to have 100 B-29s deployed by the end of the year. However, this meant accepting the bomber with identified problems, some compromising safety. Arnold personally judged the aircraft "good enough". The first of the YB-29s was delivered in July 1943 to support training. The first production aircraft flew in Wichita on 21 September.

Logistics problems with the hundreds of suppliers and thousands of engineering changes for the airframe and engine were epic. The frequent changes were too involved to introduce on production lines, so aircraft were being rolled out with significant remaining work. These were left as rework and retrofits for modification centres. They dealt with every aircraft, reaching a high of 30,000 manhours and about seven weeks per bomber before delivery to operational units. Initially, parts shortages and lingering systems problems meant aircraft were collected unfinished. Of the 97 aircraft parked in Wichita by early January 1944, only 16 were flyable and none ready to go to war. Each required substantial rework including 54 major modifications.[12] Consequently, training suffered, with the average aircraft commander having accumulated only 35hr flying time on the Superfortress when deploying overseas.

A concerted programme was undertaken to move the aircraft along, but the results were still discouraging. With 175 B-29s required in China to begin operations in April, an angry Hap Arnold instituted a high priority surge effort on 10 March 1944, the day he had expected to be seeing off the first flight of bombers. The programme moved into crisis mode with Arnold's vociferous urging from afar. High-level

Above: With combat experience suggesting that additional firepower to the front would better counter enemy tactics, the top forward gun turret of the B-29 (insert) was changed to incorporate four .50cal machine guns from the original two. This began appearing in mid-1944. The turret would later be taller but more streamlined. *Jay Miller Collection*

and knowledgeable personnel were brought in, plus hundreds of mechanics and technicians pulled from the Wichita plant, to expedite the work that went on around the clock. Daily reports were made to Arnold and passed to the President.[13] So great and stressful was this effort, with most work outdoors in severe cold, that it came to be known as the "Battle of Kansas". It saw installation of R-3350-23A "combat engines" with cylinder alterations and other changes. The five-week ordeal paid off with 100 bombers ready for their crews.

Bell began B-29 deliveries in November 1943 and Martin in June 1944. For Renton, with initial deliveries in January 1944, it proved practical to introduce some production changes to the Superfortress. Designated B-29A, these featured revised nacelles and many other internal structural changes. The inboard wing segment was built as three elements, with the centresection assembled with the mid fuselage segment, instead of dropped in as the one unit used in prior B-29s. Consequently, these aircraft had a wingspan 1.0ft (0.3m) longer than the B-29, was 706lb (320kg) heavier, and contained 213gal (806lit) less fuel.

The R-3350-13 on the initial XB-29 delivered 2,200hp (1,641kW) at 2,400rpm. They used a 17.0ft (5.2m) diameter three-blade propeller. This was the largest propeller yet used on a US

production aircraft. The YB-29s had the R-3350-21s that operated at 2,800rpm with the three-blade prop, although eventually given four-blade units. The -23 engines on the early production aircraft operated at 2,600rpm with what became the standard 16.6ft (5.1m), four-blade propeller for improved altitude performance. Beginning in November 1944, B-29s were supplied with fuel-injected -41 engines that reduced the hazard of carburetor induction fires. Late production B-29s and B-29As had the fuel-injected R-3350-57 or -59 powerplants that was back up to 2,800rpm. Curtiss reversible-pitch propellers were also installed on some late-production B-29s. By mid-production, fuel capacity had been increased from 8,168gal (30,919lit) to 9,438gal (35,727lit) by addition of centre-section tanks.

Beginning in July 1944, a four-gun turret, adapted from the Northrop P-61, replaced the top forward unit. This ensured a more effective forward-quadrant defence, answering Eglin accuracy criticism.[14] It proved beneficial as the Japanese favoured the frontal attack. A taller, streamlined variant

Peak production of the Superfortress was achieved in spring 1945 with 4.2 per day in Wichita, 8 per day total. The original goal of 50 aircraft per month was only achieved in January 1944 (54 aircraft), and a peak of 375 per month in July 1945.[16] The USAAF had a maximum 2,132 B-29s in its inventory, although by summer 1945 many were moved directly to storage upon delivery and only a bit more than 1,000 reached the combat theatre.[17]

Orders had continued to be expanded or placed anew such that 9,052 B-29s were under contract by the close of the conflict. Wartime production amounted to 3,901 machines (118 converted to photo ships). These included 3 XB-29s, 14 YB-29s, 2,181 B-29s (1,630 -BW, 357 -BA, 536 -MO), 1,050 B-29As, and 311 B-29Bs. A total 5,082 were cancelled after VJ-Day. Many of the final planes in Omaha and Wichita were broken up rather than being completed and delivered. Another 69 B-29As were finished post-war.

As the B-29 emerged and its capabilities became known, commands in all theatres began clamouring for squadrons to serve their tactical needs. Consistent with earlier national decisions, and with backing of General Marshall, Arnold held firm that these were strategic assets. He went so far as to establish a new numbered Air Force

came later. The tail 20mm was also eventually formally omitted. As the Army was stripping guns from their B-29s in-theatre, some B-29s were built new with only the tail armament, the turrets deleted and blisters fared over.

New equipment became available in 1944 that made possible a fast, unescorted B-29 for night or inclement weather blind bombing. The aircraft were stripped down 3,500lb (1,588kg), and crew trimmed to seven or eight men. Flame dampers for the engine exhausts were considered but discounted because of weight and paucity of enemy interceptors. These aircraft became the 311 B-29Bs (Model 345-3-0), production work undertaken by Bell, interspersed among typical production examples.[15] The lightened aircraft could achieve 364mph (586km/h) at 25,000ft (7,620m) altitude.

The AN/APQ-7 Eagle radar bombsight replaced the APS-13 on the B-29Bs, evidenced by an 18.0ft (5.5m) long antenna "wing" mounted below the fuselage between the bomb bays. The impact of the large installation was a loss of 412mi (663km) in range and 8mph (13km/h) in speed. The intent was to fly at around 15,000ft (4,572m) to reduce engine stress and get the most from radar accuracy. Much behind schedule, the first flight with the APQ-7 on a B-29 was performed in February 1945 in Boca Raton, Florida. The first operational aircraft flew in Seattle on 15 January 1945.

Armour and flak protection was greatly reduced in the B-29Bs, equipment

not essential to the mission removed. Armament was reduced to just the aft turret with three .50cals and increased ammunition capacity. The majority of the CFC system was replaced with the General Electric AN/APG-15B Airborne Radar Gun Sighting System, or just automatic gun-laying radar fire control system, integrated with the GE firing computer. This was characterised by a small radar scanner globe placed beneath the guns to detect and range threats approaching from behind. The system had a range of around 6,000ft (1,829m) and tests showed it improved hits by three to four times that of manual aiming. A gunner monitored a radar screen to select targets and commit to engagement, the fire control system doing the rest. However, it did not possess an IFF feature and proved difficult to maintain in the field.

Boeing B-29-25 characteristics:

span	141.3ft	weight empty	70,140lb
length	99.0ft	gross	110,000lb
height	27.8ft	maximum*	134,000lb
wing area	1,736ft²	bomb load, max.	20,000lb
fuel (int.+bay)	5,566+2,560gal	speed, cruise	230mph
service ceiling	31,850ft	max. (25,000 ft)	358mph
average climb rate	526fpm	range, (20,000 lb bombs)	3,250mi
takeoff distance* (120,000lb)	6,000ft	ferry	5,600mi
landing distance*	3,700ft	*maximums as high as 140,000lb	
*over 50ft obstacle		flown in combat	

to operate the aircraft, with himself as commander and reporting directly to the Joint Chiefs rather than theatre. The United States leadership wanted to open a strategic bombing campaign against the Japanese Home Islands with the B-29 at the earliest opportunity.

Even as the longest range bomber of the war, the vastness of the CBI and Pacific theatres challenged the ability of the USAAF to strike at Japan. Building suitable bases for the bomber became an enormous project in itself. The squadrons would initially stage from bases in India to sites in China from which the southern elements of the Japanese island chain were within reach. However, the facilities were rudimentary and most resources, including fuel and ordnance, had to be transported from India by air in B-29s or modified B-24s. This allowed a bombing mission rate of just one per week. On these combat sorties, the Superfortresses operated up to 40,000lb (18,144kg) over recommended gross.

The first "shakedown" combat mission was a 5 June attack from India on a Bangkok rail yard. At 2,100mi (3,379km) round trip, this was the longest bombing raid to that date. Japan was hit on the night of 15/16 June, the first such attack since the Doolittle Raid a little more than two years before. An attack on Sumatra oil refineries with 39 bombers (of 54 dispatched) on 10 August 1944, staging

from Ceylon, was the longest of the war at 4,030mi (6,485km) and 19hr. Some 49 missions were flown from the Chinese and Indian bases through the end of March 1945, in both day and night. With ranges to worthy targets so great, the bomb loads were comparatively light and the resources expended to launch the raids enormous. The results of most were disappointing, but improvement was evident. Experience was growing and accident rates diminishing. The situation was far from ideal but achieved the national goal of bringing the war to Japan at the earliest opportunity.

Deployed a new bomber of such complexity just 20 months after first flight was a remarkable achievement. However, it was not without its pitfalls. Operating under spartan field conditions was exceptionally difficult. Too many aircraft were turning back with aircraft issues, and more were lost to mishaps and mechanical failures than enemy action. The B-29s continued to be plagued by engine fires or overheating requiring shutdown. On hot days, where a long taxi or delay was anticipated, it was prudent to tow the aircraft to the end of the runway for engine start. Hundreds of system modifications continued to be introduced in theatre, adding to maintenance workload and requiring industry technicians to assist.[18]

The seizure of central Pacific islands

Above: Some B-29Bs were fitted with the AN/APQ-7 Eagle radar, evident here by the 18.0ft (5.5m) "vane" under the fuselage between the bomb bays. The X-band radar had superior resolution for improved radar bombing and shorter run-in on target. So equipped, these B-29Bs were employed in night attacks on priority targets. *Jay Miller Collection*

to serve as B-29 bases became an important element of the Allied war strategy, with these landings moved up from the original timetable. This was an extraordinary new complexion in warfare, with ground troops securing areas from which to launch bombers on strategic missions. The capture of the Marianas in summer 1944 was pivotal, with bases quickly prepared on three islands. These were roughly 1,500mi (2,414km) from Japan, and all points within reach. However, this was another mammoth effort as almost all materials had to be brought by sea. Over time these facilities became the largest airport complexes in the world.

The B-29 force began shifting to the Pacific on 12 October 1944 and the first bombing mission flown by the end of that month. Tokyo was hit for the first time a month later. Compared with India and China, the squadrons traded superior accommodations and resupply by sea for the hazards of long over-water flights lasting 12hr or more. The range was too great for fighter escort.

Supply and readiness problems were

still being overcome, most planes only flying three to four times a month. They ultimately reached an average 120hrs per month per aircraft, compared with 30hrs for heavy bombers in Europe. A typical mission averaged only 125 bombers, but this grew to daily attacks involving hundreds of aircraft. The most dispatched against a single target was 558 on 23/24 May 1945, and the most sent out on a single day was 836 on 1/2 August 1945. Hence, the scale of the missions against Japan was considerably less than against Germany, but with a decidedly more dramatic outcome.

Bombing altitude was lowered from 33,000 to 25,000ft (10,058 to 7,620m) or below, saving fuel, as it was observed flak was much less dense or effective than in Europe. The aircraft were depressurised, partially or fully, and the crew donned oxygen masks, prior to entering combat to avoid the effects of rapid decompression from battle damage. Another reason for lowering the altitude was to reduce the effects of what became known as the jet stream. This was a high altitude wind of 120-200mph (193-322km/h) – something previously unknown and not experienced in Europe. It could give a crosswind drift for which the Norden bombsight was unable to compensate, or a downwind ground speed of 400-500mph (644-805km/h) that did not allow enough time for lineup. Despite original expectations, high altitude and speed did not place the bombers beyond the reach of flak or fighters. The B-29s armament system continued to be criticised as too complex for the average gunner and too prone to breakdown. However, fighters had all but disappeared by summer 1945 and defences were much less sophisticated than in Europe with fewer radar and ineffective night fighters.

Although bombing accuracy improved with the latest model Norden, precision high altitude bombing, either by day, night, or radar yielded only five per cent of the bombs falling within 1,000ft (305m) of the target. This was not accurate enough to have the desired effect. Consequently, tactics were dramatically altered in March 1945 to individual, night, low level (5,000-10,000ft/1,524-3,048m) non-precision incendiary attacks.[19] The AAA could not track the fast B-29 at low altitude. As Japanese war industry had come to depend on dispersed work in homes and labor in urban areas, the targeting of general urban areas and the civilian population was judged legitimate. The incendiary attacks began with a 9 March 1945 attack on Tokyo by 270 Superfortresses. A quarter of the city was destroyed and more than 84,000 people killed. The force had suffered just four per cent losses. Within 10 days, 1,595 bombers dispensed 9,373 tons (8503 metric tons) of incendiaries to burn 32mi² (83km²) of urban areas, eliminating four of Japan's largest cities as military targets at the cost of 22 bombers. The missions were tough on the planes and crews as up and down draughts from heat convection over the target produced severe turbulence.

The capture of Iwo Jima provided an invaluable emergency landing field for the bombers and served as a base for daylight fighter escort beginning on 7 April 1945. At a minimum 1,400mi (2,253km) round trip and 8hr these P-51D sorties were among the longest and most daunting fighter escort missions of the war. However, when fighter opposition almost ceased so did escort.

The few remaining enemy interceptors were expected be executing primarily rear quarter attacks. However, with the B-29s almost unmolested after May, all defensive armament but the tail turrets were subsequently removed from many B-29s and associated crewmen left behind, lightening the aircraft by 7,500lb (3,402kg) to reduce use of full throttle and stress on the engines or increase speed 7-13mph (11-21km/h), and lowering drag for more range or greater payload.

Daylight high-altitude bombing of industrial and military centres continued in concert with the night incendiary attacks. Tactical missions were executed as urgency dictated. Among these was aerial mining of shipping channels and harbors. This was typically performed using radar at low altitude by a lone B-29 flying at night.[20]

Radar bombing was employed in 23 per cent of attacks owing to the frequency of clouds obscuring targets. However, it continued to yield poor results compared with visual bombing.

Altitude was reduced to improve results and as enemy opposition diminished. The APQ-7-equipped B-29Bs first went into action on 26 June and 15 of the night missions were flown before the end. The Japanese petroleum industry was the principal target as these were more easily identified via radar. The results were comparatively "good", with ten per cent of bombs falling within 1,000ft (305m) of the aim point.

The B-29 bombing campaign, along with other military operations, set the stage for an invasion of the Japanese home islands. Although bombing results continued to be mixed from all methods, the weight of the effort was telling. In less than a year, Japanese industry, military infrastructure, and transportation systems were staggering under the weight of the bombardment and its people were suffering frightfully. Although high altitude strategic bombing played a large role in bringing Japan to capitulation, it was not as originally envisioned. Many of the industrial facilities razed by the B-29s had already been rendered impotent by the strangling embargo by the US Navy, mining, and capture of strategic areas. Instead, the B-29's greatest contribution was low-level area bombing with incendiaries and then high-altitude release of two atomic bombs. Invasion then proved unnecessary after the Empire capitulated and the war ended. The role of the B-29 in this outcome was paramount.

The final bombing raids of the war were flown by B-29s on 14/15 August. The B-29 combat losses progressively decreased from a high of 14 per cent of dispatched aircraft to a low of 0.02 per cent owing to revised tactics, diminished Japanese defensives, improved aircraft reliability, and overall growing experience by the USAAF team. All told, B-29 operations claimed a total 360 bombers destroyed in the theatre, 147 as a direct result of combat. Another 260 aircraft were destroyed in the States through operational accidents.

Average unit cost of a Superfortress was $618,045 (three times that of a B-17F) and the entire programme totaled $3 billion. Despite the enormous cost, attrition, and hundreds of men killed, the push to get the B-29 in the field, risking built-in hazards, was roundly judged to have been worthy. Few did not agree at the time that the B-29 bombing campaign against Japan and dropping the A-bombs shortened the war and saved perhaps hundreds of thousands of lives.

The B-29 remained the premier American bomber for the next several years, continuing in combat roles until 1954 and finally being withdrawn in 1960.

Supercilious Superfortress (B-29C, B-29D)

Hardpoints in the B-29 wing segment just outboard of the fuselage could accommodate additional bomb racks. These were principally intended for one 12,000lb (5,443kg) deep-penetration bomb each, of British origin, or two 4,000lb (1,814kg) bombs each. Likewise, several B-29s were subjected to bay door modifications and other changes, making it a single bay to permit carriage of one 22,000lb (9,979kg) Grand Slam bomb, also British, partially submerged. It also saw the displaced radar moved forward, installed in place of the lower forward gun turret. The bomb had to be loaded from a pit over which the bomber was positioned. None of these combinations saw combat during the war. Similar modifications to 15 lightweight Marietta aircraft (only tail guns) were performed at Martin-Omaha under Project W-47 and Operation Pullman (MX-469) to carry the atomic bombs. The largest weapon was 10,300lb (4,672kg) and fitted entirely in the unified bay. The bomb had to be raised into the aircraft by hydraulic jacks from a pit. The bomber was rolled up beside the pit with the closest main gear truck on a turntable such that the bomber could be swung around and aligned over the pit.

An extensive armament modification to a B-29 was called Project S68 and reportedly done to evaluate turret systems. The desire may have been to explore an alternative defensive armament suite and have engineering in hand should the remote system not measure up. The B-29-25-BW 42-24441 was fitted with manned gun stations and flown in October 1944. Substituted for the four power turrets were two ventral Sperry ball turrets below and two dorsal Martin turrets above, as on the B-17. The ball turrets could not be fully

retracted, and may have been intended to model the developmental Emerson Model 110 pressurised ball that was more compatible with the B-29 mission. The aft side blisters were replaced with flat windows and a single, manually handled .50 each. An Emerson Model 126 remotely controlled barbette was

Above: Hardpoints under the inboard wing segments permitted external carriage of weapons, but did not see combat. At top, the B-29-75-BW has two 4,000lb (1,814kg) M56 Blockbuster bombs. At bottom, a B-29 hauls 12,000lb (5,443kg) Tallboy bombs for hardened targets. Note the revised APQ-13 radome, more aerodynamic and apparently not fully retractable. top *Jay Miller Collection*, bottom *Gerald Balzer Collection*

155

Left: The 22,000lb (9,979kg) Grand Slam is carried in modified bomb bays of this Superfortress (B-29-15-BW 42-63693). Removal of the radar and the separating structure created a unified bay for the unusually long weapon that remained semi-submerged, requiring door cutouts. The radar was usually relocated to the forward lower turret opening. *National Archives*

Runner Up (B-32)

Consolidated's Model 33 VHB proposal was submitted on 8 April 1940 and garnered the preliminary design contract. Two XB-32s (41-141/2) were ordered on 6 September, with the first example to be delivered within 18 months. The mockup was inspected on 6 January and an engine installation mockup likewise approved on 17 April.

The XB-32's maximum GW was estimated at 101,000lb (4,581kg). The two tandem bomb bays used roll-up panel doors as on the B-24, operated via hydraulics. The canted twin tail and high aspect ratio Davis-type wing, the latter with large-span, two-segment Fowler flaps, were classical Consolidated. Flush riveting was used only in the forward fuselage and wing.[24] Small electrical motors in the control surfaces actuated the trim tabs that helped pilots move the surfaces. The tricycle landing gear borrowed components from the B-24, although the number of the wheels were doubled. The bomber used four 2,200hp (1,641kW) R-3350 with twin B-11 exhaust-driven turbos. These were -13 models on the inboard stations and -21s outboard, the latter with an accessory drive and two large generators. The powerplants were matched with three-blade propellers of 16.6ft (5.1m) diameter. There was 1,221lb (554kg) of armour protection included.

The 9.5ft (2.9m) diameter cylindrical fuselage with rounded nose supported pressurised compartments for the crew of 8-12. The flight deck and aft fuselage compartments were joined by a 2.5ft (0.8m) diameter 'communications tunnel' above the bomb bays through which crewmen could move by pulling themselves along prone on a rope and pulley-operated trolley. With the doors to the tunnel secured, the compartments could be pressurised separately. A flight engineer was provided with a panel of instruments and controls to assist the pilots in managing the myriad systems.

grafted onto each side of the nose with a single .50calibre machine gun each. These were controlled remotely from the bombardier's station. All this made pressurisation impossible. Fortunately, resorting to such a radical change did not prove necessary.

A Superfortress was initially identified as a platform for flight testing a fuel-injected Allison R-3350 engine with reversible propellers and given a designation of B-29C.[21] The Army laid plans to build 5,000 Cs in Renton. However, these were dropped and the engines (-41 and -57) plus props were eventually introduced on the production lines without a distinct model designation change.

In 1944, plans were laid to substitute the 3,500hp (2,610kW) R-4360 in the B-29 for markedly improved performance. Given the state of the Superfortress programme with the R-3350, the proposal was welcome. A B-29A was employed as a testbed as the XB-44, first flying in May 1945.[22] Production of the

combination was to be undertaken as the B-29D (Model 345-2-1). Other changes to be introduced included a taller vertical tail, enlarged flaps, hydraulic system alterations that would provide rudder boost, revised landing gear for greater GW, and nose wheel steering. An initial order was placed in July 1945 for 200 B-29D-BNs, but this was waylaid by the war's end. It emerged postwar as the B-50.

Another aircraft contributing to Superfortress evolution was B-29-35-BW 42-24528. It received the 4.9ft (1.5m) taller vertical tail and rudder planned for the B-29D. It was already modified with the "Andy Gump" chinless cowling planned for the A-model B-29.[23] The chin scoop for the oil cooler and turbo intakes were retained, just much reduced and moved aft of the cowl flaps. The design was ultimately never introduced into the production line.

Left: This Block 25 B-29 (42-24441) was modified to test an alternative, unpressurized defensive gun suite. At top are the two dorsal manned turrets, the lower forward ball turret, and the twin, remotely controlled Emerson nose barbettes. At bottom one sees the rear ventral ball, aft dorsal turret, and one of two waist positions. Jay Miller Collection

crew of five.

The eight .50cal machine guns (500rpg) were divided between two remote-controlled and retractable fuselage Sperry turrets. These turrets were normally retracted into a single bay behind the wing and aft bomb bay, top and bottom, and enclosed by doors that slid aft. Two guns (500rpg) and a 20mm cannon (100rpg) were also placed in a turret at the aft end of each outboard engine nacelle, firing rearward. There were also two .50s (500rpg) in the wing leading edges, outboard of the propeller disks. All turrets were hydraulically powered and total .50 ammunition was 7,000 rounds. The armament was integrated with the Sperry fire control system equipped with periscopes at three aiming stations. At the forward station, the fire control officer sat on a swivel seat under a "teardrop" dome in the upper fuselage with top and bottom periscopes. An aft gunner in the tail had a top and bottom periscope while an auxiliary station at the forward end of the aft compartment had only a bottom periscope. The wing leading edge guns were controlled solely from the forward station while the nacelle weapons and turrets could be controlled from either

Below: The B-29D was to have a 4.9ft (1.5m) taller tail and rudder in addition to a new engine and other improvements. The tail configuration was tested on this Block 35 B-29 (42-24528) that also has a revised cowling chin scoop. The latter was planned for continued B-29A production but never adopted. Museum of Flight

The nominal crew was a commander, pilot, copilot, navigator, engineer, radio operator, and gunner in the forward compartment, and gunner in the aft compartment. The navigator also served as the forward gunner. The rear compartment included bunks for a relief

primary computer stations. The auxiliary station could control the bottom turret. The fire control officer controlled which station directed which guns.

A third XB-32 (41-18336) was added on 14 December 1940 and then 13 service test YB-32s ordered on 30 June 1941 for $221,700,000. However, the design and fabrication of the prototypes ran long such that the first flight was six months behind schedule. When the first XB-32 was rolled out on 1 September 1942 it was without the problematic turrets and pressurisation. This was done at Army instigation to move testing along. The gear doors were also left off when taxi testing began on 3 September and for the subsequent first flight.

The 7 September big event at Lindbergh Field proved a short flight. A pushrod for a rudder trim tab broke under oscillatory flight loads and the free tab fluttered, generating severe airframe vibration and compelled an emergency landing.

The XB-32 testing was also affected by the grounding resulting from the XB-29 crash. However, its own delays and technical problems continued to plague the B-32 programme, bringing it close to cancellation several times. Even NACA predicted the aircraft would not measure up.[25] The programme survived each time, principally as insurance should its Boeing counterpart stumble.

The 13 YB-32s were dropped in February 1943, but this was simply prelude to the award of a 300-aircraft, $221,700 production contract approved on 17 March from which test aircraft were subsumed. With first deliveries planned for September 1943, the initial 14 B-32s would be followed by two score unarmed examples to support aircrew training (TB-32s). The bombers would be built in Fort Worth.

The optimism engendered by the production order soon faded when the first XB-32 was lost on 10 May 1943 when the machine failed to get airborne near maximum GW, ran off the end of the runway and ploughed into a Marine Corps training facility. The accident cost the lives of four and injuries to 63. The exact cause of the mishap was never definitively determined but may have been a flap failure.[26]

The loss of 41-141 severely set back the testing as valuable test instruments were destroyed. The second ship took up testing, beginning with its maiden flight on 2 July. It possessed an operational pressurisation system and full armament suite. It went on to acceptance trials at Muroc AAB in February 1944. The government testers found that, in general, handling was poor, visibility from the cockpit was bad, and the XB-32 did not meet performance guarantees save for takeoff distance. Although the aircraft was 20,000lb (9,072kg) lighter than the XB-29 and powered by the same engines, it was only around 10mph (16km/h) faster and range over 1,000mi (454kg) less.

The third X-plane was first flown on 9 November 1943, also with pressurisation. Persistence of the empennage stability problem and numerous other systems issues was cause for a USAAF survey team to inspect this machine soon after it flew.[27]

Most notable of the survey team's conclusions in their 3 December report was that the aircraft was "obsolete when compared with the 1943 combat aircraft requirements". Of course, the B-32 would not be in combat sooner than 1944. Indeed, some of their recommendations reflected this near-sightedness as they derided all the advanced features shared

Consolidated XB-32 characteristics:			
span	135.0ft	weight empty	64,960lb
length	83.0ft	design gross	101,662lb
height	20.8ft	max.	113,500lb
wing area	1,422ft²	bomb load, max.	20,000lb
fuel (norm.-max.)	4,590-5,226gal	normal	8,000lb
service ceiling	30,700ft	speed, max. (25,000ft)	379mph
average climb rate	1,105fpm	normal cruise	250mph
takeoff distance*	4,000ft	range, 20,000lb bombs	1,610mi
landing distance*	2,850ft	2,000lb bombs	4,450mi
*over 50ft obstacle			

with the B-29, then shaping up as the most capable bomber in the world. They advised elimination of pressurisation, "current tactical doctrine having made it unnecessary". They judged the defensive armament to be inadequate, with too few weapons, too little ammunition, and a blind spot ahead of the wingtips. They recommended replacing the Sperry gun system with manned turrets. More understandable was their suggestion for complete redesign of the empennage to a single vertical tail, to address the flutter issue as well as improve defensive field of fire. Redesign of the nacelles, and improvements in the fuel and oil systems, would reduce stress on the engines and fire potential. Other suggestions were adoption of four-blade propellers, inclusion of an autopilot, addition of wing leading edge hot air de-icers, installation of a fully electrical bomb release system, and improving bombardier vision.

A backup to the frustratingly slow B-29 programme of high technical risk was still justifiable, so the programme soldiered on and undertook the considerable redesign advised by the survey team. The flat acceptance by Materiel Command of the recommendations demonstrated a lack of champion for the programme. The B-29 had Arnold behind it, but the B-32

was definitely second-string. A rationale may have been to achieve some of the ambitious goals of the VHB programme while reducing technical risk.

Cabin pressurisation was proving a daunting challenge for most in the industry. Although 41-142 had shown it was achievable, its practicality in service and combat had yet to be demonstrated. The Army's agitation to remove the Sperry periscope-centric gun system from the B-29 was repeated with the B-32, and Consolidated had its own reservations about the system. While Boeing kept their remote turrets, and the ability to operate at very high altitude and speed, Consolidated had to relent. Hence, Materiel Command compromised with the B-32 to hasten the road to production, supplementing Superfortress output, with some advanced capabilities if the B-29 proved ultimately unsuccessful. The resulting design gave the VHB speed and payload but not the altitude, endurance, or VLR legs.

The bombardier's station was considered wholly inadequate and work was done on a complete redesign, to include a mockup. However, higher authority decided against the change, approving more modest alterations. The twin tail had continued to frustrate

Above: The Consolidated XB-32 typified the concept of the Very Heavy Bomber with a large bomb capacity and pressurised cabin. The first airplane is shown performing taxi tests at Lindbergh Field, San Diego, during September 1941. Note the lack of main gear doors, open bomb bays, and retracted gun turrets. *San Diego Air & Space Museum*

engineers and pilots. Although it was felt to give superior directional stability, longitudinal stability could be improved and tab flutter remained a worry. The third prototype was modified with a single vertical tail, in summer 1944. The electrically powered tabs remained, but primary control surface motion was commanded conventionally. The most expedient solution was to install a B-29 empennage, flying in this configuration initially on 13 September. However, this provided inadequate directional stability. An extraordinarily tall 19.5ft (5.8m) tail and rudder was built by Consolidated, essentially extending the B-29 structure up 3.0ft (0.9m). It was later modified further by adding a second trim tab, one manual operated and one servo (geared to rudder deflection).

A few early production aircraft lacked empennage ice protection gear, but most of the first 49 featured de-icing boots on the tail leading edges. Subsequent examples employed hot air anti-ice for

159

Left: The Sperry fire control system fitted to XB-32 41-142 included, at top, retractable turrets with four .50cal guns each. The guns were aimed via periscopes at multiple stations, one periscope head visible under the aft fuselage. At bottom, the outboard engine nacelle turret displays aft-firing guns and 20mm cannon. *Air Force Flight Test Center*

F3 -820   2-28-44
CONSOLIDATED VULTEE
MODEL XB32 NO. 41-142
LEFT NACELLE TURRET.

turret (1,100 rounds). Two dorsal Martin electrical turrets (800 rounds each) initially had transparent aerodynamic fairings at the rear and rotating with the turrets, but soon discarded. Up to four 750gal (2,839lit) droppable fuel tanks could be installed in the bays. The B-32 was equipped with much the same radio, navigation, and RCM gear as the B-29. An AN/APQ-13 BTO radar was added in a retractable radome forward of the bomb bays. An AN/APQ-5B Low Level Radar Bombsight, radar altimeter, and LORAN navigation system was also installed.

An unusual feature of the B-32 flight control was a "formation stick" for fine control of the autopilot during formation flight. This was two stick columns with an arm rest beside the pilot seats by which the pilot or copilot could introduce roll an pitch commands to the C-1 unit more effectively than with the panel knobs.

A few early aircraft got R-3350-21 engines while the production standard was the -23A and -23B, all equipped with twin B-11 turbos. The A included essential changes to make the Cyclone 18 combat-worthy while the B substituted a different carburetor. These were equipped with 16.7ft (5.1m) four-blade, hollow steel props featuring automatic synchronisation. Reversible pitch on the inboard engines assisted aircraft landing deceleration and ground manoeuvering. Cuffs were frequently fitted to assist engine cooling. A bow to serviceability was made by ensuring all engines and nacelles were interchangeable.

The fundamental design changes stretched out production preparations by a year and questions continued to arise about the need to continue the programme. Consolidated, itself, was more committed to the B-24 and XB-36, but continued to respond to customer desires. Yet, by the time production began in June 1944, the Fort Worth order (-CF) had been increased to 1,713 machines that included a third contract for 500 to be built in San Diego (-CO). The California plant would generate fuselages for its

the tail, as was installed in the wing, the air being waste heat from aircraft systems. The wing anti-ice air was derived from exhaust gas heat exchangers in the outboard nacelles. Propeller anti-ice was the same as the B-29.

The tail was but one of the dramatic changes to the B-32, earning it a new Model 34 identification. A more conventional stepped windscreen and chin bombardier sighting station was substituted. With pressurisation abandoned, the tunnel above the bomb bays and turrets volume was removed. The flight engineer's station was also jettisoned, leaving the crewman to sit on the deck between the pilots, in the passageway to the nose. The remote turrets and fire control system were replaced with manned turrets. Armour

was also reduced to just turrets and engines, and the crew shrank to nine men consisting of the pilot, copilot, engineer, bombardier, radio operator, navigator, and three gunners. An APU supplemented the generators and had to be running for ground operations owing to the low generator output at low engine power settings. Reduced structural weight permitted more bombs or fuel on typical missions.

The ten .50s were paired in five turrets (5,830 rounds). These consisted of a hydraulic twin-gun Sperry ball turrets in the nose 730 rounds (space provisions for 1,200 rounds), and tail (2,000 rounds). These had a shell that rotated laterally while the nested ball rotated vertically. The ventral turret was a retractable Briggs hydraulic ball own line as well as Texas while the latter shipped wings to California. However, the B-32 faced a continuing series of design changes introduced on the production line and as retrofits that would cause unending headaches for trainers, maintainers, and operators. Its future appeared far from bright.

The first TB-32 was handed over on 27 January 1945, at which point aircrew flight training could commence. The last was completed in late March 1945 after which delivery of combat-capable aircraft began. The first of these was accepted on 17 April. By this time, Germany was close to defeat and the B-29 seemed past its worst problems, just beginning its intensive campaign against Japan.

The B-32 benefited from the R-3350 development fostered by the B-29, also aided by operating at lower weights, but was not entirely free of powerplant issues. Two aircraft were lost to engine fires and others damaged. Electrical and hydraulic problems caused other torment. All B-32s were grounded in May 1945 to correct a mechanical issue that contributed to main landing gear collapses during landings, four

experienced in a few weeks span.

Although not the aircraft the Army had initially sought, Convair hoped the B-32 would find missions. At the end of 1944, the USAAF had plans to send B-32s to Europe, replacing B-17s and B-24s. However, production remained slow, with just 14 aircraft completed by the end of 1944 and only five handed over to the Army. The few aircraft, supremacy of the Superfortress, and continuing systems problems evident in accidents once again brought calls to halt the programme. A review concluded the B-32 should continue at least through service trials.

The AAF came away from its testing in Florida and Ohio with a long list of issues that included excessive weight, cowling design that compounded the R-3350 fire potential, trimming noticeably nose-high in cruise and degrading performance, high cockpit noise level, inadequate instrument layout, and very poor bombardier station. In-service rates were low owing to numerous systems failures. It was generally unpleasant to fly with numerous handling deficiencies and performance shortfalls. Workmanship and acceptance inspections were also

criticised in some areas.[28] The overall construction was judged too light by aircrew who were shocked by the flexibility of the airframe that caused fit and leakage problems. On the positive side, cockpit layout was very good and the reversible propeller gave commendable landing performance and ground handling.[29] Some aspects of the bomber, such as the radar bombsight, was never thoroughly tested. In general, the aircraft was considered unsuitable for combat introduction. However, Convair was making continual improvements as manufacturing rolled on, yet these also introduced parts availability, training, and operational continuity issues.

The programme survived until Germany succumbed in May. By then, the B-32 was clearly superfluous and evaluations to that time found the aircraft generally inferior to the B-29. Production

Below: This image of 41-142 reveals the wing guns, one barrel protruding from the leading edge just beyond each outboard propeller arc. The upper forward periscope and main gunners station dome is also evident. The original tail shown here had advantages but suffered structural dynamics issues. *Author's Collection*

contracts were reduced in June to just 214 machines, all from Fort Worth save three San Diego aircraft. Production peaked in July at 21 that month.[30]

The B-32 was still maturing at the end of the war, but their numbers were few. Yet, some were subjected to unique modifications for specific missions. Aircraft 42-108471, the first production example, was seen with extended horizontal tail tips that were not adopted for production. It also flew a radar radome of a teardrop design that may not have been retractable. Aircraft 42-108482, a B-32-5-CF, was modified with four-gun dorsal and ventral turrets for testing purposes. Aircraft 42-108535, a B-32-20-CF, was altered at Eglin in spring 1945 to carry two 12,000lb (5,443kg) Tallboy bombs or one 22,000lb (9,979kg) Grand Slam bomb under Project Albert. However, this effort was delayed while

a suitable hoist was developed and ultimately discarded at the end of the war.

Despite an assessment that the bomber was unsuitable for combat, in April 1945 ATSC was continuing work towards conducting combat trials. However, as trained cadre and aircraft trickled out of Texas, plans to deploy the aircraft were rendered moot by the approaching end of the war in Europe and the success of the B-29. Because Arnold insisted the Superfortress be limited to strategic bombing, theatre commanders were denied the VHB capability they desired for certain targets. The unutilised B-32 offered an alternative, and they were welcomed in the Pacific to attack Japanese forces in the Dutch East Indies. The bomber certainly had significant advantages

Above: Addressing the tail criticisms and engineering problems during the B-32 redesign, the most expedient measure was to install a B-29 empennage. This proved inadequate for directional stability, but three aircraft were built with the tail, including, temporarily, the first production B-32s (42-108471 shown in Fort Worth).
San Diego Air & Space Museum

on the B-24, to include 2.5 times the payload, approximately 1,000mi (1,609km) more range, and roughly 50mph (81km/h) faster. If the combat trials proved successful, squadrons would trade in A-20s for B-32s.

Three aircraft and Convair technical support personnel were deployed to The Philippines in May 1945 for combat trials. A month of missions were executed respectably well with tolerable serviceability issues – which is to say acceptable in wartime and of limited service life. Many still considered the aircraft a "dog". Interestingly, the team noted the lack of pressurisation was a "handicap" for operations above 20,000ft (6,096m).[51] The test results were generally, if unenthusiastically, judged acceptable.

Local aircrew were already undertaking conversion training and six more aircraft were brought out. The team had relocated to Okinawa and performed one mission from there before Japan agreed to cease hostilities. This aircraft were then devoted to photography over Japan. The sortie on the 18 August saw the B-32 come away badly damaged by a fighter and with a crewman dead, becoming the last American airwar combat death in the last air battle of the conflict but also the last bomber "kill" of an enemy aircraft. The final mission on the 28th ended with two of the four bombers lost to accidents and 15 men perishing – a tragic end to the calamitous B-32 saga.

Below: The B-32 was greatly revised from the X-plane in an effort to reduce technical risk and speed production. The manned turrets (note clear fairings on dorsal units), altered nose, and new tail are evident in this image. Less evident is lack of cabin pressurisation and extensively redesigned fuselage structure. *National Archives*

Convair B-32-20 characteristics:

span	135.0ft	weight empty	60,278lb
length	82.1ft	design gross	100,000lb
height	32.2ft	max./overload	111,500/123,250lb
wing area	1,422ft²	bomb load, max.	20,000lb
fuel (norm.-max.)	5,460-6,960gal	normal	8,000lb
service ceiling	30,700ft	speed, max. (30,000ft/100,000lb)	357mph
best climb rate (100,000lb)	1,050fpm	(5,000ft)	302mph
takeoff distance* 110,000lb	6,100ft	normal cruise	290mph
landing distance*	3,100ft	range, typ. (20,000lb bombs)	2,400mi
		typ. (10,000lb bombs)	3,000mi
*over 50ft obstacle		ferry	4,400mi

The B-32 clearly had no future and all remaining orders were cancelled on 15 August. This left 1,099 -CF and 499 -CO machines cancelled. Perhaps a dozen B-32s and TB-32s were destroyed in service to all causes. Average unit cost was $731,040, considerably more than the B-29. Ultimately, 118 aircraft were accepted of 130 manufactured to include the 3 XB-32s, 74 B-32-CFs in seven blocks, a sole San Diego production example B-32-20-CO, and the 40 TB-32-CFs. Twelve nearly

complete aircraft were flown directly to storage, 10 from Texas (42-108585/94) and 2 from California (44-90487/8).[¶] Airframes in assembly (some largely complete), these being 50 in Fort Worth (42-108595/644), were broken up.[**]

¶It is indicative of wasted effort in the waste of war that, after all the work to prepare the San Diego production line, it manufactured just three B-32s that were promptly flown to the "boneyard".

** W Serial numbers up to 41-108604 are seen clearly in the accompanying photograph of the Fort Work plant.

Honorable Mention

Of the four Very Heavy Bomber competitors, the Lockheed XB-30 and Douglas XB-31 were not taken to prototype. However, they reflect what was then considered state-of-the-art and other avenues that might have lead to the VHB.

XB-30

At the time of the competition, Lockheed was already constructing the first of their four-engine Model 49 Constellation airliners. This was the most advanced commercial transport of the period and customers were awaiting deliveries. The design featured a pressurised cabin for flight up to 20,000ft (6,096m) and 35,000ft (10,668m) ceiling, 360mph (579km/h) top speed, hydraulically boosted controls, Fowler flaps, and tricycle landing gear. Four Double Wasps or Double Cyclones were planned, each delivering 2,000hp (1,491kW). As it

Right: Consolidated (later Consolidated-Vultee) developed the B-32 in competition with the B-29. However, it underwent substantial design changes to hasten production, giving up most of the unique Very Heavy Bomber features. This rare color image shows an unarmed trainer airframe, TB-32-15 42-108521, over Texas. University of Texas at Dallas

was into the hardware stage, unlike the Boeing conceptual designs, the Model 49 appeared an outstanding basis for a heavy bomber.

The Lockheed VHB design, the Model 51-81-01, was submitted in spring 1940 and designated XB-30.32 Spanning 123.0ft (37.5m), with 1,650ft² (153m²) wing area and 51,725lb (23,462kg) empty weight, the aircraft was expected

Above: The first production B-32 (42-108471) remained with Convair for the duration of the war, serving as a flight test airframe. During that time it was subject to several modifications for evaluation. Here it flies with extended horizontal stabilizers and a "teardrop" radome. Note the clear fairing behind the turrets. Jay Miller Collection

to cruise at 240mph (386km/h) and top out at 382mph (615km/h). Maximum bomb load was to be 16,000lb (7,258kg)

Above: The Convair B-32 production facility in Fort Worth is seen in the last days of the war. All these aircraft, clearly far along in assembly, would be scrapped in short order. The long assembly hall, nearly a mile, was created to permit assembly line processes for aircraft construction. *National Museum of the United States Airforce*

and range at the 88,500lb (40,143kg) GW was projected at 5,335mi (8,586km). The airliner's nose would be revised to include a bombardier station and the aft fuselage extended beyond the tails to accommodate a turret. Lockheed proposed using four R-3350-13 engines turning three-blade propellers. Armament was to be ten .50cal guns (5,000 rounds) paired in two dorsal and two ventral remote, low-profile fuselage turrets, aimed via periscopes, and a tail turret. A 20mm cannon (60 rounds) would join the tail guns. Perhaps the earliest concept had tall, manned turrets and the forward ventral turret did not exist, that quarter covered by two side turrets with two guns each. A crew of 7 and 12 was mentioned.[33]

Although Lockheed signed on 27 June 1940 to prepare preliminary engineering data for the XB-30, it withdrew on 6 September to concentrate on other programs. America's entry into the war then meant Lockheed had no commercial market for the Constellation. However, the USAAF bought the aircraft as the C-69 with R-3350-35s.

XB-31

A number of designs were explored by Douglas for the XB-31 before submitting the Model 423 or D-332F in fall 1941. For example, twin tails were eventually replaced with a single tail of enormous size. Individual "bug-eye" canopies were planned for the pilot and copilot.

The XB-31 was to be a much larger aircraft than the Superfortress and exceeded the required payload. A span of 207.0ft (63.1m), length 117.3ft (35.8m) and wing area 3,300ft² (307m²) was to be matched to 109,200lb (49,532kg) empty weight and 176,000lb (79,832kg) maximum gross to carry 13,000gal (49,210lit) of fuel and 25,000lb (11,340kg) payload distributed between two bomb bays. A larger and heavier aircraft than the XB-19, the 3,000hp (2,237kW) Pratt & Whitney X-Wasp (R-4360 Wasp Major) engines were

planned. These were to have turned three-blade propellers of 25.0ft (7.6m) diameter, although four-blade props are also shown in some concept art. Two or three low-profile, remote fuselage turrets with .50cal guns and a tail turret with two 37mm cannon would make up the armament. A periscope station for the fuselage turrets was to be just aft of the flight deck. A crew of eight or nine was planned.

After the study contract, Douglas was not rewarded with follow-on development work and the effort was shelved. One of the factors in this decision may have been the long lead-time of the R-4360 that was even earlier in its development cycle than the R-3350, having run on the test stand for the first time in April 1941, and lack of suitable alternate powerplant for the enormous aircraft. The XB-19 having already demonstrated the limited practicality of giant aircraft, the XB-31 may have appeared too risky.

In Between (B-33)

As discussed previously, a large Martin bomber grew out of the XB-33 (Model

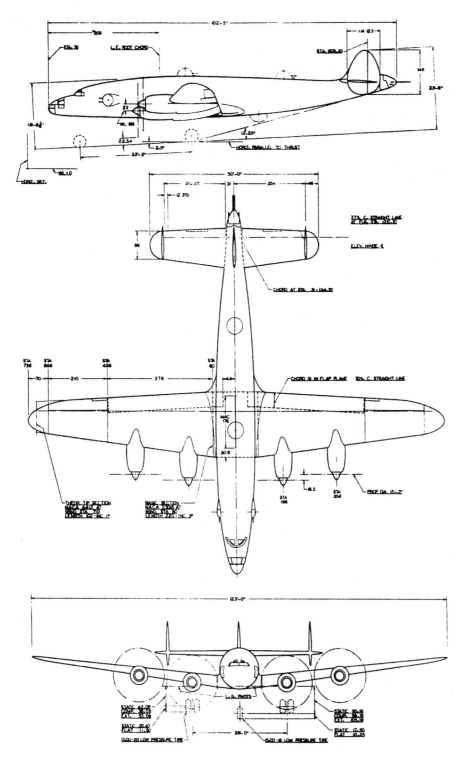

it appeared prudent to pursue a heavier design. Likewise, if the ambitious VHB projects did not pan out, the B-33 might still provide important enhancements to the bomber force.

A 5 May draft specification from Martin was followed on the 8th by a proposal with a revised Model 190-3. This had a wing spanning 114.0ft (35.8m) for an area of 1,300ft² (121m²), accommodating 12,000lb (5,443kg) of bombs for a normal gross of 67,900lb (30,799kg). An unusual design feature included engine nacelle bomb bays that could take four 100lb (45kg) bombs each. Maximum speed was to be 354mph (570km/h) and service ceiling 33,700ft (10,272m). Maximum gross with the normal bomb load of 2,400lb (1,089kg) was 80,630lb (36,573kg) for 2,890mi (4,651km) range. The remote armament would include four .50cal machine guns in an upper turret and two each in a lower and tail turret, all GE equipment.

The proposal quoted a price of $5,100,000 for two Super Marauder prototypes. Suggested initial delivery was 18 months following contract award and the second aircraft a month later. The Air Corps was authorised to proceed on 13 May. The contract, still referring to the aircraft as a Medium Bombardment Aircraft and with the same 41-28407/8 serials, was approved on 11 June for $4,538,500. It was only in August that the designation XB-33 (MX-34) was formally assigned. The Martin specification was approved 1 December 1941. The Army asked that the aircraft accommodate an alternative R-2800 engine installation as a possible upgrade during production.

Martin continued to work closely with NACA Langley for wind tunnel testing and other design assistance. During July, meetings were held to address raising concern with wing loading on the XB-29, XB-32, and XB-33. The originally planned XB-33 gross weight of 63,347lb (28,734kg) gave a wing loading of 48.6psf (10.0kg/m²), but this had grown to 68,693lb (31,159kg) and 52.8psf (10.8kg/m²) due principally to accommodating the two possible engines and a requested structural factor of 4.0 at high gross weight.[34] Maximum speed for the heavier aircraft was 353mph (568km/h) and ceiling 33,450ft (10,196m).

As a consequence of the discussions,

Above: The concept drawing of the Lockheed XB-30 shows the fundamentals of the conversion from the Constellation airliner. The bombardier nose, turrets, and periscope stations are most evident. Bomb bay doors are not shown in available period art, but would presumably have been distributed ahead and behind the wing spar. *National Museum of the United States Air Force*

189) with twin R-3350s (Chapter 4). As weight rose during preliminary design, the decision was communicated on 28 April 1941 to convert it to a four-engine aircraft with R-2600s, General Arnold himself directed the change. It would not meet the VHB or VLR goals, but would still have performance superior to the B-17 and B-24. As the suitability of these aircraft for the strategic bombardment mission had yet to be firmly established,

the target weights were reduced, normal gross down to 66,050lb (29,960kg), although a target 45psf (9.2kg/m²) was desired. The nacelle would be lightened by eliminating the requirement to mount the R-2800. The leak-proof fuel capacity would be brought down to 1,816gal (6,874lit) from 2,350gal (8,896lit), but supplemented by four 450gal (1,703lit) droppable bomb bay tanks and 250gal (946lit) droppable outboard nacelle tanks. This Model 190-8 brought wing loading down to 50.8psf (10.4kg/m²), but a cap of 74,300lb (33,702kg) maximum gross was set for the normal mission load with 2,400lb (1,089kg) of weapons. That weight would give 2,370mi (3,814km). A Model 190-9 was also conceived in the event weight continued to grow. This would have a 1,500ft² (139m²) wing spanning 123ft (38m), the fuselage lengthened 2.9ft (0.9m). At 50,115lb (22,732kg) empty weight and 67,156lb (30,461kg) normal gross, wing loading would be 45.0psf (9.2kg/m²). Range at 75 per cent power was predicted to be 2,320mi (3,733km) at 301mph (484km/h). Maximum fuel load would be 4,065gal (15,388lit). However, the schedule slip engendered by this level of redesign was not palatable.

During September 1941, the service and Martin explored an increase of 5,000-6,000ft (1,524-1,829m) in performance ceiling, with an eventual objective of 40,000ft (12.192m). The AAF was exploring the feasibility of very high altitude bombing. Various weapon load alternations were explored, some adding and some subtracting weight. General Oliver Echols, Chief of Materiel Command, made a proclamation on 24 September that all further changes to the aircraft be deferred until after December 1943 so as not to jeopardise achieving a B-33 production rate of 25 units per month by that date.

An XB-33 mockup was inspected during the week of 6 October 1941 in Baltimore, where engineering and production was to occur. Some 154 recommended changes resulted, focusing principally on visibility, instruments, radios, bomb carriage, reducing vulnerability, and armour. Most notable was the recommendation to investigate adding twin .50 gun rear-firing remote guns to each outboard

nacelle, or alternatively the inboard nacelles, to ensure suitable defence given the limited top turret field of fire with the twin tails. As all the recommended changes were seen as improving the military utility, their weight impact was felt justified. Consequently, consideration again turned to increasing wing area from 1,300ft² (121m²) to 1,500ft² (139m²) with Model 190-9. However, the requirement to maintain 8,000ft (2,438m) cabin altitude to 30,000ft (9,144m), and a constant pressure differential to the ceiling, was being reconsidered, with 35,000ft (10,668m) the new objective. Even a compromise on that objective, allowing cabin altitude to reach 18,000ft (5,486m), would be a structural weight bonanza.

On 14 October 1941, Echols recommended negotiations begin for procuring 400 B-33s, and this was further enforced in the flurry following Pearl Harbor. Negotiations completed, Martin signed the Letter of Intent on 26 December and submitted a production proposal. The 400 aircraft (42-35184/583) plus spares were priced at $288,000,000.

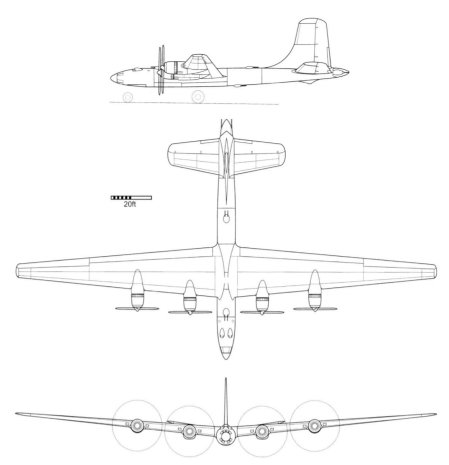

Above: The Douglas XB-31 was to exceed the B-29 in size and payload, even larger than the XB-19. Shown is the configuration reflected in the literature, but many were explored during the design process. The R-4360 engine was selected, but this would have been unavailable until very late in the war. *Author*

The 17 January 1942, $300,458,708.07 contract included the XB-33s in a total 402 machines and spares.†† This also included wind tunnel models and added a static test article (42-38279).[35] The first two production aircraft were still referred to a while longer as XB-33s although they were supposedly "identical" to the production machines and suitable for accelerated service trials. The first of the Four Engine Heavy Bombardment Aircraft would be delivered in January 1943 in a stripped-down configuration, the second in July in fully mission-capable state, and production peaking at 45 per month in March 1944 by which time 68 aircraft would have been delivered.[36]

The aircraft, as it approached the near-final configuration, retained the stepped windscreen and tailplane dihedral with

†† When formally cancelled on 24 July 1942, Martin had spent $426,733.09 on the X-planes.

167

Left: The XB-33 was to be a four-engine very heavy bomber in the class of the B-29. The Super Marauder would have been characterized by Martin's signature "pinwheel" tail. These poor but rare images show the mockup of the bomber in Baltimore, probably at the time of the October 1941 inspection. *Ray Wagner Collection*

tip fins of the Model 189, but overall dimensions increased substantially. The R-2600-15 single-speed engine offered 1,800hp (1,342kW). Each was to be fitted with two General Electric CMC-3 single-stage turbosuperchargers and turning a 15.7ft (4.8m) diameter four-blade propeller. Four GE turrets included a dorsal and ventral, a tail and nose, each with two .50cals (500rpg). All were to be remotely controlled from the pressurised cabin. There appeared to be a master gunner station above the forward fuselage and a large blister for the tail gunner in the top of the aft fuselage between the tails. Other sighting blisters are evident in the sides and bottom of the aft fuselage and ahead of the windscreen. The bombardier was to work beneath the nose turret in a chin

"sighting station". He would be one in a crew of seven.

As detail design continued, GW rose to 78,850lb (35,766kg) and the span increase to 123ft (198m) had been adopted, but Martin was still anticipating a maximum airspeed of 375mph (604km/h) and ceiling of 42,000ft (12,802m). However, by the end of 1941, they were reporting normal gross would be 80,000lb (36,287kg). Top speed was down to 355mph (571km/h), but ceiling remained unchanged. Martin was working to increase span to 134ft (216m) and aspect ratio from 10 to 12. Wing loading would then be 53.5psf (11.0kg/m²).

The first inklings of the end for the B-33 arose in fall 1942 when General Echols revealed he was negotiating

with Martin to work with Northrop on the XB-35 that had been given the "highest possible priority". Northrop had sought to borrow engineers from other firms to accelerate development, but all were saturated with work. On 2 November, the Director of Military Requirements suggested the B-33 be cancelled to reduce duplicative programs and permit Martin resources be turned to assisting higher priority efforts. The Superfortress was clearly going to reach fruition ahead of the B-33, the newest models of the B-17 and B-24 were promising marked performance improvements, and the B-29 and B-35 appeared to best meet AAF requirements. Echols directed on 9 November that work begin to convert the B-33 contract to one for Martin supporting the XB-35.

The cancellation process began on 25 November 1942 with formal action to terminate the production contract. It was revealed in a 7 December report that NACA analysis showed the B-33, as then configured, had excessive parasite drag that cut 10mph (16km/h) off the top speed it would have possessed had the drag been identical to the B-29. Airfoil selection and nacelle design were particularly criticised. The aircraft would also likely suffer unsatisfactory stability, stall, and elevator control characteristics. Although the deficiencies could probably be corrected, more time would be sacrificed. Weight had also grown substantially over the objective 66,030lb (29,951kg) normal gross to 84,060lb (38,129kg), and fuel capacity had been increased, as the Army directed changes revealed as essential from early combat experience. Consequently, top speed had dropped to 330mph (531km/h) and ceiling to 39,800ft (12,131m). The aircraft would be underpowered with the R-2600s. These revelations were followed by direction from Echols on 15 December that the B-33 work be immediately halted.

The B-33 design engineering was 90

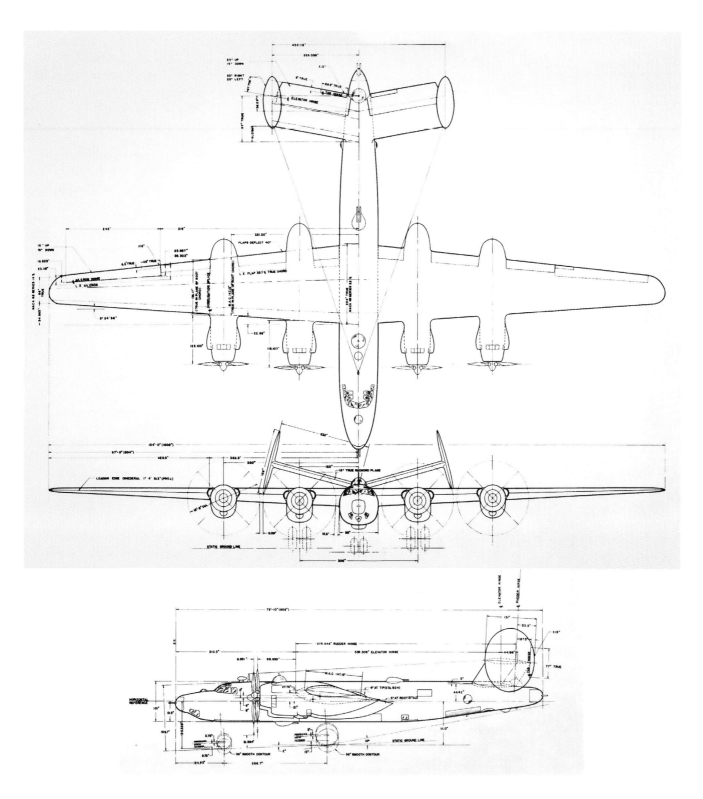

per cent complete and tool preparation 25/45 per cent complete when all efforts ceased in mid-December. Prototype construction had already begun, so these materials and associated tooling were scrapped. The 402-aircraft B-33 contract was changed on 30 June 1943 to cover Martin's contribution to the B-35 programme with 200 aircraft plus 20 per cent spares, approximately

$330,000,000 carried over. Martin also returned $5,000,000 of the advance on the Super Marauder programme. All told, the work and termination fees had cost about $8,000,000.

Above: This Martin engineering drawing of the B-33, Model 190, is useful in illustrating general characteristics of the design. The numerous turrets and gunner sighting stations are evident. The aircraft reached the stage of prototype construction before being cancelled as redundant, Martin talents better devoted to assisting the Northrop XB-35 programme. *Glenn L. Martin Maryland Aviation Museum*

Chapter Nine

Intercontinental Reach

The Impossible?

An intercontinental super heavy bomber was on the collective mind of the Air Corps since the war began. It had a dim relationship to the 1930s planned development of ever-larger bombers, the peak to be a 250ft (76m) span and 200,000lb (90,718kg) machine. The XB-19 suggested enormous bombers with great range were possible, and both the Kilner and Emmons Boards identified the need for a bomber with 6,000mi (9,655km) range. On 1 January 1940, the Assistant Chief of the Air Corps, Brigadier General Carl Spaatz, directed the Air War Plans Division to begin development of the VLR bomber with the ability to make a round-trip bombing mission against Berlin from Point Barrow, Alaska.[1]

The decision to pursue formally an acquisition was made in early 1941 by President Roosevelt in consultation with Generals Marshall and Arnold. The bomber would offer capabilities in the event land bases could not be negotiated or captured to support attacks on the German and Japanese homelands. There was real concern Great Britain might be defeated, and so unavailable for basing of American bombers in an alliance. Positioning of US aircraft in range of Japan also appeared most problematic. Hence, USAAC drafted requirements for a very heavy bomber with intercontinental reach. Just a year before, such an aircraft would have been generally considered impossible.

The principal points in the Preliminary Military Characteristics for the "Bombardment, Heavy, Long Range" aircraft were a range of 8,000mi (12,874km) minimum and 12,000mi (19,310km) desired at 25,000ft (7,620m) altitude with 4,000lb (1,814kg) of bombs, 10,000lb (4,536kg) delivered on a 5,000mi (8,046km) radius mission with 15 per cent fuel reserve, and a maximum 72,000lb (32,659kg) payload. A conservative specific fuel consumption of 0.42lb/hr/hp was stated for average cruise power setting.* Service ceiling was to be 35,000ft (10,668m) to 45,000ft (13,716m), a top speed of 350mph (563km/h) minimum to 450mph (724km/h) desired at 25,000ft (7,620m), and cruise at 200mph (323km/h) minimum and 275mph

* Specific fuel consumption is a measure of the fuel flow rate required to generate one unit of engine output power.

(443km/h) desired. Takeoff and landing over a 50ft (15m) obstacle was to be in 4,500ft (1,372m) desired or 6,000ft (1,892m) maximum. Pressurisation would ensure cabin altitude did not to exceed 10,000ft (3,048m). It was realised an escort for such a bomber was well nigh impractical, so the bomber itself would need to be exceptionally well endowed for self defence. Armament was to be a combination of .50cal guns and 20mm or 37mm cannon with 600rpg, 120rpg, or 50rpg respectively, and 200 per cent reload capacity. Fuel was to be in leak-proof tanks and 150lb (68kg) of armour would be provided for each crewman.

Barely

Preliminary design studies for the intercontinental bomber were requested on 11 April 1941 from Consolidated and Boeing, Douglas also choosing to participate. Out of a fixed fund, the contractor with the best design would get $135,445 and the other $300,178. The design data were submitted on 3 May. Boeing's concepts looked like enlarged B-29s. The Douglas model possessed just 6,000mi (9,655km) range. Consolidated's concept was based on their Model 35 study pursued in-house since September 1940. This envisioned a high wing spanning 164ft (50m) of 2,700ft² (251m²) area on a 128.0ft (39.0m) fuselage. The tail was much like the XB-32 with dihedral and tip verticals. Two wing nacelles each contained two engines in a tandem tractor/pusher arrangement. The company proposed

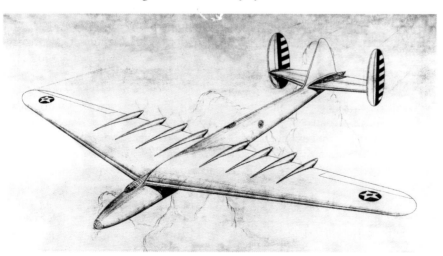

Left: The USAAC Materiel Division considered very long range "super bombers" in the earliest days of the war. Their "Long Range Bomber" concept was estimated at 264,000lb (119,748kg) gross weight with a span of 237ft (72m) and 131ft (40m) length. Dated prior to March 1940, such studies helped establish VLR requirements. *National Archives*

a 180-day Phase I design study for $150,000. Although the Army funded Consolidated's study on 9 August, none of the designs met the requirements to the extent desired. Some of the manufacturers commented that the goals were probably unachievable.

Consolidated submitted preliminary results of their design study on 16 August; although offering four-engine pushers and other layouts, they proposed the earlier push-pull arrangement be carried forward.[2] The results were somewhat lacklustre. In light of Britain's potential collapse, the decision was made to get the intercontinental bomber programme moving into high gear as a national priority. This began with a high-level AAF meeting in Washington on 19 August. It was recognised at least 2.5 years were required for development of such a super bomber and no interference with the effort could be tolerated.

The earlier characteristics were revised by the Air Staff War Plans Division based upon closer study of the problem and the offered designs. Principal changes were a 4,000mi (6,437km) tactical radius and total 10,000mi (16,092km) range with 10,000lb (4,536kg) payload at a 35,000ft (10,668m) altitude, and ceiling reduced to 40,000ft (12,192m). Average cruise speed was upped to 240mph (386km/h) minimum and 300mph (483km/h) desired while top speed remained unchanged. Runway lengths were reduced to 4,000ft (1,219m) desired and 5,000ft (1,524m) maximum. Armament was then stated as at least eight .50cal guns (1,000rpg) and six 37mm (300rpg). The 150lb (68kg) of armour was extended to each engine, and the oil would also be in self-sealing tanks. The range and speed suggested 31hr in flight for a 10,000mi flight, meaning that at least two crews would need to be carried.

The revised Preliminary Military Characteristics, CTI-310, was issued on 23 August with Boeing, Consolidated, and Douglas requested to respond in early September. Wright Field prepared its own design study showing potential design approaches and provided this to the contractors.

Boeing again proposed an enlarged B-29 but with six engines and high aspect ratio wing. Douglas offered an eight-

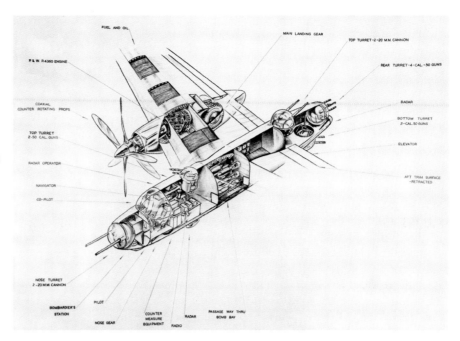

engine design, but was unwilling to reach for more range than 6,000mi (9,655km). None of these met the requirements and appeared to Wright Field engineers to be excessively large and heavy. They did not reflect as much effort as Consolidated expended. That company submitted six Model 35 variants. Of the multiple layouts offered, the six engines in the trailing edge of the wing would reduce drag and help ensure laminar flow by eliminating propeller slipstream over the wing. Wright Field recommended Consolidated be given a development contract for this configuration as it was the most likely to meet requirements. Arnold quickly approved the move.

Compromise

In reaching for their goals, the USAAC also decided to give John "Jack" Northrop his chance. President of Northrop Aircraft, he had long advocated the benefits of an all-wing or "flying wing" bomber. The firm was then flying the two-engine N-1M light aircraft all-wing testbed and developing the XP-56 tailless single-engine fighter. Considerations of such a bomber dated from January 1938, with Wright Field examining two- and four-engine designs with "buried" engines, tricycle undercarriage, 321mph (517km/h) top speed, and 8,000mi (12,875km) range.[3] At the time the intercontinental discussions were taking place both Wright Field and the War Department had recently encouraged

Above: A 1942 tailless bomber concept from Convair, designed against the B-36 requirements and with the same six engines, was used to contrast predicted performance between the two layouts. The concept pictured here, dated 3 December 1943, was for a twin-engine Navy patrol bomber and Army bomber carried forward this research. The tractor engine arrangement (R-4360 engines turning dual-rotation propeller), wingtip vertical surfaces, and elevators that arms extended out from the wing trailing edge and slid on rails in the aft fuselage, all offered stability advantages. The 90,000lb (40,823kg) aircraft was expected to carry 8,000lb (3,629kg) of bombs and fly 5,000mi (8,047km). *San Diego Air & Space Museum*

Northrop to prepare studies of bombers based on the N-1M principals. Becoming aware of the new bomber requirement, Jack Northrop sent a 13 May 1941 letter to Arnold outlining the potential benefits of flying wing bombers. General Echols visited Northrop on 22 May to discuss the work that had included goals of 400mph (644km/h) and 5,000lb (2,268kg) bomb load. The following day, Northrop stated they calculated that a 100,000lb (45,359kg) all-wing bomber could carry 10,005,000lb (4,53,804kg) of bombs and possess about 5,000mi (8,048km) range.

Given the extremely challenging intercontinental requirements, it appeared worth gambling on the radical all-wing concept, although CTI-310 and earlier requirements were never imposed. Northrop was formally asked on 27 May 1941 to submit information on their bomber concept. The initial specification for the design study was

Left: A model of the Consolidated XB-36, photographed on 14 November 1941, closely resembles the long-range heavy bomber winning design. Of particular interest are engine cooling inlets under the wing (none in the wing leading edges), the four-blade propellers, and gunner periscope protuberances. *San Diego Air & Space Museum*

an augmented version of XC-218A for the VHB.[4] It sought 4050mph (6424km/h) at 25,000ft (7,620m) and flying 5,33,000mi (8,582,874km) with 2,000lb (907kg) of bombs at a cruise speed of 2500mph (4083km/h), with 35,005,000ft (10,663,716m) service ceiling. Engines to be considered were the 2,300hp (1,715kW) R-3350, 2,600hp (1,939kW) V-3420, 2,600hp Wright R-2160, and 3,000hp (2,237kW) X-Wasp (later R-4360 Wasp Major). The defence suite of .50cal, 20mm, or 37mm weapons and armour prescribed for the intercontinental bomber were repeated. Likewise, the requirements for leak-proof tanks and armour were imposed. Like the XB-33, a 4.5 ultimate load factor was to be applied for loads analysis.

Jack Northrop presented a preliminary design at Wright Field on 2 July 1941. The more carefully analysed concept, N-9, possessed 6,000mi (9,655km) range with a 10,000lb (4,536kg) payload and 8,000mi (12,874km) with 2,000lb (907kg) at 25,000ft (7,620m) while cruising at 250mph (402km/h). Ceiling was projected at 40,000ft (12,192m). This assumed 2,50,000hp (1,86,237kW) engines.

Much supporting research was clearly necessary before detailed design of an all-wing bomber could be completed. The outlines of such a programme were

drafted at the 2 July meeting. Phase I would prepare engineering data for evaluation, Phase II would move to wind tunnel model testing and presentation of N-1M flight results, and Phase III the construction of a flying mockup at 3/10th to 4/10th scale to be delivered within a year of contract signing. Agreement on these terms was solidified in mid July.

Negotiations for a prototype all-wing bomber (MX-140) began on 6 August 1941. Northrop presented its proposal in a 9 September meeting in Echols' office with Pratt & Whitney. They arrived at a 24-month timeline to develop the bomber of 125,0085,000lb (56,693,914kg) GW to be powered by R-4360s. The engine was then still developmental. Concept N-9E of 140,000lb (63,503kg) gross was selected and Arnold approved proceeding

with the programme the same day. Considering the great uncertainty in this radical design and Arnold's hesitancy to fund research efforts in wartime, the all-wing decisions had to be based in large measure on the personal familiarity of the men involved and confidence in Jack Northrop himself.

Left For Later (XB-36)

Consolidated submitted its proposal for the super bomber on 6 October 1941. It sought $15,000,000 for two test aircraft and mockup, with work to be performed in San Diego. A contract was approved on 15 November for two XB-36 bombers (43570/1, MX-149). Recognising the time required for such an ambitious project and the probably modest priority, the USAAF requested delivered of the first aircraft in 30 months (15 May 1944) and the second six months later. Only on 22 November did the Air Forces definitely selected the six-engine pusher concept as Model 36.[5]

As proposed, the XB-36 was expected to gross 265,000lb (120,201kg), yet the projected top speed was 369mph (594km/h) with a 40,000ft (12,192m)

Right: The 28-cylinder Pratt & Whitney R-4360 Wasp Major promised 3,000hp (2,237kW), and so became the heart of intercontinental bomber designs. However, gestation of the roughly 3,500lb (1,588kg) dry weight "corncob" powerplant was lengthy and difficult. For the XB-35 application, it required a fan (like the XB-36), dual-rotation gearbox, and propeller extension shaft, and Northrop added the extensive exhaust ducting. *Gerald Balzer Collection*

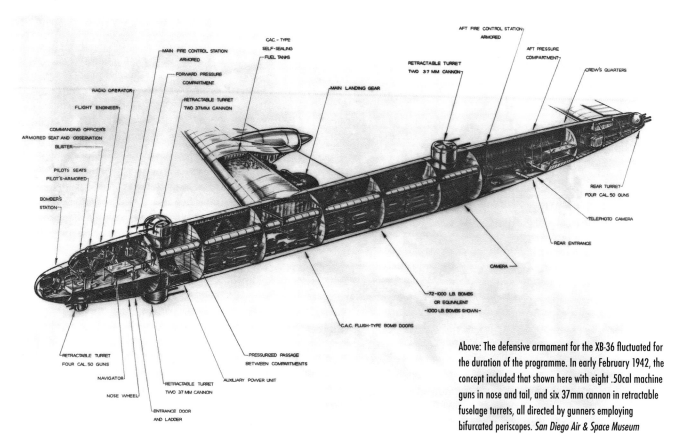

MAIN FIRE CONTROL STATION
ARMORED

CAC - TYPE
SELF-SEALING
FUEL TANKS

AFT FIRE CONTROL STATION
ARMORED

FORWARD PRESSURE
COMPARTMENT

RETRACTABLE TURRET
TWO 37 MM CANNON

AFT PRESSURE
COMPARTMENT

RADIO OPERATOR

CREW'S QUARTERS

FLIGHT ENGINEER

RETRACTABLE TURRET
TWO 37MM CANNON

MAIN LANDING GEAR

COMMANDING OFFICER'S
ARMORED SEAT AND OBSERVATION
BLISTER

REAR TURRET
FOUR CAL.50 GUNS

PILOTS SEATS
PILOT'S-ARMORED

TELEPHOTO CAMERA

BOMBER'S
STATION

REAR ENTRANCE

CAMERA

72-1000 LB. BOMBS
OR EQUIVALENT
-1000 LB. BOMBS SHOWN-

C.A.C. FLUSH-TYPE BOMB DOORS

RETRACTABLE TURRET
FOUR CAL.50 GUNS

PRESSURIZED PASSAGE
BETWEEN COMPARTMENTS

NAVIGATOR

RETRACTABLE TURRET
TWO 37 MM CANNON

AUXILIARY POWER UNIT

NOSE WHEEL

ENTRANCE DOOR
AND LADDER

Above: The defensive armament for the XB-36 fluctuated for the duration of the programme. In early February 1942, the concept included that shown here with eight .50cal machine guns in nose and tail, and six 37mm cannon in retractable fuselage turrets, all directed by gunners employing bifurcated periscopes. *San Diego Air & Space Museum*

service ceiling. It was to use six 3,000hp (2,237kW) R-4360 engines with three-blade, 19.0ft (5.8m) diameter propellers. The R-4360 had first run on the stand in April 1941 and flew in several airframes by the time of the XB-36 application. The Wasp Major had 28 cylinders in four rows of seven that gave a low frontal area for reduced drag, although of unusual length earning it the appellation "corncob engine". They would be mounted on laminar-flow wings of 230ft (70m) span and 4,772ft² (443m²) area. Slotted Fowler flaps were divided into three segments per side, separated by the nacelles, and the aileron gaps were to be sealed. The wing was so thick (7.5ft/2.3m, at the root) that the engines were to be accessible in flight for servicing. Six wing tanks totaling 21,116gal (79,933lit) of fuel were to be self-sealing while 1,200gal (4,543lit) of engine oil was planned.

Four bomb bays with 72,000lb (32,659kg) total capacity were to be incorporated into a fuselage 163.0ft (49.7m) long. Flush, sliding bay doors like the B-24 and B-32 would be adopted. Bombs would be loaded via an electric winch positioned atop the aircraft with its cables extending through a few of the

nearly 100 holes into each bay. A 3,000gal (11,356lit) jettisonable auxiliary fuel tank could be carried in the third from front bomb bay.

Forward and aft pressurised crew compartments were to be joined by a 2.1ft (0.6m) diameter "communication tube" running 80ft (24m), the crewman laying on a cart moving on rails and pulled along by hand. Approximately 1,500lb (680kg) of armour was planned for the crew of nine that included a flight engineer with his own console.

The armament suite underwent a profusion of change throughout the programme. Early on, United Machine Company pressurised turrets with twin 37mm cannon were envisioned. Later, retractable and optionally manned versions were considered. The pressurised turret would use its own supercharger or air from the pressurised cabin.[6] By 1944, the concept had changed to remote and retractable turrets. These General Electric turrets had quad .50s and were to be directed from forward and aft GE fire control stations with bifurcated periscopes. The radar-directed (AN/APG-3) tail turret contained two .50cal MGs and one 37mm cannon. Ammunition carried

was up to 10,000 bullets and 700 shells. The .60cal MG was also considered as substitution for the .50 guns.[7] The 3cm AN/APG-3 gunnery radar was ready for testing in mid 1944. Weighing 225lb (102kg), it could detect and track targets from 2200ft (2766m) out to 15,000ft (18,288m). The gunner needed only select a target to be automatically tracked and commanded firing when within range. Nose armament evolved by spring 1944 to included side barbettes with a single weapon aimed by rotating the barbette and pivoting the gun outboard. By October, more classical nose and tail turrets with twin 20mm were adopted.

Flight controls would be unpowered. They were instead free-floating and moved by flying servo tabs in the main surfaces, with some tabs electrically driven. To provide force feel to the pilot, a double-acting spring-piston in each surface compressed whenever the tab was deflected. In addition, the piston spring operated the tab to produce a dampening effect when the main surface was deflected by turbulence.

As detailed design began, the nose was reduced to a more blunt profile. The trailing edge was also swept back 3°, leaving the engines canted inboard.

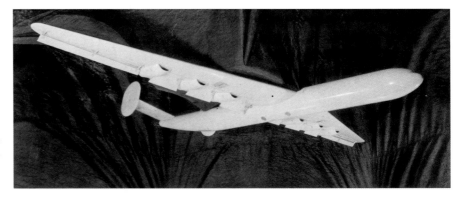

Right: A 1/26th scale wind tunnel model of the XB-36, photographed on 16 June 1942, reveals a rounded nose, one of many design changes to come, and the six flap segments. Leading edge inlets are not evident, while the twin tails and drooped ailerons were not carried to final design. *San Diego Air & Space Museum*

This may have had engine-out benefit, reducing the resulting yawing moment. The principal requirement was aligning the propellers parallel to the trailing edge to reduce asymmetrical flow into the disks that could induce vibration. The 24.ft (7.3m) tall twin tails gave way to a conventional cruciform design as static loads tests had suggested the vertical members could fail under high flight loads and a hard landing. The vertical tail stood 46.8ft (14.3m) high, unable to clear the opening of most hangars – assuming the rest of the aircraft would fit. The change also cut drag and 3,850lb (1,746kg) of weight while enhancing stability. Concurrent with that 10 October 1943 approval was agreement to a three-month slip in first aircraft delivery, or September 1944.

The nose landing gear was to be hydraulically steerable via a wheel on the console to the left of the port-seat pilot.[†] Despite lessons of the past, single main landing gear wheels and tires of an extraordinary 9.2ft (2.8m) diameter and 3.8ft (1.2m) width, the tire alone weighing 1,475lb (669kg) was chosen so that it could fit on the wing when retracted.[8] The largest tires ever fitted to an aircraft, they promised enormous surface pressure and the USAAF expressed concern for aircraft safety if one of the tires blew out on takeoff or landing. There were only three runways in the country stressed to take the load of the bomber, including Fort Worth where an 8,200ft (2,499m) runway was being built of 1.8ft (0.6m) thick concrete. Even then, the accelerate/stop distance was so great and the climb gradient of the aircraft so low as to required a minimum 10,000ft (3,048m) runway and unobstructed departure path extending 5mi (8km) beyond the departure end.[‡] The unusually large strut

components were also challenging for vendors and they were over two years in fabrication and delivery.

In fall 1942, the project was moved to Fort Worth and a new building erected there for assembly of the prototypes. The wooden mockup, complete save for one wing and tail, was initially inspected on 20 July in California and, following changes, again on 13 November 1942 in Texas. At that time, the projected weight of the XB-36 had grown such that the 10,000mi range was in jeopardy. The inspection board was firm that weight control must be rigorous to hold to the design GW of 265,000lb (120,201kg), yet firepower, armour, and crew be increased (this last to 15 men) to ensure the aircraft had tactical value. Consequently, recommendations were made for equipment removal to reduce weight. Despite these efforts, weight crept up to 271,000lb (122,923kg).

In fall 1942 the priority of the B-36 was high, but this was brief as more immediate programmes demanded resources. Even wind tunnel time was carefully managed and the B-36 had to wait long periods to collect data supporting detail design. Consequently, the programme lagged. The placement of the engines was feared to increase susceptibility to flutter, so extra effort was made to investigate dynamics. By summer 1944, the results suggested flutter speed to be just six per cent above the limit dive speed, or presenting insufficient margin.[9] Tunnel work indicated the modest wing sweep portended potentially poor stall characteristics. This was addressed by including adjustable slots ahead of the ailerons.

Weight and drag were enemies to be eliminated aggressively. This was re-emphasised repeatedly during design reviews, the 265,000lb (120,201kg) design weight held as the maximum tolerable. It was recognised that for every pound of airframe weight, two more pounds of fuel and oil were required to retain the 10,000mi range, creating a vicious cycle. Consequently, the most extensive research effort yet supporting a developmental programme was launched. Convair obtained the new, lightweight 75S aluminum, although there was initially hesitation to release the scarce material for the experimental aircraft. However, much work was done on heat-treating standard 24S alloy for greater strength to reduce material required. Lightweight magnesium was used for much of the sheet metal skin and other components, making up ten per cent of the structural weight.[§] It was also more readily available than aluminum that was carefully controlled as a "strategic" material. However, new techniques for using the metal in aircraft applications had to be developed. The designers even considered gluing aircraft exterior sheet metal skins to the underlying structure to eliminate rivet heads and the labor of drilling and placing tens of thousands of fasteners. They invested $3,000,000 in developing an adhesive that was shown to have superior fatigue life to metal fasteners. Convair would employ it postwar to install 30 per cent of the skin on the B-36.[10] Hundreds of test articles of various materials and assembly techniques were constructed and tested, with assistance of NACA Langley, in seeking the lightest structure.

---

† This wheel would become common in later transport and bomber aircraft, known as a tiller, where rudder pedal deflection alone did not provide sufficient steering fidelity during taxi.

‡ Accelerating to rotate speed and then aborting, braking to a stop in the remaining runway, determines accelerate/stop distance. Climb gradient is a function of climb rate; a low rate meaning a shallow gradient and the height of obstacles off the departure end of the runway become more critical.

§ The treated aluminum remained vital because magnesium could not be employed in pressurised areas owing to rapid fatigue and cracking under cyclical loading.

Other advances were explored during development of the XB-36. Instead of self-sealing fuel bladders, only the sides of the integral fuel cavities were fitted with self-sealing material. The lower wing skin was 3/8in (9.5mm) thick and could not be pierced by .50cal rounds from most angles. A sample fuel cell was built and subjected to gunfire tests to validate this approach. A 3,000psi (20,684kPa) hydraulic system was found necessary for the very large assemblies that had to be actuated in flight. Since standard hydraulic systems were 1,500psi (10,342kPa), Convair had to invest in hardware suitable for the higher pressure, to include lines, valves, pumps, and actuators. To meet the high electrical load demand of the aircraft, the team also adapted an AC electrical system that Wright Field laboratories had been developing to replace standard DC systems since the XB-15 experience. Apart from safety benefits that included eliminating arcing of electrical motors at high altitude, weight reduction of components like motors was also realised. However, many systems and existing equipment had to be altered to match the electrical system. The use of aluminum instead of copper wire, saving additional weight, was permitted by the AC system. The use of methyl-bromide in the fire extinguishing system, replacing the

common carbon-dioxide, also cut weight. Stopping the machine after landing required stacked brake disks, then uncommon.

The R-4365 (initially -5) had an integral shaft-driven supercharger and exhaust-driven General Electric B-1 turbosupercharger, with intercoolers, operating in parallel.[11] The engine installation was unusual and so fraught with uncertainty. Anti-icing was via ram air heated within exhaust gas heat exchangers in each nacelle, and engine exhaust channeled from the collector ring into the hollow steel propeller blades.

At Consolidated's request, P&W attempted to develop a two-speed nose gear propeller drive for the R-4360 so that speed could be shifted in flight for better efficiency. However, this ran into difficulty and was abandoned in late 1944, costing the B-36 300mi (483km) range and 21mph (34km/h) in top speed. Fuel consumption also fell short of expectations and the engine came in 576lb (216kg) overweight, subtracting another 270mi (435km).

Engine developmental delays naturally echoed in the aircraft, contributing to schedule slips to the point Convair unsuccessfully argued that another engine be considered. The Lycoming XR-7755 was recommended. This liquid-cooled design, with nine banks of four cylinders, was yielding 5,000hp (3,729kW) from 6,050lb (2,744kg) weight in its first runs

during 1944. Possibly the largest piston aero engine of all time, it was simply too late to support the XB-36.[12]

Cooling of the buried R-4360 was of great concern, as was vibration as the propeller blades cyclical passed through wing wake. An engine-driven cooling fan helped induct air into a diffuser surrounding the engine. The fan was subject to changes and moved from behind to in front of the engine. The volume of the cowling airflow inlets was revised and the wing redesigned with a change in airfoil section in summer 1942 at NACA urging. The turbosupercharger and intercooler placement plus shroud and ducting arrangements were revised, and two instead of one turbo per engine found necessary (one to support cabin pressurisation) due to the less than anticipated performance of the General Electric BM units. Instead of cowl flaps, a translating annular "air plug" altered the area between the cowling and spinner. The powerplant work drove ground tests of a full nacelle assembly on a wing segment for engine runs.

Delivery of engine data ran late and arrival of the first suitable test engine at

Below: Even the enormous XB-36 was built in wooden mockup form. This is seen in San Diego on 29 July 1942 prior a move to Fort Worth. The leading edge inlets are depicted with paint. Note the two upper turrets and the aircraft commander's scanning blister/astrodome above the flight deck. *San Diego Air & Space Museum*

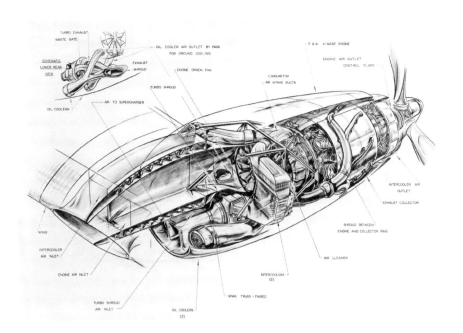

Left: The XB-36 engine nacelle underwent numerous changes seeking ideal cooling with light weight. This drawing depicts the design as it stood on 27 March 1942 with the engine-driven fan at the front of the engine. Placement of the turbo and associated hardware and ducting was still in flux. *University of Texas at Dallas*

Convair was to be May 1943, but slipped to October. It was unclear when six flight-worthy engines would be available. In June, Consolidated reported first flight would occur in September 1944, but by October this was moved right again to December. Installed ground tests with a test engine were first made on 16 April 1944, and cooling was immediately found deficient. Wind tunnel tests with the engine followed during the first half of 1944, three inlet designs and with revised fan evaluated. Cooling at certain power settings was still inadequate, driving further design changes to include a two-speed fan drive. Tests during December and January showed problems were nearly overcome.

Propeller and other systems tests extended into March. These revealed certain engine speed ranges were to be avoided as they promoted heavy vibration in the propellers and wing structure, especially at specific flap settings. The propeller was a Curtiss reversible pitch unit. Instead of electric motors or external hydraulics altering blade pitch, and to achieve the desired rapid pitch change, the energy of shaft rotation was used to operate a self-contained hydraulic pump and move the

blades per electrical command, all via a complex mechanism within the spinner. Automatic engine synchronisation was to be accomplished by reference to a "master motor", and sync retained even when throttles were advanced.

Consolidated repeatedly agitated for a production contract so it could interest vendors and suppliers in supporting the programme, and save as much as two years production design work if performed concurrent with development. On 1 August 1942, they recommended building a single transport version of the aircraft, with double-deck fuselage, to help matters along. Convair had been considering a

stripped and simplified version of the bomber to move expeditiously to testing controls, aerodynamics, and systems, so the transport fitted in with these plans while also representing a potential postwar commercial product. The USAAF decided on 8 August to fund this aircraft, the XC-99, but insisted the first XB-36 preceded the XC-99 by a minimum of three months. They still felt it was too soon to initiate production preparations.

A year later matters were more worrying as basing for even the B-29 within range of Japan looked doubtful. There was also realisation that concurrent production design and preparation would save approximately a year and help ensure the aircraft could contribute to the war. Therefore, on 19 June 1943, Arnold approved pilot production of the B-36. A $159,900,000 Letter of Intent for 100 aircraft (42004/103) plus spares was approved on 7 August 1943 with programme priority again elevated briefly. By the time a formal contract was approved a year later on 19 August 1944, delivery of the first XB-36 had slipped to September 1944 and priority was down. Combining the contract value of $160,420,000 with

Right: This hardware was built for running tests in a NACA wind tunnel. Although set for testing in summer 1945, just months before the completed aircraft was rolled out, it still has the bottom inlet aft of the leading edge whereas the final design had it flush with the leading edge. *University of Texas at Dallas*

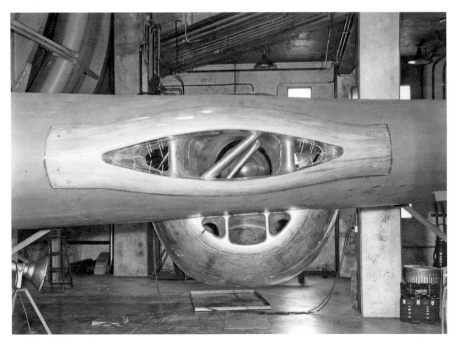

the development contract, plus perhaps another million of GFE engines, weapons, radar, etc., gave an extraordinary unit price of over $17,000,000 (not counting cost overruns). This would be the most expensive aircraft in history. First delivery was to be in August 1945 and the last in October 1946 at a peak rate of ten aircraft per month by May.

Not unexpectedly, alternatives to the main landing gear design were explored beginning as early as summer 1942. These included caterpillar tracks or dual struts on each side, one folding outboard and one inboard. However, the single wheel design appeared best for all-important drag reduction. Any change would be likely to involve substantial redesign of local wing structure. On 6 August 1945, the Army faced the inevitable and directed adoption of a multi-wheel gear – albeit without interruption to production deliveries. Although the XB-36s continued to be built with the single wheel main gear, a four-wheel dual-tandem bogie was developed for production. Although this required bulges in the upper surface of the wings and gear doors, the reduction in undercarriage weight by 1,500lb (680kg) compensated. The change made about 40 primary and alternate airfields available for the B-36.

A final solution for defensive armament was provided in January 1945. It was to consist of paired GE remote turrets with twin 20mm in upper and lower bays of the forward and aft fuselage. The side-by-side, electric turrets were stowed under sliding panels and elevated together by rotating outboard 45° upright. Each was directed from fuselage sighting blisters. A nose turret with cannons was sighted at that station and the tail turret radar directed. For these 20 cannon, the nose weapons had 400rpg while all others 600rpg, or 11,600 total.

Progress on the XB-36 had been slowed by engineering changes, higher priority design and production efforts, and late engine deliveries. Much of this had been intentional decisions of the Air Force as the course of the war made an intercontinental bomber less vital. By April 1944, the engineering stood at 74 per cent and was to be completed in September, construction had barely begun, and no engines had

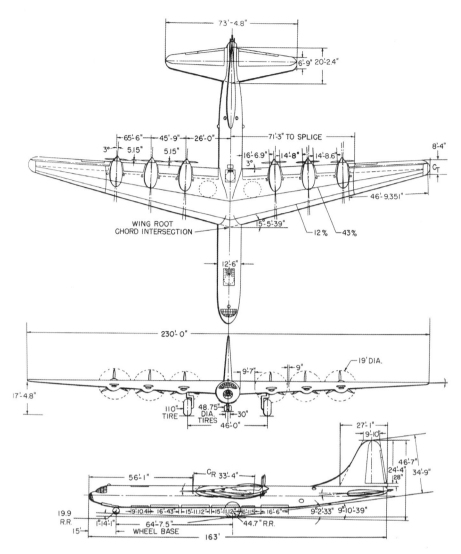

been delivered. The first production aircraft would not appear before August 1945. The production contract did not establish a programme priority, reflecting the push to get the B-32 fielded and realisation the B-36 was unlikely to contribute to the war. This effectively delayed the programme further, then already 18 months behind.

The Army decided in May 1944 to use the AN/APQ-7 Eagle with the B-36 in addition to other advanced radar, radio, and navigation gear. The equipment was expected to add 20,005,000lb (9,071,340kg) to the aircraft at the sacrifice of some range. The initial proposal was to use Douglas' narrow, 20ft (6.2m) long "vane" in the nose. A option with no drag penalty was to install an antenna inside a pressurised tube in each wing leading edge, modified with radome material, to ensure necessary scan arc. The APQ-7 and the inclusion of

Above: The near-final XB-36 design shows four hatches for turret bays. The lower aft hatch between the two rear bomb bays would be moved aft and the forward lower would be replaced by a bombing radar. The radar for the tail cannons would be in the fairing beneath the vertical tail. *San Diego Air & Space Museum*

other then-standard equipment kept the battle against weight and drag raging. The Eagle was eventually jettisoned in favour of the AN/APQ-24, the shallow, fixed radome for which eliminated the forward lower turrets and two sighting stations. The new Farrand Y-1 retractable periscopic bombsight was intended for the B-36, but the Norden adopted when that troubled development ran long.[13]

Significant changes continued to be introduced as late as fall 1944. These included moving the rear turrets behind the two aft bomb bays to permit the bays to potentially be used jointly for large ordnance, and an October redesign of the

Above: Six days following VJ-Day, the XB-36 was 82.5% complete when it was rolled outside the assembly building to be turned around and pushed back in. By this point, it was so far from representing the production design, including the impractical single-wheel main landing gear assembles, that its usefulness was limited. *San Diego Air & Space Museum*

forward compartment to accommodate the nose turret and new electronics gear. This last required raising the flight deck up under a vast domed greenhouse canopy, also improving visibility and instrument arrangement, although with a weight penalty of 3,500lb (1,588kg). Later still, nacelles were altered to extend the bottom inlet forward to the leading edge.

By October 1944, it was clear the new canopy, four-wheel trucks, nose turret, and other late changes would be deferred to prevent delaying the first XB-36. This made the aircraft only marginally suitable to evaluate production design and led, on 14 March 1945, to a USAAF decision to build the second prototype as a production-representative YB-36. However, it was also accepted that the many changes would greatly delay flight of this aircraft.

By 1945, the B-36 was still 18 months behind schedule, first flight then projected for June 1945. Many items of GFE were late and much of it overweight. Costs had more than doubled over the original X-plane contract. The service also began exploring in spring 1945 when it would be prudent to commence

Above: Even as the XB-36 was being finished, the production design was conceived with significant changes. The revised flight deck with greenhouse canopy would be incorporated into the YB-36, but the armament suite with the new nose turret was still in gestation. This mockup, with nose turret, was inspected in January 1945. *Dennis R. Jenkins Collection*

B-36 production, although this clearly would be in 1946 and a peak rate of two or four per month. Each would cost on the order of $2,720,000 each and the first 13 were considered YB-36A service test examples.[14]

Despite the battle against weight, gross had crept up 13,000lb (5,897kg) over the proposal. This cut service ceiling 1,800ft (549m), top speed 46mph (74km/h), range decremented by 640mi (1,030km), and takeoff distance was 1,100ft (335m) longer than the requirement. A speed of 369mph (594km/h) at 30,000ft (9,144m) had been guaranteed in April 1944. By July 1945, this was estimated to have shrunk to 347mph (558km/h), and later 323mph (520km/h).

Incorrect materials, failure to heat treat, and substandard workmanship were discovered in 10/20 per cent of the XB-36 structure during the last weeks of the war. A tolerance of 1/32in (0.8mm) was required on the wing contour to achieve laminar flow, but this had not been met.[15] Considerable repair and rework was necessary and structural strength was reduced by fifteen per cent, permitting flight to only 85 per cent of design loads. The resulting limitations further compromised the value of the test aircraft.

The fire control system was still in gestation as GE introduced changes to make their existing equipment compatible with the aircraft's AC electrical system. The first production-representative engine was delivered in August 1945, the sixth still months away. A near-final propulsion installation design was scheduled for further tests in the NACA Ames 40x80ft (12.2x24.4m) tunnel as the war was concluded, this to more clearly define propeller vibration and stress issues.

First prototype assembly was 82.5 per cent complete at the end of the war after expending 1,630,000 manhours, with maiden flight scheduled for March 1946. Work to establish B-36 production had begun in June. The end of the conflict did not end the B-36 programme. The war and an altered world with far-flung American commitments had taught the need for an intercontinental bomber. Advance bases need not be secured at high cost as recently demonstrated.

When finally tested, several aspects of the XB-36 were found wanting. Static testing found multiple structural design deficiencies requiring remedy. On first engine run the fabric-covered magnesium flaps came apart under propeller buffeting. They were rebuilt of aluminum, at six times the weight. In flight, engine cooling was deficient and propeller vibration accelerated fatigue of the wing structure and propeller components. Particularly the trailing edge of the wing had to be 'beefed-up' to withstand the environment. Stalls were found to be mild, making the wing slots unnecessary. The aluminum wiring proved a bad choice as it broke readily under vibration, causing hazardous system failures.

Pie in the Sky (XB-35)
Following a 12 September 1941 cost proposal for their all-wing bomber, Northrop signed a contract on 1 November for $2,910,000.88. This sought one XB-35 bomber (43603) delivered in two years and a mockup ready within nine months. The Army had initially sought two XB-35s and established an option in the

contract. Northrop initially stated they had inadequate floor space to assemble two of the large aircraft simultaneously, but soon reconsidered. The Air Corps exercised their option on 2 January 1942 (aircraft 48323). At an additional cost of $1,550,000.81, this aircraft was to follow the first by five months (April 1944).

The all-wing research effort agreed to previously was also approved on 3 October 1941 with a Northrop estimate of $314,187.50, and a contract signed 30 October. This was to provide for one aircraft, the N-9M (M for Mockup), and flight test data with the entire project completed within a year. On 10 September 1942, the Army ordered two additional N-9Ms, adding $213,841 to the contract value. The first of these was to be delivered on 15 January 1943 and the second on 15 March.[¶] This was insurance against loss of the first aircraft and an effort to accelerate data collection.

In emphasising the benefits of their design, Northrop noted that all-wing aircraft generated lift from their entire airframe with considerably less drag and superior overall lift:drag ratio. This promised remarkable performance and a more favourable ratio of gross weight to payload weight. The potential and dramatic 40 per cent reduction in drag

¶ Because the N-9M aircraft were considered flying aerodynamic mockups, essentially free-flight models, they were not given military serial numbers or civil registrations.

Above: Northrop Aircraft's radical all-wing bomber design promised considerable reduction in weight and drag for a marked improvement in performance over a comparable conventional airplane. Such a solution was worth pursuing for the very challenging intercontinental mission. However, much research would be required before the final configuration shown could be built. *Jay Miller Collection*

could yield a 30 per cent increase in range. They predicted a 700mph (1261km/h) advantage, or matching speed with just 75 per cent engine power. Theoretically, the aircraft could carry the same payload a quarter farther than a conventional aircraft. Considerable internal volume would be available, with internal mass efficiently distributed across the span, relieving structural bending stresses. It would be structurally simpler and potentially ten per cent lighter, and so possibly less costly to build. Calculations showed all these benefits increased with aircraft size. The aircraft might also be less vulnerable to aerial attack as it presented a small area in all aspects except above and below.

The challenge in designing all-wing aircraft is providing suitable stability and control without tail surfaces well aft of the CG, and lacking vertical surfaces and rudders. Wing sweep is essential to ensure the centre of lift is sufficiently aft of the CG for adequate static stability. A pusher propulsion design was considered ideal to keep the lines clean, eliminate drag-producing propwash over the wing, and permit the propeller shaft housings above the tapered aft portion of the airfoil to contribute directional stability. The turning propellers themselves tended to resist yaw. However, the buried engines challenged ability to keep them adequately cooled, and long power extension shafts were historically prone to high stresses and vibrations.

Another drawback of the flying wing is that the elevators are on the only lifting surface and so affect lift as well as creating necessary pitching moment. This requires a compensating increase in wing area with higher takeoff and landing airspeeds, and increased stall speed. Because the elevator control is not far aft of the CG but rather moves the wing centre of pressure with respect to the CG, the affective moment arm is short. This could mean limited pitch response at low speed for long takeoff roll to higher speed to achieve nose wheel liftoff, and similarly a higher landing speed for longer distances. Countering this, a large elevon or large deflections demand more pilot strength than is common. Consequences could be pitch sensitivity and easy disturbance in turbulence, potentially making the aircraft a poor bombing platform. Fore and aft CG travel limits would be about half that of a conventional aircraft because of this comparatively small control margin.[16] However, the laterally distributed payload helps reduce the detrimental fallout of the small margin. Northrop planned to ameliorate some of these effects by accepting reduced stability, 1/10th to 1/20th of that of a conventional aircraft. This was felt justified because destabilising influences of the fuselage, engine nacelles, and propwash were eliminated.[17] This would also permit smaller control surfaces.

N-9M

The N-9M was to provide controllability, manoeuvrability, and performance data for the XB-35 development to supplement those derived from wind tunnels. The N-1M work had lent confidence in designing the basic planform and wing shape, so control remained the principal area of focus.

The aircraft was 35 per cent scale in size and dynamics compared with the bomber, but weight and power were less than 20 per cent scale. Although

the XB-35 was to have four engines, there were no suitably small engines available to replicate this in scale on the N-9M. Instead, it had two engines, with selection largely determined by wartime availability. These were placed so an engine-out condition would produce the same moments as two engines out on one side of the bomber.

The N-9M was built of welded steel tube centre-section skinned with aluminum and wooden wing panels. It spanned 60.0ft (18.3m), was 17.8ft (5.4m) long and 6.6ft (2.0m) to the top of the canopy. The wing, with the same laminar-flow airfoil as planned for the XB-35, had an area of 490ft² (46m²) and 21.6° sweep at the quarter-chord line with 2° dihedral. Empty weight was 5,451lb (2,473kg) and design gross 7,000lb (3,175kg). Maximum speed was 257mph (414km/h) at 7,000ft (2,286m) altitude. It possessed tricycle landing gear and with an over-rotation strut and wheel in back.

The mockups each had two 290hp (216kW) Menasco C6S-4 Super Buccaneer, six-cylinder, inline engines. The engines turned 7.0ft (2.1m), two-blade propellers via a long shaft and hydraulic fluid-drive coupling. This coupling could be disengaged to permit the propellers to be stopped horizontally and separate from the engine to permit safe pilot bailout, but also helped reduce extension shaft loads. Each propeller shaft was tilted 9.5° up from the wing chord line and extended aft in a fairing that contributed to directional stability.

The trailing edge of the N-9M initially had, from inboard to outboard, split landing flaps, elevons (moving together as elevators and opposed as ailerons) with trim tabs, pitch control flaps for longitudinal trim, scoop drag rudders rotating out the bottom of the wing forward of the pitch flaps, and tip split speedbrakes. An "ailerudder" spoiler, intended as a lateral and directional trimming device, was installed, but deleted early on (possibly prior to flight).[18] The tip speedbrakes were clamshell surfaces opened along a line diagonally across the width of the wingtips, splitting open above and below the wing to face into the airflow. Trim change with landing flaps extension was minimised by the pitch flaps and scoops worked in concert.

The reprioritisation brought by US entry into the war meant about three months delay in the N-9M. It flew at Northrop Field, Hawthorne, California, on 27 December 1942. Most subsequent flights were conducted from dry lakebeds in the California and Nevada deserts. The first months of testing were frustrated by recurring engine problems and other mechanical issues, reducing useful data collection to almost nil. The tip speedbrakes were found largely ineffectual.

During an aft CG stall tests on 19 May 1943, the aircraft was destroyed in a crash that took the pilot's life. The cause was identified as pitch control reversal, as previously observed with the N-1M. As angle-of-attack was increased, spanwise airflow outboard inherent in the swept wing promoted early tip flow separation and reduced roll control. The airflow separation over the elevons causing the surfaces to float up. The pilot would have to quickly and powerfully push on the yoke to prevent a dramatic pitch up. However, the force required was probably too great and the full aft yoke may have trapped him in the cockpit as the aircraft entered a spin.

Fearing the flying wing had unacceptable stall and spin behaviour, models of the N-9M and XB-35 were sent to Langley for spin tunnel tests in the fall.[19] The results helped in understanding the spin behaviour and best recovery techniques. Although nothing entirely unacceptable was revealed, a single-application hydraulic boost stick-pusher was installed in all subsequent N-9Ms to ensure the stick could be moved full forward in an emergency. The addition of leading edge slots in the outer wing panels were contemplated to help prevent early flow separation.

The second testbed, designated N-9M2, took to the air on 24 June 1943. It had the same control configuration as the first machine although the speedbrakes were disconnected. Extensive testing was held up until the results of the tunnel work. When this did resume in the fall, the need for data was urgent as the XB-35 was already behind schedule. Although also plagued by engine issues, comprehensive test data finally began to be collected.

The aircraft was modified to test various control configurations while investigating the optimal design for the XB-35. Because it was built before leading edge slots were suggested, the aircraft was given slats on the outboard wing segments to help retain elevon and pitch control as stall was approached, to prevent wing-drop**. The aircraft flew reasonably well, the greatest complaints being lowly damped lateral and lateral-directional oscillations when disturbed, and large adverse yaw in roll.†† The split flaps could not be employed during takeoff as they produced a pronounced nose down pitch in ground effect, tending to oppose the climb-out. The scoop drag rudders lacked suitable effectiveness at approach speeds and there was disconcerting control lag. Further, in an engine-out case the aircraft was found to naturally stabilised itself in yaw. However, on approach (low speed), directional corrections to adjust lineup or compensate for crosswinds were very difficult. Pitch control reversal near stall remained a concern.

Auxiliary fins were briefly installed along the top of the propeller shaft housings to enhance directional stability and lateral-directional dynamic stability, but were not helpful. In addressing the longitudinal control reversal, many changes were made to ensure suitable force for moving the elevons in all circumstances. These included various balancing techniques and tab arrangements, and innovative "aero boost". This last ducted ram air from the bottom of the wing into mechanisms that assisted the pilot in moving the surface in the desired direction. The force was proportional to airspeed and so gave appropriate force feedback to the pilot. None of the solutions was entirely satisfactory, especially as they added weight.

Large split drag rudders at the wingtips was recognised as the ideal for directional control, but the purely manual control system in the N-9M2 made this impractical. Another difficulty was minimising or eliminating rolling moments induced by any solution in the directional axis.

Eventually it was clear that a full hydraulically powered control system

** Slats are a segment of a wing leading edge that slides forward or is fixed (the N-9M2 case) to increase wing camber (inflexion) and add lift. This usually creates a slot between the surface and the wing mainplane

†† Adverse yaw is a tendency to yaw away from a turn during roll. It is corrected with rudder application to "coordinate" the turn.

Above: This Northrop N-9M2 was a flying mockup of the XB-35 to provide control and performance data supporting development of the all-wing bomber. The aircraft is seen on Muroc AAB's dry lakebed with the fixed leading edge slats. The insert shows the wingtip split drag rudders that answered directional control issues. *Gerald Balzer Collection*

(as opposed to boost) would be central to the XB-35, and so this had to be tested in the N-9Ms. However, it was a source of some worry and much added work as such systems were new, component choices few, proven design guidance lacking, and such systems had a reputation for being unreliable. With only hydraulic actuators acting on the control surfaces, the pilot had no sense of the reacting aerodynamic forces, so artificial control feel became essential so that conventional piloting techniques could be employed. This was possibly the first use of an entirely "irreversible" flight control system, and certainly the first fully powered control system on an American aircraft.

The third testbed, N-9MA, was built with all the controls then planned for the XB-35 as closely represented as practical. The fixed leading edge slots were introduced. Full hydraulic power was applied to all surfaces. Emergency manual reversion capability was provided for elevons and pitch flaps. Artificial feel was added via bellows and springs. The longitudinal stick bellows was pressurised by ram air, and so resistance increased proportionally with airspeed and ambient air density. Elevon trim tabs were replaced with electrically powered biasing of the surfaces. Electric motors also moved the pitch trim flaps, these interconnected with the landing flaps and landing gear to automatically compensate for extension and retraction pitch changes. They were expected to help ameliorate the lift degradation from up elevon.[20] The tip speedbrakes and drag rudder scoops were also deleted. Directional control was instead derived

from split drag rudders within the pitch trim flap. These opened like speedbrakes above and below the parent surface to create drag on one side of the aircraft with a resulting yawing moment. The rudder pedals were not interconnected, but could be deployed together to open both drag rudders for speedbrake action.

Aircraft N-9MA first flew on 22 April 1944 and completed all required work by that fall, clearly late in supporting the bomber programme. Although Northrop was making steady progress via modification and test of the N-9Ms, solutions were not coming fast enough.

That summer, USAAF pilots flew the N-9MA and came away with confidence the XB-35 would fly acceptably well. However, remaining issues with low directional damping, considerable adverse yaw, a pitch bobble in rough air, and almost no stall warning were all perceived by the Air Forces as XB-35 risks. While it was accepted that the all-wing bomber need not have ideal flying qualities consistent with typical Air Forces standards, the less desirable characteristics could not degrade its usefulness as a bombing platform.

By summer 1944, additional testing was desired beyond that originally funded, Northrop estimating $107,068 for additional flights on top of nearly twice the planned funding spent on the

Left: The third flying wing testbed, the N-9MA, represented the control configuration of the XB-35, including automatic opening for leading edge slots at low speed and wingtip split drag rudders. While the N-9Ms provided invaluable data for the XB-35 development, this was late and required many aircraft modifications. *Gerald Balzer Collection*

second and third aircraft. Instead, focus shifted to a fourth testbed. This aircraft, the N-9MB, was ordered on 24 July 1943 at a cost of $199,339.92 to replace the first machine. It was powered by two 320hp (239kW) Franklin XO-540-7 eight-cylinder horizontally opposed engines. The aircraft was very similar to its predecessor save for further improvements to more closely represent the XB-35 as it was then to be built. Along these lines, there was automatic opening and closing of the wing slots, only opened about 20mph (32km/h) above stall. The XB-35 autopilot was tested briefly, this requiring a yaw-vane input instead of lateral acceleration or bank angle to detect sideslip.[21] First flight of N-9MB came on 26 January 1945.

XB-35

As it evolved, basics of the XB-35 remained the same. The aircraft was built conventionally of aluminum and with flush riveting. It was to span 172.0ft (52.4m) but with length of just 53.1ft (16.2m) and 20.1ft (6.1m) height. The airfoil had a centre-section 7.0ft (2.1m) thick at its deepest point, the central

chord length 37.5ft (11.4m). Leading edge sweep was 27°. A 4° washout at the tips (nose down twist) helped prevent tip stall. Although Northrop chose a laminar-flow symmetrical airfoil, they suspected they would not experience substantial areas of laminar flow in practice owing to the presence of leading edge openings for engine air, turrets, and other unavoidable surface protuberances.[22]

The bomber was to have tricycle landing gear with dual wheels on the main posts. The nose gear retracted to the left. Braking and steering were hydraulic while gear articulation was electric, the brakes

backed up by an emergency pneumatic system. Nose wheel steering was affected via a rotating pistol-grip handle to the left of the pilot. Pulling the handle aft equalised wheel brake force. There were eight bomb bays distributing the payload across span, three bays inboard of the main gear wells and another outboard on each side. Each bay was equipped with a flexible door that rolled onto a drum at the aft end of the bay.

The central portion of the wing, including an extending aft cone, contained the pressurised areas for the crew of nine. These were the pilot, copilot, navigator, bombardier, engineer, radio operator, and three gunners. A relief crew of six was projected, with bunks and a galley planned. The flight deck had the pilot elevated to see out of a bubble canopy, the copilot lower to see out windows in the leading edge, and the bombardier sighting through leading edge lower windows. A flight engineer and navigator sat to the rear. A gunner sat on an elevated platform behind the pilot to see out of the same canopy. The rear gunner sat farther back in the centre-section, and the tail gunner was at the aft end of the pressurised compartments.

Right: The XB-35 wind tunnel model at top shows the original three-blade contra-rotating propellers. Note the centreline canopy and lack of gun turret behind, and large fairings on the outboard trailing edge. The final configuration at bottom features the single long leading edge inlets and wingtip split drag rudders. The outboard leading edge slots are open, but turrets are lacking. top *Jay Miller Collection*, bottom *National Archives*

The four engines initially consisted of two R-436outboard and two -9s inboard, all of 3,000hp (2,237kW). The models were associated with different driveshaft lengths, the outboards being approximately half as long as the inboards that were 27.7ft (8.4m). Numerous changes during development drove a designation change to R-4367 and -21. Cooling and induction air to the engines were drawn in at wing leading edge openings, accelerated into a shroud around the engine by a variable-speed, engine-driven fan, and exhausted through flaps adjacent to the propeller shaft housings. Each engine had two single-stage General Electric BH-1 turbosuperchargers, augmenting the single-stage/single-speed, engine-driven superchargers integral with the R-4360. The turbos operated in parallel, allowing one to be shutdown. All four turbos and two intercoolers per side were mounted under the leading edge inlets between the two engines. These were evidenced by "flight hood" assemblies with waste gate and turbo exhausts protruding below the skin. All were interconnected and to exhaust heat exchangers, anti-icing and cabin heating systems with a maze of ducting. The propulsion system and the propellers were GFE.

The engines drove contra-rotating, pusher propellers with de-icing capabilities. The reduction and dual-rotation gearboxes were at the end of the three-segment power shafts. At first, these were to be dual three-blade propellers, but four blades were found to be more efficient. The forward four-blade unit was 15.3ft (4.7m) in diameter and the aft 15.1ft (4.6m). Reverse propeller pitch was also planned to assist landing deceleration.

The four primary, self-sealing fuel tanks were each matched to an engine but also fed a common manifold for crossfeed. Four tanks installed in the two outboard bomb bays and six auxiliary tanks in outboard cavities, all jettisonable, provided additional capacity.

The primary control surfaces evolved to inboard split landing flaps that were electrically actuated, mid-span elevons, and tip split drag rudders hinged to the electrically powered trim flaps. The trim flaps were for both pitch and roll while the neutral position of the elevons could be biased as elevator trim. The outboard leading

Above: The articulated tail "stinger" of the XB-35 is seen in mock-up form, the insert showing the fairings installed. This was to use two 37mm cannon, but war experience tended to discourage use of such large and slow-firing weapons in aircraft installation, and .50cal machine guns were substituted. *Gerald Balzer Collection*

edge slots were automatic and hydraulically powered. They opened below 140mph (225km/h) and when the undercarriage was extended. All control logic and cockpit controls were conventional.

There were two independent engine-driven sources of 3,000psi (20,684kPa) hydraulic pressure, necessary for safety redundancy given the hydraulically driven, "fully boosted" primary flight controls. Artificial feel included a ram air bellows. A button had to be depressed to allow the rudder pedals (not normally moved together) to serve as brake pedals during ground operation, with the split rudders continuing to operate. Electric motors provided emergency hydraulic pressure to the elevon actuators. Electrical demand drove insertion of considerable AC components. There were two APUs in bomb bays for AC power that served as emergency electrical power sources for the hydraulic motor.

The armament suite evolved to elimination of cannon. Instead, 20 .50cal guns (17,600 rounds) were in seven GE remote turrets and directed by their fire control system. Upper and lower centre-section low-profile four-gun turrets had

700rpg (about 650rpg reload). Two guns were in each of four turrets (1,000rpg) paired above and beneath the wing outboard of the engines. Four guns (1,000rpg) were to be in an articulated tail cone consisting of two nested cones and a fixed base. The top gunner controlled the periscope sighting station for the top three turrets. The rear gunner originally had an overhead canopy with top and bottom periscope, apparently controlling the bottom and tail turrets. There was also a manned lower ball turret at one time. This was eliminated in a revision, having the rear gunner and top periscope control only the tail gun, and adding a third aft gunner with a lower periscope controlling the bottom three turrets.

In early December 1941, Northrop had a rough mockup of the crew stations for the XB-35 to support vision evaluation and invited Army comments.

However, the prompt work represented by this step was soon arrested by America's entry into the war as emphasis shifted to rapid production of existing types. Engineering personnel were also overburdened with other Northrop projects. However, the general XB-35 mockup was completed more than a month ahead of the contracted date and inspected between 6 and 17 July. The most significant outcome was the determination that the engine installation was unacceptable.

Discussions turned to producing 13 service test YB-35s and 100 production B-35s. On 28 September 1942, development of the XB-35 and XB-36 was given "the highest possible priority". This extended to materials, wind tunnel scheduling, and other resources. However, Northrop lacked the engineering assets to accelerate the work.

In exploring the loan of staff from other manufacturers, the USAAF found resources at Martin by canceling the B-33. Initial contacts between the two engineering teams began in mid November 1942, but the exchange was initially very slow. It was certainly a new

paradigm for the industry.

With the remaining $330,000,000 in B-33 funds, Martin would provide vital engineering of the aircraft structure and engine installation while preparing a Baltimore production line. The USAAF prepared contracts for Northrop to build 100 B-35s while Martin manufactured another 100. Although the government erected a new facility in Hawthorne during 1942, it was almost fully committed to other wartime work. There was inadequate space to manufacture scores of giant bombers. Jack Northrop was also more interested in experimental aircraft development than operating vast

manufacturing works, and his company needed assistance in production design. Consequently, it fell to Martin to build all the production bombers as the Model 205.

A contract for the YB-35s (402366/78) and spares was signed on 2 December 1942 for an expected $22,773,044.69. Northrop was to build these, the first to be delivered on 30 July 1944. The firm proposed using the lighter 75ST aluminum to save 2,00,000lb (90,361kg) weight. It was, however, unclear if there would be sufficient supply of the material for all anticipated aircraft and so the Army hesitated to approve its use in the experimental examples. Also, working with the new material would require some research and tooling changes. However, this was eventually approved.

It was also 17 December before Martin had an adequate specification from Northrop. They then submitted a proposal on 6 May 1943 for the subcontract work, to include building the 200 aircraft and an equivalent of 40 in spares. They suggested the first of these would be delivered in January 1945 with production rate reaching 20 per month in September 1945 by which time 43 bombers would have been built. However, production in Middle

Right: The internal arrangement of crew stations and weapons were of concern to the AAF given the unusual layout of the XB-35 without "fuselage". This image shows a mockup of copilot and bombardier stations. The pilot sat to the left and higher so as to see out the bubble canopy. *National Archives*

River awaited completion of Northrop's experimental work. Martin's proposal was acceptable and the 200 B-35s (45126/325), the first to be delivered by June 1945, were formally ordered on a 30 June 1943 contract. The final negotiated value was for $269,697,890.84.

As 1943 progressed, it became clear the XB-35 was falling farther behind schedule and going over budget. On 18 May, Northrop informed its customer the first flight of the XB-35 would slip more than a year to December 1944. The first production aircraft was still scheduled to appear the next month, although this was recognised as probably unworkable. Contributors to the delays were legion. The adoption of a fully hydraulic control system created the issues presented earlier. The new AC electrical system required new or unique components and also constant-speed drives on the engines for the exceptional large alternators. The designers were making extra efforts to avoid high engine temperatures, the fan, drive, and diffuser work undertaken on behalf of the XB-36 also benefiting the XB-35. The airframe structure was 8,000lb (3,629kg) overweight, driving design gross up from 140,000lb (63,503kg) to 155,000lb (68,039kg). The shortage of engineering personnel continued to be a headache, Martin soon employing engineers from the Otis Elevator Company in drawing preparation.

An effort was made in summer 1944 to accelerate the programme and achieve first flight in October instead of December. This included having Martin set aside its YB-35, and by extension production design work that was of most interest to them, until the experimental design had been completed. Agreed delivery dates still appeared impossible. Efforts were also made that summer to rein in the weight growth and improve communication between Northrop and Martin. The working relationship between the two companies was not harmonious and this created delays. The service personnel sensed Martin lacked enthusiasm for the project.

An engine test stand was constructed in Baltimore for initial installed engine runs. However, this was not ready until May 1944. Another was created in Hawthorne that represented the wing section incorporating two

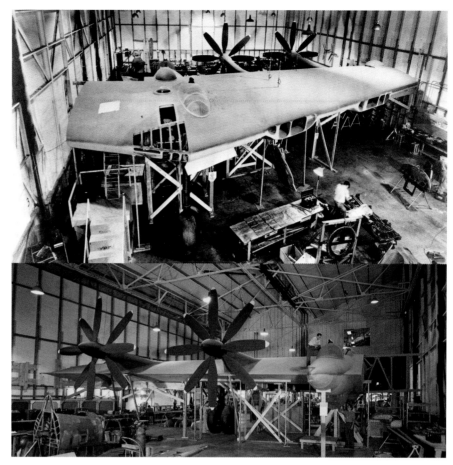

adjacent engines and the flap segment. This permitted testing of engine and propeller systems, and interaction with the airframe. The propulsion GFE was running very late. The gearbox and optimisation of the cooling fan proved major efforts that required redesign of the baseline model. Their first engine only ran in July 1943, but many changes lay between that event and delivery of a flight-worthy powerplant.

Northrop had hesitated to agree to XB-35 performance guarantees until it had enough supporting data for the unusual design. The performance guarantee adopted in fall 1943 was 401mph (645km/h) at 35,000ft (10,668m) in military power. Range with 10,000lb (4,536kg) payload was 7,600mi (12,230km). Service ceiling was to be 40,000ft (12,192m) achieved at 30 per cent of the range.

Programme acceleration efforts failed, actually losing more ground. The XB-35 engineering was only 29 per cent complete by the end of December 1943 and flight was then planned for April 1945, the first production article delivered the next month. Within two

Above: The partial mockup of the XB-35 is shown on 29 August 1942 following the government inspection. It reveals further evolution of the design with the off-centre canopy, centreline gun turret, and eight-blade propellers. There were then two engine inlets per side instead of the one long inlet finally adopted. Top *National Museum of the United States Air Force* and bottom *Gerald Balzer Collection*.

months, this slipped again to 1 August 1945 for the XB-35 and November 1945 for the B-35. By May 1944, production had moved further left to 20 August 1946.

By March 1944, the programme was estimated to be at least 1.5 years behind schedule and total programme cost expected to reach over $24,000,000. There was still no production tooling as production design had not begun. The first B-35 was to be delivered in January 1946 and the peak rate reached in seven months, by which time 39 aircraft would have been built. However, Martin thought early 1947 more reasonable for initial delivery. They were insisting that all drawings be redone to their own standards, entailing 2,330,000 manhours and a two year delay.

The slow progress and significant cost overruns prompted questions at the end of

Right: The challenging engine installation for the XB-35 compelled Northrop and Martin to built test stands for generating engineering data and prove-out the design. This image shows the Hawthorne stand with two engines operating in a mocked-up wing half. The six-blade counter-rotating propellers were eventually replaced with eight-blade units. *Gerald Balzer Collection*

Below: The XB-35 is seen on 7 May 1945 during the mating of the outer wing segments to the main assembly on an elevated platform. The surroundings suggest the vast amount of tooling, jigs, and other equipment required. The image is a good representation of American aircraft production at the war's end. *Gerald Balzer Collection*

1943, from as high as Chief of Air Staff, whether there was still merit in continuing the B-35 programme. Materiel Command had been examining a Convair flying tailless bomber design that appeared to have advantages over the XB-35.[23] Therefore, a reevaluation of the flying wing programme was undertaken during the first half of 1944. The programme was still valuable from the perspective of advancing aeronautical science and so benefiting future work. However, the B-35 was most unlikely to contribute to the ongoing war. The decision to drop B-35 production was made on 18 May, the formal contract change following on 12 June. Martin would continue its work on the XB and YB contracts into 1945.

Weight continued to grow, reaching a design gross of 162,000lb (73,482kg). Despite a mix-up in drag predictions between wind tunnels and N-9M flight data, it still appeared the XB-35's top speed would be 24mph (39km/h) and range 1,600mi (2,575km) less than previously predicted, and fall short of the guarantees. Peak speed at 35,000ft was then expected to be 386mph (621km/h) and range with 10,000lb (4,536kg) payload 4,600mi (7,402km) at 245mph (394km/h). Range was achieved with 5,000gal (18,927lit) in removable outboard wing tanks. The N-9M data suggested low dynamic damping that could reduce the aircraft's value as a bombing platform and complicate formation flying. With the assistance of USAAF laboratories, Northrop began working to acquire an artificial yaw damping system that would use rate gyro feedback to automatically command drag rudder motion countering the oscillations. A modified C-1 autopilot had four servo motors vice the common three. Instead of simply relieving pilot workload during extended cruise flight, the C-1 was to be used nearly full-time to damp the undesirable aircraft oscillations. This was one of the first such uses of stability augmentation.

Too many new systems had to be developed for the B-35, adding to delays. Yet, in summer 1944, the USAAF began considering inserting more current systems into the XB-35. They instructed Northrop to look to including radar, new radios, and RCM gear into the mockup. Space limitations made the radar especially difficult to integrate into the design, so this was set aside in the expectation that by the time of any future B-35 production, newer and smaller sets would be available.

As the end of 1944 approached, engineering for the first X-plane was 79 per cent complete and assembly twenty-four per cent, but still with significant engineering issues in the way of flight. The YB-35 engineering was less than 35 per cent complete. Many in the Air Forces' aircraft development leadership were losing faith. This performance illustrated why Arnold hesitated to pursue research projects, or programmes hinging off these during the war. In an effort to accelerate aircraft construction and place emphasis on XB-35 development, it was decided that December to build the first six YB-35s to X-plane standard, rolling out in two-month intervals after the second XB-35, then expected to fly in December 1945. This would ensure uninterrupted shop work between XB-35 construction and completed engineering for the YB-35 and get more aircraft into test sooner. Some design changes might be introduced, such as weight reduction and inclusion of aero boost, provided they did not delay delivery. The second batch of service test machines, tactically equipped, were then identified as YB-35As and any future production aircraft as B-35Bs.

Within months, the USAAF had agreed to introduce notable changes into the YB-35s. These included provisions to mount bay fuel tanks, ability to carry up to 4,000lb (1,814kg) weapons in the inboard bays, thermal de-icing in the wing leading edge, and elimination of armour to reduce weight. Radar and the tail turret were considered for the later YB-35As.

Above: The first XB-35 was photographed on "skates" during July 1945 while being turned around and rolled back into its Hawthorne building. Lacking the propulsion and control systems, it still shows the general aspect of the aircraft. Note the outboard slots and circular holes for the three upper surface turrets. *Jay Miller Collection*

With the emergence of a turbojet powered flying wing programme in March 1945, the YB-49, the B-35 programme took a back seat. The speed now seen as essential for future combat could not be achieved with propellers. The piston-powered machine would be completed for experimental purposes, but the future was in jets. In mid 1945, it was decided the second and third YB-35s would be built as YB-49s.

In May 1945, it was decided the first XB-35 would be stripped of military accoutrements. The second X-plane and the first YB-35 would be fitted with the guns and fire control system. The next two machines would be YB-49s, and the two after that fitted with the de-ice system. Configuration of the rest remained to be decided after initial flight test results, although one would probably serve as a static test article. Consideration was being given to building one with a thinner section to address flow separation issues that limited the YB-49 airspeed, and another with two R-4360s and four TG-180s that would have no restrictions.[24]

Also in May 1945, P&W announced another two-month slip in delivery of a suitable R-3350s. Even this estimate proved optimistic. The Martin contribution was also beginning to wind down toward an expected end on 31 October 1945. When Martin extricated itself, the YB-35 engineering was still preliminary, and Northrop had to essentially begin anew.

By August 1945 the first XB-35 was approaching completion, but without engines. Delivery of the R-4360s remained uncertain and they were likely to come

with significant operating restrictions. Budget overruns exceeded four hundred per cent, with much more likely to come. After years of development, and years beyond the original schedule, it had long been clear the B-35 would not fly before war's end. The programme was continuing solely for its experimental engineering value.

The first XB-35 finally flew in June 1946. Flight testing revealed stability and control deficiencies that were likely to affect bombing accuracy without corrective measures. This emphasised the important of the artificial damping then in development. The gearboxes and dual-rotation propellers were fraught with difficulties, including speed governor "hunting" and "creep" that caused wide airspeed variations, cooling fans suffering fatigue cracks, and the exhaust ducting demanded excessive maintenance attention. Propeller vibration was also a problem as was to be expected on the pusher installation, especially on a swept wing and with the propeller centre of rotation above the trailing edge. The propellers began to show cracks suggesting their service life would be as little as 80hr. The slow and problem-plagued flying wing programme was cut back and then abandoned entirely.

Chapter Ten

Late Start – Jets

Next Step

The US military began a programme in summer 1941 to develop and introduce gas turbine (jet) aircraft engines. This became a top priority in the fall after General Arnold witnessed a flight of Britain's first jet aircraft and it was understood Germany was surely pursuing similar work. The first steps were to have General Electric manufacture the British turbojet as other American powerplants were developed. Concurrently, in a vastly accelerated programme, America's first jet fighter made its initial flights in October 1942. Many other jet projects were launched and, by mid-1945, the US had built about 140 jet fighters or attack aircraft in seven models and with many other designs in development.

Although jet fighters were urgently sought very early in the war to advance speed limits and meet emergent German counterparts, thoughts of the threat the enemy jets posed to the already hard-pressed Allied bomber force was not lost on Army leadership. As the higher speed and altitude of the B-29 was an advantage against propeller-driven fighters compared with earlier heavies, so would jet-propelled bombers contend with jet fighters. Range would be sacrificed using the first generation of fuel-guzzling turbojets. It would also probably be another rung up the ladder of increasing weight and complexity of these aircraft. In all, it was going to be a tougher 'nut to crack' than the step to the super heavy bomber and jet fighter. With the strategic bombing campaign reliant on continued high-rate production of existing designs, it was late in the war before concerted efforts began along the jet track.

Jet engines emerged from growing frustration with traditional aircraft propulsion. Reciprocating engines were reaching the bounds of their practical power potential in the never-ending stretch for greater aircraft speed. The effort to keep them fed with air of sufficient density at high altitude for powerful combustion was also becoming limited. Propellers flown to higher speeds soon developed supersonic flow at the tips (matching or exceeding the speed of sound) that greatly increased drag and reduced efficiency. The combination of pistons and propellers was growing ever heavier and more complex. A prime example is the contra-rotating propellers and dual-rotation reduction gearing boxes developed substantially during the war years to meet the needs of converting ever-greater engine power to thrust within the basic limitations of high-speed propeller flight. Technically challenging, these advanced engines and propellers were the source of repeated programme delays, problems in flight testing, and burdensome maintenance.

The turbojet was refreshingly simple by comparison with the most advanced reciprocating engine and propeller installations. They promised to be more efficient in delivering thrust per unit weight of powerplant, although fuel economy was initially a third to a half less. Thrust efficiency actually increased with airspeed, and altitude performance was superior.

Just moving an aircraft through air at greater speeds introduced other challenges. Aircraft speeds approaching that of sound (Mach 1) encounter problems associated with the compression of the air into shock waves. These greatly increase drag and can generate hazardous controllability problems such as sudden trim changes, lateral control reversing sense, and nose tuck-under during dives. Straight-wing fighters were suffering such issues as they approached around 500mph (805km/h) or about 0.8 Mach at their common operating altitudes.

The goal in combating airframe high-speed difficulties was to delay the speed at which shocks formed on the aircraft, known as the critical Mach number. This suggested optimised wing airfoils and possibly introducing wing sweep. Sweep imposes additional structural complexity and tends to induce wingtip stall before root stall, compromising roll authority at low speed. There is also a forward shift in centre of pressure at stall that produces a destabilising pitch up. However, by 1945, Robert Jones at NACA Langley was becoming a proponent of the advantages of sweep, but lacked empirical data as the nation then had a dearth of suitable high-speed wind tunnels.[1] Although Allied fighters made considerable progress in dealing with compressibility problems during the war (excluding sweep), bomber design teams would be facing them anew in any jet projects.

Several approaches had been followed in the jet fighter arena that could be applicable to bombers. A tentative step added jet "boosters" to propeller-driven aircraft for surges of engagement speed. Some projects already begun as "piston jobs" were converted to jets. Others employed jets from the outset. Although the American aircraft industry had matured greatly during the war years, the high-speed jet bombers would pose considerable challenges. The design of air intakes, jet exhausts, dealing with the heat generated, and extracting power for electrical and hydraulic system operation, were just some of the added design complexities. An overarching goal for the AAF was 500mph (805km) over the target, a speed that also pressed the suitability of existing bombsights. This airspeed, it was expected, would reduce fighter intercepts to a tail chase and make only a tail turret necessary.

The Army focused on the General Electric TG-180 (later J35) axial flow turbojet for its bomber applications.* Unlike earlier rotund engines with centrifugal flow compressors, the axial flow designs had much lower frontal area. The J35's 3.1ft (0.9m) area was advantageous when compared with 4.1ft (1.3m) for the centrifugal flow units initially used in fighters. This made the axial-flow engine more suitable for nacelle installation that would be likely for multiengine bombers.[2] The General Electric powerplant had an 11-stage compressor, eight combustion chambers, and a single-stage turbine. It was an almost entirely American design and one of the few axial-flow engines to operate during the war, let alone enter production. The programme was begun in summer 1941 as MX-414 and the engine had only run in the test stand on 23 April 1944. Despite Army eagerness, it still proved frustratingly slow in maturing to a practical aircraft powerplant. The target 4,000lbf (17,793N) sea-level thrust was initially just 3,750lbf (16,681N), then raised to 3,820-3,835lbf (16,992-17,059N). It also began with a Time Between Overhaul (TBO) of just 10 operating hours, although soon brought to 35hr.

The early turbojets were temperamental, with a new set of problems to learn and overcome. They were notoriously slow to come up to speed, and so aircraft brakes had to be held until power reached around 70 per cent before beginning the takeoff roll. Too fast advancing the throttle and a compressor stall could ensue with temporary loss of thrust, or complete blowout requiring a restart. They would also occasionally shed compressor or turbine blades, which usually produced cascading failures and destruction of the engine that could endanger the entire aircraft. The lack of prop-wash over the tail surfaces meant a degradation of low-speed control effectiveness and overall reduced empennage stabilising influence.

The US Army first began exploring the potential of jet bombers with manufacturers during June 1943. The turbojet technology was secretly revealed so designers could consider the implications. Conceptual designs

* The standardised engine designation system for gas turbine engines was introduced on 10 April 1945.

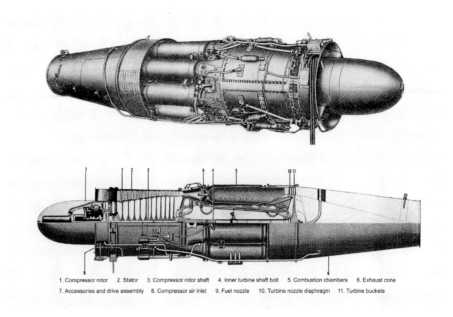

1. Compressor rotor 2. Stator 3. Compressor rotor shaft 4. Inner turbine shaft bolt 5. Combustion chambers 6. Exhaust cone
7. Accessories and drive assembly 8. Compressor air inlet 9. Fuel nozzle 10. Turbine nozzle diaphragm 11. Turbine buckets

were solicited in September, and in April 1944, the service asked the firms to begin solidifying these for multi-engine medium bombers as it firmed up formal requests.

USAAF leadership made clear in fall 1944 they saw the future of bombardment aircraft as jet-propelled machines, and they desired to acquire such aircraft at the earliest opportunity. Any manufacturer hoping to sell bombers for much longer was well advised to begin moving in that direction. Projects were soon being placed on contract. All were to find, however, that availability of the precious few jet units remained a severe bottleneck for the remainder of the war. In addition, the late-war start on bombers and sudden end of the conflict meant very few of the projects reached any substantial hardware stage prior to August 1945, and none flew before that date.

Transitional

Like the Navy, the Army saw value in adding jets to bombers with primary piston/propeller systems. However, the Army "composites" were experimental projects seeking early jet experience for the design teams and operators. The resulting data proved valuable as the US added auxiliary jet engine pods to its remaining prop-driven bombers, including the B-50, B-36, and P2V in the postwar era. This allowed some benefit of jet propulsion while pure-jet designs continued to mature in range and payload performance.

Above: Jet engines eliminated the propeller, complex moving parts, and supercharging, instead expelling compressed air for propulsive impetus. The General Electric TG-180 axial-flow turbojet engine featured eight separate combustion cans, instead of the later annular combustor. Its small frontal area and high-altitude performance made it desirable for jet bomber applications. *USAF*

Mutilation (XA-26F)

A Douglas A-26B-61 (44-34586) was converted to the sole XA-26F by fitting a General Electric I-16-3 (later J31) turbojet of 1,600lb (7,117N) thrust from the 804lb (365kg) unit of 4.1ft (1.3m) diameter. This was the first practical American version of the engine original lymanufactured in Great Britain and which underwent prolonged evolution for various fighter applications. The I-16 had already been bypassed by more advanced models, and plans existed to substitute the I-20 in the XA-26F at a later date. Douglas expected 415mph (668km/h) from the aircraft at sea level.

The J31 supplemented the two R-2800-83s with three-bladed units without the spinners that were fitted for flight. The fuselage ventral inflection was faired in to deepen the aft fuselage for the turbojet installation, the turrets and gunner's station deleted. The intake was above the spine and the long exhaust pipe issued under the tail. The 125gal (473lit) bomb bay tank was isolated for the jet's kerosene fuel, allowing 20min operation. Controls for the additional powerplant were in a supplemental

panel added to the right of the cockpit instrument panel. The loss of turrets was to be compensated with a .50cal gun in the aft end of each nacelle, aimed and fired from a sight at the starboard cockpit station. Aircraft empty weight went up 638lb (289kg), loaded weight by 7,000lb (3,175kg).[3]

The modification began in July 1945 and the project was halted briefly at the war's end until funding was reprogrammed. The jet was operated installed for the first time in October, followed soon after by first flight.[4] A maximum speed of 435mph (700km/h) at 15,000ft (4,572m) altitude was achieved with all three engines operating. This was just 32mph (52km/h) over the A-26D's top speed. The drag and weight increments accounted for the disappointing results, hardly balancing the loss of bomb bay volume. Also, the nose tended to tuck under at high speed, possibly due to the inlet influencing flow over the tail.

Hybrid (XB-42A)

In the same vein as the XA-26F was the experimental addition of two jet engines to the XB-42, essentially making it a four-engine bomber. The USAAF and Douglas first explored the installation of jet boosters on the XB-42 near the end of 1943. As the XB-43 all-jet version of the airframe was being initiated, Douglas pointed out that the composite approach could yield a valuable test aircraft at an earlier date. With AAF encouragement, the contractor made a formal proposal on 23 February 1945.

Douglas offered the options of "scabbing" the selected Westinghouse 19XB-2A (later J30) onto the wings, like under-wing tanks, or a more extensive wing rework to integrate the jet engines into the wings. The former option was selected and work initiated with a $388,090, 23 April change to the existing XB-42 contract. Douglas was expecting 488mph (785km/h) at 14,000ft (4,267m) altitude, but took a guarantee of 470mph (756km/h) at sea level.[5] First flight of the XB-42A (MX-880) was slated for March 1946.[6]

The first XB-42 (43-50224) was to be modified with "auxiliary turbojets". These 1.58ft (0.48m) diameter, axial-flow units rated at 1,600lbf (7,117N) were developed under Navy sponsorship as the first original jet engine design in the United States. They employed a six-stage compressor, annular combustor (instead of the TG-180's "canular design") and single-stage turbine. One would be installed under each wing, at roughly 25 per cent semi-span on a shallow pylon. Separate fuel, oil, and fire suppression systems were required. The Allisons and turbojets alike burned standard 100-octane fuel. It appears the wing tanks were altered as capacity was

Right: This image of the Douglas XA-26F shows to advantage the jet engine modifications. The intake over the centre fuselage fed air to the turbojet via an S-duct. An extended tailpipe exited under the tail. Hidden from view are the spinners on the four-blade propellers of the R-2800 reciprocating engines. *Ray Wagner Collection*

Above: Two J30s were added to the XB-42 as "auxiliary boosters". The XB-42A modification, with the turbojets hung like external tanks, was still underway at war's end but would appear as shown in this retouched photo. The experiment failed to give the USAAF the intended early look at a jet bomber. *Ray Wagner Collection*

Right: The XB-43 project set out to convert the extraordinary Douglas XB-42 from twin piston engines to twin jets, using TG-180 turbojets. The arrangement is illustrated here, including the side intakes and new vertical tail. Initiated in 1943, the airplane did not fly until after the war. *National Archives*

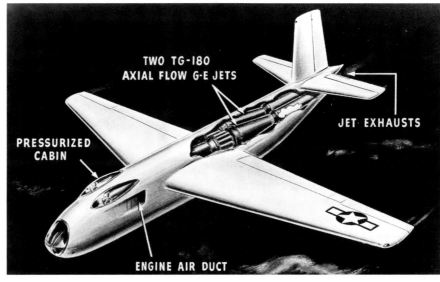

reduced from 660gal (2,498lit) to 504gal (1,908lit), but two 74gal (280lit) fuselage tanks were added to compensate.[7] The flaps behind the jets had to be redesigned and built anew. This work included segmenting and notching them along the axis of the jet to account for thermal expansion, plus making them tolerant of the high heating and pressures of the jet efflux. Douglas also took the opportunity to change to more powerful Allison V-1710-137s with 1,800hp (8,006N) in WE (water injection).[8] Empty weight increased by nearly 4,000lb (1,814kg), even with all guns removed. The landing gear may have been modified to accommodate this increased weight.[9]

Slowed after the close of the war, the modification design continued through March 1946 but then awaited engines. Initially scheduled for a November 1945 delivery, the J30s were greatly delayed. The aircraft finally flew in May 1947.

Top speed was 473mph (761km/h), well short of the expectations. Range was over 550mi (885km) off the XB-42 number. The only bright spots were takeoff distance nearly halved and ceiling increased over 6,000ft (1,829m).[10] Nacelles modifications to reduce drag were advisable, but the government demurred.

Course Changes

A possible means to accelerate acquisition of jet bombers was adapting existing aircraft to the new technology. No one was deluded into thinking it would be easy adapting an aircraft to radically different engines. Significant compromises might be necessary that

could be critically non-optimal. It also happened that the best candidates for such undertakings were airframes still under development and so likely to have maturation issues unrelated to the powerplant. However, such course changes of course appeared worth the expended resources.

Swapping (XB-43)

After the USAAF revealed the advent of turbojet engines and their eagerness to embrace the technology, Douglas saw its prospects for B-42 production slipping away. Consequently, Douglas reacted positively during an October 1943 conference at Wright Field at which the Army solicited a proposal for an XB-42 employing turbojets. The company was

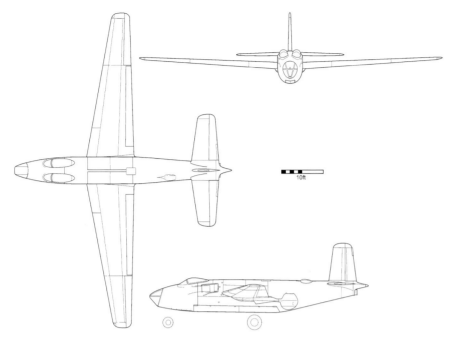

single-engine-out scenarios. The "bugeye" canopies were retained but the glazed nose modified. Three 385gal (1,457lit) bay tanks and two 550gal (2,082lit) drop tanks were planned. Included were provisions for JATO bottles under the wings to cut takeoff distance by 40 per cent.[12] Guns, armour, bomb accoutrements, bombsights, and other operational installations were left for later since the urgent focus was exploring the technical issues associated with a jet bomber.

For a 2,000lb (907kg) increase in empty weight and 4,500lb (2,041kg) in maximum weight compared with the XB-42, the XB-43 was predicted to be 100mph (161km/h) faster, climb 9,000ft (2,743m) higher, but lose around 40 per cent off range performance. Douglas signed up to performance guarantees of a maximum 503mph (809km/h) at sea level and 452mph (727km/h) at 35,000ft (10,668m), and 38,200ft (11,643m) service ceiling, at 39,997lb (18,142kg) design GW (later rounded off to 40,000lb/18,144kg). A 2,470fpm (13m/sec) climb at sea level and a ceiling of 41,800ft (12,741m) was expected at 35,900lb (16,284kg). The design mission with 8,248lb (3,741kg) payload (35,900lb/16,284kg gross) was to have a range of 1,445mi (2,325km) at 420mph (676km/h), later revised to 1,082mi (1,741km) with 8,000lb (3,629kg). Takeoff distance was to be 7,080ft (2,158m) and

asked to examine three configurations that included two engines side-by-side within the fuselage, one under each wing, and two on the wings with a third inside.[11] The next month, the AAF chose the TG-180 for the application and a specification was released. Douglas' 30 December proposal favoured the twin internal arrangement, the XB-42's original propulsion arrangement making it conducive to substituting jets while retaining much of the original airframe.

A letter supplement to the XB-42 contract was approved on 14 January 1944 to get things moving, with the formal contract change following on 31 March. This covered a mockup and two XB-43 prototypes (44-61508/9), the first to be created from the B-42 static article. This was priced at $2,683,726, but over $2,500,000 was added during 1945 owing to cost overruns. By the time of the contract change, the aircraft was being referred to as a light bomber. This became the AAF's first jet bomber programme (MX-475), maiden flight expected by 31 December 1944 (later 1 May 1945).

The basic layout of the XB-43 (Model

466) was identical to its sibling. The wing leading edge openings were sealed (promising more laminar flow), the horizontal tail moved farther aft, and vertical tail extended about 3.4in (8.6cm). The ventral fin was deleted with elimination of the propeller strike hazard. The new fuselage was similar to the old but widened 8.0in (20.3cm) to accommodate the TG-180 installation above the wing carry-through structure. The engines were easily accessed via large, hinged panels in the top of the fuselage. Simple inlets were placed on either side of the forward fuselage and given slots to bypass the boundary layer of air adjacent to the surface so this would not enter the engine. The twin exhaust pipes under the tail were adjoined, greatly limiting asymmetric thrust complications in

landing of 2,250ft (686m) all over a 50ft (15m) obstacle. Performance estimates for the alternate 2,000lb (907kg) payload mission was 2,370mi (3,814km) range at 420mph (676km/h), later revised to 1,773mi (2,853km).[13]

By 11 December 1944, the service had enough confidence in the aircraft's prospects that it sought a production proposal. It appeared the B-43s could be acquired at least a year before any other jet bombers. Even if not deployable operationally, it could serve as transitional aircraft for aircrew and maintainers gearing-up for combat-ready models to follow. By March, a cautionary order for 50 B-43s was recommended. Douglas suggested a letter contract for $20,000,000 to get things rolling and recommended making the second XB-43 production-representative. However, they cautioned that such a small buy barely justified preparing production drawings and tooling. The Army held out hope for a year's production of 1,000 aircraft and tooling would be prepared assuming a future production rate of 200 machines per month.

By this time, a more conventional canopy was adopted for the XB-42 and this was considered the best choice for the production B-43s. Both radar (AN/APQ-34) and visual bomb aiming was to be included, plus self-sealing fuel cells

and under-wing drop tanks. A remotely controlled, radar-directed aft turret with a pair of .50s (1,000 rounds) was planned and possibly retention of XB-42 aft-firing wing guns. On 15 February 1945, Douglas proposed two versions of the aircraft for joint production. The basic bomber retained the bombardier nose and 6,000lb (2,722kg) payload at 39,759lb (18,034kg) gross, to achieve 470mph (756km/h) at sea level and 429mph (690km/h) at 35,000ft (10,668m), and possess 1,140mi (1,835km) range with 2,000lb (907kg) payload. A 460mph (740km/h) sea level attack variant would have a "solid" nose, 16 forward-firing .50cal guns (300-400rpg) in place of the wing inboard fuel cells, under-wing stores, and 36 5in rockets.

The near-collapse of German resistance and growing interest in greater-capacity jet bombers caused shelving of B-43 production plans. The idea was then floated to procure 13-27 service test aircraft in either or both variants, without full production preparation, to facilitate tactics development. On 12 May 1945, Douglas submitted a quotation for $24,987,060 for 13 YB-43s, with deliveries from December 1946 through September 1947. Although the procurement was authorised on 14 May as MX-685, the proffered schedule was much later than the Air Forces had hoped,

Above: The first XB-43s was substantially complete at war's end, and the first engine run followed soon after. The engines are exposed via the hinged panels atop the fuselage and instrumentation cabling snakes away from the aircraft. Flown nine months later, it became America's first jet bomber – albeit experimental. *American Aviation Historical Society*

somewhat negating the justification. It appeared four-engine YB-45s could be had sooner. The YB-43 procurement was cancelled in July.

When Douglas took delivery of its first TG-180 in December 1944, the inexperience with the new technology and the developmental nature of the powerplant quickly became evident. Lengthy and costly changes to both the engine and airframe were necessary to get the installation right, and the War Department began to complain. Company personnel concluded GE's engine workmanship and aircraft interface design did not conform to aviation standards. Everyone was plowing new ground.

The second GE engine was delivered in July 1945, but Douglas was still struggling with pressurisation leaks. With Army consent, assembly continued without this requirement. The first aircraft was substantially complete by VJ-Day and weighed-in very close to design. Matters proceeded more deliberately

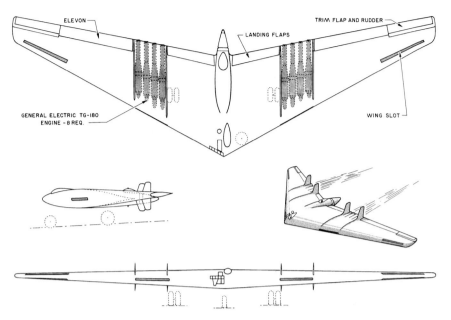

| ELEVON | LANDING FLAPS | TRIM FLAP AND RUDDER |
| GENERAL ELECTRIC TG-180 ENGINE - 8 REQ. | | WING SLOT |

Left: This three-view of the proposed YB-49 illustrates the TG-180 installation, with leading edge intakes feeding the buried engines and extended tail pipes to the trailing edge. Vertical stabilizers and wing fences compensated for loss of the stabilizing influence of the propeller shaft housings. *Jay Miller Collection*

from that point.

It was October 1945 before an engine run could be performed. The XB-43 maiden flight was performed on on May 1946 to become the first all-jet American bomber to fly. Some stability problems were uncovered that required minor modifications, but other issues associated with the experimental nature of the plane remained. Performance objectives were achieved except for excessive takeoff and landing distances. Top speeds of 515mph (829km/h) at 5,000ft (1,524m) and 32,000lb (14,515kg) gross weight were recorded.

One Step Behind (YB-49)

Northrop and the AAF began discussing a jet-powered version of the all-wing XB-35 during summer 1944. The company was provided engine data for a design study in November.[14] Seeing an inevitable future in jets for bombers, the piston-powered B-35 design dating from 1941 appeared to have a limited future. Requirements for high speed were emerging that the B-35 could not hope to meet. The significant delays in the programme, with the propulsion system a notable impediment, were other factors in considering a jet alternative. The USAAF agreed in principle during March 1945 to pursue this approach.[15]

Northrop soon made their proposal for the turbojet flying wing (NS-9) with intent to achieve the 500mph (805km/h) goal the Air Forces expected from their jet bombers.[16] Initial design

data was reviewed with the Army in May 1945. Eight TG-180s would replace the four R-4360s. Although Northrop immediately began preliminary design of this configuration, a change order to the existing YB-35 contract covering the work was not signed until 1 June 1945. This directed conversion of YB-35 ships 2 and 3 (42-102367/8) to become YB-49s (MX-661), with $1,644,603.48, as the projected cost. First flight was expected in June 1946.[17]

Conversion versus an optimised airframe somewhat limited the expected performance from the YB-49 and required a number of operational restrictions. Airspeed (no more than 0.65 Mach to preclude excessive flow separation and loss of elevon effectiveness) and engine output would have to be constrained by aerodynamics, structural, and control issues for the configuration. However, the comparative simplicity of the jet installation next to the R-4360s with its gearboxes and contraprops was like a breath of fresh air. Four turbojets were to be placed between the main landing gear and outboard fuel tanks. Air would enter through leading edge intakes and passed via ducts to the engines that would have extended tail pipes to the trailing edge. Additional fuel tanks were also to be included and a new fire extinguishing system. Two of the eight bomb bays were sacrificed to engines and fuel. Elimination of the stabilising influence of the XB-35's propeller shaft housings would require the addition of

four vertical stabilisers above and below the wings. These were to be placed near the trailing edge and at the end of fences ("separators") that discouraged detrimental spanwise airflow. Defensive weapons would be reduced to just the tail turret of four .50s. Empty weight was expected to be comparable to the YB-35 although gross would increase by about 30,000lb (13,608kg), and speed by over 100mph (161km/h), but bomb capacity would be cut by about 5,000lb (2,268kg).

Work was slowed by the general problems in the YB-35 programme, late delivery of the J35s, and issues with interfacing power extraction systems with these powerplants. Because of Martin's withdrawal from the B-35 programme, Northrop had to begin essentially anew with the YB-35 engineering process and under-utilised shops began construction using existing drawings. Consequently, the two YB-35s identified for YB-49 conversion were essentially XB-35s structurally.

The programme continued following the war at a more moderate pace but with enormous cost overruns. Efforts to "modernise" the YB-35s, and by association the YB-49s, included adding radar, jettisonable fuel tanks, and all-weather gear. None of this got far in design and so was never installed. Even had the aircraft approached an operationally representative state, the Air Forces considered the aircraft to have inadequate bomb capacity. The 16,000lb (7,257kg) maximum was less than the B-29 and no single weapon could be larger than a 4,000lb (1,814kg) bomb due to bay dimensional constraints. This made them unsuitable for then-current atomic weapons. Furthermore, crew arrangement was judged poor and six crewman considered excessive. A year after the war, the YB-49s were considered experimental subjects only.

Although the XB-49 flew in October 1947, the customer remained under-whelmed. Continuing problems with operating power generators off the J35s meant reliance on auxiliary power units. Full-time yaw damping was necessary for bombing and performance was a mixed bag given that a second generation of jet bombers was already in the wings. All the Northrop flying wing bombers had troubling control and stability characteristics that made them poor bombing platforms. They demanded enormous maintenance attention, and were likely to be very expensive to procure. There was simply too little to recommend them over other choices extant or emerging. The entire effort was finally euthanised in 1949 after nearly a decade and tens of millions of dollars expended with nothing close to an operationally suitable bomber resulting.

Attackers – Last Chance

Attack aviation was not neglected in the effort to claim the benefits of jet engines. Long thinking on how this branch might mature in the dawning era of jets and electronics brought a statement of potential revised characteristics on 23 July 1945.[18] Such aircraft were also expected to utilise the J35.

Despite these efforts, attackers would not last much beyond the war. The service began reconsidering the utility of the designation in December 1945, essentially declaring such aircraft to be light bombers.[19] No further efforts to procure attack aircraft, as such, were undertaken for decades.[20]

Lagging (XA-43)

Responding to preliminary requirements provided in September 1944, a Curtiss-Wright Corporation conceptual attack design was submitted on 14 October. This Model 100 received favourable reviews and a letter contract was inked on 24 November 1944 for the XA-43 (MX-582). Curtiss was initially permitted to proceed into Phase I with a completion date of 15 March 1945 with $2,900,000 programmed. This included preliminary design, wind tunnel testing efforts, and mockup construction in Columbus, Ohio.

Mockup inspection occurred on 19 February 1945. Responding to the comments required significant design changes to prevent weight growth, although shortfalls in TG-180 performance were a contributing factor. At USAAF urging, Curtiss investigated alternative powerplants, to include Westinghouse 24-C (later J34), but the J35 was ultimately retained.

As it shaped up, the design was to have a cigar-shaped fuselage with cruciform tail and a bubble canopy for two crewman seated in tandem. The mockup showed what appears to be a radar in the nose. The straight, mid wing would have two embedded dual-engine pods with two J35s each. The nacelle design was based on NACA research

Below: Cutaway art and model of the notional XB-49 reveals the J35 engines buried deep inside the structure. These and added fuel consumed bomb bays outboard of the landing gear in the original XB-35. The wing fences and vertical tails are clearly "scabbed-ons", while fuselage and wing turrets have been dropped. *Jay Miller Collection*, insert *National Archives*

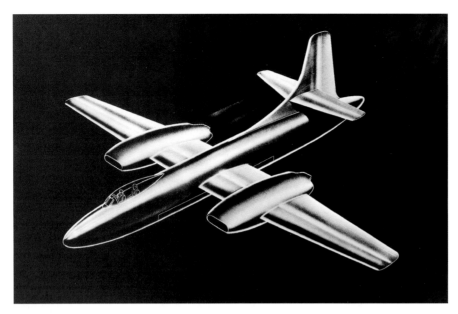

that kept drag to about that of a single, centrifugal-flow engine installation. The main landing gear was housed between the engines. Dive bombing was apparently still anticipated as dive recovery flaps were to be featured under the inboard wing segments.[21]

Typical of this period, the design eschewed manned turrets. A remotely controlled tail turret and AN/APG-3 radar would address intercept from the rear quarter. However, during the weight reduction programme, the turret and radar were deleted in favour of a remote turret on each nacelle with a single .50 gun. A gunner was then considered a possible third crewman, operating the turrets with a periscope placed amidships. A remarkable 10 fixed nose guns were to support ground attack. All told, the ship was to carry 4,700 rounds of half-inch ammunition. Eight 20mm cannon or .60cal machine guns were also considered.[22] A single 75mm or 105mm cannon centred in the nose was also reviewed, but such installations were by then much maligned and would have displaced the radar. Bombs would be within bays accommodating various weapons, potentially including pallets of additional guns or rockets.

Although the AAF was beginning to doubt the XA-43 would suitably meet requirements, the decision was made to continue the programme on at least an experimental basis. This, it was hoped, would permit Curtiss to gain experience with jet technology and respond more successfully in the future. Consequently, a supplement to the letter contract was promulgated on 22 May 1945 to cover Phase II. This would fund construction of additional wind tunnel models, a static test article, and three prototypes, in addition to bailment of a single TG-180 engine for testing. However, the Air Forces soon reconsidered and amended the contract on 27 June with reduction to two prototypes (serials 45-59600/1), one a stripped-down test bird. The effort was then valued at $5,400,000.

A wingspan of 77.6ft (23.7m) with 750ft² (70m²) area, length of 74.8ft (22.8m), and height of 22.2ft (6.8m) was planned for the most mature XA-43 design. Empty weight was projected at 39,080lb (17,726kg) and gross 62,000lb (28,123kg). A maximum 8,000lb (3,629kg) of bombs were to be carried. Projected performance included 585mph (942km/h) top speed at sea level, 1,000mi (1,609km) range with 4,000lb (1,814kg) payload, and 40,000ft (1,219m) ceiling.

The Army further revised its requirements for the attacker on 23 July 1945 with the Curtiss machine then appearing even less suitable, with range particularly deficient. The predicted 5,500ft (1,676m) takeoff distance would also have been found objectionable. It was no surprise the programme was cancelled soon after the war, 29 September, after expending about $863,959. The XA-43 work found use in the XP-87 all-weather/night fighter, one of which was built.

Raising Eyebrows (XA-44)

Having gotten wind of the impending shift to jets for attackers, Convair offered a radical 'tailless' design in the last days of the war. This employed a 1,200ft² (112m²) wing swept forward 12° at quarter-chord line with 3° dihedral and a large vertical stabiliser. The trailing edges had four control surfaces per side that appeared to include root flaps, flaperons, ailerons with fixed wing slots ahead, and tip trimming ailerons. The three J35s were to be embedded in the aft fuselage and fed air via flush fuselage inlets and ducts. The two crewman were seated in tandem under a bubble canopy. Tip tanks were originally considered and main gear retraction into the wing. Apart from up to 12,000lb (5,443kg) of bombs in a bay, weapons were to include 40 5in HVAR projectiles and a battery of a dozen .50cal MGs in the nose and eight more in turrets.[23] An interchangeable nose would offer the option to readily swap armament.[24] Convair predicted a 561mph (903km/h) top speed and 691mi (1,112km) tactical range.

This tailless design with forward-swept wing drew on recently released German research and probably American glider work with a similar layout. The unmanned Cornelius XFG-1 "fuel glider" was to be a towed fuel tank. It flew during late 1944 and into 1945 in a manned configuration for testing. Its tailless design had a 15° forward swept with dihedral adjustable between 3° and 7°, and a tall vertical stabiliser. The glider had undesirable spin characteristics that contributed to a fatal accident. Still, a preliminary design study of a medium or heavy bomber of similar configuration was begun under MX-423.[25]

No action was taken on the Convair proposal until after the close of hostilities when a requirement was issued in February 1946 for jet-powered attackers to replace A-26s.[26] It would initially be known as the XA-44 (MX-716) and later underwent a mission change to light bombardment.[27] It underwent further configuration changes and became the XB-53 in 1948, but was not taken to prototype.

Full Press

In August 1944, under direction from Materiel Command, the Production Division at Wright Field set in motion a programme to solicit jet bomber proposals from manufacturers.[28] The TG-180 was the favoured powerplant, with four or more suggested as required to achieve performance goals. In general, the USAAF was seeking aircraft with 40,000ft (12,192m) ceiling, 1,000mi (1,609km) range, and 500mph (805km/h) top speed. Only a radar-controlled or remote tail turret, with a pair of .50cal

Above: The XA-43 mockup is shown in a badly cropped photo dated 24 February 1945 and wind tunnel model inserted. Additional gun ports were below the nose that also appears to house a radar. The tailplane bullet fairing apparently was to accommodate a rear radar. *Ray Wagner Collection*, insert *Jim Hawkins Collection via Dennis Jenkins*

or 20mm, was envisioned. Normal bomb load would be 8,000lb (3,629kg). Aircraft from 80,000-200,000lb (36,287-90,718kg) were welcome. A more cautious phased approach was taken compared with other Army aircraft projects given the greater technical risk and multiple contractors expected, allowing ready termination.

The jet bomber effort began to coalesce in spring 1944 with several companies invited to bid and four projects initiated in the fall. These were kicked off with release of Addendum I to Classified Technical Instruction 1781 on 15 August 1944.[29] On 17 November, the USAAF circulated the more ambitions characteristics of 450mph (724km/h) average and 550mph (885km/h) top speed, 45,000ft (13,716m) ceiling, and 3,500mi (5,633km) range with 16,500lb (7,484kg) of weapons.[30] A requirement was added on 29 January 1945 to carry the 12,000lb (5,443kg) Tallboy bomb.[31] Then, on 2 March, a requirement to carry a single 22,000lb (9,979kg) Grand Slam bomb to 500mi (805km) was added.[†]

† While the Grand Slam was a weapon the Army wanted to deliver when necessary, the requirement may have been intended to ensure the bombers could carry the large atomic bombs then in development and too secret to reveal.

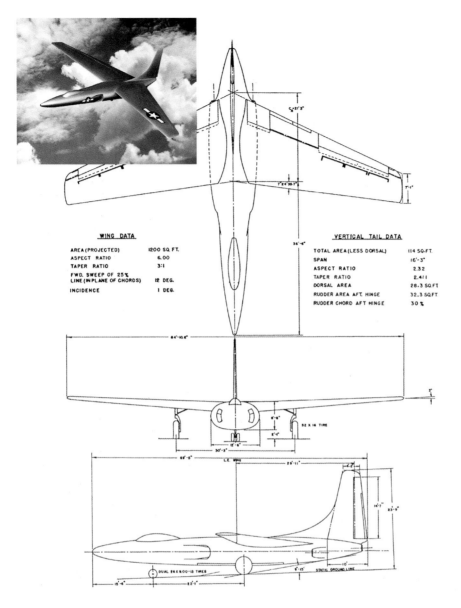

WING DATA

AREA (PROJECTED)	1200 SQ. FT.
ASPECT RATIO	6.00
TAPER RATIO	3:1
FWD. SWEEP OF 25% LINE (IN PLANE OF CHORDS)	12 DEG.
INCIDENCE	1 DEG.

VERTICAL TAIL DATA

TOTAL AREA (LESS DORSAL)	114 SQ.FT.
SPAN	16'-3"
ASPECT RATIO	2.32
TAPER RATIO	2.4:1
DORSAL AREA	28.3 SQ.FT.
RUDDER AREA AFT. HINGE	32.3 SQ.FT.
RUDDER CHORD AFT HINGE	30 %

Quads

XB-46

Answering the USAAF's offer to bid on the jet medium bomber, Convair conceived their Model 109 in San Diego, submitting this on 6 November 1944. The aircraft was to use four of the J35s, paired in wing pods, following closely the NACA nacelle design. The straight, high wing was of 113ft (34m) span and 1,285ft² (119m²) area with Davis section. The fuselage would be very slender and 105ft (32m) long. The pressurised crew compartment had the two tandem-seated pilots under a bubble canopy and the bombardier/navigator in the glazed nose. The aircraft would employ a conventional tricycle undercarriage with main gear

retracting into the inboard wing section. Empty weight was to be approximately 48,000lb (21,772kg) and gross 90,000lb (40,823kg) or more. Convair anticipated a maximum 505mph (813km/h) at 23,000ft (7,010m) and 75,200lb (34,110kg), and a service ceiling of 40,000ft (12,192m) at that weight.

Fuel would be concentrated in four fuselage tanks, paired forward and aft of the 32.0ft (9.8m) long bomb bay. Normal weapons load would be 8,000lb (3,629kg), or 22,000lb (9,979kg) maximum, and a tail turret with twin .50s (600 rounds). The turret would either be controlled remotely or via radar and the Emerson APG-27 fire control system. Bombing would employ an AN/APQ-34 radar under the nose with optical backup. Novel features included

a pneumatic system for very quick actuation of heavy hardware like landing gear, brakes, and bay doors. Electric motors powered the Fowler flaps. These stretched nearly full span with only small, 6.0ft (1.8m) ailerons. These last were "feeler" surfaces designed to provide the pilot control feedback and "guide" roll spoiler deployment. Other than at top speeds, most roll control was from the five spoiler panels stretching over 20.0ft (6.1m) on each wing. Wing and tail de-icing was planned.‡

A 17 January 1945 letter contract got the project moving and a mockup was inspected on the 29th. Satisfied, the service ordered three XB-46 prototypes (45-59582/4) and a static test article on the 12 February with estimated first flight July 1946. A related effort was to be the testing of a TG-180 on a B-24J to provide data to the Convair design team.[32]

The end of the war brought the threat of cancellation after expending $2,164,000, with 60 per cent of the engineering completed and 20 per cent of the parts fabricated. With possibly inadequate funds, the Army was more interested in Convair pursuing the XA-44 than the bomber.[33] A compromise proposed by the company was to continue with a single stripped-down XB-46 and two XA-44s. The USAAF concurred while the much-delayed B-24J testing was also dropped.

Under a more reasonable schedule, the XB-46 flew in April 1947. It possessed a respectable 505mph (813km/h) top speed at 23,000ft (7,010m).[34] Range was 1,390mi (2,237km) with the four-ton payload. It had its share of teething problems but flew well. The greatest problem was resonance between the spoilers and wings that created heavy wing oscillations at cruise speeds and

‡ Long, slender wings of conventional structural design could lack torsional rigidity sufficient to prevent inadequate roll response from ailerons that would tend to twist the wing leading edge down. This led designers to choose spoilers for crisp roll control.

nearly catastrophic failure. Turbulence or oscillating the controls fore and aft could generate disconcerting fuselage bending, and lateral control could be heavy. Although all the major problems were resolved, by the time the XB-46 was showing its capabilities the USAF had already ordered the lighter B-45 into production.

XB-45

North American also proposed a four-engine design in the USAAF's jet bomber effort. Their approach was to keep the basic airframe well within the state of the art to move quickly on design and assembly. Preliminary design of the NA-130 began late in 1943 and a mockup inspection followed in July 1944. Two prototypes and a static test article (45-59479/81) were ordered on 8 September 1944 as the XB-45.

The XB-45 was to span 89.0ft (27.1m), stretch 74.0ft (22.6m), and stand 25.1ft (7.7m). Empty weight was expected on the order of 41,000-42,000lb (18,597-19,051kg) and around 65,000lb (29,483kg) loaded. The lighter weight compared with all the competitors was

a clear advantage. The jet was to employ a straight, laminar-flow wing set high on a sleek fuselage. The four engines were paired in long pods integral to each wing, the nacelles only borrowed from the NACA design. Single-slotted Fowler flaps were placed on both sides of the nacelles. The tail plane was given a sharp dihedral to clear the surfaces from the jet exhaust. A basic tricycle undercarriage was adopted, although the new main wheels and brakes were designed to be very narrow for fitting into the wing. Unlike some of the other first-generated jet bombers, the North American wing remained thick enough (nine or 14 per cent thickness ratio) to contain fuel tanks. These, and others in the fuselage,

were all self-sealing. Additional fuel could be carried in a bomb bay tank, when fitted.

All controls were boosted with a 3,000psi (20,684kPa) hydraulic system and tabs were electrically actuated. The cockpit for the tandem-seated pilot and copilot, under a blown canopy, and forward bombardier/navigator glassed station were pressurised. The single entry and exit point for these crewmen was a forward fuselage door. An anti-ice system bled hot air from the engines' final compressor stage and passed this through insulated ducts to channels in the wing and empennage leading edges. Originally, an Emerson Electric tail turret with fire control system was to be radar-directed and fired by the copilot. However, this was dropped from the design early on when developmental tests demonstrated its unreliability. Instead, a pressurised gunner's station was incorporated to fire the twin .50s (600rpg). North American included the optical and radar bombing systems in their prototypes. Up to 14,000lb (6,350kg) of bombs could be incorporated, including the Grand Slam.

The early production of 13 service test YB-45s was explored during the early summer of 1945 as a means to get jet bombers into the hands of pilots and

Right: The programme's early 3-view of the XB-46 design, more mature than the concept art, reveals dimensions that remained largely unchanged throughout development. The tail turret is included and a radar blister under the nose that was not incorporated into the stripped-down prototype. Shown are the unusual wing control surface arrangement. *San Diego Air & Space Museum*

maintainers as soon as possible. North American suggested it could deliver these between 1 November 1946 and May 1947 at two per month. This projection was cause to drop the YB-43, but then the imminent end of the war prompted all such plans to be suspended.

The XB-45 was still in detail design as the war wrapped-up. The company's incremental approach allowed their design to fly first among the four competitors, in March 1946. It eventually demonstrated 516mph (830km/h). The only significant deficiency was lack of adequate horizontal tail area and suitable emergency egress.[35] With swept wings and atomic bomb delivery becoming the focus of the new United States Air Force, and the J35 surpassed by higher performance engines, the XB-45 already appeared obsolete. However, it seemed a practical introductory and test aircraft. Consequently, it became the first American jet bomber (by then a "light" bomber) to enter production with a modest run. Only with change of engine did it find combat roles.

Sextets

XB-48

Martin submitted their Model 223 jet medium bomber (although the size and weight of a B-24) on 9 December 1944 with an offer to perform Phase I initial design and construct a mockup for $574,826.50. The concept was judged satisfactory and a letter of intent for Phase I was promulgated. A $166,000 letter contract followed on 16 December for what was designated the XB-48 (MX-598). A formal contract was agreed to on the 12 May with a budget of $569,242.40. This covered preliminary design, wind tunnel work, and the mockup, with data delivery and mockup inspection by 1 May 1945.

The experienced Martin team wasted no time and the mockup was inspected on 19 April 1945. They kept up the fast pace with a 26 June proposal to build

prototypes, with one stripped-down for rapid move to flight testing plus one to three fully equipped aircraft. The service responded on the 30th with a supplement to the contract. This Phase II funded one stripped and one complete bomber (45-59585/6) at $8,640,482.73. The contract change authorising aircraft construction and a bomb bay mockup, with added moneys, was not approved until December 1946.

The Model 223 was to be a pressurised design possessing a high wing with six J35. Although this was an unusually large number of engines, especially for a medium bomber, the modest thrust of the early jets and the high target speed made this necessary. Three engines were combined into a single pod under each

wing-half. During detailed design, the pod became three distinct nacelles with "by-pass ducts" running between to reduce drag and weight, plus enhance lift.[36] Flak protection for the engines was conceived.[37] The pilot and copilot were to sit in tandem under a fighter-like canopy while the bombardier/navigator was in a glassed nose. Initially, the tail ball turret with twin-.50cal MGs (500rpg) would be directed by the copilot from a sighting station immediately to the rear of his seat with a bifurcated periscope. Later, a rear radar and fire control system was planned. Bombing would be facilitated with the AN/APA-59 bombing navigation computer linked with an AN/APS-23 search radar.

The XB-48 design included a number

of other unusual features. It employed a "bicycle" or "tandem" undercarriage with two main gear trucks within the fuselage (forward steerable), separated by a long bomb bay, and small auxiliary gear within the engine pods. The high-speed wing sections were too thin to house landing gear, although the inboard segments had fuel cells supplementing fuselage tanks. An engine bleed air anti-icing system was installed on the first aircraft but electric de-icing blankets were substituted on the second. Tip tanks were later suggested plus water injection for the turbojets. A "horizontal bomb bay" was also proposed and the mockup built. This was to employ a removable carrier that could be loaded separate from the aircraft with various combinations of weapons, then wheeled beneath the long, shallow bay and hoisted up to be secured. This would greatly hasten the loading task as a second carrier could be prepared between sorties. The bay doors would be pneumatically retracted into the fuselage to allow free movement of munitions personnel beneath the aircraft and reduce drag in flight. Both inboard and outboard double-slotted flaps, nearly full span, worked to enhance low-speed lift. Like the XB-46,

there were only 2.6ft (0.8m) long "feel" or "feeler" ailerons at the wingtips intended primarily to provide roll axis feedback to the pilots, but were also effective at top speeds. Most of the roll control power throughout the majority of the flight regime would come from hydraulically powered spoilers synchronised with the ailerons.

The aircraft initially had a 97.6ft (29.7m) span, but this was increased during design to 108.5ft (33.1m), bringing area to 1,330ft² (124m²) for improved takeoff performance. The rear turret and

Above: A cutaway depiction of the conceptual XB-45 shows that, unlike other teams that used very thin wings to reduce drag, the North American designers employed a laminar-flow airfoil with sufficient volume for fuel and landing gear. Note the radar and remote turret in the tail, and nacelles without individual inlets. *National Archives*

Below: This model of the XB-45 reveals the evolution to a gunner station for the tail turret, adding a fourth crewman. The engines exhaust well aft of the wing trailing edge, eased the service's concern about heating of the structure and internal fuel, in addition to predicted adverse airflow effects. *San Diego Air & Space Museum*

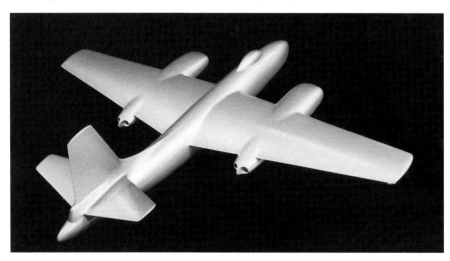

choice of controlling system vacillated for many months before simply being set aside. The objective empty weight was 58,000lb (26,308kg) and maximum gross 100,000lb (45,359kg). Martin was expecting 568mph (914km/h) at sea level and a range of 2,500mi (4,023km) with the 8,000lb (3,629kg) payload, and accepted a guarantee for 536mph (863km/h) at 35,000ft (10,668m).

Martin had many projects running and frequently shifted priorities, to the detriment of the XB-48. As work fell behind schedule and the AAF complained, Martin created a separate and lean organisation of selected individuals in Baltimore to build the XB-48. Construction was to begin without awaiting final and approved drawings. However, it does not appear any substantial assembly had begun before the end of the war. Even as German technical data became available attesting to the advantages of swept wings, the Air Forces insisted Martin keep with a low-risk approach and retain their straight wing.

A more moderate postwar pace was assumed and the aircraft flew in June 1947. A notable issue was buffet with the bomb bay doors open. A 1,340mi (2,157km) range with the 8,000lb (3,629kg) load was measured, and top speed fell well below the guarantee with 479mph (771km/h) at 35,000ft (10,668m), although achieving 516mph (830km/h) at 20,000ft (6,096m). This was well below the swept-wing Boeing

XB-47 and, combined with other deficiencies, meant the Martin design had no future.

XB-47

Boeing's path to a solid jet bomber proposal was more convoluted than the other competitors. This eventually benefited the project, as the company was able to employ design options gleaned during summer and fall 1945 from German sources. Its competitors were already committed to basic concepts by that time. To that point, Boeing had been performing conceptual design work that included wind tunnel tests to collect baseline data.[38] All had a pilot and copilot seated in tandem under a fighter-like bubble canopy and bombardier/navigator in a glazed nose. A tail turret with a pair of .50cals was mated with rear-facing radar.

Among the initial concepts, shared with the USAAF in March 1944, the Model 424 was conventional in appearance with a very thin wing and paired TG-180 engines in two pods integral with the wing. However, maximum speed was still little more than 400mph (644km/h). Seeking reduced drag to attain higher speed, the four engines were moved into a less slender fuselage. A pair of shoulder intakes fed the engines that exhausted over the top of the fuselage. The horizontal tail was raised up on the vertical stabiliser to clear it from the exhaust flow. While this Model 432

left the straight wing clean, the engines would be difficult to service and the exhaust would generate scrubbing drag and heating of the structure.

Examining the 432 when presented in December 1944, the Army also saw grave vulnerability in the event of engine fire or disintegration (the engines were above the main fuselage tank), even discounting hostile fire. Both were demonstrable concerns with the early turbojets. Little data on the efficiency of the proposed intakes existed. It was not a promising design as drag still made objective performance elusive. However, the USAAF granted Boeing a letter contract for Phase I studies on 1 February 1945 to continue conceptual design of what was then identified as the XB-47. Of the $1,500,000 programmed, Boeing was initially authorised to expend only $150,000 for wind tunnel and analytical work.

The breakthrough came with the adoption of a swept wing. As with other American aircraft manufacturers, after VE-Day Boeing was shown some of the captured German aircraft and engineering data. Additionally, the firm's chief aerodynamicist, George Schairer, was among the team visiting German facilities during May 1945, who interviewed senior personnel, and collected documents. There he found wind tunnel data substantiating Bob Jones' theories and learned the Germans had flown high-speed, swept-wing aircraft. The benefits of wing sweep in delaying compressibility effects to attain high speed, long discussed in Allied circles, was now incontrovertible. Schairer sent word back to Seattle, spurring immediate investigation of sweep for the conceptual jet bomber.

The next Boeing concept retained the portly fuselage but with a "fishmouth" nose intake and two more engines in the aft fuselage with adjoining inlets. However, the most notable feature of the Model 448 was the wing of 35° quarter-chord sweep, high aspect ratio, and

laminar-flow airfoil to increase critical Mach number. The tailplane was likewise swept back. The 448 formed the basis of a September 1945 proposal to the USAAF. Difficulties remained as the very thin airfoil did not permit storage of fuel or landing gear components, leading to complex solutions the service found unsavory. The engines did not permit sufficient tankage within the fuselage without hazardous proximity to the powerplants. Consequently, at the close of the war, the Boeing concept for the XB-47 was not a practical basis for a medium bomber, but they were on a promising track. Engine placement concepts were still being evaluated with the number of configurations considered reaching as many as 50.

Postwar, Boeing moved on to the Model 450 with two engines on each side paired in an inboard pod integral with the wing, and two others alone at the wingtips. The final step was to hang the inboard engines below the wing on

pylons, the pods projecting ahead of the leading edge. The arrangement greatly reduced drag and structural weight, with the additional advantages of delaying tip stall and pitch-up for improved low-speed aileron effectiveness. The wing was then extended beyond the outboard engines and Martin's "bicycle" landing gear adopted.

Prototypes were ordered in April 1946. After the XB-47 began flight testing in December 1947 it soon demonstrated standout performance compared with all the designs initiated during the war years. Peak speed exceeded 600mph (966km/h). The result was a production run in the hundreds and new standards

Above: To validate the "tandem landing gear" concept and gain practical experience, Martin modified a B-26G-25 (44-68221) in May 1945 to the sole XB-26H. The aircraft's undercarriage was replaced with two single-wheel main gear posts retractable into the fuselage and smaller outrigger struts retractable into the engine nacelles. San Diego Air & Space Museum

in high-speed aircraft design and bomber performance. Boeing was the only big winner of the wartime jet bomber projects.

Right: This Martin drawing of a more mature XB-48 design includes a tail radar, optical bombsight projecting from the nose, and tiny wingtip ailerons. Wingspan was later increased by 11% for a greater area to improve takeoff performance, and bombing radar radome added under the forward fuselage. The channels between the engines are evident. Glenn L. Martin Maryland Aviation Museum

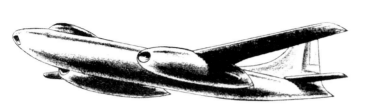

Model 424 - March 1944

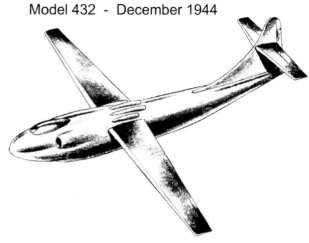

Model 432 - December 1944

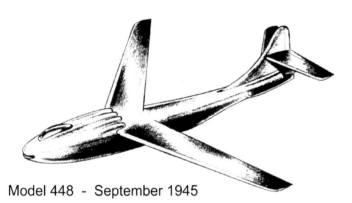

Model 448 - September 1945

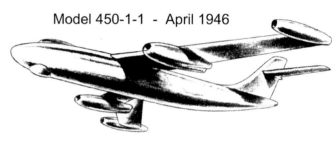

Model 450-1-1 - April 1946

Above: This montage shows the major design steps leading to Boeing's XB-47 design. The Model 448 was current at the war's end and Boeing adopted the swept wing. The last drawing is the 450-1-1 that was offered just after the conflict. One more iteration yielded the winning 450-3-3 proposal. *Author's Collection*

Right: This image reveals wind tunnel models employed during the configuration investigation for the Boeing XB-47. At top right is the Model 424, top left the Model 432, and in the foreground the final Model 450-3-3. Note the swept wing shapes in the background and landing gear on the 432. *National Museum of the United States Air Force*

Chapter Eleven

Conclusion and Prelude

Long Way, Short Time

In rounded numbers, the United States built 74,925 bombers in 20 basic types during the war, some 85 per cent of which were frontline machines and 19 per cent exported. This was 25 per cent of total US wartime aircraft production yet was more bombers than all other nations combined. Compared with a prewar 2,320 total combat aircraft, the Army took delivery of 52,500 bombers. Half of these (28,375) were four-engine heavy bombers in two just types (B-17 and B-24s), emphasising the importance the leadership placed on strategic bombardment. The sea service acquired 4,577 flying boat bombers and 4,611 landplane bombers, or 22 per cent of all Navy wartime aircraft procurement and nearly twice the total prewar complement of all naval aircraft. That the Americans began late from a background of miserly investment makes these achievements all the more remarkable. National will and rational leadership, seeking only to end the conflict quickly and at least cost to American lives, was essential to this end. Highlighting this, it ended more quickly than it began. After VE-Day, aircraft production was reduced by 30 per cent. Following VJ-Day it was reduced again to a few hundred.

Prewar procurement plans, forming the basis for this extraordinary expansion of American bomber fleets, remained remarkably consistent throughout, although altered during the conflict in response to changing requirements and available resources. Likewise, organisation

and strategy was altered in response to actual bomber delivery.[1] The support of troops in combat took a big leap forward as attackers became light bombers and medium bombers took on more of a ground attack mission, with direct attack developing techniques supplementing level bombing. Long-range patrol and anti-submarine warfare was entirely transformed. Strategic bombardment became an established fact.

The results of strategic bombing are debatable. Almost every day for nearly three years, heavy bombers cut contrails over Europe as they methodically reduced Germany's ability to wage war. The same process was repeated over Japan on a smaller scale but with similar results. "Precision bombardment" was relative. It required many hundreds of bombs from scores of aircraft to destroy an industrial target, which might then be rebuilt. The radio navigation aids and BTO radar were not accurate enough

for blind bombing of anything but large area targets. Like the British, the US also resorted to night bombing of urban areas to target distributed manufacturing facilities, transportation nodes, and the labour force. This found its ultimate application in night firebombing of Japan after daylight bombing results was judged inadequate.

Although thousands of enemy fighters were claimed destroyed by American bomber gunners, the cost of the relative successes in strategic bombardment was enormous, as it was in all other bombing missions.[2] Even in their most heavily armed configurations the bombers suffered grave losses in Europe. In heavy and long-range bombers alone, the US Army lost 12,000 aircraft (roughly half the total procurement) and tens of thousands of crewmen. In the year between summer 1943 and 1944, units in the ETO flying heavy bombers suffered 98 per cent aircraft attrition.[3]

Right: Army intent to build an enormous fleet of bombers while meeting foreign demands led to an tremendous national undertaking. Some types were built at multiple sites and by multiple manufacturers. This image is of B-24Es in final assembly at the mile-long Consolidated plant in Ft. Worth, Texas. *National Museum of the United States Air Force*

As the RAF had found, the veil of night was not enough to turn the trick either as night fighters and the hazards of night operations took a terrible toll as well. Losses in the ETO during the day were actually less than at night. The prewar notion of the bomber's splendid invincibility as it battered the miscreant foe into submission was clearly mistaken. During 1943 it appeared a disheartening war of attrition was developing, with young men slaughtering each other in their clever machines at the command of their national leaders with unclear progress towards victory. This was only reversed with the introduction of effective fighter escort and enemy opposition was slowly reduced to a shadow of its former self. Likewise, Japan's early air dominance that so effectively met Allied bombing raids was only slowly eroded and by many means.

None of the strategic bombing provided a knockout blow, completely crippling enemy war-making capability or resolve. During the nine-month bombing campaign against the Japanese home islands, B-29s dropped only 11 per cent of the tonnage delivered on Germany, but the impact was more

telling. Japan's ability to wage a modern war was essentially obliterated, with industrial output cut by more than seventy-five per cent. These operations reduced 178mi² (461km²) of urban area to ash and killed 330,000 civilians.[4] However, by August 1945 the B-29s had eliminated most of the assigned targets and the enemy continued to resist.

Similarly, tactical conditions were seldom changed profoundly by interdiction and air support. Had the atomic bombings not convinced Japan to surrender, a bloody and protracted land campaign would likely have ensued, as it had in Europe. In this scenario,

the effectiveness of the thousands of bombers planned to be amassed against the islands appeared minimal. Nonetheless, bombing in all its forms was a vital contribution to ultimate victory.

Little glamour was felt for these aircraft at the time. The bombers were utilitarian, built to the task. Maintaining them was dirt, dreary work performed in all weather with sometimes makeshift equipment. Operating the aircraft was exhausting, with high noise, vibration, and extremes of temperature, disregarding being shot at. The missions were long and grueling (8-12hr for strategic and patrol bombers), swinging between boredom and terror. The enemy always had tactics or technology responding to each Allied innovation. If it wasn't the enemy, it was inexperienced pilots or weather contributing to midair collisions, impact with terrain, or losing their way and exhausting fuel supply. The task was brutal, sowing terror on the ground as the war moved from airmen killing each other to mass slaughter of civilians via mechanised warfare. Even for those not receiving the bombs directly, others were at risk from spent bullets and shell fragments falling about

Right: American bombers tended to be more rugged and survivable than their foreign counterparts. Many tales are told, supported by photographs like this one, of aircraft returning to base over hundreds of miles with gaping holes, missing components, and casualties onboard from flak or enemy fighters. *San Diego Air & Space Museum*

them along with casings, links, pieces of aircraft, and pieces of people. Few of the men who operated and maintained these bombers would have wished a similar activity on their children.

The work wore down men and machines alike. A few months in service, if they survived that long in combat, generally exhausted an airframe and engines, demanding ever more maintenance and spares. Severe climates, operating from unpaved fields, battle damage repair, and maintenance outdoors contributed to deterioration. With the added requirement that aircraft be built quickly, often by semi-skilled workers, the machines were not generally durable. A year was generally the limit of a bomber's useful life as new models typically appeared in that time. However, some did complete 50-100 missions.

By the end of the war the US armed forces had a comparative wealth of materiel with their steady rise to dominance. This was partially an expression of the mammoth resources America enjoyed and industries free from enemy bombs. Although war is wasteful by nature, the Americans found it practical in some circumstances to simply discard unserviceable equipment, like aircraft engines, rather than apply the manpower, time, and parts supply to repair them. Bomber deliveries eventually ran ahead of needs, and hundreds were stored after completion.

By Comparison

The American aircraft industry was exceptionally experienced by the end of World War 2, having developed numerous model variations and new designs in a short period. The United States excelled in some things while foreign nations led in others. This was partially the outcome of prewar development (varying political and fiscal commitment), matters of national circumstances like range from adversary, available resources, division of effort with allies, selected strategy and tactics, different weighing of attributes like defence and safety, and leadership preferences. Hence, direct comparison of individual bomber capabilities is not entirely meaningful. On a whole, however, America stood essentially

Above: The Americans had an "embarrassment" of materiel wealth in the final year of the war compared with the opposition. The end of hostilities left them with thousands of excess bombers and thousands of tons of associated gear. This desert "bone yard" contains some brand new B-29s sent directly to storage. *National Archives*

shoulder-to-shoulder with Great Britain and Germany, although always on a larger scale, and well ahead of Italy, Japan, and the USSR.

American bombers were used by all allied nations and evaluated by the opposition. They were generally judged advanced, sound and very capable. However, they were also seen as perhaps needlessly complex and with too much left to crew actions. More weight was devoted to defensive systems, armour, and safety features. All this also required more crewmen.[5] Two pilots in even medium bombers was criticised, the RAF practice being different and even US Army studies showing copilots were unnecessary except to reduce fatigue.[6] The bombers initially lagged behind combat needs when introduced into Europe. Even as they were improved and became fully combat-worthy, major operators like Great Britain and the USSR continued to prefer their own equipment built to their particular circumstances. This was all the better for US forces who wanted as many of the bombers as they could get.

The American lead in the insertion of the latest technology for all-weather operations, precision bombing, and flight safety. In areas of long range, heavy payload, defence, system safety, and pressurised systems, the US was

in a class by itself integrating all these into successful warplanes. Only the United States built practical pressurised bombers in large numbers and employed them during routine bombing missions.

Although radical designs were offered by American industry teams, these were usually rejected because of the greater technological risk, time required for supporting research and development, and longer period to fielding. This was particularly at variance with Germany whose Nazi leadership was enraptured with advanced weapons and spent considerable resources on long-term projects that yielded nothing or contributed little. However, no new US bomber project begun after 1941 reached combat. The war was won with upgrades of existing designs and engines, and a few ongoing projects that flew only after America entered the conflict.

Of the advanced projects, the flying wing led nowhere. Other nations dabbled with such designs, but the American advanced farthest, even to prototype assembly of a bomber.

Right: The war brought the rapid rise of heavily armed, propeller-driven bombers with capabilities unattainable just a few years before. At the end, the equally quick demise of such airplanes was in sight. Airplanes like this B-24, bristling with guns and turrets and driven by reciprocating engines (R-1820 shown), were becoming passé. *San Diego Air & Space Museum*, insert *National Archives*

Likewise, only the United States took an intercontinental bomber to prototype assembly while others drew conceptual sketches. While the US came late to jet engine development, it was neck-to-neck with Britain by the end of the war and a few months behind Germany. Although Germany did some work in jet bombers, this did not reach prototype stage and they fielded only a light bomber conversion of a reconnaissance aircraft. The Americans' more practical designs underway at the end laid the foundation for the first post-war bombers.

By mid-1944 it was clear all such advanced aircraft developments were not going to be essential to victory, and leadership showed restraint in assigning them resources. Instead, work focused on enhancing capabilities and safety. Standards by then were higher than at the beginning, with more careful selection and testing. Some of the earlier bombers would probably have been rejected just three years later.

The Future Beckons

After the end of the war in Europe, the USAAF began to look to requirements beyond the conflict. The rapid technological advance had set the stage for truly world-spanning and efficient aircraft, and strategic weapons of cataclysmic destructive potential. By the end of the war some of the path forward was becoming clear. The economic and geopolitical outcome of the conflict placed the United States in a superior position to exploit the technological gains and sustain the momentum for postwar military and commercial benefit. Likewise, the combat organisations of all services had reached a pinnacle of professionalism and technical acumen. This readied them for the coming postwar challenges of increasing aircraft complexity and worldwide missions.

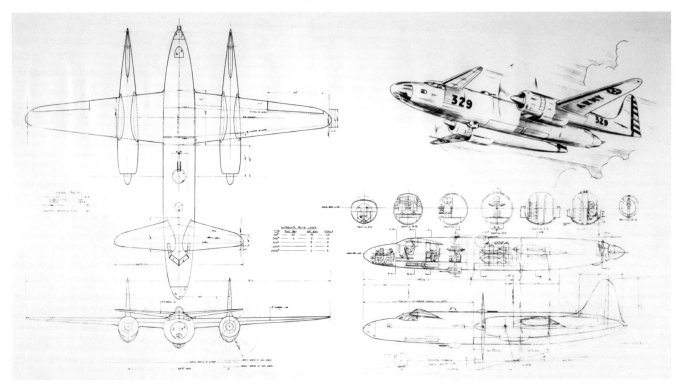

The bombers that helped win the war represented a peak of unpressurised, propeller-driven, turreted design, and soon disappeared. Since jet bombers could not yet match the range and payload of reciprocating-engine bombers, the B-36 continued to production. It was possibly the only true intercontinental bomber as those that followed relied upon aerial refueling. The B-36 was a remnant of the war, the ultimate World War 2 bomber although destined never to fight in that conflict. It was the largest and heaviest bomber ever fielded, a complicated beastie costly to maintain and difficult to operate.

Jet bombers with more electronic systems were clearly going to be superior in time, and the new United States Air Force emphasised their development. Their speed would lessen requirements for defensive armament. Although

Left: Martin's efforts to foster B-26 follow-on work and meet requirements for a high-altitude medium bomber brought forth many Model 189 variations, including this Design No. 4 (18 March 1941 drawing). Many such radical designs were offered by the nation's aeronautical firms, but the services resisted them to ensure rapid development and production. Glenn L. Martin Maryland Aviation Museum

accuracy and reliability remained wanting, the bomb-nav radar still promised all-weather combat and so was pursued with determination.[7] Likewise, the efficiency of multiengine landplanes equipped with radar and specialised anti-submarine weapons rendered the flying boat bomber a curiosity with diminishing mission application. The advent of atomic weapons made the prospects of strategic and even maritime bombing more promising. The destructive potential of these weapons rendered fleets of thousands of bombers anachronistic. Never again were they built in World War 2 numbers. The elusive goal of precision bombing seemed no longer necessary as the massive blast of an atomic detonation was sure to obliterate the target, along with the surrounding area.

All the jet bomber programmes survived the drastic demobilisation cutbacks, but proceeded at a much reduced pace. Many of the resulting aircraft failed to measure up or were challenging to operate. They remain, however, a remarkable wartime result and the first of a breed that continues today as among the most potent warplanes. The insertion of nav-bombing

Above: By war's end, jet bombers were the clear future in meeting speed demands. This drawing of the XB-45 shows how the nacelles have evolved with separate inlets and the overall shape appears to be slimmer. The aft fuselage shows where the radar was replaced by a then-anachronistic manned station. San Diego Air & Space Museum

radar, radar-directed guns or cannon, electronic navigation aids, electronic warfare systems, and flight safety subsystems continued to increase along with efforts at reducing weight and achieving greater reliability. Such has continued to the present day.

By comparison to today's aircraft, America's World War 2 bombers would be considered shockingly unsafe, exceptionally unreliable and maintenance intensive, and massively inefficient. They were a product of their time and wartime circumstances. These and the conflict established new standards for human carnage and set the stage for the weapons focus during the Cold War that followed. That over 65 years have past without repeating the death and destruction of the 20th century's two world wars suggests some hopeful maturing of humankind. Yet, bombers remain.

Endnotes

Chapter One

1. *The Development of the Heavy Bomber*, 49.
2. Cash-and-Carry required that aircraft not be flown across US borders for delivery to belligerents. This produced such spectacles as the aircraft being flown to an airstrip on the Canadian border and then rolled across or towed by draft horses. Although any belligerent could ostensibly purchase weapons from the United States, the fascist regimes' war industries had been working at high capacity for some years and these countries did not require or want American products. Only the democratic nations were lagging and required foreign arms. This arrangement suited American sensibilities.
3. W. Wolf, *Boeing B-29 Superfortress*, 131.
4. M. Gorn, Expanding the Envelope, 361.
5. *The Development of the Heavy Bomber*, 25, 30, and 86. The rejection included the observation that no military requirement existed for such a bomber. The objectives were later applied to the programme spawning the XB-29 and XB-32.
6. R. Francillon, *Lockheed Aircraft Since 1913*, 122 and 129.
7. The dawn of precision guided munitions was explored and saw some modest operations use. Few of the efforts to develop manually or autonomously guided munitions made it to the field, and those that did were marginally successful, at best. This subject is best left for another text.
8. N. Friedman, *US Naval Weapons*, 266.
9. Heavy bomber self-defensive armament had its greatest expression in the "bomber escort" or "convoy protector aircraft". This envisioned more heavily armed examples of a bomber flying in a formation of like-type aircraft and lending heavy fire in all quadrants of the sphere around the machine. An XB-40 was created from a B-17F and an XB-41 from a B-24D, each with added powered turrets and enormous quantities of ammunition. These were followed by 13 YB-40s that were deployed to Europe and flew nine missions in summer 1943. The aircraft were so heavy they could not carry bombs, were difficult to handle in formations, and could not keep up with the formation during the return leg. It was no substitute for long range fighter escort, and the concept was dropped. However, on 23 August 1941, it had been decided that each new bomber would have a variant that could serve as a formation escort, at least until suitable long-range fighters became available. Hence, the fourth YB-29 (41-36597) was modified with added turrets to explore Superfortress potential as an escort. This remained the only expression of the policy, which was subsequently set aside.
10. F. Johnsen, *Boeing B-17 Flying Fortress*, 15-16, and *Development of Aircraft Gun Turrets in the AAF*, 95 and 154.

Chapter Two

1. Claims that B-18As were provided to Canada, supplementing the Digbys could not be substantiated.
2. W. Wolf correspondence, author of *Douglas B-18 Bolo*.
3. W. Wolf, *Douglas B-18 Bolo*, 119.
4. B. Kinzey, *B-25 Mitchell*, 17.
5. N. Avery, *North American Aircraft 1934-1998*, 91.
6. W. Wolf, *North American B-25 Mitchell The Ultimate Look*, 59.
7. K. Darling, North American B-25 Mitchell, pp.26-27
8. R. Waag, *Thunder from the Sky*, 49 and 51.
9. R. Dorr, *North American B-25 Variant Briefing*, 133.
10. The first flight date is frequently seen as 29 November, even in seemingly authoritative text.
11. The introduction of multi-engine trainers was one answer to this shortcoming. The step from the single-engine AT-6 trainer to a sophisticated multi-engine had become too great.
12. J. Breihan, et al, *Martin Aircraft 1909-1960*, 105.

Chapter Three

1. J. Cuny, *AAHS Journal*, Spring 1968, 2.
2. These are the most commonly quoted values. However, R. Caruana in *Douglas A-20 Boston/Havoc*, 25, states 16 were destroyed, which appears to be well supported. The 22nd is also occasionally given as the date of the DB-7's combat debut, but this is also refuted. Additionally, 134 combat sorties also reported.
3. R. Wagner, *American Combat Planes of the 20th Century*, 206.
4. S. Thompson, *Douglas Havoc and Boston*, 41.
5. Ibid, pp.278 and 280..
6. The armament is frequently stated as 20mm.
7. S. Thompson, *Douglas A-26 and B-26 Invader*, 32.
8. Several sources offer the serial 44-34776, a late-production A-26B-71-DL, as a A-26D prototype and state that only two Ds were created. This aircraft is so late in the production cycle that it is unlikely to have been modified. Likewise, reports of the prototypes being identified with a prefix X appear to be in error.
9. Thompson, 45-46.
10. The aircraft is most often attributed with six .30cal guns, with the wing MGs seldom mentioned in the literature. Photos reveal two mocked-up gun barrels protruding from the starboard wing and one from the port wing, outboard of the propeller arc and inboard of the landing light.
11. Some sources state that all F1 and F2 aircraft were delivered by April 1940 or July. Others sources state only 25 of the F2s were in Morocco at commencement of the spring offensive.
12. Model Designations, The Glenn L. Martin Co., p.15.
13. J. Breihan, et al, *Martin Aircraft 1909-1960*, 124, describes this as freezing at high altitude. However, C. Shores, *Martin Maryland & Baltimore Variants*, 231, offers the more likely explanation as great difficulty with horizontal motion owing to awkward ammunition boxes and feed installation.

Chapter Four

1. *Development of Aircraft Gun Turrets in the AAF*, 135-136.
2. *Case History of XB-33 and B-33 Aircraft*, summary 1.
3. Ibid, document summary entry 11.
4. Ibid, document summary entry 6.
5. The change from one to two prototypes reflects a general trend in aircraft development at that time. Prewar, funding would only permit a single flying example, but this placed the programme at risk if the aircraft was damaged or lost – a none-too infrequent outcome.
6. *Case History of XB-33 and B-33 Aircraft*, document summary entry 11.

7. E. Johnson, *Aviation History*, January 2004, 12, states it was purely coincidental that the numbers associated with the A and B designations were identical.

8. *Report of Preliminary Flights, XB-42 Aircraft*, 1, and *Flight, Test, Incidents and Accidents on Selected Multi-engine Bombers*, 112.

9. *Air Force Developmental Aircraft*, 164c.

10. W. Boyne, *Airpower*, September 1973, provides much of this detail of flight test findings, that author having the benefit of unpublished flight test reports from the USAAF test pilots.

Chapter Five

1. *The Development of the Heavy Bomber*, 47-48. This was soon raised to 1,000 per month, a goal achieved in October 1943, 128.

2. *The Development of the Heavy Bomber*, 85.

3. The acronym BVD was actually a bit of rye humor since this was also the name of a popular brand of under shorts.

4. A more natural solution would have been a larger diameter propeller, but the existing design dimensions did not permit this without interference.

5. *Development of Aircraft Gun Turrets in the AAF*, 226.

6. A. Lloyd et al, *B-17 Flying Fortress, Part 1*, 5.

7. W, Hess, *Wings of Fame* Vol. 6, fold-out.

8. R. Freeman, *American Bombers of World War Two* Vol. 1, 20.

9. M. Bowman, *Boeing B-17 Flying Fortress*, 83.

10. F. Johnsen, *Boeing B-17 Flying Fortress*, 72.

11. Ibid, 76.

12. Inference from P. Borchers, et al, *Flight Research at Ames*, 7, and R. Scherrer and L. Rodert, AAR No. A420, 3.

13. This effectively scuttled a notion to have an American manufacturer produce Short Stirlings or the Handley Page Halifax. J. Lake, *International Air Power Journal*, No. 15, 160.

14. F. Johnsen, *B-24 Liberator*, 42.

15. British preference for their own weapons, despite being lighter, was puzzling to some aircrew who found the .50s more effective. Concentrated fire from twice the number of lighter rounds was a philosophy found wanting. However, for night operations the brighter muzzle flash of the .50 was undesirable and the longer range of little practical value as it was beyond sight of the gunner.

16. Other 'mod' centres undertaking considerable "Lib" rework was the Consolidated facilities in Louisville, Kentucky, Nashville, Tennessee, and Tucson Modification Center, Northwest Airlines in St. Paul, Minnesota, and Vandalia, Ohio, United Airlines in Cheyenne, and Bechtel at the Birmingham Modification Center in Alabama.

17. G. Swanborough and P. Bowers, *United States Military Aircraft Since 1909*, 182.

18. F. Johnsen, *B-24 Liberator*, 75.

Chapter Six

1. The crews carried pencils to be wedged into holes from popped rivets and then broken off.

2. B. Gunston, *The Encyclopedia of Russian Aircraft 1875-1995*, 19. The quantity has never been clear, "several hundred" often quoted. The factory was eventually overrun by the Germans in October 1941 and records lost.

3. From 1 November 1941, the US Coast Guard was under the operational control of the US Navy with rescue, coastal patrol, convoy escort, and ASW roles. Their equipment included USN flying boats.

4. The NAF was largely an experimental engineering facility, but maintained a manufacturing capacity to remain abreast of current production practices and gain insight into costs underlying contractor bids.

5. W. Trimble, *Wings for the Navy*, 241.

6. R. Ragnarsson, *US Navy PBY Catalina Units of the Atlantic War*, 51.

7. R. Creed, PBY, The Catalina Flying Boat, p. 166.

8. B. Kinzey, *PBY Catalina*, 66.

9. B. Smith, *Wings*, August 1990, 14.

10. Radar installation information from B. Smith, 16 and 54, and N. Freidman, *US Naval Weapons*, 252 and 254.

11. A. Pearcy, *Aviation News*, 4. This appears the most authoritative source, with details contradicting others.

12. M. Bracho ed., *Squadron 13 and the Big Flying Boats*, 171.

13. P. Bowers, *Wings*, December 1984, 14.

14. Ibid.

15. P. Bowers, 54, and J. Breihan, et al, *Martin Aircraft 1909-1960*, 168 and 206.

16. C. Hansen, *AAHS Journal*, Spring 1985, 52.

17. R. Wagner, *American Combat Planes of the 20th Century*, 381.

Chapter Seven

1. Reports that the PBO-1s were equipped with R-1920-40s engines instead of the A-29's R-1820-87 engines cannot be confirmed, and appear erroneous.

2. *Pilot's Flight Operating Instructions Army Model RB-37*, 1.

3. R. Francillon, *Lockheed Aircraft Since 1913*, 203.

4. R. Francillon, *Lockheed Aircraft*, 203. B. Slayton, *AAHS Journal*, Fall 1999, 217, gives this as the XB-34D.

5. J. Scutts, *PBJ Mitchell Units of the Pacific War*, 49.

6. R. Wagner, *American Combat Planes of the 20th Century*, 251.

7. A. Warnock, *Air Power Versus U-Boats*, 6.

8. R. Wagner, *American Combat Planes of the 20th Century*, 387.

9. F. Johnsen, *B-24 Liberator*, 73.

10. J. Wegg, *General Dynamic Aircraft and Their Predecessors*, 90.

11. J. Lake, *Wings of Fame*, No. 19, 139.

Chapter Eight

1. Press Release, *World's Largest Plane, XB-19A, to Carry Air Cargo*, 2.

2. H. Bunker, *Development, Test and Acceptance of the Douglas XB-19 Aircraft*, 26.

3. The title Hemisphere Defence Weapon dated from 1934 and so catered to the sensibilities of the isolationists, such that it would not appear to be an offensive weapon, and avoided calling it a heavy bomber. However, a War Department study of hemisphere defence had been delivered on 1 September 1939 that made clear foreign long-range bombers placed America at risk and could only be answered in kind.

4. *Case History of XB-33 and B-33 Aircraft*, summary entry 71.

5. The R-3350 also received some Navy funding for planned aircraft projects.

6. *The Development of the Heavy Bomber 1918-1944*, 91.

7. The BTO radar was so widely installed on the fleet that the Superfortress was called the "radar bomber" by some.

8. W. Wolf, *Consolidated B-32 Dominator*, 164.

9. W. Craven, ed., *The Army Air Forces in World War II*, Volume Five, 7, and Volume Six, 209. Numbers from 1064-1,665 have been published, with even seemingly authoritative sources differing or self-contradictory. Tracing out the exact order quantities has proven elusive.

10. E. Gillum, *AAHS Journal*, Fall 2000, 233.

11. G. White, *Allied Aircraft Piston Engines of World War II*, 370-371.

12. C. LeMay and B. Yenne, *Superfortress*, 70.

13. Gillum, 233.

14. W. Wolf, *Boeing B-29 Superfortress*, 161.

15. It is often reported that the B-29B used R-3350-51 engines. Although there was a proposal to install these model R-3350s on the Superfortress, it was never actually consummated. White 364.

16. Wolf, 72.

17. Craven, Volume Six, 209, is source for the production total.

18. LeMay, 81.

19. Tests in March 1943 with incendiaries against a carefully replicated Japanese urban area constructed at Dugway Proving Ground, Utah, had demonstrated the effectiveness of this attack technique. Further testing from mid-May to early September 1943 identified the most suitable weapons, the M-69 resulting by the end of the year. A December 1944 B-29 attack on Hankow also employed incendiaries to great effect.

20. Wolf, 321.

21. Allison Engineering Company was a division of General Motors Corporation.

22. Another alternative to the R-3350 was explored in the Allison V-3420 inline engine tested on the XB-19A and later on a modified YB-29, redesignated XB-39. It flew in December 1944 and showed promise, but war progress made this substantial change unnecessary.

23. Andy Gump was a comic character of the era known for his chinless visage.
24. S. Harding and J. Long, *Dominator*, 5.
25. Craven, Volume Six, 210.
26. The flaps appeared to observers on the ground to be up rather than in the 20° takeoff position. Interference between the headset and microphone chord and the flap leaver may have been the cause.
27. The tail instability was at least partially attributed to "an unsatisfactory aerodynamic condition around the inboard nacelles which was adversely affecting the empennage". *Development of the Heavy Bomber*, 94.
28. Although the American workforce is highly praised for their contributions during the war, the hasty training of unskilled workers and tremendous pressure to produce aircraft quickly had its negative side effects. Inspections and production testing were critical in catching deficiencies, but many still got through. Operational units devoted much time to correcting problems related to poor workmanship at all levels in the supply chain. Fortunately, there was generally enough personnel for such activities, although not always sufficient materiel. Readiness suffered.
29. The aircraft could actually be turned sharply and then backed into its hardstand, although this was not advisable due to the potential for engine overheating. The featured proved so popular and useful that placement at all four powerplant stations was planned for late blocks that, ultimately, were never produced.
30. Wolf, *Consolidated B-32 Dominator*, 258.
31. Ibid, 243.
32. R. Francillon, *Lockheed Aircraft Since 1913*, 229, also refers to this as the Model 249.
33. *Army Aircraft Characteristics, Production and Experimental*, 18a, appears the most authoritative source, but other credible references provide conflicting figures. The crew of seven given by the Army document appears too low while the 11-12 found in other sources is more reasonable.
34. This is not well explained in the available literature on the XB-33 and several confusing terms are used like "margin factor" and "ultimate load factor". It is believed to refer to a payload factor, that is to assume loading four times the design payload weight. This practice ensures the structure is over-designed to provide a margin on analysis for uncertainties, service wear, loading variabilities, etc. However, 4.0 is unusually high and would lead to excessive structural weight.
35. The static article was originally to be flyable for the sole purpose of delivery to Wright Field for ground testing. This, however, was revised on 1 October 1942 to a shippable article in the interest of saving time and money. *Case History of XB-33 and B-33 Aircraft*, summary entry 40. This source plus *Historical Record of XB-33 and B-33 Aircraft Project* and *History of XB-33 Aircraft* form the basis of this section.
36. *Case History of XB-33 and B-33 Aircraft*, summary entry 29.

Chapter Nine

1. W. Craven, ed., *The Army Air Forces in World War II*, Volume Six, 244.
2. *Case History of XB-36 Aircraft Project*, document summary 7.
3. *The Development of the Heavy Bomber*, 88.
4. A. Morrow, *Case History of the YB-35, YB-49 Aircraft*, Document 5.
5. This was based partially on War Department study MX-159. All designs considered were called Model 35. "Model 36" was applied to the winning variant in December 1941 only after the USAF designated the aircraft the XB-36 and to avoid confusion with the XB-35.
6. M. Jacobsen, *Convair B-36*, 253.
7. Ibid, 249.
8. It has been stated that suitable brakes for multi-wheel bogies were initially proving difficult for the industry to design, and this influenced the choice of the single wheel gear. It was only when the technology was suitably developed that the multi-wheel bogie was adopted. This does not ring true, especially considering the B-29 and other aircraft already had a two-wheel bogie with twin brakes and there was conceptually no great technological hurdle that had to be overcome.
9. Historical Division, Air Materiel Command, *Case History of XB-36 Aircraft Project*, document summary 67.
10. D. Jenkins, *Magnesium Overcast*, 6-7.
11. Graham White, *R-4360, Pratt & Whitney's Major Miracle*, 52, 230, and 246. The R-4360-25 was an Army designation for the -5 model engine. The -5 is generally associated with the experimental B-36s and -25 with early production aircraft. Both model designations are found in the literature for the XB-36 and YB-36.
12. The XR-7755 received a USAAF development contract in 1941. It featured an overhead camshaft with two sets of cams, with shifting between these in flight (takeoff and cruise) for better efficiency. Its two-speed hydraulic gearcase designed for contra-rotating propellers acknowledged that such would be required to transmit the enormous power output to thrust. It was 10.0ft (3.0m) long and 5.0ft (1.5) diameter. Takeoff fuel flow was expected to be 580gph (2.196lit/h) but with a respectable specific fuel consumption of 0.485lb/h/hp at cruise. It possessed an integral single-stage/single-speed supercharger and two General Electric BH-2 turbosuperchargers. Only two of the XR-7755s were built but never flown, the programme cancelled before a production decision. Even the giant XB-36 would have found it exceptionally large and heavy.
13. Jenkins, 45.
14. *Case History of XB-36 Aircraft Project*, document summary 90 through 94.
15. These issues are examples where training and use of previously unskilled labour, the impact of the draft on experienced manpower, spotty record keeping, allowing

material substitutions, and the shifting of personnel with programme priorities, had a grave deleterious effect.
16. J. Northrop, *The Development of All-Wing Aircraft*, The Royal Aeronautical Society, 501.
17. B. Young and G. Balzer, *Northrop N-9M Flying Wing, Part I: Description*, AAHS Journal, 255.
18. Young and Balzer, 250.
19. The spin tunnel, then a recent innovation, is vertically oriented with airflow upward. A statically balanced model is hand-launched into this flow with a desired initial dynamic conditions (inverted right spin, for example) and the resulting motion observed. Models could be fitted with control surfaces set prior to launch or controlled remotely to test spin recovery techniques.
20. W. Sears, *Flying Wing Aircraft*, AIAA 80-3036, 57.
21. Northrop, 505.
22. Sears, 58.
23. *The Development of the Heavy Bomber*, 96-97. Presented in August 1943, this design had retractable horizontal trailing surfaces to simplify low-speed stabilization yet still enjoy high lift with low drag. It was to feature a pressurised cabin of more conventional layout, leading edge slots and slats, and full-span trailing edge slotted flaps for good field performance, four turbosupercharged engines in a tractor arrangement turning independently featherable counter-rotating propellers via extension shafts, and a maximum GW of 180,000lb (816,466kg). Convair predicted a service ceiling of 43,000ft (13,106m), 374mph (602km/h) at 30,000ft (9,144m), and 407mph (655km/h) in WE. Range was predicted to be 7,500mi (12,070km) with 5,000lb (2,268kg) payload and 240mph (386km/h) cruise, or 40,000lb (18,144kg) to 3,500mi (5,633km). Defensive turrets were to be manned and pressurised. Although encouraging, it was apparently judged rather late to embark upon another such high-risk project.
24. A. Morrow, *Case History of the YB-35, YB-49 Aircraft (Supplement to Case History of the XB-35 Aircraft)*, Routing and Record Sheet "Evaluation of Projects MX-140, MX-661, and MP-13", 28 May 1945, Major F. E. Loudy.

Chapter Ten

1. Sweep had been employed in aircraft previously, but primarily to move the centre of lift with respect to the CG for stability benefits. The aerodynamic benefits had been discussed for many years, including in a paper presented in 1935 by German engineer Adolf Busemann. Germany went on to actively explore the design choice and was developing aircraft incorporating substantial wing sweep to achieve high speed. The technology was never seriously explored or incorporated into any official designs by the Allies before summer 1945.
2. The Air Forces, NACA, and the manufacturers appear to have tended toward considering

engine nacelles integral with the wing as the natural installation for a jet bomber, despite the fact propeller clearance was no longer a concern. To some extent, the designers did not want to stretch the credulity of senior Army officers with unusual or unexpected proposals. However, most of the proposed designs and those pursued with developmental contracts featured only these nacelle arrangements, even when there were less drag-producing solutions. The dual-engine nacelles risked losing both powerplants in an uncontained turbine disintegration as well as possible fuel cell penetrations. After the German work was revealed, with most of these employing integrated nacelles and the work considered "cutting edge", that approach may have been even further enforced as orthodox.

3. R. Francillon, *McDonnell Douglas Aircraft Since 1920*, 355.
4. S. Thompson, *Douglas A-26 and B-26 Invader*, 50.
5. W. Boyne, *Airpower*, September 1973, 11.
6. *Army Aircraft Characteristics, Production and Experimental*, 20.
7. There is much confusion on the matter of fuel tanks, with some sources repeating mention of external tanks that apparently never appeared on the aircraft. See *Army Aircraft Characteristic*, 11a and 20, Boyne, 67, and *Handbook of Erection and Maintenance for Model XB-42A Aircraft*, 11.
8. *Handbook of Erection and Maintenance for Model XB-42A Aircraft*, 9. Also given as V-1710-133, which, according to G. White, *Allied Aircraft Piston Engines of World War II*, 284-285, is essentially identical to the -137 except the later uses the -103 extension shaft and reduction gearing.
9. *Army Aircraft Characteristics*, 20, this being uncertain.
10. R. Schrader, *Air Classics Special*, 1990, 10.
11. *Case History of XB-43 Aircraft*, document summary 4.
12. Auxiliary fuel and JATO details gleaned from R. Williams, *Douglas Service*, January/February 1982, 32.
13. There were several slight shifts in the guarantees as the final weights and engine specifications became clear. These are too cumbersome to detail and were minor.
14. G. Pape, and J. Campbell, *Northrop Flying Wings*, 149.
15. *Case History of XB-35 Aircraft Project*, document summary 87.
16. F. Anderson, *Northrop, An Aeronautical History*, 100.
17. *Army Aircraft Characteristics*, 20.
18. Yip, W., *AAHS Journal*, Spring 2007, 73.
19. Ibid, 72.
20. The Attack category was dropped completely in 1948, all projects already underway under that designation assuming Bomber identities. It took nearly twenty years, but the Air Force finally discarded the A distinction that, by the end of World War 2, had lost its meaning. Single-engine attackers became fighters with ground attack as a supplemental mission, and multi-engine attackers were essentially light bombers that could strike targets on the battlefield or farther removed.
21. *Army Aircraft Characteristics*, 11.
22. The developers would likely have found surrounding a radar with guns or cannon would have created a vibration environment during firing detrimental to electronics serviceability. These were all new with little practical experience, empirical data, or industry standards.
23. W. Boyne, *Wings/Airpower*, date unknown, 10. None of the concept art shows turrets and the configuration would have made their inclusion, even of a tail turret, very problematic. Other sources suggest all 20 guns were to be in the nose.
24. *Army Aircraft Characteristics*, 11.
25. G. Cully, and A. Parsch, *Designations of U.S. Air Force Projects*, MX-423 entry.
26. S. Libis, *The Martin XB-51*, 3.
27. This change occurred in 1947. C. Roger Cripliver, correspondence with W. Yip, 15 January 1996, mentions serials assigned for two XB-53s with 1945 prefixes (45-59583/4).
28. *AAHS Journal*, Summer 1992, 150.
29. J. Miller, *The XB-48 Jet Bomber*, 1.
30. Knaack, 101.
31. G. Martin, *International Air Power Review*, No. 23, 165.
32. Knaack, 524.
33. Ibid.
34. A 520mph (837km/h) average speed on a flight from San Diego to Dayton, Ohio, was favoured with a strong tail wind. Some sources credit the aircraft with up to 545mph (877km/h), but the most reputable sources and Convair estimates suggest otherwise.
35. The XB-46 and XB-48 also had the single crew entry and exit points. Its inadequacy was demonstrated via a fatal XB-45 flight test accident and rectified with among the first uses of ejection seats.
36. Adjoining surfaces with acute or right angles, and especially narrow channels, historically produce high drag, and NACA warned against adopting this approach. However, wind tunnel testing suggested the Martin design's potential benefits outweighed the risks. Yet, the drag was found to be quite high during later flight testing.
37. *Army Aircraft Characteristics*, 20.
38. A. Lloyd, *Boeing's B-47 Stratojet*, 15, points out that Boeing, alone among the bomber manufactures, had the advantage of possessing its own a high-speed wind tunnel. Completed in spring 1944, it could achieve 0.95 Mach.

Chapter Eleven

1. For example, as the Very Heavy bombers were still in active development when the strategic bombing campaign against Germany began, plans to convert Heavy units in Europe to Very Heavy in summer 1944 were reformulated, and the task was ultimately prosecuted with prewar Heavy types.
2. W. Wolf, *Boeing B-29 Superfortress*, 171, states that each fighter destroyed required an average 10,000 rounds of bullets and shells from the bombers.
3. H. Stapfer, *B-26 Marauder in Action*, 4. Additionally, only a quarter of strategic bomber crews completed their 25-mission combat tour.
4. Former US Defence Secretary Robert McNamara, who served on the headquarters staff planning and executing the bombing campaign against Japan, said they speculated that, should the United States lose the war, they would likely be prosecuted as war criminals for the unprecedented toll in civilian lives and property.
5. An American heavy bomber at the end of the war would typically have a crew of ten men while RAF bombers, operating at night with less opposition, had a crew of seven.
6. W. Wolf, *North American B-25 Mitchell*, 66.
7. C. LeMay and B. Yenne, *Superfortress*, 110. Radar bombing became more prevalent after early 1943, eventually accounting for 50 per cent of the bombs dropped on Germany by the USAAF. Even with the APQ-13, accuracy was inferior to optical means, with only one per cent of bombs falling within 1,000ft (305m) of the aim point when released from high altitude. Resolution simply was not generally adequate to locate a target except with very sharp surface feature contrast, like a coastal target. Also, as these radar relied upon vacuum tube technology, their reliability was relatively low; as little as 25 per cent serviceability rate but typically ten per cent.

Bibliography

Books

Aircraft of the Second World War, The Development of the Warplane 1939-45, ed. Philip Jarrett, Putnam Aeronautical Books, 1997.

Airwar, Edward Jablonski, Doubleday & Company, 1971.

Allied Aircraft Piston Engines of World War II, Graham White, Society of Automotive Engineers, Inc., 1995.

American Attack Aircraft Since 1926, E. R. Johnson, McFarland & Company, 2008.

American Bombers of World War Two, Roger A. Freeman, Hylton Lacy Publishers Limited, Windsor, 1973.

American Combat Planes of the 20th Century, Ray Wagner, Jack Bacon & Company, 2004.

The Army Air Forces in World War II, Volume V Men and Planes, Wesley F. Craven, and James L. Cate, editors, The University of Chicago Press, 1955.

The Army Air Forces in World War II, Volume VI The Pacific: Matterhorn to Nagasaki June 1944 to August 1945, Wesley F. Craven, and James L., Cate, editors, The University of Chicago Press, 1955.

B-24 Liberator, Frederick A. Johnsen, Motorbooks International, 1993.

B-36 Photo Scrapbook, Dennis R. Jenkins, Mike Moore and Don Pyeatt, Specialty Press, 2001.

Boeing Aircraft Since 1916, Peter M. Bowers, Naval Institute Press, 1989.

Boeing B-17 Flying Fortress, Martin W. Bowman, The Crowood Press, Ltd., 1998.

Boeing B-17 Flying Fortress, Production Line to Frontline 2, Michael O'Leary, Osprey Publishing., 1998.

Boeing B-29 Superfortress, Peter M. Bowers, WarbirdTech Series, Volume 14, Specialty Press, 1999.

Boeing B-29 Superfortress, Steve Pace, The Crowood Press Ltd., 2003.

Boeing B-29 Superfortress, The Ultimate Look: From Drawing Board to VJ-Day, William Wolf, Schiffer Publishing Ltd., 2005.

Boeing's B-47 Stratojet, Alwyn T. Lloyd, Specialty Press, 2003.

The Bomber War, The Allied Air Offensive Against Nazi Germany, Robin Neillands, The Overlook Press, 2001.

A Brief History of the Boeing Company, Boeing Historical Services, Boeing, 1998.

Consolidated B-24 Liberator, Martin W. Bowman, The Crowood Press, 2004.

Consolidated B-24 Liberator, Frederick A. Johnsen, WarbirdTech Series Volume 1, Specialty Press, 2001.

Consolidated B-24 Liberator, Production Line to Frontline 4, Michael O'Leary, Osprey Publishing, 2002.

Consolidated B-32 Dominator, The Ultimate Look: From Drawing Board to Scrapyard, William Wolf, Schiffer Publishing Ltd., 2006.

Consolidated PB2Y Coronado, Naval Fighters Number 85, Richard Hoffman, Steve Ginter, 2009.

Consolidated-Vultee PB4Y-2 Privateer, The Operational History of the U.S. Navy's World War II Patrol/Bomber Aircraft, Alan C. Carey, Schiffer Publishing, 2005.

Convair B-36, A Comprehensive History of America's "Big Stick", Meyers K. Jacobsen, Schiffer Publishing Ltd., 1997.

Convair B-36 "Peacemaker", Dennis R. Jenkins, WarbirdTech Series Volume 24, Specialty Press, 2001.

Convair B-36 Peacemaker, A Photo Chronicle, Meyers K. Jacobsen, Schiffer Publishing Ltd., 1999.

Curtiss Aircraft 1907-1947, Peter M. Bowers, Naval Institute Press, 1987.

Curtiss Fighter Aircraft, A Photographic History 1917-1948, Francis H. Dean, and Dan Hagedorn, Schiffer Publishing Ltd., 2007.

Dominator, The Story of the Consolidated B-32 Bomber, Stephen Harding, and James I. Long, Pictorial Histories Publishing Company, 1983.

Douglas A-26 and B-26 Invader, Scott Thompson, The Crowood Press Ltd, 2002.

Douglas A-26 and Invader, Frederick A. Johnsen, WarbirdTech Series Volume 22, Specialty Press, 1999.

Douglas B-18 Bolo, The Ultimate Look: from Drawing Board to U-Boat Hunter, William Wolf, Schiffer Publishing, 2007.

Douglas A-20 Boston/Havoc, Warpaint No.32, Richard J. Caruana, Hall Park Books Ltd, undated.

Douglas Havoc and Boston, The DB-7/A-20 Series, Scott Thompson, The Crowood Press Ltd, 2004.

The Dragon's Teeth?: The Creation of United States Air Power for World War II, Benjamin S. Kelsey, Smithsonian Institute Press, 1982.

The Encyclopedia of Russian Aircraft 1975-1995, Bill Gunston, Motorbooks International, 1995.

Encyclopedia of U.S. Air Force Aircraft and Missiles, Volume II Post-World War II Bombers 1945-1973, Marcelle Size Knaack, Office of Air Force History, United States Air Force, 1988.

Expanding the Envelope, Flight Research at NACA and NASA, Michael H. Gorn, The University Press of Kentucky, 2001.

The Fighting Flying Boat, A History of the Martin PBM Mariner, Richard A. Hoffman, Naval Institute Press, 2004.

Flight Research at Ames, 1940-1997, Paul F. Borchers, James A. Franklin and Jay W. Fletcher, National Aeronautics and Space Administration, SP-1998-3300, 1999.

Flying Cats, The Catalina Aircraft in World War II, Andrew Hendrie, Naval Institute Press, 1988.

The Flying Wings of Jack Northrop, A Photo Chronicle, Garry R. Pape, John M. Campbell, and Donna Campbell, Schiffer Publishing Ltd., 1994.

Foreign Invaders: The Douglas Invader in Foreign Military and US Clandestine Service, Dan Hagedorn and Leif Hellström, Midland Publishing Ltd., 1994.

Fortress in the Sky, Peter M. Bowers, Sentry Books, 1976.

General Dynamics Aircraft and their Predecessors, John Wegg, Naval Institute Press, 1990.

Historic Naval Aircraft, Norman Polar, Potomac Books, 2004.

A History of U.S. Coast Guard Aviation, Arthur Pearcy, Airlife Publishing, 1989.

The History of the US Nuclear Arsenal, James Norris Gibson, Schiffer Publishing Ltd., 1996.

Jack Northrop and the Flying Wing: The Real Story Behind the Stealth Bomber, Ted Coleman with Robert Wenkam, Paragon House, 1988.

Lend-Lease Aircraft in World War II, Arthur Pearcy, Motorbooks International, 1996.

Lockheed Aircraft Since 1913, René J. Francillon, Naval Institute Press, 1988.

Lockheed Hudson in World War II, Andrew Hendrie, Airlife Publishing, 1999.

Lockheed Hudson Mk.I to Mk.VI, Warpaint Series No.59, Alan W. Hall, Warpaint Books, undated.

Lockheed P2V Neptune, An Illustrated History, Wayne Mutza, Schiffer Publishing, 1996.

Magnesium Overcast, The Story of the Convair B-36, Dennis R. Jenkins, Specialty Press, 2001.

The Making of the Atomic Bomb, Richard Rhodes, Simon and Schuster, 1986.

Martin Aircraft 1909-1960, John R. Breihan, Stan Piet and Roger S. Mason, Jonathan Thompson, 1995.

Martin B-26 Marauder, Warpaint Series No. 69, Ken Darling, Warpaint Books, undated (approximately 2008).

Martin B-26 Marauder, Frederick A. Johnsen, WarbirdTech Series, Volume 29, Specialty Press, 2000.

Martin Baltimore, Ali Straniere in Italia 3, Marco Gueli, La Bancarella Aeronautica, 2004.

Martin Mars XPB2M-1R & JRM Flying Boats, Naval Fighters Number 29, Steve Ginter, Steve Ginter (publisher), 1995.

Martin P4M-1/-1Q Mercator, Naval Fighters Number Thirty-Seven, Steve Ginter, Steve Ginter (publisher), 1996.

McDonnell Douglas Aircraft Since 1920: Volume I, René J. Francillon, Putnam Aeronautical Books, 1988.

The Navy's Air War, A Mission Completed, The Aviation History Unit, ed. A. R. Buchanan, Harper & Brothers Publishers, undated.

The New Encyclopedia Britannica, 15th Edition, Robert McHenry, general editor, Encyclopedia Britannica Inc., 1992.

North American Aircraft 1934-1998, Volume 1, Norm Avery, Narkiewicz/Thompson, 1998.

North American B-25 Mitchell, Frederick A. Johnsen, WarbirdTech Series, Volume 12, Specialty Press, 1997.

North American B-25 Mitchell, Warpaint Series No. 73, Ken Darling, Warpaint Books, 2009.

North American B-25 Mitchell The Ultimate Look: From Drawing Board to Flying Arsenal, William Wolf, Schiffer Publishing, 2008.

Northrop, An Aeronautical History, Fred Anderson, Northrop Corporation, 1976.

Northrop Flying Wings, Edward T. Maloney, Planes of Fame Publications, Inc., 1990.

Northrop Flying Wings, A History of Jack Northrop's Visionary Aircraft, Garry R. Pape and John M. Campbell, Schiffer Publishing Ltd., 1995.

Nuclear Weapons of the United States, An Illustrated History, James N. Gibson, Brompton Books Corporation, 1989.

PBY, The Catalina Flying Boat, Roscoe Creed, Naval Institute Press, 1985.

Pilot's Handbook for the Flying Wings of Northrop, Leo J. Kohn, Aviation Publications, 1984.

PBJ Mitchell Units of the Pacific War, Combat Aircraft 40, Jerry Scutts, Osprey Publishing, 2003.

PV Ventura/Harpoon Units of World War 2, Combat Aircraft 43, Alan C. Carey, Osprey Publishing, 2002.

R-4360, Pratt & Whitney's Major Miracle, Graham White, Specialty Press, 2006.

Radical Wings & Wind Tunnels: Advanced Concepts Tested at NASA Langley, Joseph R. Chambers and Mark A. Chambers, Specialty Press 2008.

Rockwell, The Heritage of North American, Bill Yenne, Crescent Books, 1989.

Squadron 13 and the Big Flying Boats, ed. Mary Bracho, Hellgate Press, 2005.

The Story of Boeing, Harold Mansfield, *Vision*, Popular Library, 1966.

The Story of the PBY Catalina, Aero Biographies Volume 1, Ray Wagner, Flight Classics, 1972.

Stearman Aircraft, A Detailed History, Edward H. Phillips, Specialty Press, 2006.

Superfortress, The Boeing B-29 and American Airpower in World War II, Curtis LeMay, and Bill Yenne, Westholme, 2007.

Testing for Combat, Eric Brown, Airlife Publishing, 1994.

Thundering Peacemaker, The B-36 Story in Words and Pictures, Frederick A. Johnsen, Bomber Books, 1978.

United States Army in World War II, Special Studies, Buying Aircraft, Matériel Procurement for the Army Air Force, Irving Brinton Holley, Jr., Center of Military History, United States Army, 1989.

United States Military Aircraft Since 1909, Gordon Swanborough, and Peter M. Bowers, Putnam Aeronautical Books, 1989.

U.S. Aerial Armament in World War II, The Ultimate Look, Vol. 1: Guns Ammunition, and Turrets, William Wolf, Schiffer Publishing, 2009.

U.S. Army Aircraft, 1908-1946, James C. Fahey,

Ships and Aircraft, 1946.

U.S. Bombers, Lloyd S. Jones, Aero Publishers, Inc., 1974.

US Bombers of World War Two, Robert F. Dorr, Arms and Armour Press, 1989.

U.S. Experimental & Prototype Aircraft Projects, Fighters 1939-1945, Bill Norton, Specialty Press, 2008.

U.S. Military Aircraft Designations and Serials 1909 to 1979, John M. Andrade, Midland Counties Publications, 1997.

US Naval Weapons, Norman Freidman, Conway Maritime Press, 1983.

US Navy PBY Catalina Units of the Atlantic War, Osprey Combat Aircraft 65, Ragnar J. Ragnarsson, Osprey Publishing, 2006.

Vee's for Victory: The Story of the Allison V-1710 Aircraft Engines 1929-1948, Daniel D. Whitney, Schiffer Publishing Limited, 1998.

War Planes of the Second World War, Volume 5: Flying Boats, William Green, Doubleday and Company, 1962.

Wings of Gold, The U.S. Naval Air Campaign in World War II, Gerald Astor, Random House, 2004.

Wings for the Navy: A History of the Naval Aircraft Factory, 1917-1956, William F. Trimble, Naval Institute Press, 1990.

World Encyclopedia of Aero Engines, Bill Gunston, Patrick Stephens Ltd., 1987.

Monographs

A-20 Havoc in Action, Aircraft Number 144, Jim Mesko, Squadron/Signal Publications, 1994

A-26 in Action, Aircraft No. 134, Jim Mesko, Squadron Signal Publications, 1993.

Aero Biographies: The Story of the PBY Catalina, Flight Classics Volume 1, Ray Wagner, Flight Classics, 1972.

Air Power Versus U-Boats, Confronting Hitler's Submarine Menace in the European Theater, The U.S. Army Air Forces in World War II, A. Timothy Warnock, Air Force History and Museums Program, 1999.

B-17 in Action, Aircraft No. 63, Larry Davis, Squadron Signal Publications, 1984.

B-17 Flying Fortress, Part 1 Production Versions, In Detail & Scale Vol. 2, Alwyn T. Lloyd and Terry D. Moore, Detail & Scale, 1981.

B-17 Flying Fortress, Part 2 Derivatives, In Detail & Scale Vol. 11, Alwyn T. Lloyd, Detail & Scale, 1983.

B-17 Flying Fortress, Part 3 More Derivatives, In Detail & Scale Vol. 20, Alwyn T. Lloyd, Detail & Scale, 1986.

B-24 Liberator in Action, Aircraft No. 80, Larry Davis, Squadron Signal Publications, 1987.

B-24 Liberator, In Detail & Scale Vol. 64, Bert Kinzey, Squadron/Signal Publications, 2000.

B-25 Mitchell in Action, Aircraft No. 34, Ernest R. McDowell, Squadron Signal Publications, 1978.

B-25 Mitchell, In Detail & Scale Vol. 60, Bert Kinzey, Squadron/Signal Publications, 1999.

B-26 Marauder in Action, Aircraft No. 50, Steve Birdsall, Squadron Signal Publications, 1984.

B-26 Marauder in Action, Aircraft No. 210, Hans-Heiri Stapfer, Squadron Signal Publications, 2008.

B-29 Superfortress, Part 1 Production Versions, In Detail & Scale Vol. 10, Alwyn T. Lloyd, Detail & Scale, 1983.

B-29 Superfortress, Part 11 Derivatives, In Detail & Scale Vol. 25, Alwyn T. Lloyd, Detail & Scale, 1987.

B-29 Superfortress in Action, Aircraft No. 165, Larry Davis, Squadron Signal Publications,

1997.

B-36 in Action, Aircraft No. 42, Meyers K. Jacobsen and Ray Wagner, Squadron Signal Publications, 1980.

B-36 Peacemaker, In Detail & Scale Vol. 47, Wayne Wachsmuth, Squadron/Signal Publications, 1997.

Boeing XB-15 Douglas XB-19, Air Age Technical Library, Warplane Research, Group II—No. 3B, no author stated, Air Age Inc., 1944.

The Boeing B-17E & F Flying Fortress, Profile Number 77, Charles D. Thompson, Profile Publications Ltd., 1966.

The Boeing B-29 Superfortress, Profile Number 101, Mitch Mayborn, Profile Publications Ltd., 1966.

The Boeing B-47, Peter M. Bowers, Profile Number 83, Profile Publications Ltd, 1966.

C-47 Skytrain in Action, Aircraft No. 149, Larry Davis, Squadron Signal Publications, 1995.

The Consolidated B-24J Liberator, Profile Number 19, Roger A. Freeman, Profile Publications Ltd., 1965.

The Consolidated PBY Catalina, Profile Number 183, Everett Cassagneres, Profile Publications Ltd., date unknown.

Consolidated PBY-5A Catalina Walk Around, Larry Davis, Squadron Signal Publications, 2009.

The Douglas A-20 (7A to Boston III), Aircraft Profile 202, Harry Gann, Profile Publications Ltd., 1967.

Fax File #1, Lloyd S. Jones, Aerolus Publishing, 1987.

Fax File #2, Lloyd S. Jones, Pacific Aero Press, 1988.

Fax File #3, Lloyd S. Jones, Pacific Aero Press, 1989.

Fax File #5, Lloyd S. Jones, Pacific Aero Press, 1989.

Fax File #6, Lloyd S. Jones, Pacific Aero Press, 1991.

Fax File #8, Lloyd S. Jones, Pacific Aero Press, 1991.

Images of America, Sikorsky, John W. R. Taylor, Tempus Publishing, 1998.

Lockheed Neptune, Warpaint Series No. 51, Kev Darling, Warpaint Books, date not specified.

The Lockheed Hudson Mks I to VI, Profile Number 253, Christopher F. Shores, Profile Publications Ltd., April 1973.

The Lockheed P2V Neptune, Number 204, Homes G. Anderson, Profile Publications, date not specified.

The Martin B-26B & C Marauder, Number 112, Ray Wagner, Profile Publications, date not specified.

The Martin XB-51, Air Force Legends Number 201, Scott Libis, Steve Ginter, 1998.

Martin JRM Mars Flying Boat, Commercial Projects of 1944, American Aerospace Archive 1, Jared A. Zichek, MagCloud, 2008.

Martin Maryland & Baltimore Variants, Aircraft Profile 232, Christopher F. Shores, Profile Publications Ltd., December 1971.

The North American B-25G to G Mitchell, Aircraft Profile 59, Ray Wagner, Profile Publications Ltd., 1965.

P2V Neptune in Action, Aircraft No. 68, Jim Sullivan, Squadron Signal Publications, 1985.

PBM Mariner in Action, Aircraft No. 74, Bob Smith, Squadron Signal Publications, 1986.

PBY Catalina in Action, Aircraft No. 62, W. E. Scarborough, Squadron Signal Publications, 1983.

PBY Catalina, In Detail & Scale Vol. 66, Bert Kinzey, Squadron/Signal Publications, 2000.

Pedigree of Champions, Boeing Since 1916, The Boeing Company, Sixth Edition, May 1985.

Periodicals

A-20 Havoc: A Douglas "Great", no author stated, *Air Enthusiast*, No. 36, May-August 1988, pp. 25-38.

A-20 Production List, William T. Larkins, *AAHS Journal*, Vol. 5 No. 1, Spring 1960, pp. 52-53.

A-20, the Douglas Attack Bomber, Part I, John Alcorn, *Historical Aviation Album*, Volume 15, 1977, pp. 287-298.

A-20, the Douglas Attack Bomber, Part II, John Alcorn, *Historical Aviation Album*, Volume 16, 1980, pp. 63-81.

A-26/B-26 Invader, David Willis, *International Air Power Review*, No. 18, 2005, pp. 104-127.

Aerial Oddities, E. R. Johnson, *Aviation History*, January 2004, pp. 12-16.

The Aero-Engine That Won World War II in the Pacific, William Wolf, *AAHS Journal*, Vol. 54 No. 2, Spring 2009, pp. 27-38.

Air Apaches, Lawrence J. Hickey, *Airpower*, September 1985, pp. 24-35.

Aircraft Design Analysis No. 4, A-20 "Havoc", T. R. Smith, *Aviation*, January 1944, pp. 125-143.

Aluminum Overcast, Michael O'Leary, *Aeroplane*, September 2009, pp. 14-19.

America's First Jet Bomber, no author stated, *Air Classics Special*, Volume 1, 1990, pp. 78-87.

America's Mystery Bomber, Robert Trimble, *Air Classics*, date unknown, pp. 16-26.

An Analysis of the Skipping Characteristics of Some Flying Boats, Mitch Mayborn, *AAHS Journal*, January-March 1958, pp. 1-7.

As if it Were Yesterday, Combat Tales from a Liberator Pilot, Robert G. DeGroat, *Flight Journal*, August 1998, pp. 60-66.

Atom Bomber Base, Wendover Army Air Base, Utah, Lou Thole, *Air Enthusiast*, No. 108, November/December 2003, pp. 28-33.

B-15 Granddaddy of the B-17, Freeman Westel, *Air Classics*, July 1966, pp. 12-15 and 60-61.

B-17 Military Operators, Jim Winchester, *Wings of Fame*, Volume 6, 1997, pp. 96-103.

B-29: Boeing's Super Fortress, no author stated, *Take Off*, Part 104, 1990, pp 2908-2915.

B-29 Bombardier, Wilbur H. Morrison, *Take Off*, Part 58, 1989, pp 1605-1611.

B-32 Crash, 10 March '45, D. R. Fox, *AAHS Journal*, Vol. 13 No. 3, Fall 1968, p. 224.

B-32 Crash 27 Aug. '44, William T.Y'Blood, *AAHS Journal*, Vol. 13 No. 3, Fall 1968, pp. 223-224.

B-32 Dominator, "The Alternative to the B-29 Superfortress", George A. Larson, *Friends Journal*, Summer 1999, pp. 45-49.

B-36: Billion Dollar Blunder or the Real Beginning of Strategic Airpower!, James Gibson, *Wings* or *Airpower*, date unknown, pp. 36-51.

The B-36: Production Begins, 1946-1948, Meyers K. Jacobsen, *AAHS Journal*. Vol. 17 No. 3, Fall 1972, pp. 163-173.

B-36 Production, Part 2, Meyers K. Jacobsen, *AAHS Journal*. Vol. 18 No. 3, Fall 1973, pp. 166-174.

B-36 Revealed Turret Guns Only When Needed, Frederick A. Johnsen, *Wings*, December 2003, pp. 56-57.

B for Bomber, no author stated, *Airpower*, March 1998, pp 8-39.

Be Prepared!, Anson McCullough, *Airpower*, January 2000, pp. 8-39.

"The Beast", Living with the 3350, E. M. Gillum, *AAHS Journal*, Fall 2000, Vol. 45 No. 3, pp. 231-237.

Before the B-2, Northrop's Flying Wings, The XB-35 and XB-49, Francis Allen, *Air Enthusiast*, No. 106, pp. 2-12.

Big Iron, Big Engines & Bigger Headaches: Building the First Experimental Strategic Bombers!, Freman Westell, *Airpower*, Vol. 29 No. 6, November 1999, pp. 8-23 and 48-55.

Blackhawk, A Fighter for all Weather … Curtiss XP-87, Walter Boyne, *Wings/Airpower*, Date unknown, pp. 31-39 and 5?.

Boeing B-17 Flying Fortress, Queen of the Skies, William N. Hess, *Wings of Fame*, Volume 6, 1997, pp. 38-95.

Boeing B-17D-BO 40-3097: Better Known As "The Swoose", Albert Hansen, *AAHS Journal*, Volume 54 Number 1, Spring 2009, pp. 65-67.

Boeing B-29 and B-50 Superfortress, David Willis, *International Air Power Review*, No. 22, 2007, pp. 136-169.

Boeing's B-29: Birth of a Bomber, Edward H. Phillips, *Aviation History*, May 1998, pp. 38-44 and 66.

The Boeing B-50, Bill Jesse, *FlyPast*, No. 172, November 1995, pp. 77-79.

Boeing's Battle Wagon, The B-17 Flying Fortress – An Outline History, Ken Wixey, *Air Enthusiast*, No. 78, November/December 1998, pp. 20-33.

Boeing's Battle of Wichita, Ed Phillips, *Airpower*, July 1981, pp. 36-49 and 51.

Boeing's 'Forgotten' Monster: XB-15, A Giant in Search of a Cause, Patrick Boniface, *Air Enthusiast*, No. 79, January/February 1999, pp. 64-67.

Boeing's Lone Ranger, Patrick Boniface, *Aeroplane Monthly*, January 1997, pp. 54-57.

The Boeing PB-1, Robert C. Mikesh, *AAHS Journal*, Summer 1964, Vol. 9 No. 1, pp. 42-45.

Bomber 47: Indispensable Forerunner and Outlook on the Future!, Walter Boyne, *Wings*, August 1981, pp. 8-27 and 46-51.

Bombardier, Fred Huston, *Airpower*, March 1985, pp. 44-54.

Bombing Behemoth, Robert L. Trimble, *Air Classics*, date unknown, pp. 29-41.

Born to Lose, The Story of North American's High Flying Hawk … The XB-28 Bomber, C. M. Daniels, *Airpower*, May 1975, pp. 36-39.

Breaching the Walls of Fortress Europe, Warren M. Bodie, *Airpower*, September 1973, pp. 36-55.

Burning Japan to the Ground, Chester W. Marshall, *Wings*, date unknown, pp. 8-24 and 36.

Case History of the B-42 Aircraft Project, no author stated, Historical Office, Air Materiel Command, Wright-Patterson AFB, January 1948, reproduced in *AAHS Journal*, Vol. 37 No. 2 Summer 1992, pp. 140-154.

Case History of the B-43 Aircraft, no author stated, Historical Office, Air Materiel Command, Wright-Patterson AFB, November 1948, reproduced in *AAHS Journal*, Vol. 39 No. 2 Summer 1994, pp. 82-93.

Case History of the XF-87 All-Weather Fighter, no author stated, Historical Office, Air Technical Service Command, January 1950, reproduced in *AAHS Journal*, Vol. 38 No. 1 Spring 1993, pp. 20-31.

'Cause a PBY Don't Fly That High', William E. Scarborough, *Proceedings*, date unknown, pp. unknown.

Cheaper by the Thousands!, The Logbook of the Consolidated B-24 Liberator, Jack Dean, *Wings*, December 1991, 10-45.

Confessions of a PBM Pilot, D, C, Quinn, *Air Classics*, May 1976, pp. 72-79.

Consolidated B-24 Liberators, Part One: Development and Allied Operations, 1939-1943, Robert F. Dorr and Jon Lake, *International Air Power Review*, Volume 4, 2002, pp. 125-163.

The Consolidated Model 31/XP4Y-1 "Corregidor" Flying Boat, Chuck Hansen, *AAHS Journal*, Summer 1982, pp. 136-147.

The Consolidated PBY, Part II, William E. Scarborough, *AAHS Journal*, Summer 1971, pp. 113-123.

Conquistador Turned Merchant, Consolidated's PB2Y Coronado, Daniel Ford, *Air Enthusiast*, No. 57, Spring 1995, pp. 16-21.

Convair B-36 Peacemaker, Bill Yenne, *International Air Power Review*, Vol. 13, Summer 2004, pp. 116-151.

Convair's Contribution, Liberators and Privateers Join the Fray, Frederick A. Johnsen, *Airpower*, July 2003, pp. 28-35 and 48-56.

Convair's Needle-Nosed Orphan, Walter Boyne, *Wings/Airpower*, Date unknown, pp. 8-16 and 19-20.

"Cry Havoc", Pt I, Designing and Building the A-20, Walt Boyne, *Wings*, June 1976, pp. 22-39 and 52-54.

"Cry Havoc", Pt II, The A-20 Goes to War!, Walt Boyne, *Airpower*, July 1976, pp. 50-66.

The Curtiss-Wright XA-43 Attack Aircraft, Wai Yip, *AAHS Journal*, Vol. 52 No. 1 Spring 2007, pp. 68-73.

Database: Consolidated B-24 Liberator, Robert F. Dorr, *Aeroplane* Monthly, December 2002, 61-81.

Defending the Fortress, Inside the B-17, Ted Mayer, *Airpower*, January 2000, pp. 40-55.

Design Analysis of the Martin PBM-5 "Mariner", E. G. Riley, *Industrial Aviation*, September 1945, pp. 7-20 and 97.

Design Development of the XB-36, Part I, Meyers K. Jacobsen, *AAHS Journal*. Vol. 15 No. 4, Winter 1970, pp. 224-235.

Design Development of the XB-36, Part II, Meyers K. Jacobsen, *AAHS Journal*. Vol. 16 No. 2, Summer 1971, pp. 124-130.

Design Development of the Douglas XB-42, Carlos C. Wood, *Aviation*, February 1947, pp. 37-42.

Details of the Coronado PB2Y-3 Design, Ernest G. Stout, *Automotive and Aviation Industries*, 15 July 1945, pp. 18-22, 116, and 118.

Development of the "Straight-Through" Turbojet Engine, Peter Berry, *AAHS Journal*, Vol. 47 No. 3, Fall 2002, pp. 198-203.

Dog of War, Part 1, Peter M. Bowers, *Airpower*, January 1996, pp. 10-47.

Dominator, The Last and Unluckiest of the Hemisphere Bombers, Frederick A. Johnsen, *Wings*, Vol. 4 No. 1. February 1974, pp. 8-17.

Douglas Airview, Entire issue devoted to XB-19, date unknown.

The Douglas B-18, The Forgotten Warrior, George A. Larson, *AAHS Journal*, Spring 2001, pp. 25-31.

Douglas B-23 Dragon, George A. Larson, *AAHS Journal*, Winter 2004, pp. 255-261.

Douglas DB-7 in French Service, Jean Cuny, *AAHS Journal*, Spring 1968, pp. 2-15.

Douglas B-23 Dragon, Arthur Pearcy, publication unknown, date unknown, pp. unknown.

The Douglas B-23 Dragon, R. E. Williams, *Douglas Service*, November/December 1979, pp. 22-27.

The Douglas DB-7s in French Service, J. Cuny, *AAHS Journal*, Vol. 13 No. 1 Spring 1968, pp. 2-15.

The Douglas DB-7/A-20 Boston/Havoc, Robert E. Williams, *AAHS Journal*, Vol. 35 No. 1 Spring 1990, pp. 2-15.

The Douglas Invader Story, René J Francillon, *Air Enthusiast*, No. 7, July-September 1978, pp. 215-236.

The Douglas XB-19, Ray Wagner, *Aeroplane Monthly*, date unknown, pp. 232-235.

Douglas XB-19A, author not stated, *AAHS Journal*, Vol. 27 No. 3, Fall 1982, p. 160.

The Douglas XB-42 "Mixmaster", R. E. Williams, *Douglas Service*, date unknown, pp. 32-34.

The Douglas XB-43, R. E. Williams, *Douglas Service*, January/February 1982, pp. 30-35.

Down the Pickle Barrel, H. R. Black, *Air Enthusiast*, No. 75, May-June 1998, p. 78.

ERCO, Engineering and Research Corporation, Chuck Hansen, *AAHS Journal*, Vol. 30 No. 1, Spring 1985, pp. 42-57.

The Excalibur, Peter Berry, *AAHS Journal*, Winter 1975, pp. 236-238.

Eye in the Sky: The Being F-13, Research Project 7807, David B. Morse, *AAHS Journal*, Vol. 26 No. 2 Summer 1981, pp. 150-168.

Elegant Failure, Richard K. Schrader, *Air Classics Special*, Volume 1, 1990, pp 6-13.

Experimental Bomber, Long Range: Boeing XB-15 and Douglas XB-19, Bill Yenne, *International Air Power Review*, Vol. 5, 2002, pp. 164-171.

Farewell to 'Grandpappy', no author stated, *Air Force*, October 1945, p. 41.

Fighter Fortress!, no author stated, Son of Fabulous Flying Flops!, *Air Classics* special edition, Vol. 1 1990, pp. 18-23.

The First, the Last, and the Only: The Douglas XB-42/42A/43, Walter Boyne, *Airpower*, September 1973, pp. 6-15 and 67.

Fledgling Neptunes, A Portfolio of Early Series Lockheed P2Vs, no author stated, *Air Enthusiast*, No. 84, November/December 1999.

Flying Frigates of the Forties, Don Gumz, *Wings*, pp. 18-25.

The Flying Wing's Unsung Prototypes!, Gerald Balzer, *Wings*, April 1997, pp. 12-45.

A Fortress is Forever, Peter M. Bowers, *Wings*, February 1977, pp. 24-51 and 64.

Fortress Over the Atlantic, Don Downie, *Airpower*, March 1988, pp. 9-33.

Fortunes of War, Alan F. Crouchman, *FlyPast*, March 2008, pp. 68-73.

From Three to Two: Australian Use of the Do 24 and PBM-3, James Ritchie Grant, *Air Enthusiast*, No. 64 July/August 1996, pp. 60-64.

The Ghost of Coronado, Peter M. Bowers, *Wings*, February 1972, pp. 36-49.

Gone, and All But Forgotten, Leo Kohn, *Armchair Aviator*, October 1972, pp. 43-48.

The Great Bolo Boondoggle, Frederick A. Johnsen, *Wings*, August 1973, pp. 8-19.

The Grim Reapers, Part I, John S. Alcorn, *AAHS Journal*, Spring 1975, Vol. 20 No. 1, pp. 6-15.

The Grim Reapers, Part II, John S. Alcorn, *AAHS Journal*, Fall 1975, Vol. 20 No. 3, pp. 187-193.

Guess What?, Cole H. Morrow, *Air Line Pilot*, July 1978, p. 43.

Harpoon, On Patrol in a Lockheed PV-2, Charles L. Scrivner, *Airpower*, date unknown, pp. 49-59.

Havoc, Don Berliner, *American Aircraft Modeler*, November 1970, pp. 40-43 and 58.

High Altitude 'Mitchell', no author stated, *Royal Air Force Flying Review*, December 1962, 47.

How P2V Meets Patrol Objectives, John B. Wassall, *Aviation Week*, 25 July 1949, pp. 20-28.

The Hudson Ventura Saga, Neal Rawlings, publication unknown, date unknown, pp. 34-39.

Invader, author unknown, publication unknown, date unknown, pp. 32-44.

The Last Great Bomber Fly Off, Joe Mizrahi, *Wings*, June 1999, pp. 8-21 and 24-55.

The Last to Die, Stephen Harding, *Air & Space*, November 2008, pp. 66-71.

The Latest in Killers, no author stated, *Popular Aviation*, date unknown, pages unknown.

LB-30's in Latin America, Allan G. Blue, *AAHS Journal*, Spring 1970, Vol. 15 No. 1, pp. 27-29.

Lease-Lend Flying Boats, Coronado and Mariner in RAF Service, Arthur Pearcy, *Aviation News*, date unknown, p. 4.

Liberator Logbook, A Gallery of B-24 Bomber Types, no author stated, *Wings*, February 1985, pp. 24-31.

The Lockheed Constellation: A History, Part I, Louis Barr, *AAHS Journal*, Fall/Winter 1983, Vol. 28 No. 3/4, pp. 190-205.

Lockheed P-2 Neptune, Ronald Drucker, *Scale Aircraft Modeling*, December 1983, pp. unknown.

Lockheed's Make Over Bomber, Freeman Westell, *Wings*, December 1996, pp. 46-55.

The Lockheeds That Never Were, Part I, Bill Slayton, *AAHS Journal*, Vol. 44 No. 1, Spring 1999, pp. 65-73.

The Lockheeds That Never Were, Part II, Bill Slayton, *AAHS Journal*, Vol. 44 No. 2, Summer 1999, pp. 103-113.

The Lockheeds That Never Were, Part III, Bill Slayton, *AAHS Journal*, Vol. 44 No. 3, Fall 1999, pp. 208-219.

The "Lone Ranger", Peter M. Bowers, *Wings*, December 1984, pp. 8-29.

The Magnificat, In Praise of the Consolidated PBY, Part One, no author stated, *Air Enthusiast*, No. 38, January-April 1989, pp. 1-18.

The Magnificat, In Praise of the Consolidated PBY, Part Two, no author stated, *Air Enthusiast*, No. 39, May-August 1989, pp. 19-28.

Magruder's Marauder, Part I, Walt Boyne, *Wings*, April 1973, pp. 18-37.

Magruder's Marauder, Part II, Walt Boyne, *Airpower*, May 1973, pp. 8-21.

The Makeshift Armada, Peter M. Bowers, *Wings*, April 1984, pp. 26-41.

Mariner Pilot, Frederick Johnsen, *Wings*, December 1972, pp. 19-20.

The Mars – Long Lasting Flying Boat, Karl E. Hayes and Eamon C. Power, *Air-Britain Digest*, July-August 1981, pp. 75-80.

Martin 167 in French Service, J. Cuny, *AAHS Journal*, Spring 1965, Vol. 10 No. 1, pp. 34-41.

Martin Flying Boats: Mariner, Mars and Marlin, Robert F. Dorr, *Wings of Fame*, No. 7, 1997, pp. 114-133.

The Martin "Mars" Patrol Bomber, no author stated, *Aero Digest*, August 1942, p. 194.

Martin's Mighty Monarch of the Globe – PBM Mariner, Peter Bowers, *Wings*, December 1972, pp. 6-17.

Martin Model 167W General Purpose Bomber, no author stated, *Aero Digest*, December 1939, pp. ? and 74.

Martin Model 187 Dive Tests, Kent A. Mitchell, *AAHS Journal*, Vol. 39 No. 1, Spring 1994, pp. 46-49.

Martin P4M Mercator, no author stated, *Take Off*, No. 114, 1990, p. 3197.

Martin P4M Mercator: Cold War Elint-gathering Operations, Jon Lake, *Wings of Fame*, No. 19, 2000, pp. 139-149.

Martin's Mercenaries, Walt Boyne, *Airpower*, January 1975, pp. 16-27 and 52.

Martin's PBM Mariner 1937-1956, Bob Smith, *AAHS Journal*, Fall 2003, pp. 196-214.

Martin's PBM Mariners, Bill Gunston, *Aeroplane Monthly*, May 1976, pp. 228-233.

Medium with the Mostest – the B-25 Mitchell (Part 2), Jerry Scutts, *Air International*, March 1993, pp. 144-151.

Mitchell Memory, Gerald H. Balzer, *AAHS Journal*, Winter 1960, Vol. 5 No. 4, pp. 314-315.

A Monster from Santa Monica, Bill Gunston, *Aeroplane Monthly*, December 1991, pp. 718-721.

Mother was an A-26 or was it a B-26!", Jack Dean, *Air Combat*, unknown date, pp. 6-15.

The Narrow Margin, Jay Spenser, *Airpower*, January 1984, pp. 10-23 and 50-53.

News & Comment from Our Members: "The Douglas B-18", Bob Hirsch, *AAHS Journal*, Summer 2001, Vol. 46 No. 2, p. 159.

The North American Aviation B-25H Project NA-98X, Norm Avery, *North American Aviation Retiree Bulletin*, Summer 2001, p. 5.

North American B-25 Variant Briefing, Robert F. Dorr, *Wings of Fame*, No. 3, 1996, pp. 118-141.

North American B-25 Transports, Norman L. Avery, *AAHS Journal*, Summer 1977, Vol. 22 No. 2, pp. 136-141.

North American's Flying Gun, The Story of the B-25 from Paper Aircraft to Legendary Bomber!, Jack Dean, *Wings*, August 1993, pp. 10-45.

North American NA-116, Scott Lowther, *Aerospace Projects Review*, November-December 2002, 32.

The North American XB-28, Jim Tuttle, *AAHS Journal*, Summer 1979, Vol. 24 No. 2, pp. 82-89.

Northrop B-35 Landing Gear, C. J. Dunn, *Aero Digest*, May 1948, pp. 59-60.

Northrop Flying Wing XB35 Bomber, no author stated, *The Northrop News*, 1 May 1946, entire issue.

Northrop N-9M Flying Wing, Part I: Description, Bill Young and Gerald Balzer, *AAHS Journal*, Winter 1993 Vol. 38 No. 4, pp. 242-259.

Northrop N-9M Flying Wing, Part 2: Flight Testing, Bill Young and Gerald Balzer, *AAHS Journal*, Spring 1994 Vol. 39 No. 1, pp. 32-45.

The Northrop XB-35 Flying Wing Superbomber, John K, Northrop, *Aviation*, August 1946, pp. 55-68.

Northrop's Flying Wing Bombers, no author stated, *Aerophile*, Vol. 1 No. 4, May 1978, pp 188-213.

Northrop's Flying Wings, Bill Gunston, *Wings of Fame*, No. 2, 1996, pp. 24-37.

Northrop's Winged Wonders, Bob O'Hara and Gary Bradbrook, *Air Classics*, date unknown, pp. 58-70.

Old Grandpappy, Leo J. Kohn, *Armchair Aviator*, Vol. 2 No. 2, February 1973, pp. 35-38.

Old Man of the Sea, Robert L. Trimble, *Air Classics*, date unknown, pp. 14-26 & 75.

On Patrol, Flying the Martin PBM Mariner in WWII (Pt. I), Bob Smith, *Wings*, August 1990, pp. 10-27 and 46-55.

On Patrol, Flying the Martin PBM Mariner in WWII (Pt. II), Bob Smith, *Airpower*, September 1990, pp. 10-21 and 50-55.

On Top of Old Smokey, The Amazing Story of 'JATO', Scott Libis, *Wings*, June 2005, pp. 20-27.

On Wings Alone!, Jack Dean, *Airpower*, March

2000, pp. 43-55.

Pacific Privateers, VPB-121 in World War II, Joseph C. Woolf, *AAHS Journal*, Vol. 21 No. 2, Summer 1976, pp. 118-125.

Parallel Development with PBY, Harvey H. Lippincott, *AAHS Journal*, Vol. 16 No. 2, Summer 1971, pp. 118-120.

P-Boat, The Consolidated PBY "Catalina" Design, Development, and Production, William E. Scarborough, *Wings*, April 1975, pp. 8-29 and 52-55.

P-Boat, Flying the PBY Catalina / Part II, William E. Scarborough, *Airpower*, May 1975, pp. 8-21 and 54-55.

PBM Mariner, no author stated, *Naval Aviation News*, April 1977, pp. 20-21.

PBO-1 Hudson, Hal Andrews, *Naval Aviation News*, March-April 1990, pp. 16-17.

Peacemaker, Meyers K. Jacobsen, *Airpower*, November 1974, pp. 8-27 and 50-55.

The Post-WWII USAF Bomber Designs That Never Flew, E. R. Johnson, *AAHS Journal*, Vol. 49 No. 4, Winter 2004, pp. 285-296.

Precision Aerial Bombardment of Strategic Targets: Its Rise, Fall, and Resurrection, Daniel L. Haulman, *Air Power History*, Winter 2008, 24-33.

RAF Liberators at War, Part 1: UK-Based Operations, Jon Lake, *International Air Power Review* Volume 15, 2005, pp. 158-173.

RAF Liberators at War, Part 2: Service Abroad, Variants and Operations, Jon Lake, *International Air Power Review*, Volume 16, 2005, pp. 156-173.

Pioneers & Prototypes: North American B-45 Tornado, Guy Martin, *International Air Power Review*, No. 23, 2007, pp. 162-173

Plane Facts: An Unconventional Pair, no author stated, *Air International*, August 1975, pp. 100-101.

Plane Facts: North American Twins, no author stated, *Air International*, April 1979, pp. 189-190.

Rating the Major Air Forces of World War II, Jack Dean, *Airpower*, May 2000, pp. 8-21 and 34-55.

RCT Armament in the Boeing B-29, J. Brown, *Air Enthusiast Quarterly*, No. 3, undated, pp. 80-83.

Recollections of a Naval Liberator Pilot, Owen D. Windall. *AAHS Journal*, Vol. 18 No. 3, Fall 1973, pp. 184-191.

The Reluctant Dominator (Part 1), Stephen Harding, *Aeroplane Monthly*, April 1989, pp. 204-208.

The Reluctant Dominator (Part 2), Stephen Harding, *Aeroplane Monthly*, May 1989, pp. 264-268.

The Reluctant Dragon, Peter M. Bowers, *Wings* or *Airpower*, date unknown, pp. 29-40.

Requiem for Heavyweights, no author stated, *Wings*, June 1990, pp. 10-26 and 33-55.

Rival to the B-29, Alan Crouchman, *Air Enthusiast*, No. 48 December 1992 to February 1993, pp. 48-53

Round and 'Round, Mike Machat, *Wings*, April 2005, pp. 28-45.

The Second String, William T. Y' Blood, *AAHS Journal*, Vol. 13 No. 2, Summer 1968, pp. 80-92.

The Secret Weapons of World War II, Nick T. Spark, *Wings*, October 2004, pp. 40-56.

The Silverplate B-29s, World's First Atomic Bombers, Steve Pace and Dick Campbell, *Wings*, August 2002, pp. 42-55.

Shirt-Lived Dragon: The Douglas B-23, William Jesse, *Air Enthusiast*, No. 81 May/June1999,

pp. 70-72.

"Sighted Sub, Sank Same", Thomas F. Gates, *AAHS Journal*, Vol. 54 No. 2, Summer 2009, pp. 109-122.

Six Days, Ben Warner, *AAHS Journal*, Spring 1994, pp. 68-74.

Sky Guns, Joe Mizrahi, *Wings*, June 2000, pp. 8-47.

Solitary 'Dragon': The North American XB-21, Bradley Engbrecht, *Air Enthusiast*, No. 92 March/April 2001, pp. 10-12.

Super Bomber, Peter M. Bowers, *Wings*, October 1973, pp. 10-39.

The Super Superfort, Lindsay Peacock, *Air International*, April 1990, pp. 204-208.

Supercharged, Wayne Eleazer, *Airpower*, November 2001, pp. 26-61.

Tailless Bomber, no author stated, *Air Enthusiast*, March 1972, p. 150.

Target Germany Part 1, no author stated, *Take Off*, 15, 1988, pp. 401-409.

Target Germany Part 2, The Big Raids, no author stated, *Take Off*, 16, 1988, pp. 429-435.

Target Germany Part 3, Attack at Will, no author stated, *Take Off*, 17, 1988, pp. 457-463.

Target Germany Part 4, Race for the Reich, no author stated, *Take Off*, 18, 1988, pp. 487-491.

Thunder from the Sky, The Story of North American's B-25 Mitchell, Robert J. Wagg, *Wings*, Vol. 2 No. 3 June 1972, pp. 36-59 and 66.

Transatlantic Coronados, Peter Berry, *AAHS Journal*, Summer 2002, pp. 108-111.

The Truculent Turtle, Bob O'Hara, *Air Classics*, date unknown, pp. 27-26 & 48.

Two Classics Revisited, Another Look at the Bell YFM Airacuda and the Douglas B-18 Bomber, author not stated, *Wings*, June 1977, pp. 28-43.

Unwanted and Unloved, The Consolidated B-32, William T. Y' Blood, *Air Power History*, Fall 1995, pp. 59-71.

Ventura … The Borrowed Bomber, Peter M. Bowers, *Wings*, February 1975, pp. 40-53

We Flew the Convair B-36 "Peacemaker", George A. Larson, *Friends Journal*, Winter 1995-96, pp. 21-25.

What, No Propeller?, Rex Hardy, *AAHS Journal*, Vol. 41 No. 1, Spring 1996, pp. 12-16.

Why the Boeing B-29 Bomber, and Why the Wright R-3350 Engine?, Robert E. Johnson, *AAHS Journal*, Fall 1988, Vol. 33 No. 3, pp. 174-189.

Widow Maker, Ken Wixey, *FlyPast*, November 1990, pp. 58-61.

XB-48 … Martin's Pipe Dream—Pipe Organ Bomber!, Walter Boyne, *Wings/Airpower*, Date unknown, pp. 8-21.

Yesteryear … The Douglas XB-19, R. E. Williams, unknown publication, unknown date, pp. 24-31.

Reports

Air Force Developmental Aircraft, no author stated, Air Research and Development Command, United States Air Force, April 1957.

Army Aircraft Characteristics, Production and Experimental, Report No. TSEST – A2, no author stated, ATSC, United States Army, 1 April 1946.

B-32 Design Data, Report No. FZM-33-020, Service Engineering Department, Consolidated-Vultee Aircraft Corporation, 15 February 1944.

Case History of A-26 Aircraft, no author stated, Historical Division, Air Technical Service Command, U.S. Army Air Forces, October 1944.

Case History of B-26 Aircraft Project, no author stated, Historical Office, Materiel Command, U.S. Army Air Forces, 1945.

Case History of Norden Bombsight and C-1 Autopilot, Historical Office, Air Technical Service Command, January 1945.

Case History of XB-33 and B-33 Aircraft, no author stated, Historical Office, Air Technical Service Command, U.S. Army Air Forces, November 1944.

Case History of XB-35 Aircraft Project, no author stated, Historical Office, Air Materiel Command, U.S. Army Air Forces, Spring 1946.

Case History of the YB-35, YB-49 Aircraft (Supplement to Case History of the XB-35 Aircraft), Ardath M. Morrow, Historical Office, Air Materiel Command, United States Air Force, February 1950.

Case History of XB-36 Aircraft Project, no author stated, Historical Division, Air Materiel Command, U.S. Army Air Forces, August 1946.

Case History of XA-42, XB-42, and XB-42A Aircraft, Raymond J. Snodgrass, Historical Office, Air Materiel Command, United States Air Force, March 1948.

Case History of XB-43 Aircraft, no author stated, Historical Office, Air Materiel Command, United States Air Force, November 1948.

Case History of XB-43 Aircraft, no author stated, Historical Office, Air Materiel Command, United States Air Force, November 1948.

Development of Aircraft Gun Turrets in the AAF, 1919-1944, Army Air Forces Historical Studies: No. 54, Captain Irving B. Holley, Jr., AAF Historical Office, Headquarters, U.S. Army Air Forces, June 1947.

The Development of the Heavy Bomber 1918-1944, no author stated, US Air Force Historical Study No. 6, Historical Division, Air University, United States Air Force, August 1951.

Development, Test and Acceptance of Douglas XB-19 Aircraft, AAF No. 38-471, Air Corps Technical Report No. 4803, Howard G. Bunker, Materiel Division, 18 July 1942.

A Flight Investigation of Fuselage Static-Pressure-Vent Airspeed Installations, Richard Scherrer and Lewis A. Rodert, National Advisory Committee for Aeronautics, ARR No. 3K16, November 1943.

Final Report on Test of Armament Installation in XB-41 Aircraft, 6-43-1-2, Colonel Dudley W. Watkins, Proof Department, Army Air Forces Proving Ground Command, Eglin Field, 16 March 1943.

Flight Tests on the Consolidated-Vultee XB-32 Aircraft, AAF NO. 41-142, Engineering Division Memorandum Report Serial No. ENG-47-1715-A, Paul F. Bikle, Flight Test Engineering Branch, 15 March 1944.

Historical Record of XB-33 and B-33 Aircraft Project, Major H. W. Case, United States Army Air Forces, 21 March 1945.

History of the Development and Production of USAF Heavy Bombardment Aircraft, 1917-1949, Study No. 195, Mary R. Self, Historical Office, Executive Secretariat, Air Materiel Command, December 1950.

Longitudinal and Lateral Dynamic Stability Derivatives of the N-8MB Flying Wing Aircraft as Obtained from Flight Test, Edwin A. Kidd, Report No. TB-559-F-1, Cornell Aeronautical Laboratory, 7 October 1949.

Memorandum Report on History of XB-33 Aircraft, Serial No. EXP-N-50-722, Army Air Forces Materiel Center, H. Allan Sullivan, 7

September 1942.
Pilot's Observations on the N9MB Flying Wing, Glen W. Edwards, Air Technical Service Command, 3 May 1946.
Power-Off Tests of the Northrop N9M-2 Tailless Aircraft in the 40- by 80-foot Wind Tunnel, Victor I Stevens, Jr., and Gerand M. McCormack, Memorandum Report A4L14, National Advisory Committee for Aeronautics, 14 December 1944.
Report of Preliminary Flights, XB-42 Aircraft, no author stated, source unknown, undated.
Service Test Requirements and Manual on XB-15 Aircraft, E. H. Beebe and C. F. Greene, Material Division, 1 July 1948.
Summary of the XB-40 Project, unknown author, unknown date.
Summary of the XB-41 Project, unknown author, unknown date.
Tests of Thermal-Electric De-Icing Equipment for Propellers, Richard Scherrer and Lewis A. Rodert, National Advisory Committee for Aeronautics, ARR No. 4A20, January 1944.
XA-42, XB-42, and XB-42A Aircraft, Raymond J. Snodgrass, Historical Office, Air Materiel Command, United States Air Force, March 1948.
The XB-48 Jet Bomber, Martin J, Jr. Miller, Historical Office, Air Materiel Command, United States Air Force, July 1950.

Technical Papers
The Development of All-Wing Aircraft, John K. Northrop, 35th Wilbur Wright Memorial Lecture, The Royal Aeronautical Society, 29 May 1947, printed in 1947 proceedings pp. 481-510.
Flying-Wing Aircraft: The XB-35/YB-49 Program, W. R. Sears, American Institute of Aeronautics and Astronautics, AIAA 80-3036, 1980.
The Flying Wings, Max Stanley, *Society of Experimental Test Pilots Twenty-Fourth Symposium Proceedings*, 24-27 September 1980, pp. 237-256.
From New Technology Development to Operational Usefulness – B-36, B-58, F-111/FB-111, Forrest E. Armstrong, AIAA 83-1046.
N-1 to B-2: Fifty Years of Flight-Testing Northrop's Flying Wings, Bill Flanagan, *Society of Experimental Test Pilots Forty-Eight Symposium Proceedings*, September 2002, pp. 222-248.

Correspondence
B-32 Flight Tests, B-32 Aircraft, AAF No. 42-108473, Memorandum Report On TSCEP5E, O. J. Ritland and Paul F. Bikle, Flight Section, Headquarters, Air Technical Service Command, 1 November 1944.
Flight Tests of the Consolidated-Vultee XB-32 Aircraft, AAF No. 41-142, Memo Report Serial No. Eng-47-1715-A, Paul F. Bikle, Flight Test Engineering Branch, Engineering Division, 15 March 1944.
Notes on Flight of Northrop B-35 Flying Model (N9MA), 28 June 1944, Frank R. Cook.
XB-32 Armament, R. C. Sebold to H. A. Sutton, Consolidated Aircraft Corporation, 17 October 1942.
C. Roger Cripliver correspondence with W. Yip, 15 January 1996, subject XA-44 and XB-53, resident in the University of Texas, Dallas, archives.

Manuals
B-18 Bolo, Douglas Aircraft Corp., undated.
B-23 Dragon, Douglas Aircraft Corp., undated.
Plane Captain's Handbook for PV-2 Aircraft, First Edition, Lockheed Aircraft Corporation, undated.
Flight Handbook, USAF Series B-26B TB-26B B-26C TB-26C Aircraft, T.O. 1B-26-1, 1 July 1957, United States Air Force.
Flight Handbook, USAF Series B-36H-III Aircraft, T.O. 1B-36H (III)-1, 26 November 1954, United States Air Force.
Handbook of Erection and Maintenance for Model XB-42A Aircraft, no author stated, Douglas Aircraft Company, undated.
Handbook, Flight Operating Instructions, USAF Model YB-35 Aircraft, Northrop Aircraft, AN 01-15EAA-1, 15 July 1948.
Handbook, Flight Operating Instructions, USAF Series RB-36F Aircraft, AN 01-5EUF-1, 30 March 1951, United States Air Force.
Handbook of Service Instructions for the Model XB-19 Long Range Bombardment Aircraft, T. O. No 01-40ED Volume I, Field Service Section, Materiel Division, undated.
Pilot's Flight Operating Instructions Army Model RB-37, U.S. Army, T.O. NO. 01-75EA-1, 20 July 1943.
Pilot's Handbook, U.S. Navy, Model PBM-3R, Class VPB, The Glenn L. Martin Company, June 1943.
Pilot's Handbook, U.S. Navy, PB2Y-3 Aircraft, Consolidated Aircraft Corporation, June 1942.
Pilot's Handbook of Flight Operating Instructions for the Model XB-42 Aircraft, Douglas Aircraft Company, 7 August 1945.
Pilot's Pocket Manual, Model PV-2 Aircraft, First Edition, Lockheed Aircraft Corporation, undated.
Preliminary Handbook of Operation and Servicing Instructions, Central-Station Fire-Control System Model 2CFR55A1 for the B-29 Aircraft, General Electric, GEI-17708, May 1943.
Preliminary Pilot's Flight Operating Instructions for Army Model XB-32, Consolidated Vultee Aircraft Corporation, 23 October 1943.
Service Instructions for Jet Propulsion Engines Models J35-1 and J35-3 (Former Type TG-180), AN 02-105CA-2, no author stated, 5 August 1945, Rev 20 November 1945.

Internet Sources
Designations of U.S. Air Force Projects, George Cully and Andreas Parsch, http://orbat.com/site/andreas/U_S_%20Air%20Force%20Projects.htm.
Designations of U.S. Military Electronic and Communications Equipment, Andreas Parsch, http://www.designation-systems.net/usmilav/html.
Lockheed PBO Hudson, Lockheed R4O Super Electra, Jack McKillop, http://www.microworks.net/pacific/aviation/PBO_Hudson.htm.
NavSource Online: Service Ship Photo Archive, www.navsource.org/archives.htm.
US Navy Auxiliary Ships: Catapult Lighter AVC-1, www.shipscribe.com/usnaux/AVC/AVC01.html.
World Aircraft Carriers List Photo Gallery, Aviation Oddities, Part III: Barges, Landing Ships, and Other Platforms, www.hazegray.org/navhist/carriers/odd/index3.htm.

Other
Aircraft Characteristics & Performance, Model PBM-3D, Bureau of Aeronautics, Navy Department, 1 May 1945.
Aircraft Characteristics & Performance, Model PBM-3S, Bureau of Aeronautics, Navy Department, 1 October 1944.
Aircraft Characteristics & Performance, Model PBM-5, Bureau of Aeronautics, Navy Department, 1 August 1945.
Aircraft Characteristics & Performance, Model PV-1, Bureau of Aeronautics, Navy Department, 1 December 1943.
The Century of Flight: Airpower and Armies 1939-1945, Nugus/Martin Productions for BBC, 1997. (video)
The Century of Flight: Airpower and Navies 1939-1945, Nugus/Martin Productions for BBC, 1997. (video)
The Century of Flight: The Bomber as a War Winner?, Strategic Bombing 1939-1945, Nugus/Martin Productions for BBC, 1997. (video)
Data on New B-19 Army Bomber, press release, War Department, 22 March 1940.
The Douglas DB-7/A-20 Boston/Havoc, R. E. Williams, unpublished manuscript (magazine format).
Epilogue, Gerald Balzer, unpublished Northrop flying wing paper, 2009.
Flight, Test, Incidents and Accidents on Selected Multi-engine Bombers, Historical Division, Air Materiel Command, April 1957.
The Glenn L. Martin Co. Presents to the U.S. Air Forces the B-48, Glenn L. Martin Company, undated (brochure).
Historical Planes of the Martin Company, The Maryland (GLM Model 167): Attack Bomber and Reconnaissance, Release #910-N, no author stated, The Glenn L. Martin Company, undated.
History of the B-36, no author stated, Convair, undated.
The Mariner Newsletter, 50th Anniversary Edition XPBM-1's First Fight February 18, 1939, February 1989.
Model XB-48, A Medium Bombardment Aircraft, Glenn L. Martin Company, 14 April 1945 (brochure).
Reflections, Courtland D. Perkins, unpublished autobiography, prepared approximately 1989.
Standard Aircraft Characteristics, YB-49 Flying Wing, Northrop, no author stated, Air Materiel Command, U.S. Air Force, 20 December 1949.
Summary of Handling Characteristics, NACA Wind Tunnel Prediction, 7 x 10 ft. Tunnel, Figure 14, (XA-42), National Advisory Committee for Aeronautics, date probably late 1943.
Tailless Aircraft, An Historical Perspective, Captain Paul Metz, undated briefing slides.
World's Largest Plane, XB-19A, to Carry Air Cargo, press release, Public Relations Office, Air Technical Service Command, 8 March 1945.

Index

221

222

223